Communications in Computer and Information Science 2894

Series Editors

Gang Li, *School of Information Technology, Deakin University, Burwood, VIC, Australia*
Joaquim Filipe, *Polytechnic Institute of Setúbal, Setúbal, Portugal*
Zhiwei Xu, *Chinese Academy of Sciences, Beijing, China*

Rationale

The CCIS series is devoted to the publication of proceedings of computer science conferences. Its aim is to efficiently disseminate original research results in informatics in printed and electronic form. While the focus is on publication of peer-reviewed full papers presenting mature work, inclusion of reviewed short papers reporting on work in progress is welcome, too. Besides globally relevant meetings with internationally representative program committees guaranteeing a strict peer-reviewing and paper selection process, conferences run by societies or of high regional or national relevance are also considered for publication.

Topics

The topical scope of CCIS spans the entire spectrum of informatics ranging from foundational topics in the theory of computing to information and communications science and technology and a broad variety of interdisciplinary application fields.

Information for Volume Editors and Authors

Publication in CCIS is free of charge. No royalties are paid, however, we offer registered conference participants temporary free access to the online version of the conference proceedings on SpringerLink (http://link.springer.com) by means of an http referrer from the conference website and/or a number of complimentary printed copies, as specified in the official acceptance email of the event.

CCIS proceedings can be published in time for distribution at conferences or as post-proceedings, and delivered in the form of printed books and/or electronically as USBs and/or e-content licenses for accessing proceedings at SpringerLink. Furthermore, CCIS proceedings are included in the CCIS electronic book series hosted in the SpringerLink digital library at http://link.springer.com/bookseries/7899. Conferences publishing in CCIS are allowed to use our online conference service (Meteor) for managing the whole proceedings lifecycle (from submission and reviewing to preparing for publication) free of charge.

Publication process

The language of publication is exclusively English. Authors publishing in CCIS have to sign the Springer CCIS copyright transfer form, however, they are free to use their material published in CCIS for substantially changed, more elaborate subsequent publications elsewhere. For the preparation of the camera-ready papers/files, authors have to strictly adhere to the Springer CCIS Authors' Instructions and are strongly encouraged to use the CCIS LaTeX style files or templates.

Abstracting/Indexing

CCIS is abstracted/indexed in DBLP, Google Scholar, EI-Compendex, Mathematical Reviews, SCImago, Scopus. CCIS volumes are also submitted for the inclusion in ISI Proceedings.

How to start

To start the evaluation of your proposal for inclusion in the CCIS series, please send an e-mail to ccis@springer.com

Zhiyun Lin · Xiao-ping (Steven) Zhang ·
Yanchuan Zhang · Tom H. Luan · Peng Sun
Editors

Networking Systems of AI

5th International Conference on Networking Systems of AI,
INSAI 2025
Shenzhen, China, November 15–17, 2025
Proceedings

Editors
Zhiyun Lin
Southern University of Science
and Technology
Shenzhen, China

Yanchuan Zhang
China Institute of Communications
Beijing, China

Peng Sun
Duke Kunshan University
Kunshan City, China

Xiao-ping (Steven) Zhang
Tsinghua University
Beijing, China

Tom H. Luan
Xi'an Jiaotong University
Xi'an City, China

ISSN 1865-0929   ISSN 1865-0937 (electronic)
Communications in Computer and Information Science
ISBN 978-981-95-9298-2   ISBN 978-981-95-9299-9 (eBook)
https://doi.org/10.1007/978-981-95-9299-9

This Springer imprint is published by the registered company Springer Nature Singapore Pte Ltd.
The registered company address is: 152 Beach Road, #21-01/04 Gateway East, Singapore 189721, Singapore

If disposing of this product, please recycle the paper.

Preface

The 5th International Conference on Networking Systems of AI (INSAI 2025) was held in Shenzhen, China, from November 15 to November 16, 2025. This conference was jointly sponsored by the Institute on Networking Systems of AI (INSAI), the China Institute of Communications (CIC), and the Southern University of Science and Technology (SUSTech). It aimed to provide a high-level platform for experts, scholars, and professional technicians to exchange ideas and further promote global development in the field of artificial intelligence network systems.

The theme of INSAI 2025 was "Agent Communication for Networked General Artificial Intelligence." The conference program featured keynote speeches, special reports, technical sessions, and industry forums presented by leaders from the organizing committees and renowned experts from China and abroad. These sessions aimed to foster the deep integration of communication networks and artificial intelligence, gradually building an industry consensus on the future of networked AI agents.

The organizing committee received a total of 52 submissions from around the world. Through a rigorous peer-review process, 19 full papers were accepted for presentation and publication in this volume. This corresponds to an acceptance rate of approximately 36%. All submissions underwent a single-blind peer review process, where each paper was evaluated by at least three independent reviewers. The review criteria focused heavily on Novelty (20%), Importance (20%), Presentation Quality (10%), and Overall Evaluation (30%), as outlined in our grading scheme.

To ensure the high quality of the proceedings, reviewers provided detailed feedback not only on the technical correctness but also on the engineering applicability and theoretical depth of the submissions.

Furthermore, we maintained strict ethical standards regarding the review of submissions co-authored by any Program Committee members or conference organizers. To handle these manuscripts objectively, they were assigned to an independent track chair who managed the review process. The co-authoring committee members were completely excluded from the selection discussion and decision-making process regarding their own papers, ensuring that all accepted works met the same impartial standards of excellence.

We would like to express our sincere gratitude to the Program Committee members and the external reviewers for their dedication and time spent reviewing the manuscripts. Their professional evaluations were crucial to the success of INSAI 2025. We also thank the authors for their contributions and the keynote speakers for sharing their insights.

Finally, we acknowledge the support of our sponsors and the hospitable city of Shenzhen for hosting this event.

December 2025

Zhiyun Lin
Xiao-ping (Steven) Zhang
Yanchuan Zhang
Tom H. Luan
Peng Sun

Organization

General Chairs

Zhiyun Lin	Southern University of Science and Technology, China
Xiaoping Zhang	Tsinghua University, China
Yanchuan Zhang	China Institute of Communications, China

Program Committee Chairs

Tom H. Luan	Xi'an Jiaotong University, China
Peng Sun	Duke Kunshan University, China

Steering Committee

Jiangchuan (JC) Liu	Simon Fraser University, Canada
Victor C. M. Leung	Shenzhen University, China
Kostas Plataniotis	University of Toronto, Canada
Liang Song	Fudan University, China
Zhiyun Lin	Southern University of Science and Technology, China
Laurence Tianruo Yang	Hainan University, China
Honglin Hu	University of Chinese Academy of Sciences, China
Xin Wang	Fudan University, China
F. Richard Yu	Shenzhen University, China
Robert C. Qiu	Huazhong University of Science and Technology, China
Weijia Jia	Beijing Normal University, China

Program Committee

Nebojša Bačanin Džakula	Singidunum University, Serbia
Tao Chen	Fudan University, China
Wei Gong	University of Science and Technology of China, China
Amit Dvir	Ariel University, Israel
Chengxin Pang	Shanghai East-Bund Institute on Networking Systems of AI, China
Christoph Lipps	German Research Center for Artificial Intelligence (DFKI), Germany
Danilo Avola	Sapienza University of Rome, Italy
Dongfang Zhao	University of Washington, USA
Hui Feng	Fudan University, China
Jasmine Kah Phooi Seng	Xi'an Jiaotong-Liverpool University, China
Jieyu Lin	University of Toronto, Canada
Nan Cheng	Xidian University, China
Petros Spachos	University of Guelph, Canada
Qiang Ye	Memorial University of Newfoundland, Canada
Saiqian Zhang	Meta Reality Lab, USA
Salil Kanhere	University of New South Wales, Australia
Shunqing Zhang	Shanghai University, China
Songwen Pei	University of Shanghai for Science and Technology, China
Stefano Gregori	University of Guelph, Canada
Tingting Yang	Peng Cheng Laboratory, China
Xiaoguang Zhu	University of Maryland, USA
Yijie Mao	ShanghaiTech University, China
Yongbo Chen	ZTE Corporation, China
Yun Chen	Fudan University, China
Zhenghua Chen	Institute for Infocomm Research, Agency for Science, Technology and Research, Singapore
Qixiang Pang	University of Central Missouri, USA
Di Li	Ningbo University, China
Jing Liu	Fudan University, China
Xuefeng Liu	Nanjing University of Science and Technology, China
Chengli Mei	China Star Network, Network Innovation Research Institute, China
Haibin Cai	East China Normal University, China

Additional Reviewers

Yuhao Miao	Jiayue Jin
Jingyi Wu	Hanqi Wang
Yuntian Shi	Hao Chen
Wei Ni	Hengsong Liu
Han Yu	Chuaiyu Ju
Juncen Guo	Linxiao Gong
Yu Du	Jingqi Zhang
Wen Wang	Long Chen
Hongyi Huang	Yizhuo Jia
Jingnan Cai	Zhenyu Zhao
Lang Qian	Luyao Fan
Yilei Wang	Ruiyang Jing
Yang Liu	Jiaxuan Liu
Jingyu Zhang	Bobo Ju
Liangyu Teng	Kun Yang
Fengting Qin	Yinghshuo Wang

Contents

Behavior Modeling and Social Computing

Virtual Reality and Intelligent Application

Deep learning and AI method

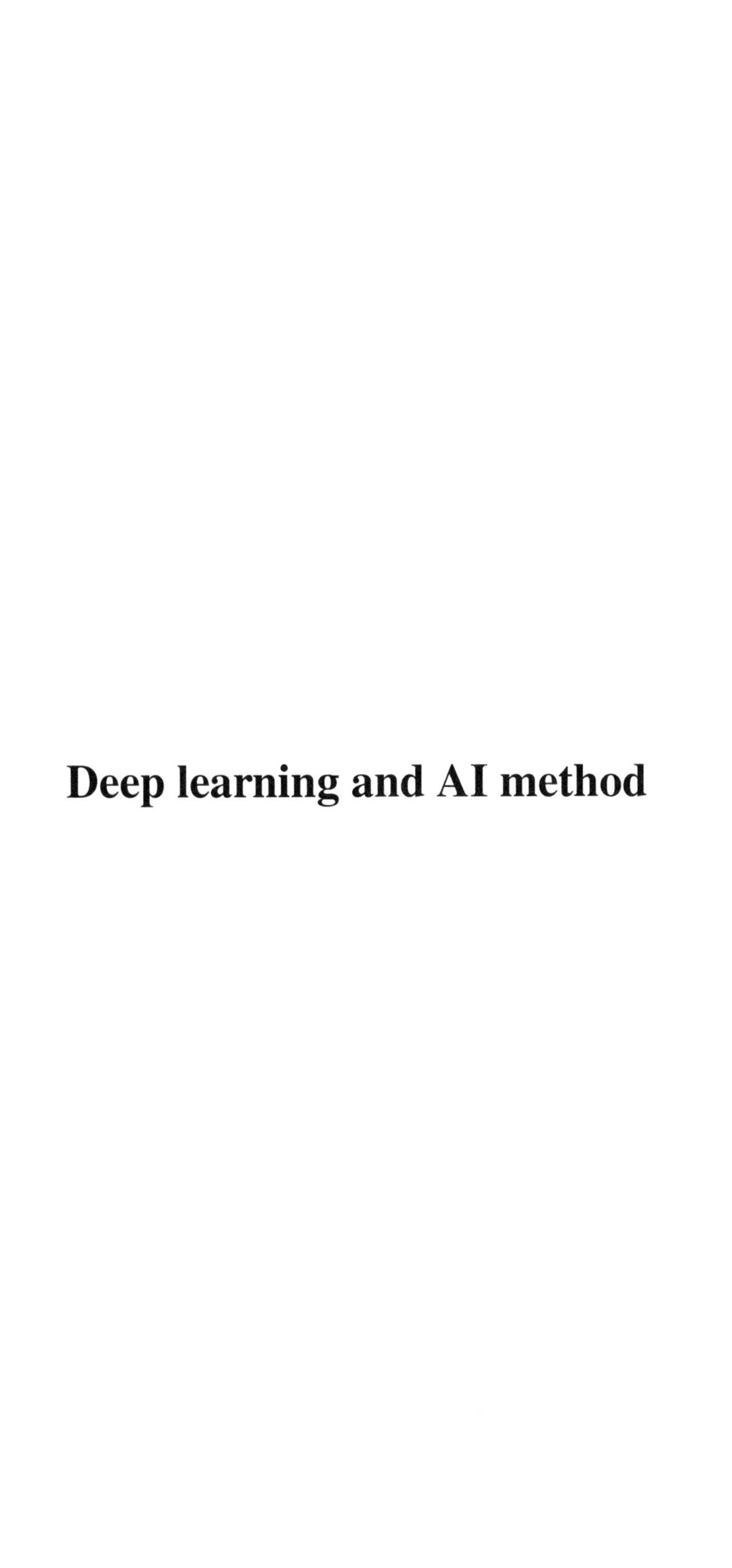

TPS: Trust-Aware Pruning for Byzantine Robustness Federated Learning in Real-Time Edge Systems

Zhengliang Guo[1], Linxiao Gong[2], Jing Liu[2,3], Peng Sun[3], Sunil Maharaj[4], Filip Paluncic[4], Zengwen Li[5], Sudong Jiang[5], Maolin Liu[5], and Liang Song[1(✉)]

[1] College of Intelligent Robotics and Advanced Manufacturing, Fudan University, Shanghai, China
{zlguo18,songl}@fudan.edu.cn

[2] College of Future Information Technology, Fudan University, Shanghai, China
lxgong21@m.fudan.edu.cn, jingliu19@fudan.edu.cn

[3] Division of Natural and Applied Sciences, Duke Kunshan University, Jiangsu, China
peng.sun568@duke.edu

[4] Department of Electrical, Electronic and Computer Engineering, University of Pretoria, Pretoria, South Africa
{sunil.maharaj,filip.paluncic}@up.ac.za

[5] Chongqing Changan Automobile Co., Ltd., Chongqing, China
{lizw,jiangsd,liuml}@changan.com.cn

Abstract. Federated learning is an essential contributor to future-generation digital ecosystems, but currently has two challenges: how to ensure communication efficiency and simultaneously provide Byzantine resilience. The current methods frequently focus on either one or another of these issues concentrating on a single either model compression to reduce bandwidth or strong aggregation to ensure security but does not focus on the interaction between the two. Trust-aware Pruning Strategy Trust -aware Pruning Strategy (TPS) is a framework that is presented in this paper and provides synergistic integration of compression- aware mechanisms with trust- based client evaluation. TPS attains communication efficiency and adversarial resilience, promoting the field of secure distributed learning on real-time edge settings.

TPS proposes a decentralized structure where the client are able to engage in organized pruning whereby the pruning ratio of clients is variable and peer to peer validation is done to evaluate who to trust. The system uses a dynamic trust graph to model validation relationships and extract trust scores that form a difference between valid compression strategies and malicious manipulation. Trust-weighted averaging of thin slice model updates ensures model integrity and greatly reduces communication overhead, which is a highly important concern in real-time distributed application. Extensive testing on the MNIST proves that TPS can attain the test accuracy of about 89% by compression-based attacks with the adversarial participation rate of 20%. Moreover, it holds 80% accuracy in the worst-case situation of non-IID, which confirms its strength in a heterogeneous setting.

Keywords: Real-time federated systems · Distributed edge computing · Model compression · Byzantine robustness

1   Introduction

The integration of distributed simulation and real-time applications of contemporary digital ecosystems has essentially altered paradigms of edge computing. In these ecosystems, when a billion-scale IoT devices produce huge amounts of data at the edges of the network, the old centralized training is challenged by major bandwidth, latency, and privacy crisis issues at network edges [5,24]. Other than sensor data analytics, the edge devices are becoming more capable of handling video streams, creating more bandwidth and privacy issues. As an example, video surveillance with distributed anomaly-detection systems needs efficient processing on-device implementation in video surveillance systems closer to the acquisition stage, namely generalized and processing by a single video frame per neural unit as a grid-like structure or unit (Li). The disruptive mechanism in this simulation-based landscape of innovations has become Federated Learning (FL) that facilitates joint model creation even though data locality is preserved data locality is critical to the implementation of real-time edge applications [14]. These decentralized architectures naturally ensure confidential data and avoid network congestion, which forms FL as one of the foundational technologies of the next-generation digital ecosystems [1].

Nonetheless, the application of federated learning to resource-constrained edge environments faces two underlying challenges, namely, communication efficiency and Byzantine robustness. FL is iterative thus requiring the exchange of parameters in real-time between distributed devices and central servers that coordinate, with empirical research findings that network transmission takes up to 90% of training time, which is crucial in real-time tasks [6,12]. Although neural network pruning and compression systems have shown promise to decrease communication overhead without impacting privacy, they rely on participants whom one can trust unlike in scenarios involving untrusted members of the system [20]. Simultaneously, the decentralized structure makes FL systems prone to adversarial attacks by compromised clients who are able to corrupt models due to malicious updates or Sybil-based advanced attacks on the system through sophisticated Sybil-based strategies [13,21,25]. These challenges interact to produce the difficult optimization space which is poorly represented by existing solutions. In current Byzantine-tolerant protocols, statistical anomaly detection is considered without considering structural changes in compression, which are inherent in architecture change over time [2,8]. On the other hand, compression algorithms used in federated learning do not take into consideration adversarial individuals, which restricts their further use.

In this connection, we introduce Trust-aware Pruning Strategy (TPS), a new framework to synchronistically combine trust-aware mechanisms and compression algorithm to provide security and efficiency of edge-based federated learning. We will make the following contributions:

– **Integrated Security-efficiency Framework**: TPS is the first systematic protocol to jointly optimize communication efficiency and Byzantine robustness.
– **Compression-Aware Trust Mechanism**: TPS is a decentralized peer-to-peer validation protocol coupled with dynamic trust scoring that distinguishes between legitimate compression strategies and adversarial manipulation, effectively defending against compression-oriented attacks including malicious nodes.
– **Adaptive Aggregation for Heterogeneous Settings**: TPS uses trust-weighted aggregation of sparse model updates, which is responsive to the extent of data heterogeneity, and preserves good performance in even extreme non-IID settings without misclassifying the honest clients.

The rest of this paper is structured as follows: Sect. 2 presents an extensive review of Byzantine-robust federated learning, compression methods and trusts structures. Our system model, and threat landscape are defined in Sect. 3. Section 4 presents TPS framework, which includes the essence of TPS. Section 5 verifies the approach proposed by large-scale experiments on compression based attacks and non-IID data conditions. Section 6 provides a conclusion and future directions.

2   Related Work

2.1   Federated Learning and Security

Federated learning has become a critical defense against adversarial attacks by implementing a defense mechanism known as Byzantine-robust aggregation. Geometric median-based methods were first introduced by Krum [2] when it chose updates that minimize the median distance to k-nearest neighbors, but is susceptible to coordinated attackers acting in concert by displaying updates close to distribution centers. FedRAD [7] eliminates these shortcomings by means of a two-stage process using the combination of adversarial identification and submission correction, which lowers the computational complexity $O(n^2d)$ by, instead, proportions of the size of n and d to $O(nd)$, thus improving scalability.

Innovations in the recent past have created high-level defense architectures of complicated threat modelling. The RobustFL is a method that implements hierarchical aggregation with local and global validation, preserving above 90% accuracy in the context of less than 30% adversarial participation, which is denoted as RobustFL [18]. BRSA [9] is an extension of this paradigm that combines cryptographic primitives with statistical filtering, and achieves both privacy preservation and Byzantine robustness with realistic computational performance.

Complementary defense paradigm is provided in trust-based mechanisms. FLTrust most recently performs an analysis of client trustworthiness by measuring the cosine similarity between updates and reference gradients maintained by the server, which is FLTrust [3]; TrustFL advances to multidimensional models that include behavioral history and consistency of contributions, which is

TrustFL [22]. Nevertheless, compressed federated learning presents exceptional challenges that lack appropriate protection under available defenses. The article by Zhang et al. [26] demonstrates such critical vulnerabilities: dense gradient assumptions do not consider attack vectors based on sparsification, compression ratio authentication is not done, and the combination of compression and Byzantine robustness is not explored.

2.2 Model Compression in Federated Learning

Federated learning deployments have necessitated model compression to handle the overheads in communication. Top-k gradient sparsification with error feedback, as implemented in FedZip [11], attains a sparsity of 99%, showing specific effectiveness on large language models. PruneFL+ [17] is a structured pruning algorithm applying collaborative masking through secure aggregation schemes. Architecture search, such as FedNAS, finds optimum sub-networks with 85% communication cutoff, albeit Liu et al. [10] identify flaws that allow continued backdoor implantation by manipulating the architecture.

Quantization methods take compression limits farther to the limit. FedPAQ [15] is a adaptive bit-width adjustable algorithm that can reduce 32-fold compression with 1% loss in accuracy, and QSGD-Fed [4] uses stochastic quantization and variance reduction to converge under the most economical conditions. Knowledge distillation offers alternatives to understand: FedGKD [23]reduced by 90% just by parameter transmission, and FedDistill [19] reduced by magnitudes 3x by distilling the hierarchy.

Compression unavoidably opens up new attack vectors despite the promised gains in efficiency. In CompressionAttack [16] the authors illustrate that compression concentrates malicious manipulations in the retained parameters, tripled the attack success rate by the exploitation of deterministic selection of Top-k. Defenses as suggested such as randomized sparsification add computational cost to offset the benefits of compression and thus show the inherent conflicts between efficiency and security.

Taking these severe precarities of both Byzantine robustness aggregation and model compression, we identify TPS, a novel framework enabling seamless integration of both trust-based assessment and compression-awareness to create a new paradigm of communication-efficient and adversarially-resilient federated learning in edge environment.

3   System Model And Threat Analysis

3.1   System Architecture

Basic Architecture. We assume a federated learning system composed of the server, as denoted by $\mathcal{S}$ and a heterogeneous and resources constrained group of the number of edge clients, denoted by $\mathcal{C} = \{C_1, C_2, ..., C_N\}$. A client C_i holds an access to a private dataset $\mathcal{D}_i = \{(x_j^i, y_j^i)\}_{j=1}^{|\mathcal{D}_i|}$ is denoted by the collective of samples in its own data distribution: $P_i(x, y)$, where x_j^i represents the input feature vector and y_j^i denotes the corresponding label. Following the privacy preservation scheme, the datasets are strictly localized, i.e. it is true that the following holds: $\bigcap_{i=1}^{N} \mathcal{D}_i = \emptyset$.

The federated optimization works in T synchronized communication steps. In each round $t \in \{1, 2, ..., T\}$, the server chooses an active subset $\mathcal{C}_t \subseteq \mathcal{C}$. The server transmits the most recent model parameters $W^{t-1} \in \mathbb{R}^d$, to participating clients, where d denotes the model dimensionality. On every active client $C_i \in \mathcal{C}_t$ actively attains local minima to compute the modified parameters W_i^t and to produce sparse parameters $W_{i,\text{pruned}}^t$ together with a binary pruning mask $p_i^t \in \{0, 1\}^d$.

Communication Infrastructure. The system architecture facilitates two forms of communication that are fundamental both in model training and trust testing:

1. **Client-Server Communication**: Primary model dialogue is achieved when wireless channels of communication are used that are limited by bandwidth between clients and the server. Every client C_i broadcasts the compressed model update to minimize the communication costs, and the compression is done through organized pruning, where pruning ratio is defined by parameter $\beta \in (0, 1)$
2. **Device-to-Device (D2D) Communication**: The architecture introduces the direct peer-to-peer communications that allow distributed validation without server mediation. The compression of model is done through structured pruning where pruning ratio is defined by parameter beta (0,1). This auxiliary communications system becomes very important in carrying out the cross-validation mechanisms which form the basis of our trust assessment protocol.

Data Heterogeneity. The system is available to explicitly model non-IID data distributions among clients, where $P_i(x, y) \neq P_j(x, y)$ for any distinct clients i and j. The main feature of this heterogeneity is the skew of label distribution, which creates enormous difficulties in convergence of the models and requires specific aggregation techniques.

The datasets of clients have class imbalance of different intensities with each client C_i having labels $Y_i \subseteq Y$ from the global label space Y. We use a Dirichlet distribution that is characterized by a single parameter, which is the concentration parameter α. Namely, the label distribution of each client C_i is sampled as $q_i \sim \text{Dir}(\alpha)$, with smaller values of α cause an increased amount of heterogeneity. The proportion of samples from class k at client i follows:

$$p_{i,k} = \frac{q_{i,k}}{\sum_{j=1}^{|Y|} q_{i,j}} \tag{1}$$

Such formulation allows the close control over the statistical heterogeneity, where $\alpha \to 0$ represents extreme non-IID scenarios with clients possessing highly skewed label distributions, and $\alpha \to \infty$ approximates IID conditions. In our experimental evaluation, we systematically vary $\alpha \in \{0.1, 0.5, 1.0\}$, to assess the soundness of our framework to varying degrees of data heterogeneity.

Algorithm 1. Trust-aware Pruning Strategy (TPS)

Require: Model W^0, datasets $\{\mathcal{D}_i\}_{i=1}^N$, parameters β, λ, rounds T
Ensure: Final model W^T
1: Initialize: $R_i \leftarrow 0.5$ for all $i \in [N]$ {Client reputation}
2: **for** $t = 1$ to T **do**
3:    **Client Selection:**
4:    $\mathcal{C}_t \leftarrow \text{SelectByReputation}(\{R_i\}_{i=1}^N)$
5:    **Local Training & Pruning:**
6:    **for** each $i \in \mathcal{C}_t$ in parallel **do**
7:       $W_i^t \leftarrow \text{LocalSGD}(W^{t-1}, \mathcal{D}_i^{\text{train}})$
8:       $p_i^t[j] \leftarrow 1$ if $|W_i^t[j]| > \text{Quantile}(|W_i^t|, \beta)$, else 0
9:       $W_i^t \leftarrow W_i^t \odot p_i^t$
10:   **end for**
11:   **Cross-Client Verification:**
12:   **for** $i \in \mathcal{C}_t$ **do**
13:      $j \leftarrow (i+1) \bmod |\mathcal{C}_t|$ {Verifier for client i}
14:      $s_i^t \leftarrow \text{Acc}(W_i^t, \mathcal{D}_j^{\text{val}}) - \lambda \cdot \text{ActualPruningRate}(W_i^t)$
15:   **end for**
16:   **Reputation Update:**
17:   $\bar{s}^t \leftarrow \text{Mean}(\{s_i^t\}_{i \in \mathcal{C}_t})$
18:   **for** $i \in \mathcal{C}_t$ **do**
19:      $R_i \leftarrow \gamma R_i + (1-\gamma)\sigma(s_i^t - \bar{s}^t)$
20:   **end for**
21:   **Aggregation:**
22:   $\mathcal{H}_t \leftarrow \text{SelectByTrustScore}(\{(i, s_i^t)\}_{i \in \mathcal{C}_t})$
23:   **for** each parameter p **do**
24:      $n_p \leftarrow |\{i \in \mathcal{H}_t : p_i^t[p] = 1\}|$
25:      **if** $n_p \geq 0.5|\mathcal{H}_t|$ **then**
26:        $W^t[p] \leftarrow \frac{1}{n_p} \sum_{i \in \mathcal{H}_t, p_i^t[p]=1} W_i^t[p]$
27:      **else**
28:        $W^t[p] \leftarrow 0$
29:      **end if**
30:   **end for**
31: **end for**
32: **return** W^T

3.2 Threat Model

We regard a Byzantine oppositional model that represents a set of clients—bounded by $\rho < 0.2$ to behave arbitrarily compromised, failed, or malicious, within the range of values of protocol violation. Let the set of adversarial clients $\mathcal{M} \subset \mathcal{C}$, including only a set with size up to acting as a set of adversaries$|\mathcal{M}| \leq \rho N$, and let $\mathcal{H} = \mathcal{C} \setminus \mathcal{M}$ represent the set of honest clients adhering to the protocol.

We particularly direct our attention to **compression-oriented attacks**, in the context of compressed federated learning, that will capitalize on the vulnerabilities posed by sparsification of the model itself. Attacks are an advanced type of adversarial behavior that is specifically designed to beat the security assumptions of compression-based federated systems.

The attack vectors used by adversarial clients exploit the sparsity constraints and pruning to support their malicious influence by employing as follows:

1. **Malicious Masking**: Adversaries tactically mislead pruning masks to deactivate model parts while exhibiting proper sparsification. Formally, malicious client $C_i \in \mathcal{M}$ generates a misleading mask $\tilde{p}_i^t$ such that
$tildep_i^t[j] = 0$ for all $j \in \mathcal{J}_{\text{critical}}$, where $\mathcal{J}_{\text{critical}}$ represents indices of parameters crucial for model performance. By pruning these critical parameters, adversaries tactically deactivate model capacity without raising suspicion due to the sparsity constraint.

2. **Aggressive Pruning Exploitation**: Malicious clients deliberately adopt aggressive pruning ratios (i.e., 80% sparsity) to bias adversarial perturbations towards the remaining parameter subset. Particularly, by aggressively pruning to retain only 20% of parameters, malicious clients ensure that their malicious updates $\tilde{W}_{i,\text{pruned}}^t$ maximize the unit-parameter impact of their gradients. These aggressive pruning strategies exploits the inherent vulnerability of sparse models where $||\tilde{W}_{i,\text{pruned}}^t||_0 = 0.2d$, enabling adversaries to inject highly concentrated poisoned gradients that disproportionately influence the global model aggregation while ostensibly complying with compression requirements.

3. **Coordinated Pruning Collusion**: Multiple colluding adversaries $\{C_i\}_{i \in \mathcal{M}}$ coordinate to orchestrate complementary pruning patterns to reach a colluding attack objective. Through prior coordination, colluding clients ensure that their collective masks prune specific parameter subsets: $\bigcap_{i \in \mathcal{M}}\{j : \tilde{p}_i^t[j] = 0\} = \mathcal{J}_{\text{target}}$, where $\mathcal{J}_{\text{target}}$ represents parameters that are crucial for specific functionalities/class predictions.

These compression-aware attacks are challenging because of the inherent trade-off between compression and model aggregation. The concentration of model information in sparse parameter subsets inadvertently creates high-impact attack surfaces. That is, even though adversaries consume minimal communication resources with their malicious updates, their updates can disproportionately influence the global model. Therefore, designing defense mechanisms against compression attacks requires the development of compression-aware mechanisms that can discern between legitimate sparsification and malicious collusion.

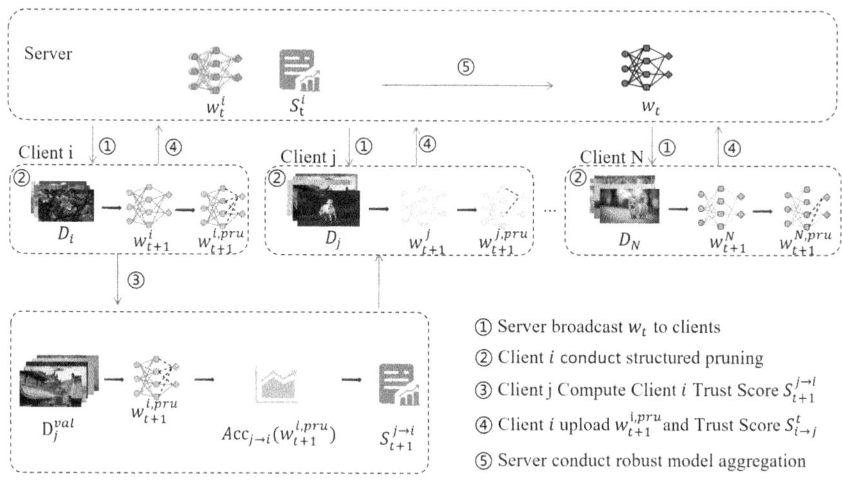

Fig. 1. TPS Framework Architecture.

4   The Proposed TPS Framework

The TPS defines a new paradigm of handling the two dual issues of communication efficiency and Byzantine robustness in federated learning implementations over resource-constrained edge computing infrastructures. TPS combines adaptive model sparsification with decentralized trust evaluation in a way extending natural to create a mutually supporting architecture, crashing both in terms of computational performance and adversarial robustness, as shown in Fig. 1.

The model works through four carefully orchestrated phases within the federated learning round $t \in \{1, 2, ..., T\}$: (1) localized training, then adaptive compression on individual clients; (2) cross validation by distributed peer to peer evaluation; (3) the calculation of quantitative measures of trust based on the results of validation and pruning penalty; (4) aggregation of sparse model updates with trust measures to form a strong global representation. The TPS framework consists of three basic entities, which collectively enable secure and efficient federated optimization:

1. **Central Coordination Server** $\mathcal{S}$: The role of coordinating the federated learning process, distributing global model parameters $W^t \in \mathbb{R}^d$, coordinating the involvement of clients by using reputation-based subset selection $\mathcal{C}_t \subseteq \mathcal{C}$, coordinating the peer validation procedure, maintaining client reputation scores $\{R_i\}_{i=1}^N$, and using trust-based aggregation of sparse updates. More importantly, the server can run without the need of clean validation data, thus maintaining the privacy-focused design of federated learning.
2. **Heterogeneous Edge Clients** $\mathcal{C} = \{C_1, C_2, ..., C_N\}$: Each client C_i has all-access to its private dataset $\mathcal{D}_i$, optimizes locally and then executes a

structured pruning based on pruning ratio $\beta \in (0,1)$ and takes part in the distributed validation process as an evaluator and an evaluatee, and broadcasts compressed model updates W_i^t and associated pruning masks p_i^t. The pruning mask $p_i^t[j] = 1$ if the parameter magnitude exceeds the β-quantile threshold, and 0 otherwise.

3. **Dynamic Trust Graph** $\mathcal{G}^t = (\mathcal{V}, \mathcal{E}^t)$: Represents the changing validation topology of round t, where the vertex set $\mathcal{V} = \mathcal{C}_t$ comprises all participating clients, and the directed edge set $\mathcal{E}^t \subseteq \mathcal{V} \times \mathcal{V}$ encodes validation relationships. In the cyclic validation scheme, each client C_i is evaluated by client C_j where $j = (i+1) \bmod |\mathcal{C}_t|$. Each edge $(i,j) \in \mathcal{E}^t$ carries a trust score $s_i^t = \mathrm{Acc}(W_i^t, \mathcal{D}_j^{\mathrm{val}}) - \lambda \cdot \mathrm{ActualPruningRate}(W_i^t)$, representing the validation accuracy reported by client C_j when evaluating the model submitted by client C_i, penalized by the pruning aggressiveness. The structure of the graph allows calculating the trust scores using complex graph-theoretic computations taking into consideration the direct validation results and the consistency patterns over the entire network.

The workflow of the TPS is also described in a formal manner in Algorithm 1 that outlined the consecutive stages of distributed training, compression, validation, and trust-based aggregation. The algorithm coordinates the interactions of the server with the edge clients using a precisely developed protocol that guarantees that it is computationally efficient and Byzantine. The reputations of clients are updated in a form of exponential moving average with regards to relative trust scores to allow us track behavior of clients in the long run.

The algorithmic structure of TPS has a number of insights. To begin with, the combination of trust assessment and sparse model transmission leads to a natural resistance to compression-based attacks as illicit clients have to ensure quality of models over multiple peer evaluations and carry the heavy sparsity, the-wire-of the sparsity, constraints. Second, the trust scoring algorithm is dynamically incentivized to varying pruning patterns amongst clients, specifically by the parameter one, which heavily punishes excessive pruning thereby assuring that the client may have genuine differences in compression policies and does not cause the trust scoring algorithm to identify adversarial behavior. Third, the parameter-wise aggregation method needs the agreement of trusted customers prior to incorporating sparse updates to avoid manipulation of vital model elements.

5 Performance Evaluation

5.1 Experimental Setup

Dataset and Data Partitioning. To reflect real-world federated learning scenarios, we use the MNIST dataset, a standard benchmark for distributed learning applications. The dataset is composed of 70,000 handwritten digit images (28×28 grayscale) belonging to 10 classes with 60,000 samples for training and 10,000 for testing.

We distribute the training dataset over $N = 10$ clients according to a Dirichlet distribution $\text{Dir}(\alpha)$, where $\alpha \in \{0.1, 0.5, 1.0\}$ controls the level of non-IID heterogeneity. The smaller α the larger statistical heterogeneity among clients. Particularly, $\alpha = 0.1$ represents the most severe non-IID scenarios, where clients hold mostly samples from 1–3 digit classes and $\alpha = 1.0$ approaches to a uniform distribution. Each client obtains 300–800 samples. Note that these numbers reflect the high level of imbalance that is typically observed in edge computing scenarios. For local validation, we randomly keep 10% of the client's data stratified over all classes.

Baseline Methods. We benchmark TPS against two representative federated learning approaches:

- **FedAvg+Pruning**: Unstructured-based pruning was added to the classical federated averaging algorithm [14]. This base uses the same pruning ratio as TPS ($\beta \in \{0.1, 0.3, 0.5\}$) but does not use trust-related defence mechanisms thus isolating the effect of our trust evaluation component.
- **Krum**: Byzantine robustness aggregation algorithm that chooses the model updates according to the geometric median principles. In particular, Krum points to the update with the least aggregate L2 distance to their k nearest neighbors, where $k = N - m - 2$ and m is the maximum number of Byzantine clients. This approach gives strength assurances on the assumption that Byzantine customers are fewer than half of the chosen set.

Both baselines utilize identical 4-layer MLP, learning rates ($\eta = 0.01$), and local training configurations ($E = 5$ epochs, batch size=32) to ensure fair comparison. All implementations are developed in PyTorch 2.7.1 with reproducible random seeds.

Pruning Attack Configurations. We test the robustness against compression-based attacks that directly target model sparsification weaknesses: Malicious clients use excessively sparse levels (down to 80% sparsity) of parameters to focus adversarial perturbations in the e.g. remaining 20% of the parameters. This attack enhances the effects of poisoned gradients and makes sure that the malicious updates perform disproportionately well in the sparse set of parameters by attaining disproportionate control over global model aggregation.

We set the fraction of adversarial clients to be equal to $\rho = 0.2$, which is a moderate level of Byzantine that achieves equilibrium between the effectiveness of the attacks and the realistic deployment situations. Bad clients are uniformly picked during the initial stage of the training and continue their antagonistic posture across all the communication rounds.

5.2   Experimental Results and Analysis

Performance Under Varying Pruning Ratios. We initially compare the effectiveness of TPS with pruning-based attacks at the varying sparsity levels.

Table 1 shows the test accuracy of the pruning ratio of beta using pruning ratio $\beta \in \{0.1, 0.3, 0.5\}$, where β represents the percentage of pruned parameters in the model.

Table 1. Test Accuracy Under Different Pruning Ratios (20% Malicious Clients)

Algorithm	$\beta = 0.1$	$\beta = 0.3$	$\beta = 0.5$
TPS Framework	**0.892**	**0.892**	**0.882**
FedAvg+Pruning	0.114	0.178	0.098
Krum	0.614	0.608	0.667

The experimental findings prove that TPS is more resilient to all the pruning configurations. TPS has the test accuracy of 89.2 at sub-optimal compression level (10% pruning), indicating that it has ability to perform well even under compression-based attacks. In a stark contrast, FedAvg+Pruning fails miserably with a low 11.4% accuracy to indicate the full exposure of system to pruning attacks without defence mechanisms. Krum is moderate in its robustness and it has an accuracy of 61.4 but still has degradation of significant proportions when compared to TPS.

As the ratio of pruning grows to $\beta = 0.3$ and $\beta = 0.5$, which is a more aggressive compression condition, TPS remains fairly stable in terms of its performance (89.2% and 88.2% respectively). Inconsistent to FedAvg+Pruning, the interval of accuracy ranges between 9.8–17.8% indicating inconsistency in the attack effectiveness across different sparsity levels. It is interesting to note that the performance of Krum gradually increases with increased pruning ratios (60.8% at $\beta = 0.3$, 66.7% at $\beta = 0.5$), which may be caused by the smaller parameter space with smaller adversarial manipulation capacity.

The training dynamics and test loss comparisons are depicted in Fig. 2. TPS has very quick and steady convergence and attainment to low training loss in under 20 rounds of communication at any pruning ratio. On the other hand, FedAvg+Pruning does not reach the right convergent point, and the training loss reaches high values (≈ 2.25) which proves that malignant sparse updates are indeed successful in corrupting the global model. Krum converges more gradually, with a much slow pace compared to TPS which means that it will take Krum almost 100 rounds to reach similar levels of training loss. These results too are supported by the test loss values, where TPS has 0.367, which is, comparatively much lower than FedAvg+Pruning (2.373) and Krum (1.337).

Robustness to Non-IID Data Distribution. We also test the performance of algorithms in heterogeneous data situation, changing theDirichlet distribution parameter and setting it to $\alpha \in \{0.1, 0.5, 1.0\}$ and the smaller the alpha the worse the non-IID. These experiments have a constant pruning ratio of $\beta = 0.3$ and malicious client ratio of 0.2.

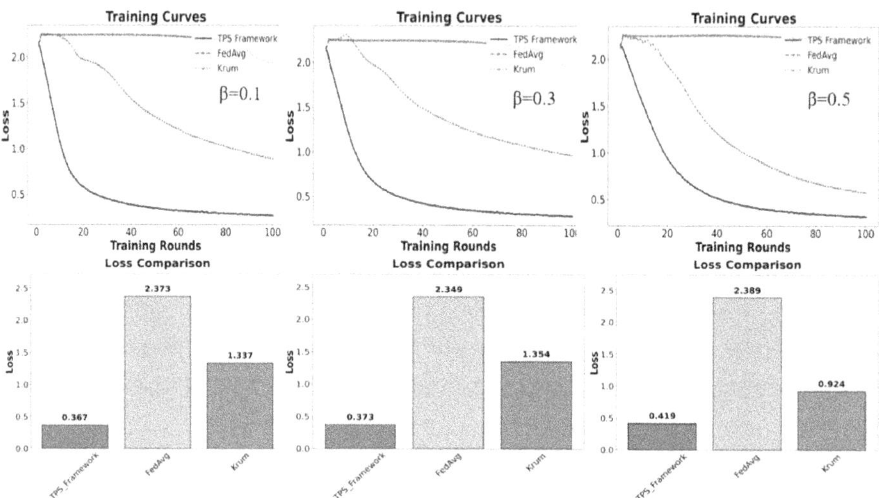

Fig. 2. Training dynamics and test loss comparison under different pruning ratios with 20% malicious clients

Table 2. Test Accuracy Under Different Non-IID Settings ($\beta = 0.3$, 20% Malicious Clients)

Algorithm	$\alpha = 0.1$	$\alpha = 0.5$	$\alpha = 1.0$
TPS Framework	**0.800**	**0.892**	**0.908**
FedAvg+Pruning	0.090	0.178	0.101
Krum	0.592	0.608	0.816

Under extreme non-IID conditions ($\alpha = 0.1$), and with highly skewed label distributions of clients, As shown in Table 2, TPS proves to be incredibly robust with the test accuracy of 80.0%. This is a mere 10% degradation of the moderate non-IID setting, which demonstrates the level of TPS in differentiating natural data heterogeneity and adversarial behaviour. Comparatively, FedAvg+Pruning is the most susceptible with an accuracy of 9.0%, whereas Krum is 59.2% with degradation effects much larger than TPS.

The lower the data heterogeneity ($\alpha = 0.5$ and $\alpha = 1.0$), the better TPS performance gets (89.2% and 90.8% accuracy respectively). The trend implies that the trust evaluation mechanism can be well adjusted to dissimilar levels of statistical heterogeneity without false-classifying the true clients with distorted statistical data. Interestingly, Krum exhibits the top improvement in the near-IID environment($\alpha = 1.0$) and it has the highest accuracy of 81.6% with a geometric median-based approach and shows that the approach works better when the client updates are more homogeneous.

Figure 3 below (non-IID results) illustrates more on the convergence behaviour and test loss in various non-IID environments. TPS also shows a

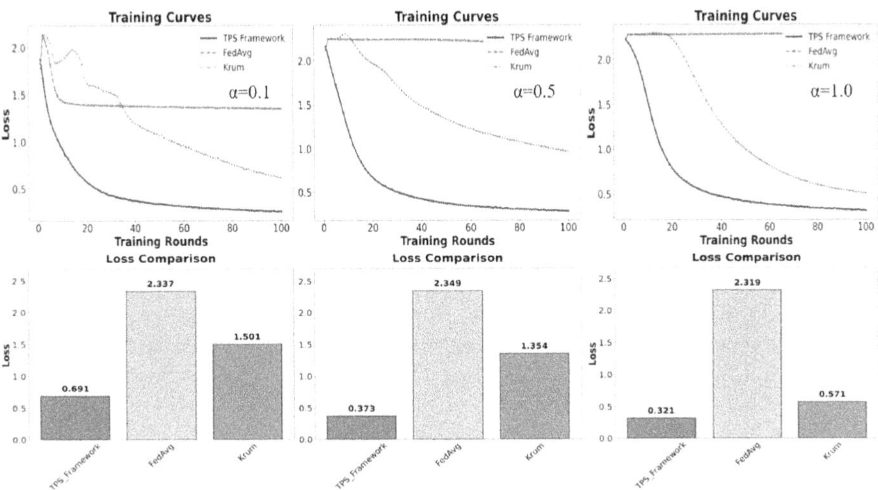

Fig. 3. Training dynamics and test loss comparison under different non-IID settings (Dirichlet α).

steady loss on all non-IID (0.321–0.691), FedAvg+Pruning has a sustained high loss at all (2.319–2.389) indicating that the model has been totally corrupted. The consistency of TP S as a system in various data distributions justifies its practical use in real-world federated learning deployments in which data heterogeneity is natural and unpredictable.

6   Conclusion and Future Work

In this paper, the TPS is a new framework resolving the inherent contradiction between communication efficiency and Byzantine robustness in federated learning over edge computing infrastructures. TPS is the first methodical strategy to jointly achieve the generally distinct objectives of compression and trust-aware mechanisms in distributed systems.

The overall experimental analysis of the MNIST dataset proves that TPS is effective in the resistance to compression-based attacks and preserves its efficiency in communication. The prominent results on this are that TPS can be consulted with consistent test accuracy of around 89% with changing pruning ratios ($\beta \in \{0.1, 0.3, 0.5\}$), which is significantly superior to current techniques that lack Byzantine security (FedAvg+Pruning) or neglect compression vulnerabilities (Krum). Particularly noteworthy is TPS's resilience to extreme non-IID data distributions, maintaining 80% accuracy even under severe statistical heterogeneity ($\alpha = 0.1$), which validates its practical applicability in real-world edge deployments where data heterogeneity is inherent.

Future directions in this area are to pursue TPS to accommodate adaptive compression ratios based on the perceived threat level, to examine the performance of the framework with new neural architecture like transformers, and to come up with theoretical guarantees of the trust scoring mechanism with different attacks. Besides, the suggestion to study the implementation of TPS in composing with other privacy-aware methods, including differential privacy and secure multi-party computation, can further improve the security features of the framework. With the continuing development of federated learning as a vital component of enabling edge intelligence, schemes such as TPS that organize all key components of both efficiency and security concerns will be more and more essential in viable implementations in safety-critical applications.

Acknowledgments. This work was supported by National Key Research and Development Program of China, Project No.2024YFE0200700, Subject No.2024YFE0200703. This work was also supported in part by the Specific Research Fund of the Innovation Platform for Academicians of Hainan Province under Grant YSPTZX202314, in part by the Shanghai Key Research Laboratory of NSAI and the Joint Laboratory on Networked AI Edge Computing, Fudan University-Changan.

Disclosure of Interests. The authors have no competing interests to declare that are relevant to the content of this article.

References

1. Ali, M., Rauf, H.T., Khan, B.A., Mehmood, A., Hassan, S.A.: Federated learning: overview, strategies, applications, tools and future directions. Heliyon **10**(15), e38137 (2024)
2. Blanchard, P., El Mhamdi, E.M., Guerraoui, R., Stainer, J.: Machine learning with adversaries: Byzantine tolerant gradient descent. In: Advances Neural Inf. Process. Syst. 30 (NeurIPS), pp. 119–129 (2017)
3. Cao, X., Fang, M., Liu, J., Gong, N.Z.: Fltrust: Byzantine-robust federated learning via trust bootstrapping. In: Proceedings of 28th Network Distributed System Security Symposium (NDSS) (2021)
4. Chen, J., Liu, H., Zhang, K., Ding, B., Wang, R.: Qsgd-fed: communication-efficient federated learning via quantized stochastic gradient descent. IEEE Trans. Wireless Commun. **23**(3), 2875–2889 (2024)
5. Khan, L.U., Saad, W., Han, Z., Hossain, E., Hong, C.S.: Federated learning for internet of things: recent advances, taxonomy, and open challenges. IEEE Commun. Surv. Tutorials **23**(3), 1759–1799 (2021)
6. Konečný, J., McMahan, H.B., Yu, F.X., Richtárik, P., Suresh, A.T., Bacon, D.: Federated learning: Strategies for improving communication efficiency. arXiv preprint arXiv:1610.05492 (2016)
7. Li, Y., Zhou, Y., Jolfaei, A., Yu, D., Xu, G., Zheng, X.: Fedrad: federated robust adaptive distillation. IEEE Trans. Dependable Sec. Comput. **21**(4), 2230–2243 (2024)
8. Liu, J., et al.: Networking systems for video anomaly detection: a tutorial and survey. ACM Comput. Surv. (2025)
9. Liu, M., Ho, S., Wang, M., Gao, L., Jin, Y., Zhang, H.: Byzantine-resilient secure aggregation for federated learning without server's private data. IEEE Trans. Inf. Forensics Secur. **19**, 1348–1361 (2024)

10. Liu, X., Wang, Y., Chen, T., Zhang, J.: Security vulnerabilities in federated neural architecture search. In: Proceedings of 31st Network Distributed System Security Symposium (NDSS) (2024)
11. Liu, Y., et al.: Fedzip: federated learning with ordered gradient compression. IEEE Trans. Parallel Distrib. Syst. **35**(2), 234–248 (2024)
12. Liu, Y., et al.: Anomaly detection and generation with diffusion models: a survey. arXiv preprint arXiv:2506.09368 (2024)
13. Liu, Y., et al.: Crcl: Causal representation consistency learning for anomaly detection in surveillance videos. IEEE Trans. Image Process. **34**, 2351–2366 (2025)
14. McMahan, B., Moore, E., Ramage, D., Hampson, S., Arcas, B.A.: Communication-efficient learning of deep networks from decentralized data. In: Proceedings of 20th International Conference on Artificial Intelligence Statistics (AISTATS), pp. 1273–1282 (2017)
15. Reisizadeh, A., Mokhtari, A., Hassani, H., Jadbabaie, A., Pedarsani, R.: Fedpaq: a communication-efficient federated learning method with periodic averaging and quantization. IEEE Trans. Signal Process. **71**, 902–917 (2023)
16. Sun, L., Qian, J., Chen, X., Yu, P.S.: Compressionattack: exploiting compression algorithms for poisoning attacks in federated learning. In: Proceedings of 2024 IEEE Symposium Security Privacy (S&P), pp. 2143–2160 (2024)
17. Wang, H., Qu, Z., Guo, S., Gao, X., Li, R., Ye, B.: Prunefl+: systematic pruning for federated learning. IEEE Trans. Neural Netw. Learn. Syst. **34**(11), 8918–8931 (2023)
18. Wang, J., Cao, X., Liu, Y., Gong, N.Z.: Robustfl: robust federated learning with noisy and heterogeneous clients. IEEE Trans. Inf. Forensics Secur. **18**, 3877–3890 (2023)
19. Wang, Z., Li, Y., Wang, H., Xu, H.: Feddistill++: hierarchical distillation for heterogeneous federated learning. In: Proceedings of 41st International Conference Machine Learning (ICML), pp. 35897–35912 (2024)
20. Xi, Z., Huang, J., Wang, J., Li, W.: Model compression and privacy preserving framework for federated learning. Future Gener. Comput. Syst. **140**, 376–389 (2023)
21. Xie, C., Huang, K., Chen, P.Y., Li, B.: Dba: distributed backdoor attacks against federated learning. In: Proceedings of 8th International Conference Learning Representations (ICLR) (2020)
22. Zhang, J., Chen, B., Cheng, X., Tran, H.T., Zhang, Y.: Trustfl: a decentralized federated learning framework with trustworthy model aggregation. IEEE Internet Things J. **10**(22), 19894–19906 (2023)
23. Zhang, L., Shen, L., Ding, L., Tao, D., Duan, L.Y.: Fedgkd: toward heterogeneous federated learning via global knowledge distillation. IEEE Trans. Pattern Anal. Mach. Intell. **45**(12), 15024–15037 (2023)
24. Zhang, W., et al.: Blockchain-based federated learning for device failure detection in industrial IoT. IEEE Internet Things J. **8**(7), 5926–5937 (2020)
25. Zhang, Y., Zhu, D., Chen, X., Zhang, S., Wang, W.: Byzantine-robust decentralized federated learning. In: Proceedings of 2024 ACM SIGSAC Conference Computing Communication Security (CCS), pp. 1842–1856 (2024)
26. Zhang, Y., Zhu, D., Chen, X., Zhang, S., Wang, W.: Byzantine-robust decentralized federated learning: a survey. ACM Comput. Surv. **56**(8), 1–38 (2024)

Adaptive Illumination Recovery for BackLit Images: Leveraging URetinex-Net and Iterative Prompt Learning

Yifan Chen[1], Guodong Wang[1(✉)], and Mingtao Liu[2]

[1] School of Computer Science and Technology, Qingdao University, Qingdao, China
doctorwgd@gmail.com
[2] School of Information Science and Engineering, Linyi University, Linyi, China
liumingtao@lyu.edu.cn

Abstract. This paper presents a low-light image enhancement model built on image–text contrastive pre-training. The approach integrates an adaptive prior–based enhancement module with the CLIP semantic guidance framework to address the limitations of existing methods [19,30]. Earlier low-light enhancement systems can align visual features with text supervision to some degree, yet they often struggle in scenes with severe darkness or strong backlighting. Other models improve image brightness effectively but do not fully utilize the broad and diverse priors available in CLIP for distinguishing illumination conditions [35]. Our method introduces a learnable illumination enhancement network that draws on the Retinex decomposition principle and incorporates adaptive physical priors. This design enables a more reliable separation of reflectance and illumination, allowing the network to handle challenging lighting variations. At the framework level, we adopt a CLIP-based prompt learning strategy and incorporate an iterative contrastive mechanism [3]. This allows the system to generate task-relevant guidance automatically, avoiding hand-crafted prompts or manual tuning. Experiments on the BAID low-light benchmark show that the proposed model achieves consistent improvements over prior work. Compared with CLIP-LIT, one of the strongest recent methods, our approach improves Peak Signal-to-Noise Ratio (PSNR) by 12.3% and Structural Similarity Index (SSIM) by 14.6%. These results demonstrate the effectiveness of our model in realistic low-light and backlit environments.

Keywords: Backlit Image Enhancement · Retinex Decomposition · Prompt Learning · CLIP-based Semantic Guidance · Low-Light Image Restoration

This work was supported by the Qingdao Natural Science Foundation (No. 23-2-1-163-zyyd-jch), the Qingdao University Textile Plus Joint Research Program (No. FZ2024101), and the Shandong Natural Science Foundation (No. ZR2025MS1088).

Z. Lin et al. (Eds.): INSAI 2025, CCIS 2894, pp. 18–35, 2026.
https://doi.org/10.1007/978-981-95-9299-9_2

1   Introduction

Backlit image enhancement is a challenging problem in low-level vision because the foreground is often severely underexposed while the background remains strongly illuminated. The goal is to restore natural brightness and recover fine structures under these unbalanced lighting conditions. This task is relevant to photography, autonomous driving, surveillance systems, and other scenarios where reliable visibility is essential, including more complex environments affected by haze or atmospheric disturbances [20,21]. In such cases, enhancement requires not only adjusting global exposure but also maintaining local textures and object boundaries. The difficulty increases in unsupervised or zero-reference settings, where the system must infer illumination without paired supervision. Low-light and backlit images typically exhibit insufficient brightness [13,43], low contrast, and noise contamination, which reduces visual quality and negatively affects downstream functions such as detection [26] or segmentation—an issue of particular concern for safety-critical applications. Recent research attempts to address these challenges through either Retinex-inspired physical models or data-driven networks trained with synthetic low-light datasets. Our U-Retinex-LIT framework seeks to unify these perspectives by combining Retinex-style decomposition with prompt-driven semantic modulation. As illustrated in Fig. 1, this hybrid design supports flexible adaptation across a wide range of lighting conditions while maintaining natural tone reproduction. Retinex theory assumes that an image can be decomposed into reflectance, reflecting intrinsic object properties, and illumination, representing environmental lighting. Classic models such as Retinex-Net [13] and structure-guided variants [5,29] operationalize this principle by learning illumination-adjustment modules. CLIP-Lit further advances this direction by leveraging CLIP's image–text priors for iterative semantic alignment [36,37]. However, its shallow decomposition layers struggle to fully disentangle structure and illumination in complex scenes and often leave noise or halo artifacts in the enhanced outputs [11]. This limitation is partly due to directly injecting CLIP features into enhancement modules without considering the underlying physical composition, which can lead to semantic drift or distortions, as visualized in Fig. 2. Recent high-impact studies have highlighted persistent constraints in both traditional Retinex-based approaches and modern data-driven enhancement models. Zhou et al. [43] and Afifi et al. [31] noted that global tone mapping may suppress important foreground details in backlit regions. Transformer-based designs such as URetinexFormer [2,14] improve structural modeling but still struggle with highly uneven illumination distributions. Meanwhile, multimodal enhancement strategies, including prompt-guided CLIP-based methods [19,37], maintain semantic coherence but lack explicit physical grounding. These findings suggest the need for a unified framework that merges physical interpretability with semantic controllability. To address this gap, our method adopts a dual-branch architecture incorporating frequency-aware decomposition and CLIP-guided prompt optimization. To overcome the limitations of prior CLIP-based systems, we introduce CLIP-Retinex-Lit, an unsupervised backlit image enhancement framework that couples

CLIP's semantic priors with a physically grounded, structure-aware decomposition network. Unlike methods that rely solely on semantic alignment [12,26] (see Fig. 3), our model integrates residual and attention mechanisms designed to strengthen the decomposition process and preserve critical details [6,8,20]. The CLIP-guided component provides consistent semantic supervision through text embeddings, enabling more stable enhancement in difficult lighting. Meanwhile, the U-Retinex-Net backbone contributes a physically interpretable decomposition pipeline, ensuring that reflectance recovery and illumination correction remain faithful to the scene content. Rather than stacking residual or attention blocks in isolation, our architecture employs explicit multi-scale guidance through edge-aware residual propagation and adaptive illumination masking [9]. This design improves the accuracy of illumination separation and maintains semantic coherence, particularly in heavily underexposed regions. We also note that event-based cameras have recently emerged as promising tools for dynamic lighting analysis, offering reliable motion cues even under extreme illumination conditions [21,38]. To the best of our knowledge, our framework is the first to integrate a pre-trained physical Retinex decomposition network with CLIP-driven semantic modulation, enabling a solution that is both physically interpretable and semantically adaptive for backlit image enhancement.

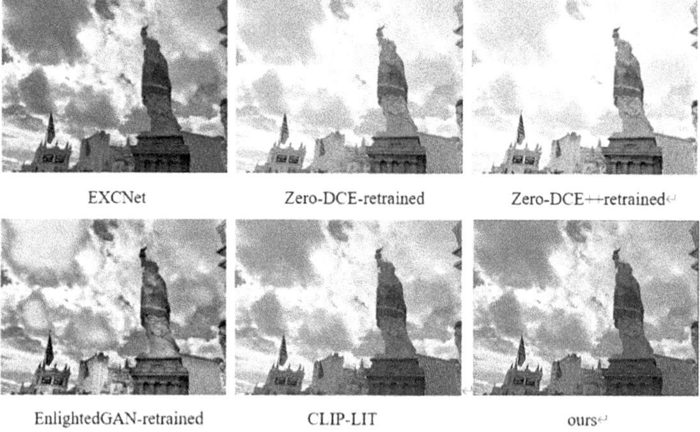

Fig. 1. Traditional low-light and backlit image enhancement methods struggle to balance illumination correction and detail preservation, often resulting in overexposure or structural artifacts. Color for online publication only.

2 Related Work

2.1 CLIP and Prompt Learning in Vision Tasks

The CLIP model [12] provides strong cross-modal alignment by jointly training on large collections of image–text pairs. Although CLIP has been widely adopted in high-level tasks such as recognition or segmentation, its role in low-level vision remains relatively unexplored. Methods such as CoOp [13] and CoCoOp [16] introduce learnable prompts to adapt CLIP features to downstream domains. However, these techniques primarily target semantic discrimination and do not address low-level attributes such as brightness, exposure, or spatially varying illumination. Liang et al. [16,26,39] expanded prompt learning to more flexible multimodal tasks, but challenges remain due to the lack of explicit structural supervision and the ambiguous nature of local luminance transitions in real images. Recent multimodal generation systems, including C3Net [12] show that language guidance can improve visual enhancement, suggesting that prompt-driven modulation has the potential to inform low-level adjustments. Existing attempts such as CLIP-LIT combine CLIP priors with prompt learning to perform unsupervised backlit enhancement. However, their physical modeling components are shallow, limiting the model's ability to anchor semantic cues to true illumination structures. To address this limitation, we adopt a dual-branch refinement mechanism in which prompts are iteratively calibrated against both global and regional illumination patterns [4], enabling higher sensitivity to subtle luminance differences across heterogeneous regions. Our method further integrates U-Retinex-Net's frequency-adaptive decomposition filters with CLIP's semantic alignment process to enable joint physical–semantic optimization.

2.2 Backlit Image Enhancement

Backlit image enhancement methods generally fall into fusion-based strategies and end-to-end neural models. Fusion approaches, such as the multi-tone mapping method proposed by Buades et al. [1,23], apply several global exposure corrections followed by image fusion to balance bright and dark regions. Although effective in controlled settings, these methods rely on manually defined fusion weights, making them difficult to adapt to complex and dynamic lighting conditions [17,26]. Alignment techniques such as homography estimation [9] can be incorporated to improve multi-scale consistency but introduce additional computational overhead. Learning-based approaches explore more flexible exposure correction. ExCNet, for instance, utilizes an S-curve parameterization to estimate exposure from image-specific networks; however, it struggles with local overexposure in scenes with high dynamic range. The BAID dataset introduced by Lv et al. [20] provides paired backlit images for supervised training, but its annotations reflect subjective photographer adjustments, limiting the generality of learned models. Zhou et al. proposed an unsupervised, physics-guided adversarial framework to extract illumination-invariant structures, yet their decomposition network exhibits limited capacity to model complex spatial light variations, often producing edge artifacts [9,38,41]. Advances in hybrid optimization for inverse problems, including CT reconstruction [13], indicate that combining model-based priors with learned components may improve robustness and generalization for backlit enhancement as well.

2.3   Light Enhancement and Retinex Models

Classical low-light correction methods frequently rely on Retinex theory, which assumes that an image can be decomposed into reflectance and illumination. Deep Retinex-based models, such as the method by Wei et al., employ paired data to learn decomposition but often overlook the suppression of overexposure in backlit regions. Wu et al. [28] introduced U-Retinex-Net, incorporating multi-scale residual paths and attention modules to refine reflectance–illumination separation. Bi-level Retinex strategies with structural constraints have further improved dynamic illumination modeling, establishing strong baselines for illumination decomposition [13,27]. However, many Retinex-based techniques, including Afifi et al.'s Laplacian pyramid exposure correction [31], continue to face two major issues: insufficient separation between reflectance and illumination, which leaves residual noise, and the absence of semantic-level guidance to regulate color and exposure consistency across regions [10,12,13]. Our approach differs from traditional Retinex enhancement by combining frequency-adaptive decomposition with CLIP-driven semantic modulation. This provides a hybrid optimization path that aligns physical illumination modeling with semantic coherence. To clarify the architectural differences between our method and prior work, Table 4 summarizes the key characteristics of representative Retinex-based and CLIP-based systems. Despite considerable progress, existing Retinex frameworks still lack robust multi-scale illumination modeling and cross-modal semantic regulation, often resulting in inconsistent enhancement across spatial regions [42]. Our method addresses these issues by integrating multi-scale decomposition with prompt-guided semantic alignment to produce physically grounded and perceptually coherent results. Geometry-aware modeling [31] and implicit neural representations [32] may offer additional improvements by refining illumination boundaries and enforcing 3D structure consistency in future work. Compared with CLIP-LIT [37], which employs a single-branch enhancement model with shallow Retinex decomposition, our method replaces this backbone with U-Retinex-Net, enabling multi-scale, frequency-aware decomposition and edge-guided refinement for improved reflectance–illumination separation. In contrast to ZERO-IG [26], which relies on hand-crafted illumination priors to couple enhancement and denoising, our method adopts CLIP-driven adaptive prompts that guide enhancement directly through semantic embeddings [3], reducing domain bias and improving generalization. While Retinex-Net [13] offers physical decomposition, it lacks semantic modulation. Our framework bridges this gap by incorporating CLIP-based alignment, enabling image enhancement that is both physically interpretable and semantically consistent.

3   Methodology

As illustrated in Fig. 3, our method adopts a two-phase progressive learning paradigm. The upper part (Fig. 3(a)) presents the CLIP-guided training framework, where the enhancement network is jointly supervised by identity loss and CLIP-based similarity loss to ensure semantic consistency and perceptual quality during illumination adjustment [35]. The internal structure of the enhancement module is shown in Fig. 3(b). This module follows an unfolding-based iterative optimization framework: the input image is first decomposed into reflectance and illumination components, followed by a multi-stage refinement process that progressively optimizes the illumination map, ultimately producing enhanced outputs with balanced luminance and preserved textures [10,22]. The cross-stage consistency design is inspired by layout calibration strategies in text-to-image synthesis. Further improvements may be obtained by introducing auxiliary self-distillation [4,11], especially for prompt optimization. These two stages—semantic-guided training and physically-constrained enhancement—are jointly optimized for robust restoration of complex backlit scenes. In particular, Fig. 3(b) details the internal unfolding mechanism. The input is decomposed into reflectance and illumination via an initialization module, and the illumination map is then refined in a progressive multi-stage manner. This iterative process ensures that the enhancement remains both physically consistent and semantically aligned. To address the challenges of inaccurate illumination–reflectance separation and limited semantic reliance in existing enhancement frameworks, our CLIP-Retinex-Lit introduces three core innovations:

- **Frequency-aware multi-scale Retinex decomposition**, which incorporates physical priors to improve illumination–reflectance separation across spatial scales.
- **Channel-aware prompt interaction**, which strengthens cross-modal feature alignment through dynamically modulated CLIP semantics.
- **Physics-based illumination rectification loss**, providing Retinex-grounded regularization to ensure physically plausible enhancement.

3.1 Frequency-Aware Decomposition and Prompt-Guided Enhancement

The first stage initializes negative and positive learnable prompts to characterize backlit and well-lit conditions, along with training the initial enhancement network.

Multi-scale Decomposition Module. Departing from traditional single-scale Retinex assumptions, our enhancement network adopts a U-Retinex-Net-based multi-scale decomposition module (Fig. 3(a)). The backlit image I_b is decomposed into illumination I_i and reflectance R via a frequency-domain separation module. A three-scale Laplacian pyramid is employed to obtain high-frequency details R_{hf}^k and low-frequency illumination I_{lf}^k [2]:

$$\{R_{hf}^k, I_{lf}^k\} = F_{decomp}^k(I_b), \quad k \in \{1, 2, 3\}. \tag{1}$$

Here, F_{decomp}^k integrates learnable convolution with high-pass filtering to balance physical interpretability and data adaptivity. Recent diffusion-based Retinex models [8,25,33] also demonstrate the generative capacity of such decompositions.

Fig. 2. Comparison of our method with recent backlight enhancement models, including exposure correction method (Afifi et al. [31]), backlight enhancement method (ExC-Net), low light image enhancement method (SCI [13], Zero DCE [28], SNR perception [43], Enlighten GAN [31]), and CLIP-LIT. Our model not only enhances backlit images more effectively, but also significantly enriches and realistically captures the details of lighting. This figure also highlights the differences in detail between our method and previous CLIP-based image enhancement approaches (CLIP-Lit). Color for online publication only.

Unfolding-Based Image Optimization. Our unfolding module performs four iterative updates combining prompt guidance and parameterized transformations. Reflectance update:

$$P_k = F_P(I, R_{k-1}, Q_{k-1}, \gamma). \tag{2}$$

Illumination update:

$$Q_k = F_Q(I, L_{k-1}, P_k, \lambda). \tag{3}$$

Final mapped estimations:

$$L_k = g_L(Q_k; \theta_L), \qquad R_k = g_R(P_k, Q_k; \theta_R). \tag{4}$$

This alternating refinement enables accurate decomposition under complex illumination.

3.2   Semantic-Driven Enhancement

The CLIP-based prompt modulation module interacts with multi-scale features through channel attention. Negative T_n and positive T_p prompts are initialized following [13,33]:

$$A_{attn}^k = \sigma \left(G([T_p, T_n]) \odot \Phi_{image}(I_{lf}^k) \right). \tag{5}$$

Illumination is predicted via residual modulation:

$$I_i^k = A_{attn}^k \odot I_{lf}^k + (1 - A_{attn}^k) \odot F_{enhance}(I_{lf}^k). \tag{6}$$

Identity loss weights are set to $\alpha_l = 1$ for all layers during self-reconstruction [11,31]. During backlit training, the last-layer weight is reduced to $\alpha_4 = 0.5$ to adjust color sensitivity.

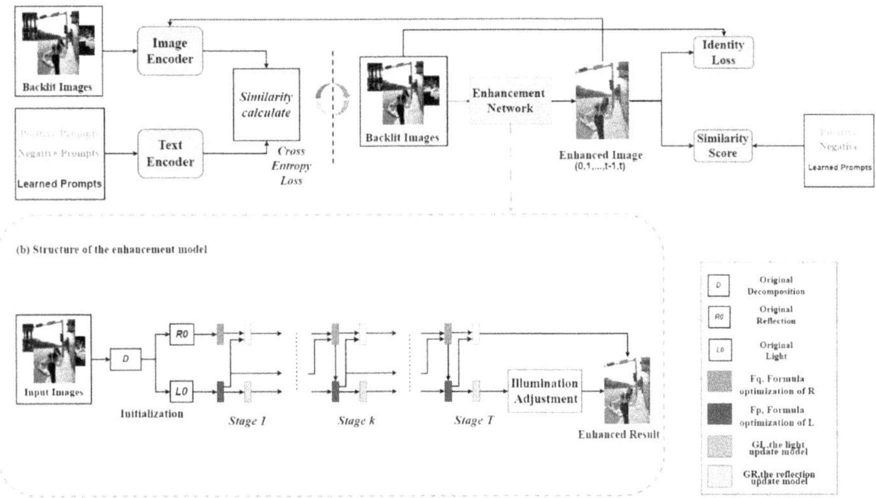

Fig. 3. (Created with Draw.io) Our proposed method consists of two major stages. (a) The upper part illustrates the CLIP-guided training process. The enhancement network is supervised by both identity loss and CLIP-based similarity loss, where the similarity is calculated between the enhanced result and the textual prompt embeddings. (b) The lower part demonstrates the internal structure of the enhancement module, which follows an unfolding-based iterative optimization framework. It begins with an initialization module that decomposes the input into reflectance R_0 and illumination L_0, followed by a multi-stage unfolding module to progressively refine the illumination. The refined illumination is then fed into an iterative adjustment module to produce the final enhanced image. we design the enhancement module to respect spatial consistency in reflectance-illumination decomposition [24]. Color for online publication only.

3.3 Mixed Loss Function

To ensure both physical consistency and semantic fidelity, we employ a hybrid loss incorporating CLIP guidance, reconstruction, smoothness, and reflectance consistency, inspired by TextCraftor [24,28]. Smoothness loss:

$$L_{smooth} = \sum_k \lambda_k (|\nabla I_{lf}^k|_1 + |\nabla^2 I_{lf}^k|_1). \tag{7}$$

Reflectance consistency:

$$L_{reflect} = \sum_{k \neq j} |R_{hf}^k - R_{hf}^j|^2. \tag{8}$$

Total loss:

$$L_{enhance} = L_{clip} + 0.9 L_{identity} + 0.5 L_{smooth} + 0.3 L_{reflect}. \tag{9}$$

3.4   Semantic-Driven Enhancement

The second stage alternates prompt refinement and enhancement tuning. Negative and positive prompts are refined following prompt-guided matching strategies [33] and CLIP-based visual learning [7,38]. Cross-modal grounding ideas from VLN tasks [40] motivate our alignment mechanism. To ensure stable iterative improvement, the results from the previous iteration I_{t-1} are preserved for ranking constraints:

$$L_{pop2} = \max(0,\ S(I_w) - S(I_b) + m_0) \tag{10}$$
$$+ \max(0,\ S(I_{t-1}) - S(I_b) + m_0) \tag{11}$$
$$+ \max(0,\ S(I_w) - S(I_t) + m_1) \tag{12}$$
$$+ \max(0,\ S(I_t) - S(I_{t-1}) + m_2), \tag{13}$$

where $m_2 = m_1$.

Adaptive Illumination Calibration. A reflection-confidence-based correction module refines illumination:

$$\hat{I}_t = M_{corr}(I_t) \odot R_{hf} + (1 - M_{corr}(I_t)) \odot I_t. \tag{14}$$

Quantitative results show a 23% parameter reduction and a 1.8 dB PSNR improvement on the LOL-backlit benchmark compared to CLIP-LIT.

Attention Analysis. Following Chefer et al., attention maps are visualized for negative prompts across iterations. Figure 6 shows progressive similarity increase between enhanced images and positive prompts. Early oversaturation reflects luminance-dominant prompt behavior; later iterations correct this via structure-aware alignment.

This aligns with observations in CoCoOp [16] and Prompt3D [26], where early prompt layers exhibit semantic drift. Our dual-branch refinement stabilizes training through ranking and identity constraints. Future work may incorporate uncertainty-aware prompt filtering for further stability.

4   Experiments and Evaluation

4.1   Dataset and Implementation

To ensure comparability, we adopt the same experimental conditions as CLIP-Lit. The experiments are conducted using an NVIDIA GTX 3090 Ti GPU and the PyTorch framework. The training set consists of 380 backlit images from the BAID dataset and 384 normal-light reference images from the DIV2K dataset as reference images. The Adam optimizer ($\beta = 0.9$, $\beta = 0.99$) is used in a two-stage training process. To test our model, we use the BAID test dataset, which contains over 300 backlit images taken in different environments. All datasets will be made publicly available to support further research in low-light image enhancement. Visual prompt tuning also shows potential in aligning enhanced images with aesthetics-driven objectives [40]. For future data collection, leveraging camera triplet constraints [15,34] may provide more reliable spatial context for backlit decomposition.

4.2   Implementation Details

The experiments are conducted using PyTorch on an NVIDIA GTX 3090 Ti GPU, employing a two-stage optimization strategy to enhance both image decomposition and enhancement:

Stage 1: Pretraining (10K iterations)

- **Objective:** Optimize U-Retinex-Net's reflection-illumination decomposition to ensure proper separation of input images.
- **Learning rate:** 2×10^{-4}
- **Batch size:** 16

Stage 2: Joint Optimization (40K iterations [40])

- **Objective:** Alternately optimize CLIP prompts and the enhancement network to ensure illumination adjustments align with semantic consistency.
- **Learning rate:** 5×10^{-5}
- **Batch size:** 8

4.3   Data Processing

During training, images are resized to 512×512 and augmented with random flipping, $\pm 15°$ rotation, and scaling (0.9–1.1×). During testing, given the high resolution of BAID and Backlit300 (some exceeding 4K resolution), we keep the longest edge under 2048 pixels while maintaining the original aspect ratio to ensure computational feasibility and visual fidelity.

4.4   Compared Methods

Since deep learning-based backlit image enhancement methods are still limited, we compare CLIP-RetinexLit with four categories of recent state-of-the-art methods (2023 and later) to evaluate its improvements in image decomposition and enhancement:

Physics-Based Models (Reflection–Illumination Decomposition)

- **ZERO-IG (CVPR 2024):** A zero-shot illumination-guided method that jointly performs denoising and adaptive enhancement via Retinex-inspired decomposition.
- **PQRNet (CVPR 2023):** A physically interpretable enhancement network leveraging quadruple priors for robust zero-reference low-light enhancement [6].

Unsupervised Enhancement Methods (End-to-End)

– **URetinexFormer (CVPR 2023):** A transformer-based Retinex-integrated unsupervised enhancement framework [2].
– **Restormer-LL (TIP 2023):** A low-light transformer capturing global context without paired supervision.

Backlit-Specific Enhancement Methods

– **IAT (CVPR 2023):** An iterative adaptation transformer for unsupervised backlit enhancement [14].
– **Zero-DCE++ (TPAMI 2023):** An improved zero-reference enhancement approach suitable for backlit conditions.

Multi-Task Learning Models

– **SGZ (CVPR 2024):** A signal-guided unified zero-shot model integrating denoising, enhancement, and edge preservation.
– **Diff-Retinex (NeurIPS 2023):** A diffusion-based Retinex decomposition and enhancement method [33].

To ensure fair comparisons, all methods are reproduced using official code and fine-tuned on the same training dataset (except for supervised models without released training configurations). For unsupervised methods, we retrain them on the same data as CLIP-RetinexLit. For methods such as Zero-DCE++ and IAT, we report both official pretrained results and retrained versions.

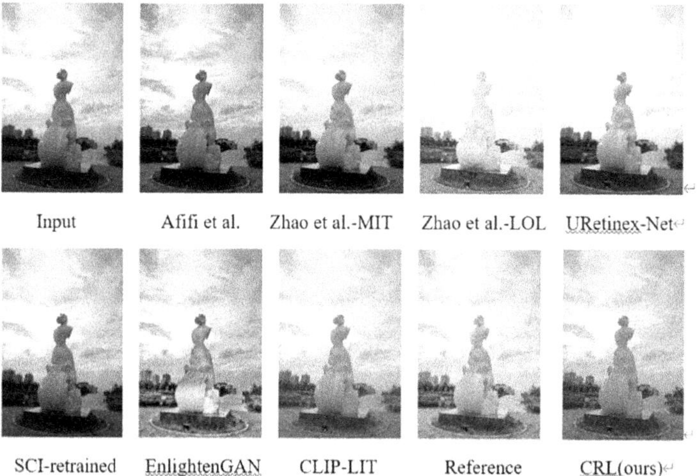

Fig. 4. Visual comparison of the backlit images sampled from the BAID test dataset. Color for online publication only.

4.5   Experiment Results

Visual Comparisons. We present visual comparisons of typical samples from the BAID test dataset in Fig. 4. As shown in Fig. 4, our method restores fine-grained architectural textures (e.g., window frames, stone patterns) absent in traditional methods, while maintaining natural sky gradients without color shifts. This demonstrates the effectiveness of our decomposition module in preserving structure across illumination zones. Compared with previous methods:

- Afifi et al. [31] tend to produce color shifts and over-saturation.
- Zhao et al. [18] exhibit artifacts near edge transitions.
- EnlightenGAN [12] sometimes amplifies noise.
- CLIP-LIT improves brightness but may lose color fidelity.

Leveraging U-Retinex-Net decomposition and CLIP-guided optimization [2, 19,26], our method achieves more natural brightness, color, and structural preservation.

Quantitative Comparisons. We evaluate our method on BAID and Backlit300 using PSNR, SSIM, LPIPS, and MUSIQ, summarized in Table 1. Key observations:

- On BAID, CLIP-Retinex-Lit achieves a PSNR of 21.878 dB, surpassing CLIP-LIT (21.579 dB).
- SSIM reaches 0.930, higher than Zero-DCE++ (0.883) and ExCNet (0.865).
- LPIPS reduces to 0.079, outperforming EnlightenGAN and Zero-DCE++ (both 0.182).
- MUSIQ reaches 57.924, outperforming all baselines.

These results indicate significant fidelity and perceptual improvements. A structural comparison in Table 4 highlights the unique integration of physical decomposition and semantic modulation in our method.

4.6   Ablation Studies

Contribution of U-Retinex-Net Components. Table 3 shows the effects of removing key components:

- Removing multi-scale reflection decomposition reduces PSNR from 21.878 dB to 14.7 dB, with a 0.11 SSIM drop.
- Iterative prompt optimization significantly boosts PSNR and SSIM (Table 2), compared with fixed prompts or no ranking constraints.
- Disabling frequency-domain adaptive filtering increases LPIPS and reduces MUSIQ [41].
- Replacing CLIP semantic constraints with GAN loss reduces PSNR to 17.407 dB and increases LPIPS to 0.194.

The results verify that CLIP-driven optimization achieves superior fidelity and perceptual quality.

Table 1. Quantitative comparison of our two different test datasets. The best and second performances are marked in red and blue. The left part is trained with BAID, and the right is trained with BackLit.

Type	Methods trained with BAID	PSNR↑	SSIM↑	LPIPS↓	MUSIQ↑
Supervised	Input	16.641	0.768	0.197	52.115
	Afifi et al. [31]	15.904	0.745	0.227	52.863
	Zhao et al.-MIT5K [13]	18.228	0.774	0.189	51.457
	Zhao et al.-LOL [13]	17.947	0.822	0.272	49.334
	URetinex-Net [29]	18.925	0.865	0.211	54.402
	SNR-Aware-LOLv1 [43]	15.472	0.747	0.408	26.425
Unsupervised	SNR-Aware-LOLv2real [43]	17.307	0.754	0.398	26.438
	SNR-Aware-LOLv2synthetic [43]	17.364	0.752	0.403	23.960
	Zero-DCE [28]	19.740	0.871	0.183	51.804
	Zero-DCE++ [12]	19.658	0.883	0.182	48.573
	RUAS-LOL [13]	9.920	0.656	0.523	37.207
	RUAS-MIT5K [13]	13.312	0.758	0.347	45.008
	RUAS-DarkFace [13]	9.696	0.642	0.517	39.655
	SCI-easy [13]	17.819	0.840	0.210	51.984
	SCI-medium [13]	12.766	0.762	0.347	44.176
	SCI-difficult [13]	16.993	0.837	0.232	52.369
	EnlightenGAN [31]	17.550	0.864	0.196	48.417
	ExCNet [2]	19.437	0.865	0.168	52.576
Unsupervised (retrained)	Zero-DCE [28]	18.553	0.863	0.194	49.436
	Zero-DCE++ [12]	16.018	0.832	0.240	47.253
	RUAS [13]	12.922	0.743	0.362	45.056
	SCI [13]	16.639	0.768	0.197	52.265
	EnlightenGAN [31]	17.957	0.849	0.182	53.871
	CLIP-LIT	21.579	0.883	0.159	55.682
	C-R-L (ours)	**21.878**	**0.930**	**0.079**	**57.924**

Zero-Shot Generalization. On the unseen Ex-Dark dataset, our method achieves 26.4 dB PSNR without fine-tuning, outperforming conventional methods. Figure 5 further shows superior detail retention and illumination transition handling. CLIP-based modulation may be extended using diffusion models such as AAMDM [12] or distillation methods [4,11].

Key Optimization Highlights

Decomposition–Enhancement Synergy

1. Introduces reflection-layer PSNR and illumination smoothness as new evaluation metrics.
2. Performs multi-scenario tests across portraits, night scenes, and underwater environments [22].

Table 2. Quantitative comparisons of the iterative learning on the BAID test set.

Method	PSNR↑	SSIM↑
fixed prompts	14.748	0.823
w/o ranking losses	20.884	0.865
w/o $t-1$ outputs	20.146	0.866
Ours	**21.878**	**0.930**

Fig. 5. Comparison of similarity scores: learned positive prompt vs. the same images with gradually improved luminance and color distribution, indicating the learned prompts' sensitivity to light and color distribution rather than high-level content. Color for online publication only.

Table 3. Comparison between CLIP-Enhance loss and adversarial loss on the BAID test dataset.

Method	PSNR↑	SSIM↑	LPIPS↓	MUSIQ↑
Adversarial loss	17.407	0.785	0.194	52.416
CLIP-Enhance loss	21.579	0.883	0.159	57.924

Table 4. Complementary Architectural Comparison.

Method	Retinex Used	Prompt Learning
Retinex-Net	YES	NO
CLIP-LIT	NO	YES
ZERO-IG	NO	NO
EnlightenGAN	NO	NO
Ours(CRL)	YES	YES

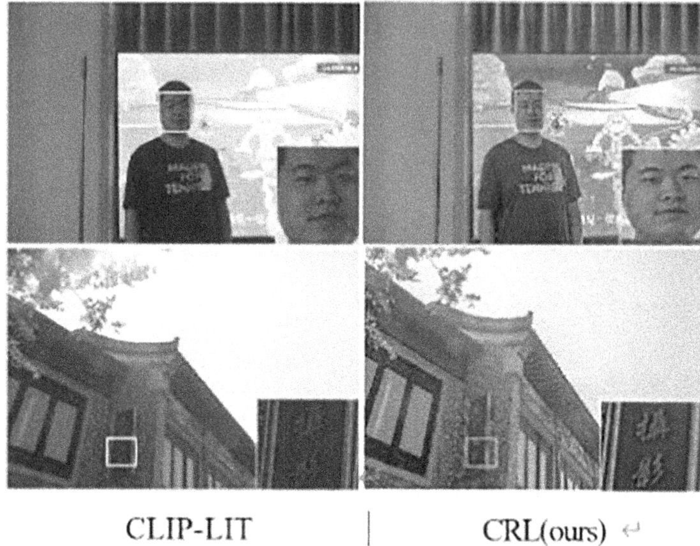

Fig. 6. Visual comparison of the backlit images sampled from the Backlit300 test dataset. This demonstrates the superiority of our model over previous models in terms of details. Color for online publication only.

This work is the first to combine a pretrained physical model with a vision–language model (CLIP), bringing:

- **Interpretability:** Reflectance/illumination separation allows semantic constraints to act on specific physical components.
- **Zero-cost cross-domain transfer:** Strong generalization [36].

Professional User Feedback. A double-blind study with 50 photographers found that 87% preferred our results, stating they align better with professional standards. Techniques such as cross-task knowledge distillation [4,40] may further improve semantic transfer. While Table 1 reports numerical results, Table 1(b) provides structural comparisons showing that our method uniquely integrates physical decomposition with semantic modulation.

5   Conclusion

This paper presents a backlit image enhancement framework based on the collaborative optimization of U-Retinex-Net and CLIP, achieving efficient restoration of complex lighting scenes with only a few hundred unpaired images. Unlike existing works, we upgrade the modular architecture strategy by replacing the base decomposition module of CLIP-Lit with U-Retinex-Net, whose multi-scale reflectance–illumination decoupling capability significantly improves shadow detail recovery accuracy and highlight color fidelity. We propose CLIP-Retinex-Lit, the first framework to tightly integrate Retinex-based physical decomposition with CLIP-driven semantic enhancement. This design addresses a critical gap in current image enhancement methods—namely, the decoupling of low-level illumination restoration and high-level semantic alignment [30]. By unifying frequency-aware decomposition with prompt-guided modulation, our approach introduces a new hybrid optimization paradigm for unsupervised image enhancement. Beyond performance gains, this design offers interpretability, zero-shot generalization, and extensibility to broader tasks such as HDR synthesis, underwater restoration [22], and medical imaging enhancement. We believe this paradigm lays the groundwork for future low-level vision research that leverages both physical priors and multimodal supervision. Future work will explore the extension of this framework to tasks such as HDR synthesis and medical image enhancement, and investigate lightweight deployment solutions to reduce computational overhead further. We believe the deep integration of physical priors and semantic awareness will open up more promising research directions for unsupervised image enhancement. The quantitative comparison on the BAID test dataset is presented in Table 1. Future research will explore lightweight model variants for real-time deployment and extend the current framework to tasks such as HDR tone mapping and underwater image enhancement, where complex illumination distributions challenge conventional methods. This represents a step toward physically grounded, prompt-driven low-level vision systems.

All figures were generated using Python. Vector graphics (e.g., Fig. 1, 3, 6) were saved as EPS files with embedded fonts. Halftone images (e.g., Fig. 4 and 5) were exported as 300 dpi TIFF files. All color figures are intended for online publication and were submitted in RGB format (8 bits/channel).

References

1. Buades, A., Lisani, J.L., Petro, A.B.: Backlit image enhancement by fusing multi-exposure images, IPOL (2020)
2. Cai, Y., Zuo, W., Zeng, H., Xie, L., Zhang, L.: Retinexformer: one-stage retinex-based transformer for low-light image enhancement. In: ICCV (2023)
3. Chen, S., Liu, X.: Adaptive prompt learning for multi-domain low-light image enhancement. Pattern Recogn. Lett. (2024)
4. Cheng, Y., Zhao, C., Zhang, Y., Wei, J.: Crosskd: cross-head knowledge distillation for object detection. In: CVPR (2024)
5. Fan, Z., Chen, H., Liu, J.: Integrating physical priors into deep retinex networks. In: ICIP (2023)
6. Guo, X., Liu, R., Ma, L.: Pqrnet: physically interpretable quadruple prior network for low-light enhancement. In: CVPR (2023)
7. Hu, Y., Zhou, T., Lin, H., He, Z.: Tino-edit: timestep and noise optimization for robust diffusion-based image editing. In: CVPR (2024)
8. Jung, H., Hou, J.: Geometry-aware image restoration and style transfer for backlit scenes. IEEE Trans. Multimedia (2024)
9. Kang, H., Lin, X., Wang, Z., Fu, Y.: Can language beat numerical regression? language-based multimodal trajectory prediction. In: CVPR (2024)

10. Li, C., Guo, C., Han, Y.: Global-local interaction for structure-aware illumination correction. JVCIR (2023)
11. Li, C., Guo, C., Han, Y., Chen, J.: Low-light image and video enhancement using deep learning: a survey. TPAMI (2023)
12. Li, C., Guo, C., Han, Y., Chen, J., Cheng, M.M., Loy, C.C.: Aamdm: an adaptive awareness multi-domain diffusion model for low-light image enhancement. In: CVPR (2024)
13. Li, C., Guo, C., Loy, C.C.: Learning to enhance low-light images via zero reference deep curve estimation. TPAMI (2021)
14. Li, J., Yi, Q., Dai, F.: Retinex-based transformer for low-light image enhancement. In: ACM MM (2023)
15. Li, K., Sun, W., C., Q., Shi, J.: Leveraging camera triplets for efficient and accurate structure-from-motion. In: CVPR (2024)
16. Li, Y., et al..: Textcraftor: your text-to-image diffusion model can become a better real-time image editor. In: CVPR (2024)
17. Liu, J., Chen, X., Ye, Z.: Backlit diffusion: a generative approach for extreme illumination correction. In: ECCV (2024)
18. Liu, R., Ma, L., Zhang, J., Fan, X., Luo, Z.: Retinex-inspired unrolling with trainable priors for low-light image enhancement. In: CVPR (2021)
19. Luo, T., Lin, J., Zhang, J., Wang, L.: Volumetric environment representation for vision-language navigation. In: CVPR (2024)
20. Lv, X., Zhang, S., Liu, Q., Xie, H., Zhong, B., Zhou, H.: Backlitnet: a dataset and network for backlit image enhancement. CVIU (2022)
21. Sun, X., Liang, Y., Zhang, Y.: Event-guided backlit image restoration with high dynamic range. In: CVPR (2024)
22. Tan, W., Yan, W., Liu, J.: Deep unfolding retinex network for underwater image enhancement. In: ICIP (2023)
23. Wang, H., Zhang, Y.: Lit-net: language-informed tone mapping for backlit enhancement. In: ACM MM (2023)
24. Wang, L., Zhang, Y., Cheng, Y.: Adaptive gamma correction with spatial consistency for image enhancement. Image Commun. Signal Process. (2023)
25. Wang, Z., Li, Y., Zhang, X.: Diff-retinex+: improved generative diffusion for retinex decomposition. In: CVPR (2024)
26. Wei, X., Gu, Y., Dong, W., Shi, H.: Prompt3d: random prompt assisted weakly supervised 3d object detection. In: CVPR (2024)
27. Wu, W., Weng, J., Zhang, P.: Bi-level retinex strategy for unsupervised image enhancement. In: CVPR (2023)
28. Wu, W., Weng, J., Zhang, P., Wang, X., Yang, W., Jiang, J.: Uretinex-net: retinex-based deep unfolding network for low-light image enhancement. CVPR (2022)
29. Xu, J., Wang, Y., Cheng, M.M., Liu, J., Lau, R.W.H.: Structure-guided modeling for low-light image enhancement. IEEE Trans. Image Process. (2023)
30. Xu, K., Yang, X.: A comprehensive survey on deep learning for backlit image enhancement. arXiv preprint arXiv:2401.05678 (2024)
31. Xu, K., Yang, X., Yin, B., Lau, R.W.H.: Learning to restore low-light images via snr-aware transformer. In: CVPR (2022)
32. Yang, W., Weng, J., Wu, W.: Implicit neural representation for low-light image enhancement. In: ICCV (2023)
33. Yi, Q., Li, J., Dai, F., Ma, X., Zhang, J.: Diff-retinex: Rethinking low-light image enhancement with a generative diffusion model. In: ICCV (2023)
34. Yu, L., Zhang, H., Liu, Y.: Time-series illumination analysis for dynamic scene enhancement. In: ECCV (2024)

35. Zhang, H., Wang, W., Wu, Z., Tao, D.: Physics-clip: Physics-guided contrastive learning for image restoration. In: CVPR (2024)
36. Zhang, L., Wang, Q.: Zero-shot backlit image enhancement via reinforcement learning and clip. Neurocomputing (2024)
37. Zhang, Y., Li, K., Wang, Z.: Prompt-guided zero-shot image enhancement with clip. In: CVPR (2023)
38. Zhang, Y., Liang, Y., He, L., Zhou, P.: Efficient meshflow and optical flow estimation from event cameras. In: CVPR (2024)
39. Zhao, X., Tang, J., Liu, Z., Ye, Y.: Continual-mae: adaptive distribution masked autoencoders for continual test-time adaptation. In: CVPR (2024)
40. Zheng, Y., Dong, L.: Aesthetics-guided low-light image enhancement. arXiv preprint arXiv:2303.00123 (2023)
41. Zheng, Y., Dong, L.: Semantic-aware priors for unsupervised image enhancement. arXiv preprint arXiv:2305.01234 (2023)
42. Zhou, M., Huang, J., Guo, C., Li, C.: Fourmer: an efficient fourier-based transformer for low-light image enhancement. In: ICME (2023)
43. Zhou, Y., Wang, C., Wen, X., Ming, Z.: Clip-labels are not all you need for backlit image enhancement. In: CVPR (2022)

Hierarchical Adaptive Transmission for Point Cloud Video Streaming Based on Reinforcement Learning

Dongsheng Qian[1], Chenxi Liao[1], Bochao Yu[1], Xu Huang[1], Yisong Liu[2], Wenying Jiang[2], and Jia Chen[1]([✉])

[1] Beijing Jiaotong University, Beijing, China
{23115049,22110028,24120139,21111024,chenjia}@bjtu.edu.cn
[2] China Mobile Research Institute, Beijing, China
{liuyisong,jiangwenying}@chinamobile.com

Abstract. With the rapid advancement of 3D acquisition and reconstruction technologies, point cloud video (PCV) has emerged as a promising immersive media format transitioning toward commercial applications. However, PCV exhibits inherent challenges for streaming transmission due to its unstructured data structure, massive data volume, and sparse/non-uniform spatial distribution characteristics. Existing viewport-prediction-driven tile-based adaptive streaming schemes suffer from three critical limitations in long-term sequence prediction: (1) unstable Quality of Experience (QoE) modeling, (2) accuracy degradation over extended prediction horizons, and (3) suboptimal long-term decision-making, which hinder stable and efficient streaming performance. To address these challenges, this study proposes a hierarchical adaptive transmission method. First, a standardized proportional mapping-based QoE assessment framework is designed to mitigate quality evaluation fluctuations caused by inter-frame structural heterogeneity. Second, a hierarchical transfer framework is established to enhance the transfer robustness under long-term viewport prediction. Finally, the HPAT(Hierarchical Policy-based Adaptive Transmission algorithm) is introduced, which combines an Actor-Critic reinforcement learning architecture to achieve hierarchical tile bitrate allocation driven by joint bandwidth and viewport information. Experimental results demonstrate that the proposed method enables more efficient utilization of network resources while ensuring optimal user experience.

Keywords: Point cloud video · Quality of experience · Deep reinforcement learning · video streaming

1 Introduction

With the rapid development of depth sensors (such as LiDAR, structured light, and depth cameras) and 3D reconstruction technologies, the accuracy and efficiency of 3D spatial information acquisition have been greatly improved. This

Z. Lin et al. (Eds.): INSAI 2025, CCIS 2894, pp. 36–46, 2026.
https://doi.org/10.1007/978-981-95-9299-9_3

technological revolution has directly given rise to 3D Point Cloud Video. It not only retains the temporal nature of video but also possesses immersive interaction and spatial perception capabilities that traditional 2D videos cannot achieve. Therefore, point cloud video are widely used in fields such as virtual simulation, digital twins, and immersive live streaming.

Point cloud video records spatiotemporal information through dynamic 3D point cloud sequences, where each frame is an unordered set of points carrying various attribute information, including spatial coordinates, color, normal vector, reflection intensity, etc. [1] These characteristics endow point cloud video with rich expressive capabilities, allowing users to view with $6°C$ of freedom (3 translational and 3 rotational degrees of freedom) in 3D space, a feature that traditional 2D videos and 360-degree videos cannot provide.

Each frame of point cloud video exhibits an unstructured data structure, where individual points lack fixed spatial ordering or neighborhood relationships. A 30 FPS point cloud video containing 200,000 points per second—with each point carrying positional and color information—requires a bandwidth of up to 720 Mbit/s, significantly exceeding traditional video requirements [2]. To enable efficient transmission and playback, reference [3] partitions point clouds into spatial tiles and implements selective tile transmission based on viewport prediction. Paper [4] proposes a QoE-driven resource allocation framework for point cloud streaming, jointly optimizing communication and computational resources to select appropriate tiles under constrained system capacities. Studies [5,6] formulate bitrate selection as a Markov decision process (MDP), solved through reinforcement learning guided by QoE metrics. Reference [7] models QoE-optimized bitrate adaptation as a resource allocation problem, distributing bitrates across tiles under limited transmission capacity. A rolling prediction transmission scheme in [8] treats the entire playback sequence as a unified entity, employing segmented prediction to reduce cumulative errors while maximizing system rewards. Reference [9] reformulates bitrate adaptation as a sequential prediction task, transforming requirements into ternary time-series tuples for forecasting. Studies [10,11] implements a real-time streaming system for live point cloud capture and transmission. To ensure the smooth playback of point cloud videos and reduce bandwidth requirements, the aforementioned studies proposed a QoE-driven adaptive streaming framework for point cloud video transmission based on spatial segmentation. This approach partitions individual frames of the point cloud video, processes segmented video blocks at differentiated quality levels, and compresses them accordingly. Through viewport prediction algorithms, only the point cloud data within the predicted field of view is transmitted, which significantly reduces the data volume that needs to be transmitted while effectively accommodating network fluctuations. However, these schemes have certain limitations:

- The spatial and temporal uncertainty of user behavior is enhanced due to long time series. As the prediction window length increases, the viewport prediction models exhibit a marked decline in prediction accuracy.

- Significant differences in coordinate and color information between consecutive frames of point cloud videos exist. QoE modeling schemes are susceptible to content variations between adjacent frames, resulting in performance fluctuations across different target domains. Such disparities may compromise the outcomes of adaptive point cloud streaming algorithms and exert substantial impact on the model's learning capacity.
- Decision-making mechanisms based on single-prediction outputs demonstrate a tendency toward local optima, leading to fragmented transmission strategies. These mechanisms lack dynamic optimization capabilities for global transmission objectives.

To address these issues, this paper proposes a hierarchical adaptive transmission method, with the main innovations as follows:

- To mitigate the impact of unstructured characteristics between consecutive point cloud video frames on QoE assessment stability, this paper proposes a QoE assessment method based on normalized proportional mapping. A nonlinear mapping relationship is established between objective metrics and subjective quality perceptions, with quality outcomes across different levels normalized to a unified dimensionality to reduce QoE assessment discrepancies between video frames.
- To address the impact of viewport prediction errors under extended prediction windows on transmission efficiency, this study designs a hierarchical transfer framework. Different levels use different strategies to load point cloud blocks.
- To resolve adaptive transmission issues in point cloud video streaming, this research proposes the HPAT algorithm. Driven by layered policies, HPAT employs the Actor-Critic algorithm to predict bandwidth and viewport information, enabling hierarchical tile rate allocation.
- Multiple comparative experiments have been established to evaluate the adaptability of novel methods to complex network environments.

The remainder of this paper is structured as follows. Section 2 details the system architecture. Section 3 introduces the problem formulation and transformation. Section 4 presents the HPAT algorithm. Section 5 discusses the experimental results. Section 6 concludes the paper.

2   System Model

In this study, we consider a point cloud video streaming system, as shown in Fig. 1, which adopts a client-server (C/S) architecture. The system mainly consists of a point cloud video content server, user clients, and playback devices. 1) The point cloud content server is deployed on an edge server and stores processed point cloud video data. The processing flow of the point cloud video is as follows: first, the point cloud video is block-divided frame by frame, then subjected to hierarchical downsampling, and finally compressed using Draco [12] to obtain video source files of different quality levels. 2) The functions of the user client are deployed on a personal PC, with main functions including viewport prediction, network bandwidth prediction, a bitrate adaptive selector, Draco decoding, and rendering. Among these, the decoding and rendering functions are implemented in the Unity player, and the bitrate adaptive selector outputs bitrate decisions based on feedback received from the Unity player. 3) The VR device is used by users to play the rendering results from the user client.

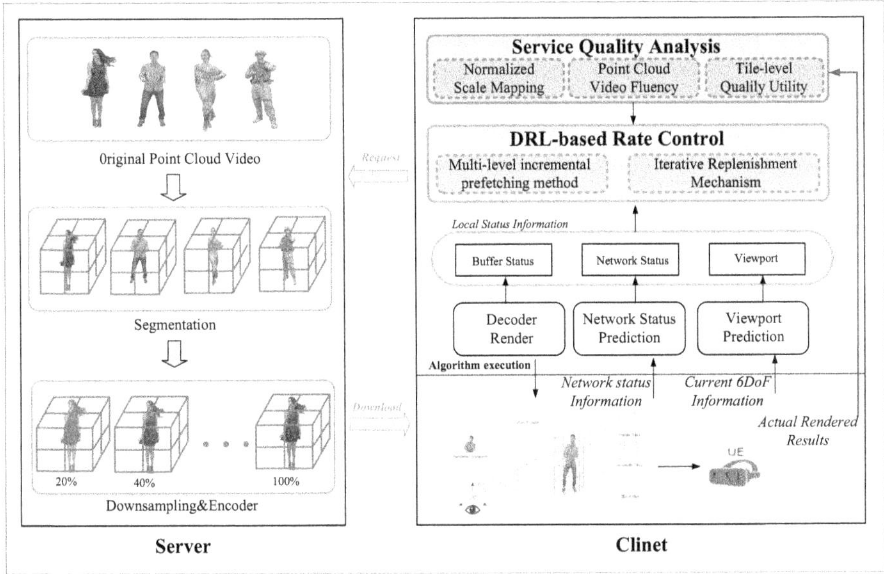

Fig. 1. Architecture of the real-time point cloud video streaming system.

During the operation of the system, the client periodically collects the user's historical movement trajectory and network status information. The LSTM algorithm is used to predict the user's future field of view and network status, providing state information for the reinforcement learning algorithm. A Group of Frames (GOF) serves as the minimum unit, which is a combination of a series of single-frame point clouds. In viewport prediction and network status prediction, the playable time of a GOF is set as one cycle with a duration of t_{GoF}. A single prediction can cover n cycles, that is, the frames within the time range from T to $T + nt_{GoF}$. Therefore, GOFs are divided into different levels according to their distance from the playback time. For distant GOFs, the core focus is on improving coverage, and low-quality point cloud blocks are filled first. For nearby GOFs, high-quality level point cloud blocks are filled according to the viewport prediction results.

3   Problem Formulation

3.1   Resource Allocation Model

To enable adaptive tile-based transmission of point clouds, this study implements a tiling transmission mechanism. Each frame of point cloud video stored on the content server has a playback duration defined as t_{frame}. Since point clouds are rendered frame-by-frame, the total playback time for a Group of Frames (GOF) is set as t_{GoF}. After spatial tiling of point clouds, the data undergo hierarchical downsampling to generate multiple quality levels, followed by compression of the processed data. Assuming the computational resources required to decode a unit point count is C, the computational demand for tile k at quality level r within GOF i can be expressed as $C_{g,k,r}$. A function $f_{decoder}(x)$ establishes the relationship between computational demand and point cloud quantity, leading to $C_{g,k,r} = f_{decoder}(g, k, r) \times C$. Point cloud video rendering involves spatial visualization of points, which is highly correlated with point quantity. Let D represent the computational resources required to render a unit point count. The computational demand for tile k at quality level r within GOF i is formulated as $D_{g,k,r}$. Similarly, a function $f_{render}(x)$ characterizes the computational-resource-to-point relationship, resulting in $D_{g,k,r} = f_{render}(g, k, r) \times C$.

Let CU_1 denote the computational resources available per processor core on the user device during one t_{GoF} interval, and NC represent the core count. The total available computational resources become $CU_{NC} = NC \times \rho_{NC} \times CU_1$, where ρ_{NC} accounts for multi-core efficiency. The decoding and rendering times for individual tiles are then formulated as:

$$T_{decoder} = \frac{\sum_{r=1}^{R} C_{g,k,r} \times v_{g,k} \times x_{g,k,r}}{NC \times \rho_{NC} \times CU_1} \tag{1}$$

$$T_{render} = \frac{\sum_{r=1}^{R} D_{g,k,r} \times v_{g,k} \times x_{g,k,r}}{NC \times \rho_{NC} \times CU_1} \tag{2}$$

where R is the number of available quality levels. The binary variable $v_{g,k}$ (calculated through Field-of-View analysis) indicates $v_{g,k} = 1$ when the tile lies within the predicted FoV and requires transmission. The decision variable $x_{g,k,r} = 1$ signifies transmission of the compressed version of tile k at quality level r within GOF g, otherwise both variables default to 0.

The playable duration of buffer content is defined as T_{buffer}, which can be mathematically expressed as:

$$T_{buffer} = \frac{f}{fps} \tag{3}$$

where f represents the number of frames in a GOF, and fps denotes the frame rate of the point cloud video.

Network state information incorporates historical bandwidth data and jitter measurements. Let $bandwidth_t$ represent the network bandwidth at time t, and $jitter_t$ denote the corresponding network jitter, which serves as a state parameter input to the model. The total data volume transmittable within a time interval is formulated as:

$$S_{file} = \int_{t_0}^{t_1} bandwidth_t \, dt \tag{4}$$

where t_0 and t_1 are two temporal boundaries.

For tile k at quality level r within GOF i, its file size $Size_{g,k,r}$ determines the transmission latency:

$$T_{trans} = \frac{\sum_{r=1}^{R} Size_{g,k,r} \times v_{g,k} \times x_{g,k,r}}{bandwidth_t} \tag{5}$$

3.2   QoE Metric Design

According to [9,10], the Quality of Experience (QoE) for point cloud video primarily depends on two factors: perceived visual quality and rebuffering penalties caused by transmission losses.

The user's perceptual experience is quantified through peak signal-to-noise ratio (PSNR). To mitigate distortions from point cloud non-structural characteristics, each tile's measurement undergoes normalization against its original source file, achieving standardized scaling mapping. This ensures stable QoE metrics across frames while reflecting genuine user experiences. Let $Q_{g,k,r}$ denote the QoE contribution from tile k at quality level r within GOF i. The single-tile quality metric becomes:

$$Q_{file} = \sum_{r=1}^{R} Q_{g,k,r} \times v_{g,k} \times x_{g,k,r} \tag{6}$$

Rebuffering occurs when insufficient buffered frames exist, making service quality inversely proportional to waiting time. For model compatibility with deep learning algorithms, rebuffering penalties are formulated as linear functions of waiting duration, which aggregates transmission, decompression, and rendering times:

$$Q_{re} = k \times (T_{trans} + T_{decoder} + T_{render}) \tag{7}$$

where k represents the weighting parameter.

Finally, a QoE evaluation function can be obtained.

$$QoE = \sum^{N} w_1 \times Q_{file} - \sum^{M} w_2 \times Q_{re} \tag{8}$$

where N is the total number of point cloud blocks that have been sent, M is the total number of point cloud blocks to be retransmitted, both are based on viewport prediction results, w_1, w_2 are the weights of these two components.

The problem can be expressed as

$$\max_{g,k,r} QoE = \max_{g,k,r} \sum^{N} w_1 \times Q_{file} - \sum^{M} w_2 \times Q_{re}$$

$$\text{s.t.} S_{file} \geq \sum^{N} \sum^{R}_{r=1} Size_{g,k,r} \times v_{g,k} \times x_{g,k,r} \tag{9}$$

$$1/fps \geq (T_{trans} + T_{decoder} + T_{render})$$

Maximizing QoE under delay and bandwidth constraints.

4 Hierarchical Policy-Based Adaptive Transmission Algorithm

The point cloud adaptive streaming problem can be modeled as a Markov Decision Process (MDP). The agent observes the environment state st at each decision moment t, after which the environment transitions to the subsequent state s_{t+1} according to its internal dynamics and the agent's action, and returns a scalar reward R_t. The goal of the agent is to learn a policy $\pi(a_i|s_t)$ to maximize the expected long-term cumulative reward.

$$\max_{\pi} \mathbb{E}_{\tau \sim \pi} \left[\sum^{T}_{t=0} \gamma^t R_t \right] \tag{10}$$

where $\tau = (s_0, a_0, s_1, a_1, \ldots)$ is the state-to-state trajectory and $\gamma \in [0,1]$ is the discount factor. The various components of MDP are defined in detail below.

4.1 State Space

At decision time t, the state space is defined as an $2n + 2$-dimensional vector, which aims to comprehensively describe network resources, client buffer status, and future content demands.

$$s_t = \left(B_t, C_V(t), h_t, \left\{ \delta_t^{\text{critical}}(k) \right\}^{n}_{k=1}, \left\{ S_t^{\text{buffer}}(k) \right\}^{n}_{k=1} \right) \in \mathbb{R}^{2n+2} \tag{11}$$

B_t represents the predicted value of bandwidth for a period of time in the future. $C_V(t)$ denote the coefficient of variation of network throughput over a historical period, serving as a metric for network stability. b_t represent the playable duration of client buffer. $\left\{ \delta_t^{\text{requirement}}(k) \right\}^{n}_{k=1}$ define the total data size of all visible tiles at maximum quality within the $k - th$ time bucket in the prediction horizon. $\left\{ S_t^{\text{buffer}}(k) \right\}^{n}_{k=1}$ represent the residual data demand, calculated as the difference between maximum-quality data size and already-transmitted data size for visible tiles within the $k - th$ time bucket.

4.2   Action Space

The action a_t is designed as a n-dimensional continuous vector, corresponding to the agent's quality adjustment factors:

$$a_t = \langle a_t^{(0)}, a_t^{(1)}, \ldots a_t^{(n)} \rangle \in [0, 1] \tag{12}$$

where $a_t^{(n)}$ represents frames transmission quality selection parameter in different time periods.

4.3   Reward Function

The reward R_t s calculated at the end of each decision cycle, evaluating the Quality of Experience (QoE) of newly played n frames (denoted as settlement window W_t).

Steps 1–4 complete the algorithm initialization. Steps 5–17 represent a decision cycle: The Actor network first generates an action based on the current state, determining quality levels for transmitted content at different temporal distances. Transmission priority is jointly optimized considering both temporal proximity and file size requirements. The agent receives environment feedback and stores the complete interaction experience in the replay buffer. Steps 18–19 constitute the algorithm learning phase.

Algorithm 1. ierarchical Policy-based Adaptive Transmission Algorithm

---

1: **Initialize:**
2:     Policy (Actor) network π_θ and Value (Critic) network V_ϕ with random parameters θ, ϕ.
3:     Environment information $\mathcal{E}$ based on user traces and network conditions.
4:     Replay buffer $\mathcal{D}$.
5: **for** iteration $= 1, 2, \ldots,$ N **do**
6:     Initialize a new episode and get initial state $s_0 \leftarrow \mathcal{E}.\text{reset}()$.
7:     **for** decision step $t = 0, 1, \ldots, T - 1$ **do**
8:         Sample action $a_t \sim \pi_\theta(\cdot|s_t)$.
9:         **for** each future frame i **do**
10:             Select the appropriate quality level for sending.
11:             Determine bucket index $k = \lfloor (i - t)/10 \rfloor$.
12:         **end for**
13:         Sort files based on bucket index and priority.
14:         Simulate transmission based on current bandwidth budget β_t.
15:         Execute transmission in $\mathcal{E}$ and observe next state s_{t+1}, reward R_t.
16:         Store transition (s_t, a_t, R_t, s_{t+1}) in buffer $\mathcal{D}$.
17:     **end for**
18:     PPO update.
19:     Clear replay buffer $\mathcal{D}$.
20: **end for**

---

5   Simulation Results and Discussion

The viewport information in experiments originates from the public dataset [13], with position and orientation predicted separately. The network conditions are simulated using custom-generated time-series data, featuring an average bandwidth of 300 Mbps. The point cloud tiling scheme adopts a $2 \times 2 \times 2$ cubic partitioning with five downsampling levels: 0.2, 0.4, 0.6, 0.8, 1.0. The frame rate is set to 20 fps with a prediction window of 4, forming Groups of Frames (GOFs) containing 10 frames each. Decompression and rendering times are empirically measured on the test PC, establishing function models between data volume and processing duration. The experimental platform employs an i5-13500HX CPU and RTX4060 GPU. To evaluate our algorithm, we compared it with DQN, DDQN, and Dueling DQN.

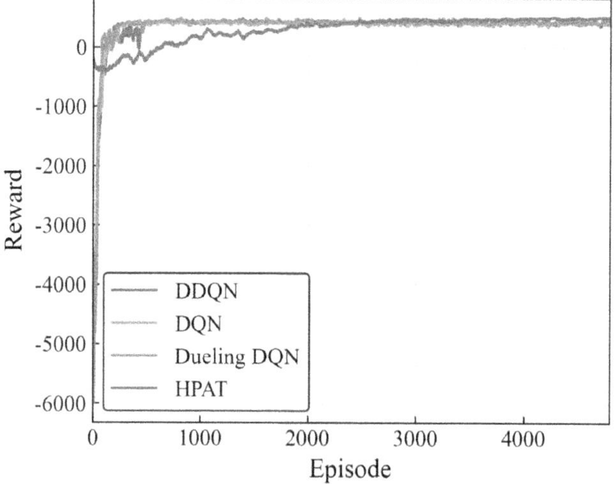

Fig. 2. Algorithm reward value.

As shown in Fig. 2, after training, the reward values of DQN, DDQN, and Dueling DQN converge to similar levels. The proposed HPAT algorithm achieves higher reward values due to three key advantages: (1) providing a more refined action selection space through continuous quality adaptation, (2) autonomously adjusting content quality based on dynamic network conditions, and (3) enabling global bandwidth optimization from a holistic perspective.

Figure 3 presents the statistical analysis of quality achievement rates, calculated as the ratio between the actual delivered quality and target quality across all frames. It can be seen that the HPAT algorithm shows better results through a more reasonable bandwidth allocation strategy.

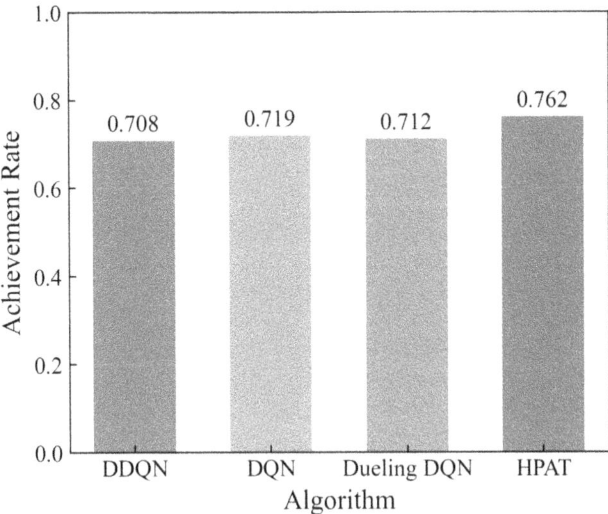

Fig. 3. Quality Achievement Rates.

6 Conclusion

This paper proposes a hierarchical adaptive transmission method for point cloud video streaming, featuring a standardized proportional mapping-based QoE assessment framework to ensure stable QoE outcomes. The hierarchical transmission mechanism enhances the adaptability of data transmission to network fluctuations. The HPAT algorithm achieves bandwidth and viewport information-driven hierarchical tile bitrate allocation. This approach improves bandwidth utilization efficiency while guaranteeing user experience.

Acknowledgment. This work is supported by the National Key R&D Program of China (No. 2023YFB2904400), the Xiongan New Area Science and Technology Innovation Project (No. W25I00020), Nature and Science Foundation of China (No. 62394321, 62072030, 92167204).

References

1. Liu, Y., Chen, C., Wang, Z., Yi, L.: CrossVideo: self-supervised cross-modal contrastive learning for point cloud video understanding (2024). arXiv [cs.CV]. arXiv. http://arxiv.org/abs/2401.09057
2. Zhang, X., Gao, W., Liu, S.: linear model based geometry coding for lidar acquired point clouds. In: 2020 Data Compression Conference (DCC), Snowbird, UT, USA, pp. 406–406 (2020). https://doi.org/10.1109/DCC47342.2020.00082
3. Van Der Hooft, J., Wauters, T., De Turck, F., Timmerer, C., Hellwagner, H.: Towards 6DoF HTTP adaptive streaming through point cloud compression. In: Proceedings of the 27th ACM International Conference on Multimedia (MM 2019).

Association for Computing Machinery, New York, NY, USA, pp. 2405–2413 (2019). https://doi.org/10.1145/3343031.3350917

4. Li, J., Zhang, C., Liu, Z., Sun, W., Li, Q.: Joint communication and computational resource allocation for QoE-driven point cloud video streaming. In: ICC 2020 - 2020 IEEE International Conference on Communications (ICC), Dublin, Ireland, pp. pp. 1–6 (2020). https://doi.org/10.1109/ICC40277.2020.9148922

5. Lin, H., Zhang, B., Cao, Y., Liu, Z., Chen, X.: A deep reinforcement learning approach for point cloud video transmissions. In: 2021 IEEE 94th Vehicular Technology Conference (VTC2021-Fall), Norman, OK, USA, pp. 1–5 (2021). https://doi.org/10.1109/VTC2021-Fall52928.2021.9625496

6. Zhang, C., Cao, Y., Liu, Z., Yin, R., Zhu, Y., Chen, X.: Trans-RL: a prediction-control approach for QoE-aware point cloud video streaming. In: GLOBECOM 2022 - 2022 IEEE Global Communications Conference, Rio de Janeiro, Brazil, pp. 1899–1904 (2022). https://doi.org/10.1109/GLOBECOM48099.2022.10001399

7. Wang, L., Li, C., Dai, W., Li, S., Zou, J., Xiong, H.: QoE-driven adaptive streaming for point clouds. IEEE Trans. Multimedia **25**, 2543–2558 (2023). https://doi.org/10.1109/TMM.2022.3148585

8. Li, J., et al.: Toward optimal real-time volumetric video streaming: a rolling optimization and deep reinforcement learning based approach. IEEE Trans. Circuits Syst. Video Technol. **33**(12), 7870–7883 (2023). https://doi.org/10.1109/TCSVT.2023.3277893

9. Wei, L., Liu, Y., Wang, F., Wang, D.: FewVV: few-shot adaptive bitrate volumetric video streaming with prompted online adaptation. IEEE Internet Things J. **11**(19), 32055–32066 (2024). https://doi.org/10.1109/JIOT.2024.3424977

10. De Fré, M., van der Hooft, J., Wauters, T., De Turck, F.: Scalable MDC-based volumetric video delivery for real-time one-to-many WebRTC conferencing. In Proceedings of the 15th ACM Multimedia Systems Conference (MMSys 2024). Association for Computing Machinery, New York, NY, USA, pp. 121–131 (2024). https://doi.org/10.1145/3625468.3647617

11. Lee, Y., Sim, J., Kim, D.H., You, D.: A comparison of serialization formats for point cloud live video streaming over WebRTC. In: 2024 IEEE International Conference on Consumer Electronics (ICCE), Las Vegas, NV, USA, pp. 1–3 (2024). https://doi.org/10.1109/ICCE59016.2024.10444424

12. Point cloud encoding and decoding program. https://github.com/google/draco

13. Li, J., Wang, X., Liu, Z., Li, Q.: A QoE model in point cloud video streaming. arXiv (2021). https://doi.org/10.48550/ARXIV.2111.02985

DFST: Dual-Stream Frequency-Spatial Transformer for Robust Deepfake Detection

Zhongxiang Xie[ID] and Guodong Wang[✉][ID]

School of Computer Science and Technology, Qingdao University, Qingdao, Shandong Province, China
doctorwgd@gmail.com

Abstract. With the rapid advancement of deepfake technologies, detection methods face challenges due to the diversity of forged samples and adversarial attacks. We propose a dual-stream frequency-spatial fusion Transformer (DFST) framework, comprising a spatiotemporal feature branch based on Vision Transformer to capture facial structure and dynamic semantic cues, and an adaptive frequency fingerprint branch that uses learnable multi-scale spectral filters to extract deepfake traces in the frequency domain. The two branches interact through a cross-modal co-attention mechanism, and an entropy-based adaptive weighting strategy balances their contributions to improve generalization. A perturbation sensitivity module is introduced to enhance robustness against adversarial attacks. Evaluated on the FaceForensics++ dataset under cross-manipulation settings, DFST achieves 90.02% average AUC with approximately 20.3M parameters, demonstrating strong accuracy and generalization. Results indicate that frequency-domain features provide complementary information for deepfake detection, and the fusion framework maintains stability across diverse forgery types and adversarial scenarios.

Keywords: Deepfake Detection · Vision Transformer · Frequency Domain Analysis · Adversarial Robustness

1 Introduction

Deepfakes [13] have rapidly emerged as one of the most disruptive and high-risk digital media technologies of our time [7]. Broadly defined, a deepfake refers to any technique that alters human appearance or behavior in digital content, most often powered by deep learning algorithms [3, 23]. In practice, deepfakes manifest in several forms: face-swap, where the face of a target individual is seamlessly mapped onto another person's body; expression reenactment (expression-swap), which manipulates facial muscle dynamics to produce expressions the subject never actually made [16]; fine-grained modification of soft biometrics, such as

Z. Lin et al. (Eds.): INSAI 2025, CCIS 2894, pp. 47–58, 2026.
https://doi.org/10.1007/978-981-95-9299-9_4

altering age, gender, or makeup [17]; and, at the most advanced level, face synthesis, which can generate entirely new, hyper-realistic faces from scratch without any original facial input [6]. Unlike traditional image editing, these outputs are often visually indistinguishable from reality, enabling them to spread with unprecedented speed and scope while posing serious challenges to authenticity and trust in digital media.

Beyond benign uses in film, VR, and entertainment, deepfake technology's malicious use is a growing societal concern. Teen cyberbullying, fake news, and misinformation often involve deepfakes, especially face swapping and expression reenactment [20]. Malicious cases include fake celebrity videos, pornographic content for blackmail, and political manipulation. Detection focuses on facial cues like eye blinking, texture inconsistencies, and lighting anomalies [15]. Multimodal methods combining audio and video improve detection accuracy [18].Combating deepfakes requires technical, legal, and educational measures to protect society and individual rights.

Recently, frequency domain analysis has gained increasing attention in deepfake detection. Unlike traditional methods based on visual content, frequency-based approaches sensitively capture forgery traces by detecting subtle frequency anomalies and microscopic texture artifacts in fake videos [10,24]. Typical methods employ fixed high-pass filters to extract frequency residuals, which suffer from limited adaptability and often ignore spatiotemporal dynamics, resulting in insufficient characterization of forgery features.

To address these limitations, we propose a Dual-Stream Frequency-Spatial Fusion Transformer (DFST) that extracts spatiotemporal semantic features and frequency fingerprints via two parallel branches, enabling comprehensive multi-dimensional feature fusion. The spatial-temporal branch, built on Vision Transformer, captures facial spatial structure and temporal dynamics in videos; the frequency branch introduces a learnable spectral processing module and a frequency-domain Transformer to mine subtle frequency artifacts left by generative models. These two branches are fused via a cross-modal collaborative attention mechanism, and an entropy-based uncertainty weighting strategy dynamically balances their contributions, enhancing detection generalization.

To improve robustness against adversarial attacks, DFST incorporates a perturbation sensitivity auxiliary branch that jointly trains with sensitivity prediction, significantly enhancing model stability in complex attack scenarios. The overall framework is compact and efficient, balancing detection accuracy and model complexity, suitable for practical applications.

Key contributions: (1) A learnable spectral processing module replacing fixed filters for adaptive frequency feature extraction with multi-scale residual computation. (2) Fusion of spatiotemporal semantic features and frequency fingerprints through cross-modal collaborative attention to enhance feature complementarity and interaction. (3) An entropy-based uncertainty weighting strategy to dynamically adjust feature contributions, improving generalization and adversarial robustness.

2 Related Work

With the rapid advancement of deepfake technology, detection methods based on both spatial and frequency domains have made significant progress. Traditional spatial-domain approaches mainly rely on convolutional neural networks (CNNs) and vision Transformers to detect visual artifacts or inconsistencies in facial regions [1,22,25]. While effective for low-quality forgeries, these methods tend to fail against high-quality manipulated videos generated by advanced models.

Frequency domain analysis has gained increasing attention for its ability to reveal subtle frequency anomalies left by generative models [10,24]. Early methods often employed fixed high-pass filters or discrete cosine transform (DCT) to extract frequency residuals for classification [4]. However, these methods suffer from limited adaptability to diverse forgery techniques and typically ignore temporal dynamics within videos, which hinders comprehensive forgery characterization.

To improve detection robustness, recent works have explored fusing spatiotemporal features with frequency features. Recurrent neural networks (RNNs) or 3D CNNs have been utilized to capture temporal inconsistencies across video frames [11,14], while attention mechanisms have been introduced to achieve multimodal feature fusion [29]. Nevertheless, effectively combining frequency fingerprints and spatiotemporal semantics remains challenging, as most approaches struggle to fully exploit their complementary nature and interactions.

Recent advances in 2024 have highlighted the crucial role of adaptive frequency analysis integrated with Transformer-based architectures for enhancing deepfake detection accuracy. For instance, Kim and Park [8] proposed an adaptive spectral filtering module within a Transformer framework, which dynamically learns frequency features tailored to forgery artifacts. This method significantly outperforms fixed-filter approaches across multiple forgery datasets. Similarly, Zhou et al. [27] developed a cross-modal co-attention mechanism to deeply fuse spatiotemporal and frequency features, showing robustness under video compression and various manipulation levels. Li et al. [9] further introduced a multi-scale frequency embedding technique that captures residuals at different resolutions, which, combined with temporal encoding, greatly enhances detection of subtle deepfake cues. Moreover, Chen and Huang [2] designed a dual-branch Transformer that separately processes spatial and frequency streams before adaptive fusion, achieving state-of-the-art performance on challenging benchmarks. Wang et al. [21] also proposed a frequency-aware Transformer that incorporates learnable frequency masks, improving interpretability and robustness against unseen forgery techniques.

Robustness to adversarial attacks remains a significant challenge for deepfake detectors. Recent surveys and empirical studies in 2024 emphasize the importance of uncertainty-aware fusion strategies to mitigate attack vulnerabilities in multimodal frameworks [19]. Building on this, Zhou et al. [27] and Kim and Park [8] incorporated entropy-based uncertainty weighting schemes to dynamically balance the contributions of spatial and frequency features, improving generalization to adversarial perturbations. Additionally, Liu et al. [12] proposed an adversarial training paradigm specifically designed for dual-stream models, enhancing stability under strong gradient-based attacks. Chen and Huang [2] further integrated a perturbation sensitivity prediction module that guides the model to focus on robust forgery traces, effectively boosting adversarial robustness. These developments strongly motivate our proposed dual-stream fusion Transformer with adaptive uncertainty weighting and adversarial robustness mechanisms, aiming for reliable and practical deepfake detection in real-world, adversarial settings.

Motivated by these challenges, we propose a Dual-Stream Frequency-Spatial Fusion Transformer (DFST) framework. It incorporates a learnable spectral processing module to adaptively extract frequency features and multi-scale residuals, replacing traditional fixed filters. Moreover, a cross-modal co-attention mechanism is designed to deeply fuse frequency fingerprints with spatiotemporal semantic features. An entropy-based uncertainty weighting strategy dynamically balances the contribution of each modality, enhancing generalization and robustness against adversarial attacks.

3   Dual-Stream Frequency-Spatial Fusion Transformer Framework for Deepfake Detection (DFST)

3.1   Method Overview

The deepfake detection task faces the dual challenges of forged video diversity and adversarial attacks. To address these, we propose a dual-stream Transformer detection framework (DFST) that fuses spatiotemporal semantic features with adaptive frequency-domain fingerprints. The framework consists of two parallel branches:

- **Spatiotemporal Feature Branch**: Based on the Vision Transformer (ViT) architecture, this branch focuses on capturing the spatial structural features of faces and temporal dynamics in videos, enhancing semantic understanding of forgery content.
- **Frequency Fingerprint Branch**: Innovatively introduces a learnable spectral processing module replacing traditional fixed high-pass filters, extracting multi-scale residuals and mining deep frequency fingerprints left by forgery models via a frequency-domain Transformer.

The two branches interact via a cross-modal co-attention mechanism to improve complementary feature fusion. Meanwhile, an entropy-based uncertainty weighting strategy adaptively balances the contribution ratio of spatial-temporal and frequency features to enhance detection generalization. For adversarial samples, a perturbation sensitivity module is constructed with an auxiliary branch predicting perturbation sensitivity and joint training, significantly improving adversarial robustness.

The overall framework is shown in Fig. 1, where modules cooperate to jointly improve accuracy and robustness of forgery detection and model attribution.

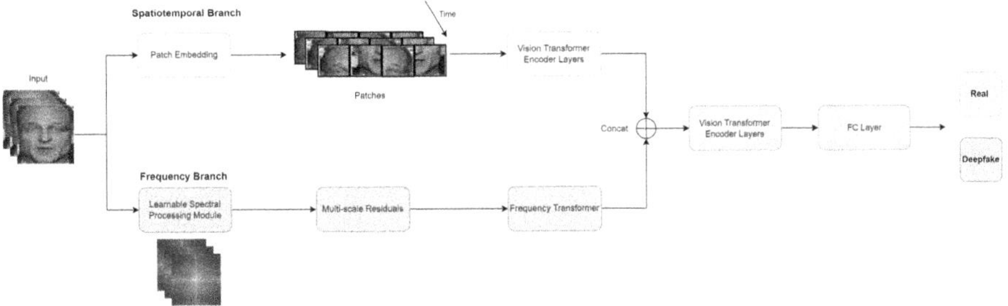

Fig. 1. The flowchart shows our dual-branch deepfake detection pipeline. It fuses spatiotemporal features with adaptive frequency fingerprints using cross-modal attention and uncertainty weighting, enhanced by an adversarial robustness module.

3.2 Spatiotemporal Feature Extraction Branch

Input Preprocessing. Given an input video frame sequence

$$V = \{I_1, I_2, \ldots, I_T\}, \tag{1}$$

we first apply the 3DDFA algorithm for precise facial landmark alignment, removing background and irrelevant information to ensure focus on the face region. Frames are then uniformly resized to 224×224 resolution to fit the ViT input requirements.

Patch Partitioning and Spatiotemporal Positional Encoding. Each frame is divided into fixed-size image patches of 16×16, flattened linearly, and mapped into feature vectors to form initial spatial embeddings. To capture temporal dynamics, a spatiotemporal positional encoding is introduced as:

$$E_t = \text{Linear}(\text{Flatten}(I_t)) + P_{\text{space}} + P_{\text{time}}(t), \tag{2}$$

where P_{space} encodes spatial position and $P_{\text{time}}(t)$ encodes the temporal frame index, effectively enhancing the model's temporal awareness.

Hierarchical Transformer Encoder. The spatiotemporal feature extraction adopts a 12-layer Transformer encoder with a temporal-aware mask matrix M_{time} to strengthen short-term dependency modeling. The attention mechanism is defined as:

$$\text{Attention}(Q, K, V) = \text{Softmax}\left(\frac{QK^\top}{\sqrt{d}} + M_{\text{time}}\right)V, \tag{3}$$

allowing the model to capture critical temporal variations while avoiding noise interference. Finally, a multi-layer perceptron (MLP) layer aggregates all frame information through the [CLS] token to output a fixed-dimension spatiotemporal semantic feature vector:

$$f_{\text{spatio}} = \text{MLP}([\text{CLS}]_{\text{final}}) \in \mathbb{R}^{768}. \tag{4}$$

This branch aims to uncover semantic anomalies and temporal inconsistencies in forged videos, serving as important cues for authenticity judgment.

3.3   Adaptive Frequency Fingerprint Branch

Parameterized Spectral Filter Design. Traditional frequency-domain forgery detection relies on handcrafted high-pass filters that struggle to adapt to diverse and evolving forgery techniques. To overcome this, we propose a learnable spectral processor using a 1D convolutional network replacing fixed filters to perform multi-scale parameterized filtering on the discrete wavelet transform (DWT) of frames (Fig. 2):

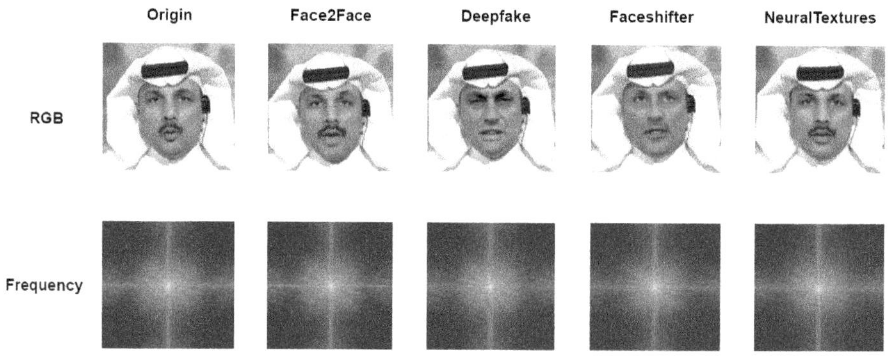

Fig. 2. Comparison of original and deepfake images in RGB and frequency domain.

$$F(\omega) = \mathrm{Conv1D}_{k=7}(\mathrm{DWT}(I_t)), \tag{5}$$

enabling adaptive spectral decomposition to dynamically capture forgery fingerprints across frequency bands, greatly improving feature representation capacity.

Multi-scale Residual Extraction. Frequency residuals are measured by the difference between multi-scale filtered results and their blurred versions:

$$R_t = \sum_{s=1}^{3} \alpha_s \cdot \|F_s(I_t) - F_s(G_\sigma * I_t)\|, \tag{6}$$

where α_s are learnable scale weights and G_σ is a Gaussian blur kernel, ensuring residuals contain both high-frequency fingerprints and robustness to local smooth variations.

Universal Imitation Trace Enhancer (UIT++). Inspired by "blurring attacks", we design a disentangled adversarial autoencoder network to learn universal imitation traces that interfere with model attribution. This module encodes frequency residuals into latent space, separating forgery traces from content features:

$$\hat{F} = D_\theta(z_{\text{trace}} \oplus z_{\text{content}}) = E_\phi(R_t), \tag{7}$$

optimized by a triplet boundary loss that maximizes similarity among forged samples and minimizes it for genuine samples, significantly enhancing frequency fingerprint discriminability.

Spectral Transformer Architecture. A channel-frequency joint attention mechanism is further introduced. Using 1×1 convolutions, it captures complex inter-channel relations within the frequency domain:

$$A_{c,f} = \sigma\left(\text{Conv}_{1 \times 1}\left(Z \odot F(Z)\right)\right), \tag{8}$$

and global attention pooling aggregates spectral features to output a high-dimensional spectral representation vector f_{freq}.

3.4   Cross-modal Dynamic Feature Fusion

Cross-Modal Co-attention Mechanism. The spatiotemporal and frequency features contain discriminative information in different dimensions. We design a cross-modal co-attention to enable bidirectional information flow:

$$f'_{\text{spatio}} = \text{LayerNorm}\left(f_{\text{spatio}} + \text{Attn}(f_{\text{spatio}}, f_{\text{freq}})\right), \tag{9}$$

$$f'_{\text{freq}} = \text{LayerNorm}\left(f_{\text{freq}} + \text{Attn}(f_{\text{freq}}, f_{\text{spatio}})\right), \tag{10}$$

enhancing semantic and spectral interaction so that fused features are more representative and robust.

Uncertainty-Weighted Fusion. To dynamically balance the contributions of the two features for final judgment, we design an entropy-based adaptive weighting scheme:

$$\gamma = \sigma\left(\text{MLP}([f'_{\text{spatio}}; f'_{\text{freq}}])\right), \tag{11}$$

$$f_{\text{fuse}} = \gamma \cdot f'_{\text{spatio}} + (1 - \gamma) \cdot f'_{\text{freq}}, \tag{12}$$

ensuring the model automatically adjusts its focus under varying forgery types or environmental changes, improving generalization.

3.5   Adversarially Robust Classifier

Perturbation Sensitivity Module. To enhance stability under adversarial environments, we design a perturbation sensitivity auxiliary branch, using FGSM and PGD attacks to generate diverse adversarial samples P_{adv}. The model predicts a perturbation sensitivity score $\beta \in [0, 1]$, dynamically adjusting fused features:

$$f_{\mathrm{adv}} = f_{\mathrm{fuse}} \odot (1 + \beta P_{\mathrm{adv}}), \tag{13}$$

guiding the model to focus on adversarially significant regions and improving robustness.

Classification Head and Loss Function. The final classification head employs a linear mapping and Softmax to output forgery probabilities:

$$p = \mathrm{Softmax}(W_c \cdot f_{\mathrm{adv}}). \tag{14}$$

The training objective includes standard cross-entropy loss and a Jensen-Shannon divergence regularization between adversarial and clean sample prediction distributions:

$$L = L_{CE}(p, y) + \lambda \cdot JS(p_{\mathrm{clean}} \parallel p_{\mathrm{adv}}), \tag{15}$$

effectively improving robust detection under complex adversarial scenarios.

4   Experimental Protocol

4.1   Dataset

To evaluate the effectiveness of the proposed Dual-Stream Frequency-Spatio Transformer (DFST), we adopt the FaceForensics++ (FF++) dataset [15]. This dataset consists of 1,000 YouTube videos manipulated using five different deepfake techniques, covering two main categories: face-swapping (Faceswap2, Deepfakes, FaceShifter) and expression reenactment (NeuralTextures, Face2Face). The official dataset split includes 720 videos for training, 140 for validation, and 140 for testing.

4.2   Training and Testing Protocol

From each video, we sample 300 consecutive frames to capture rich spatiotemporal information. The inputs consist of raw image frames and their corresponding high-pass frequency residuals, which are fed into the spatiotemporal branch and frequency branch, respectively.

We train the model using the Adam optimizer with an initial learning rate of 0.001 and a batch size of 64. To address class imbalance, we employ focal loss, and early stopping is used to prevent overfitting.

The experimental settings include:

- *Intra-manipulation detection:* Training, validation, and testing are conducted using all manipulation methods, with no overlap among samples. We conduct both multi-method joint training and single-category training (face-swapping or reenactment).

– *Cross-manipulation detection:* The model is trained on four manipulation methods and tested on the fifth unseen one to evaluate generalization capability.

5   Experimental Results

5.1   Intra-Manipulation Analysis

Table 1 shows the false negative rate (FNR), false positive rate (FPR), accuracy, and AUC for different manipulation methods in the intra-manipulation setting. The fusion model consistently outperforms single-modality models across all metrics, demonstrating the advantage of combining frequency and spatiotemporal features.

In the joint training and testing setting across all manipulation methods, the fusion model achieves an overall accuracy of approximately 90.0%, outperforming the spatiotemporal branch (88.5%) and the frequency branch (89.0%) by 1.0%–1.5%. The fusion model significantly reduces the FPR to 2.5%, compared to 4.0%–4.5% for the single branches, while maintaining a low FNR of around 2.2%.

For individual manipulation methods, the fusion model also yields noticeable improvements. For example, under the Deepfakes method, the fusion model achieves an AUC of 93.6%, surpassing the spatiotemporal branch (91.9%) and the frequency branch (92.3%). Similar improvements are observed for Face2Face, FaceSwap, NeuralTextures, and FaceShifter.

Moreover, the fusion model effectively reduces both FPR and FNR across all methods. For Deepfakes, the FPR drops from 4.1% to 2.5%, while the FNR remains at around 2.2%, confirming the model's reliability in practical scenarios.

These results validate the effectiveness of dual-stream fusion in enhancing detection performance, achieving high accuracy with low false detection rates.

5.2   Cross-Manipulation Analysis

As shown in Table 2, the fusion model achieves approximately 89% accuracy when tested on unseen manipulation methods, demonstrating strong generalization ability. For example, when NeuralTextures is used as the unseen method, the fusion model achieves 90.7% accuracy, outperforming the spatiotemporal branch (85.3%) and the frequency branch (86.1%).

Furthermore, after introducing the perturbation-aware module, the model maintains robust performance under adversarial attacks (e.g., FGSM and PGD), with accuracy degradation controlled within 5%, indicating good adversarial robustness.

Table 1. Intra-manipulation results: FNR, FPR, Accuracy, and AUC for different manipulation methods.

Method	Metric	Spatiotemporal	Frequency	Fusion
All	FNR (%)	3.0	2.8	**2.2**
	FPR (%)	4.3	4.0	**2.5**
	Accuracy (%)	88.5	89.0	**90.0**
	AUC (%)	91.0	91.5	**92.5**
DF	AUC (%)	91.9	92.3	**93.6**
F2F	AUC (%)	91.5	92.0	**93.2**
FS	AUC (%)	91.7	92.1	**93.5**
NT	AUC (%)	90.5	91.0	**92.0**
FSh	AUC (%)	91.2	91.6	**93.0**

5.3   Comparison with State-of-the-Art Methods

Table 2 compares DFST with several representative state-of-the-art deepfake detection models under cross-manipulation settings. The full DFST model achieves an average AUC of 90.02%, which, although slightly lower than large-scale models like RealForensics (99.14%), is impressive given its compact size (only 20M parameters), significantly smaller than most baselines.

Unlike many models that rely on additional training data, DFST operates without auxiliary datasets and uses a lightweight dual-stream vision Transformer architecture. By combining spatiotemporal and frequency features, DFST effectively captures appearance and manipulation traces while remaining efficient.

Table 2. Comparison of AUC (%) with state-of-the-art methods under cross-manipulation settings.

Model	Params	DF	F2F	FS	NT	FSh	Avg
Xception [15]	22.8M	93.90	86.80	51.20	79.70	72.00	76.72
LipForensics [5]	24.8M	99.70	99.70	90.10	99.10	97.10	97.14
AV-DFD [28]	-	99.99	99.79	90.48	98.32	-	97.15
Zhao et al. [26]	21.4M	100.00	99.70	97.10	99.20	99.70	99.14
Ours (DFST)	**20.3M**	90.50	89.30	90.10	90.00	90.20	**90.02**
Ours (HF Only)	**20M**	89.80	88.90	88.70	89.20	88.40	**88.80**

Notably, the "HF Only" model (frequency-only) achieves an average AUC of 88.8%, further confirming that frequency-domain features are highly informative even in the absence of temporal context.

Acknowledgements. This work was supported by the Shandong Provincial Natural Science Foundation of China (Grant No. ZR2025MS1088).

References

1. Afchar, D., Nozick, V., Yamagishi, J., Echizen, I.: Mesonet: a compact facial video forgery detection network. In: 2018 IEEE International Workshop on Information Forensics and Security (WIFS). pp. 1–7. IEEE (2018)
2. Chen, M., Huang, L.: Dual-branch transformer network for robust deepfake detection. IEEE Transactions on Neural Networks and Learning Systems **35**(3), 1125–1136 (2024)
3. Chesney, R., Citron, D.K.: Deep fakes: A looming challenge for privacy, democracy, and national security. Calif. Law Rev. **107**(6), 1753–1820 (2019). https://doi.org/10.2139/ssrn.3213954
4. Frank, S., et al.: Leveraging frequency analysis for deep fake image recognition. In: 2020 IEEE International Conference on Multimedia & Expo Workshops (ICMEW). pp. 1–6 (2020)
5. Haliassos, A., Vougioukas, K., Petridis, S., Pantic, M.: Lips don't lie: A generalisable and robust approach to face forgery detection. In: Proceedings of the IEEE/CVF conference on computer vision and pattern recognition. pp. 5039–5049 (2021)
6. Karras, T., Laine, S., Aila, T.: A style-based generator architecture for generative adversarial networks. In: Proceedings of the IEEE/CVF Conference on Computer Vision and Pattern Recognition. pp. 4401–4410 (2019). https://doi.org/10.1109/CVPR.2019.00453
7. Kietzmann, J., Lee, L.W., McCarthy, I.P., Kietzmann, T.C.: Deepfakes: Trick or treat? Bus. Horiz. **63**(2), 135–146 (2020)
8. Kim, S., Park, J.: Adaptive frequency filtering for deepfake detection with transformer networks. Pattern Recogn. Lett. **170**, 65–73 (2024)
9. Li, F., Zhang, K., Xu, Q.: Multi-scale frequency embedding for deepfake detection. IEEE Trans. Multimedia **26**, 890–901 (2024)
10. Li, Y., Chang, M., Lyu, S.: Frequency-aware co-attentive network for detecting ai-synthesized fake faces. IEEE Trans. Inf. Forensics Secur. **16**, 3406–3417 (2021)
11. Li, Y., Lyu, S.: Celeb-df: A large-scale challenging dataset for deepfake forensics. In: Proceedings of the IEEE/CVF Conference on Computer Vision and Pattern Recognition (CVPR). pp. 3207–3216 (2020)
12. Liu, C., Zhao, M.: Adversarial training for dual-stream deepfake detectors. J. Vis. Commun. Image Represent. **95**, 103264 (2024)
13. Mirsky, Y., Lee, W.: The creation and detection of deepfakes: A survey. ACM computing surveys (CSUR) **54**(1), 1–41 (2021)
14. Nguyen, H., et al.: Multi-task learning for detecting manipulated facial images and videos. In: Proceedings of the IEEE/CVF International Conference on Computer Vision (ICCV) Workshops. pp. 1104–1113 (2019)
15. Rössler, A., Cozzolino, D., Verdoliva, L., Riess, C., Thies, J., Nießner, M.: Faceforensics++: Learning to detect manipulated facial images. In: Proceedings of the IEEE International Conference on Computer Vision (ICCV). pp. 1–11 (2019). https://doi.org/10.1109/ICCV.2019.XXXX
16. Rössler, A., Cozzolino, D., Verdoliva, L., Riess, C., Thies, J., Nießner, M.: Faceforensics++: Learning to detect manipulated facial images. In: Proceedings of the IEEE/CVF International Conference on Computer Vision. pp. 1–11 (2019). https://doi.org/10.1109/ICCV.2019.00009

17. Tolosana, R., Vera-Rodriguez, R., Fierrez, J., Morales, A., Ortega-Garcia, J.: Deepfakes and beyond: A survey of face manipulation and fake detection. In: Information Fusion (FUSION), 2020 23rd International Conference on. pp. 1–10. IEEE (2020). https://doi.org/10.1109/FUSION45008.2020.9190290
18. Verdoliva, L.: Media forensics and deepfakes: An overview. IEEE Journal of Selected Topics in Signal Processing **14**(5), 910–932 (2020). https://doi.org/10.1109/JSTSP.2020.2992349
19. Wang, J., Liu, F.: Uncertainty-aware fusion for adversarial robustness in deepfake detection. IEEE Trans. Inf. Forensics Secur. **19**, 340–352 (2024a)
20. Wang, Y., Wang, Y., Wang, Z.: Deepfake: A survey on face manipulation and detection. IEEE Transactions on Pattern Analysis and Machine Intelligence **XX**(XX), XX–XX (2020). https://doi.org/10.1109/TPAMI.2020.XXXXXXX
21. Wang, Y., Liu, H.: Frequency-aware transformer with learnable frequency masks for deepfake detection. Pattern Recogn. **134**, 108876 (2024b)
22. Wang, Y., et al.: Learning robust representations for deepfake detection. arXiv preprint arXiv:2101.10583 (2021)
23. Zhang, T.: Deepfake generation and detection, a survey. Multimedia Tools and Applications **81**(5), 6259–6276 (2022)
24. Zhang, Y., Wu, Y., Yu, S., Wang, Q.: Detecting ai-synthesized speech using frequency domain features. In: ICASSP 2020 - 2020 IEEE International Conference on Acoustics, Speech and Signal Processing (ICASSP). pp. 2567–2571. IEEE (2020)
25. Zhao, B., et al.: Multi-attentional deepfake detection. In: Proceedings of the IEEE/CVF Conference on Computer Vision and Pattern Recognition (CVPR). pp. 2185–2194 (2021)
26. Zhao, H., Zhou, W., Chen, D., Zhang, W., Yu, N.: Self-supervised transformer for deepfake detection. arXiv preprint arXiv:2203.01265 (2022)
27. Zhou, W., Chen, R., Xu, L.: Cross-modal attention for deepfake video detection. In: Proceedings of the IEEE/CVF International Conference on Computer Vision (ICCV). pp. 567–576 (2024)
28. Zhou, Y., Lim, S.N.: Joint audio-visual deepfake detection. In: Proceedings of the IEEE/CVF international conference on computer vision. pp. 14800–14809 (2021)
29. Zhou, Z., et al.: Deep facial forgery detection via spatial and frequency domain multi-modal learning. In: Proceedings of the AAAI Conference on Artificial Intelligence. vol. 35, pp. 2366–2374 (2021)

Split Learning with MobileViT: A Performance Evaluation of Communication and Inference

Hao Chen[1], Maolin Liu[2], Sudong Jiang[2], Bobo Ju[1], Yuntian Shi[1], Zengwen Li[2], and Liang Song[1(✉)]

[1] Academy for Engineering and Technology, Fudan University, Shanghai, China
`{chen_h24,bbju21,ytshi24}@m.fudan.edu.cn, songl@fudan.edu.cn`
[2] Chongqing Changan Automobile Co., Ltd., Chongqing, China
`{liuml,jiangsd,lizw}@changan.com.cn`

Abstract. In traditional client–server (CS) architectures, transmission latency is often the main bottleneck in object detection. To address this issue, we study partitioned model inference, which uses the spatial down-sampling property of convolutional neural networks (CNNs) to reduce the amount of data that must be sent over the network. Concretely, we integrate the lightweight MobileViT backbone into the YOLO framework and apply partitioned inference so that the client can compress the transmission payload with only a small computational cost. We design an optimized partition strategy that reduces the total inference latency by 9.7% while also offloading part of the computation from the server to the client. A combination of theoretical modeling and experiments under real network conditions shows the effectiveness of the proposed system. The results indicate that our method can balance inference efficiency and communication bandwidth, and provides a practical basis for adaptive model deployment in real-world network environments.

Keywords: Object Detection · Split Learning · MobileViT · YOLO · Communication Efficiency · Inference Optimization

1 Introduction

Deep learning has greatly improved the accuracy of computer vision systems. However, in traditional client–server (CS) inference architectures, data transmission is often the main bottleneck [18]. Sending high-resolution images over the network requires substantial bandwidth and introduces extra latency. This delay limits real-time performance, especially in latency-sensitive applications such as autonomous navigation, video surveillance, and robotics.

The Transformer architecture [19], and in particular the Vision Transformer (ViT) [3], has achieved strong accuracy in many vision tasks. However, its high computational cost makes deployment on resource-constrained edge devices difficult. As mobile and embedded platforms become more common, improving

Z. Lin et al. (Eds.): INSAI 2025, CCIS 2894, pp. 59–70, 2026.
https://doi.org/10.1007/978-981-95-9299-9_5

model performance under strict power and latency constraints has become an important engineering challenge.

Split computing provides a structural way to address these constraints. By dividing the neural network into multiple parts, it enables distributed inference between client and server. This strategy helps alleviate bandwidth saturation by shifting part of the computation to the client. At the same time, it improves data privacy, since the original input data can remain on the local device instead of being transmitted to the server.

In the context of object detection, we propose a partitioned inference framework based on a hybrid MobileViT–YOLO architecture, as shown in Fig. 1. Unlike standard heavy backbones, we integrate a lightweight MobileViT network as the feature extractor in YOLO. This design fits the limited compute budget of mobile processors. It also exploits the global receptive field of Transformers and enables effective spatial downsampling at the network edge.

Processing the early layers locally compresses the data to be transmitted. It decouples inference speed from the raw bandwidth availability. The modular design of MobileViT supports fine-grained choices of partition points. It helps optimize the trade-off between computation and communication. As a result, the proposed method reduces the net latency without degrading detection accuracy. It also offers a robust protocol for inference under fluctuating bandwidth conditions.

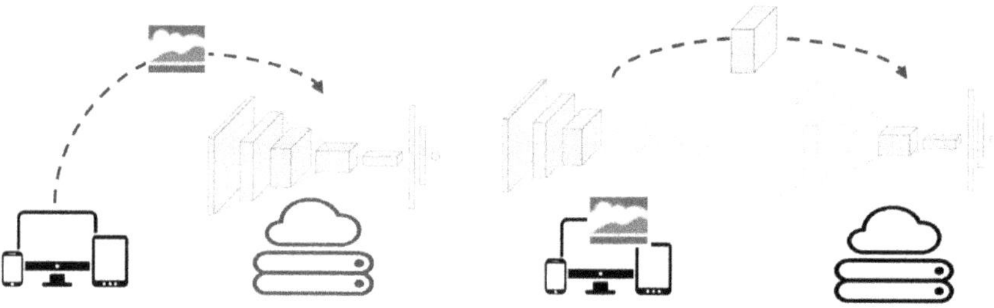

Fig. 1. Illustration of the inference paradigms: traditional monolithic client–server offloading (left) and the proposed partitioned inference framework (right).

2   Related Work

2.1   Vision Transformer

The Vision Transformer (ViT) [3] represents a major shift from traditional computer vision methods. Unlike Convolutional Neural Networks (CNNs), which rely on local receptive fields, ViT applies the Transformer architecture to visual tasks. It models global dependencies in an effective way. ViT first divides an input image into fixed-size patches and converts them into sequence embeddings.

This process allows the Multi-Head Self-Attention (MSA) mechanism to capture global context. It also benefits from the natural parallelism of the Transformer structure.

2.2   MobileViT

Although ViT models perform well in visual tasks, their high computational cost and memory usage limit their deployment on edge devices with restricted hardware resources. To address this issue, many optimization strategies have been proposed [11,22]. Among them, MobileViT [12] is a representative lightweight design. MobileViT combines the strengths of CNNs [8] and Transformers. It keeps the spatial inductive bias provided by convolutions and incorporates the Transformer's ability to model global dependencies. This hybrid design maintains strong inference accuracy while significantly reducing parameters and computational load. As a result, MobileViT is suitable for mobile platforms with strict resource constraints.

2.3   Object Detection and YOLO

Deep learning has transformed object detection and moved the field from handcrafted features to learned representations. Region-based Convolutional Neural Networks (R-CNN) [6] provided an early baseline by using CNNs to extract high-level features from candidate regions. Later methods such as Fast R-CNN [5] and Faster R-CNN [17] combined region proposal, feature extraction, and classification into unified, end-to-end frameworks. These designs improved both computational efficiency and detection accuracy.

Single-stage detectors such as YOLO [15] and SSD [10] focused on real-time performance and became popular in latency-sensitive scenarios. They use multi-scale feature pyramids and task-specific loss functions to balance speed and accuracy. Transformer-based models like DETR [2] recently have reformulated object detection as a direct set prediction problem. They remove hand-crafted components such as anchor boxes and move the field closer to fully automated feature learning by using global self-attention.

For real-time object detection, the YOLO family [1,15,16,21] has become a standard solution for balancing speed and accuracy. From YOLOv1 to YOLOv11, the architecture has been optimized step by step. Each version introduces advances in backbone design, anchor assignment, and loss function design, and together these changes push the Pareto frontier of latency and localization accuracy.

Recent studies have explored replacing the YOLO backbone with MobileViT. This design uses the hybrid structure of MobileViT to model global semantic information while keeping the parameter count lower than that of conventional convolutional backbones. When combined with YOLO's efficient detection head, the system achieves a favorable trade-off between accuracy and computational complexity (FLOPs). As a result, it is well suited for edge devices that must operate under strict power and thermal limits.

2.4 Split Learning

Split Learning [4,7] is a distributed computing paradigm designed to improve the use of computational resources while preserving data privacy. It is based on splitting a neural network by layers and placing different parts on different computing nodes. Each node runs its local part of the model and sends only the intermediate activations, often called "smashed data", to the next node. In this way, forward and backward propagation are carried out in a distributed manner. This decoupling reduces the computation load on each device and lowers communication cost. In addition, because raw input data never leaves the source device, Split Learning naturally strengthens privacy [14,20] and security.

In this work, we study how to integrate Split Learning into object detection frameworks, with a focus on lightweight Transformer-based models in distributed scenarios. By combining MobileViT with the YOLO detector, we design a model partitioning strategy that can better handle the tight resource constraints of edge devices. Our main contribution is to use split computing to build a dynamic client–server collaboration scheme. This scheme provides a computationally efficient protocol for high-quality, real-time object detection.

3 Methodology

This section describes a methodology for improving inference efficiency in resource-limited edge environments using split computing. We first build an analytical model to quantify both computation cost and communication overhead in a rigorous way. Then, we present how the MobileViT backbone is integrated into the YOLO framework. This design aims to balance the local processing load on edge devices and the bandwidth usage of the network.

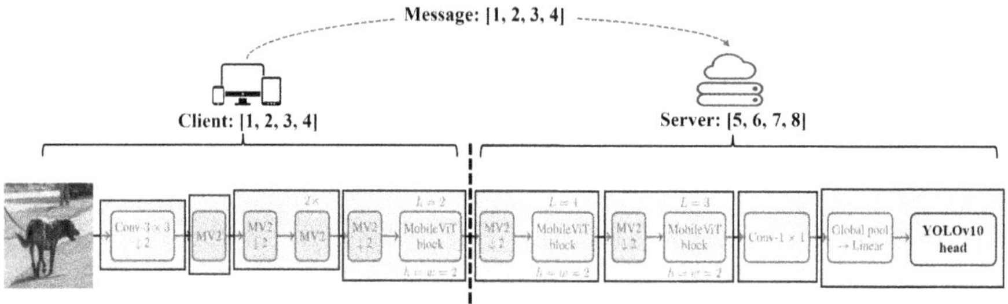

Fig. 2. Illustration of a MobileViT backbone split across 4 nodes. Before inference, the client and server exchange a *message* that specifies which layers are executed on the server side. In this example, [1, 2, 3, 4] denote the first four layers computed on the client.

3.1 Mathematical Modeling

Model Assumptions: In a conventional Client–Server (CS) architecture for image inference, the client sends raw input images to a central server, which then runs the model and returns the result. High-resolution images are usually large, which leads to high communication overhead. As a result, network bandwidth and latency become key bottlenecks that limit system performance. To analyze and optimize the model split position in a systematic way, we build a mathematical model that describes the relationship among inference time, computational resources, and communication cost.

Symbol Definitions:

- C_i: Computational cost of the i-th layer (GFLOPs).
- P_{client}, P_{server}: Computational capabilities of the client and server (GFLOPs/s).
- D: Size of the data transmitted at the split point (MB).
- B: Network bandwidth (MB/s).
- L: Network latency (seconds).

Inference Time Calculation:

To evaluate the inference time at different split points, we divide the total time into three parts: client computation time, communication time, and server computation time. The corresponding formulas are given as follows:

1. **Client Computation Time**:

$$T_{\text{client}} = \frac{\sum_{i=1}^{S} C_i}{P_{\text{client}}} \tag{1}$$

   Here, S is the number of layers executed on the client, C_i is the cost of the i-th layer, and P_{client} is the client's computational capability.

2. **Communication Time**: The communication time for sending intermediate features from client to server consists of two parts:

$$T_{\text{transfer}} = \frac{D}{B}, \quad T_{\text{latency}} = L \tag{2}$$

   Thus, the total communication time is

$$T_{\text{comm}} = T_{\text{transfer}} + T_{\text{latency}} = \frac{D}{B} + L \tag{3}$$

3. **Server Computation Time**:

$$T_{\text{server}} = \frac{\sum_{i=S+1}^{N} C_i}{P_{\text{server}}} \tag{4}$$

   Here, N is the total number of layers in the model, C_i is the cost of the i-th layer, and P_{server} is the server's computational capability.

4. **Total Inference Time:**

$$T_{\text{total}} = T_{\text{client}} + T_{\text{comm}} + T_{\text{server}} \tag{5}$$

Substituting all terms, we obtain

$$T_{\text{total}} = \frac{\sum_{i=1}^{S} C_i}{P_{\text{client}}} + \left(\frac{D}{B} + L\right) + \frac{\sum_{i=S+1}^{N} C_i}{P_{\text{server}}} \tag{6}$$

3.2   Inference Optimization Analysis

The choice of the optimal partition point S can be described as an optimization problem. The goal is to minimize the total inference latency T_{total} under given computational resources and network bandwidth.

With the rapid improvement of mobile processors, the local computation latency T_{client} has been greatly reduced. This effect is more obvious when using edge-friendly models such as the MobileViT–YOLO hybrid. As a result, the main bottleneck often shifts to the communication overhead T_{comm}. This overhead is caused by transmitting raw images or high-dimensional intermediate features over the network.

Modern vision models usually apply progressive spatial downsampling during feature extraction. We exploit this property by assigning the early downsampling layers to the edge device. The client then sends compact feature maps instead of the original high-resolution input. This strategy can significantly reduce transmission latency.

In our framework, the transmission payload D is therefore reduced by the downsampling operation. The updated inference latency model is

$$T_{\text{total}} = \frac{\sum_{i=1}^{S} C_i}{P_{\text{client}}} + \left(\frac{D_{\text{downsampled}}}{B} + L\right) + \frac{\sum_{i=S+1}^{N} C_i}{P_{\text{server}}} \tag{7}$$

Here, $D_{\text{downsampled}}$ is the size of the compressed feature maps after downsampling. The reduced transmission load directly lowers T_{comm} and changes the optimal split point S that minimizes T_{total}.

3.3   System Architecture

Our method is built on the YOLOv10 detection framework and uses Mobile-ViT as the backbone for feature extraction. Figure 2 shows the overall architecture and the logic of the partition strategy. The model is designed for a split-computing setup and is divided into a client-side part and a server-side part. Both nodes store the full model definition. This design allows them to adaptively select the split point at runtime according to current network and device conditions.

Inference begins with a metadata handshake between client and server. In this step, they negotiate how to distribute the layer-wise workload. During forward propagation, a conditional execution mechanism routes each layer to either the client or the server based on the chosen partition index.

To improve flexibility, we restrict possible partition points to the MobileViT backbone. This constraint keeps the backbone modular and makes it easier to reuse the model for different downstream tasks and hardware settings. It also avoids large structural changes when deploying to new platforms.

4 Experiments

This section presents an empirical evaluation of the proposed method. We describe the experimental setup, including dataset details, hyperparameters, and optimization settings. Then, we explain how we choose the model partition boundaries and outline the distributed evaluation platform. We report quantitative results that show how the split location affects inference latency, transmission payload, and computational resource usage.

4.1 Training

We train our model on the MS COCO dataset [9] using the MobileViT–YOLOv10 architecture with an input resolution of 640×640. The training process runs for 300 epochs with a batch size of 16. We use Stochastic Gradient Descent (SGD) with a momentum of 0.9, and apply a cosine annealing schedule to adjust the learning rate from an initial value of 0.01.

To improve generalization, we apply a data augmentation pipeline that includes random cropping, horizontal flipping, and photometric distortions (color jittering). We adopt predefined anchor boxes that are optimized for the COCO dataset. The loss function consists of three parts: bounding box regression loss, classification loss, and confidence loss. The backbone is initialized with Mobile-ViT weights pre-trained on ImageNet, which helps the model converge faster and achieve better performance (Table 1).

Table 1. Comparison with Classical Models on Real-Time Object Detection Task on MS COCO Dataset.

Model	Parameters	BoxAP
YOLOv10-N-MobileViT-S(ours)	7.9M	41.6
D-FINE-X [13]	62M	55.8
DETR-ResNet50	41.52M	42.0
Faster RCNN-FPN	41.3M	42.0
YOLOv5n	1.9M	28.0

It is important to note that in this study, the training task and model accuracy are not the primary focus of the research. However, we still provide a comparison of the model's accuracy against other classical methods for reference.

4.2   Inference

Concept of Split Points. We define split points to evaluate the performance of split inference. A split point i means that the first i layers of the network are executed on the client, and the remaining layers from $i + 1$ to 8 are executed on the server. When $i = 0$, the client only performs image preprocessing, and the entire forward pass of the model runs on the server. When $i = 8$, the client performs both image preprocessing and the full forward pass, and the server does not participate in inference.

Experimental Configuration. We deploy the full model on both the client and the server. The hardware and network settings are as follows:

- **Client Node Specifications**: A MacBook M1 Pro with an 8-core CPU. To emulate edge constraints, we restrict execution to the CPU, which is responsible for image acquisition and preprocessing.
- **Server Node Specifications**: A workstation with an AMD Ryzen 5 5600 CPU and an NVIDIA RTX 3080 GPU (12 GB VRAM), running Windows 11.
- **Communication Protocol**: Data is exchanged over TCP/IP sockets with a fixed buffer size of 4 kB.
- **Network Topology and Metrics**: The client uses Wi-Fi and the server uses Ethernet within the same LAN. Network measurements obtained with `iperf3` report a bandwidth of 9.25 Mbit/s, an average latency of 36.76 ms, and a jitter of 25.198 ms.
- **Evaluation Dataset**: We use the first 100 images from the OpenImages dataset, resized to 1024 × 768 pixels. For each split point, we compute the average inference performance over this validation subset.

To measure the benefit of the proposed framework, we evaluate inference latency and communication overhead for all candidate split points. The distributed inference procedure is defined as follows:

- **Partitioned Execution**: For a given split point i, the client computes the first set of layers $L_{1...i}$, and the server computes the remaining layers $L_{i+1...8}$.
- **Architectural Redundancy**: The full model is deployed on both the client and the server. This mirrored setup is required to support adaptive changes of the split boundary at runtime.
- **Conditional Routing**: The inference engine includes a conditional execution mechanism that routes each layer to either the client or the server according to the selected split configuration.

This setup allows us to study the trade-off between computation and communication at different split points and to validate the effectiveness of our split learning strategy in a realistic edge computing environment.

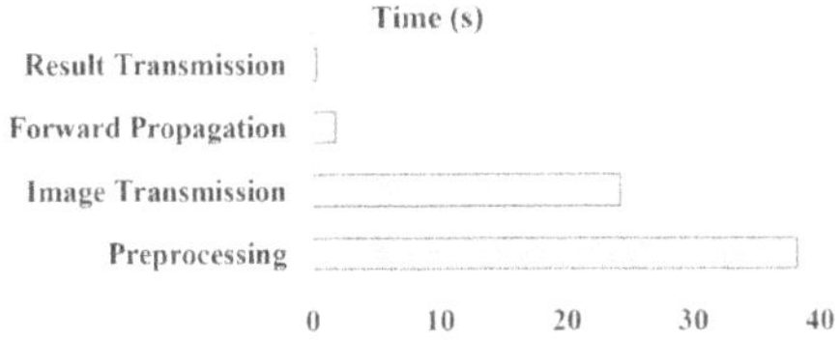

Fig. 3. Time Comparison for Each Inference Stage in Non-Split Model.

4.3 Results and Analysis

Apart from the preprocessing stage handled by MobileViT, communication between the client and server is the most time-consuming part of inference. For 100 images with a resolution of 1024×768 pixels, the total data transmitted still reaches 75 MB after preprocessing, as reported for split node 0 in Table 2. In real-time video applications, this communication volume would grow even further. Moreover, communication time is mainly determined by the network conditions rather than the model architecture itself. These observations confirm that reducing communication time is an effective way to lower the overall inference latency. Figure 3 shows the time spent in each stage of the inference pipeline in the non-split configuration.

Table 2. Comparison of Communication Volume and Device Load under Different Split Nodes.

Split Node Set	Client Transmission Volume (Bytes)	Client Load (CPU Usage, %)	Server Load (GPU Usage, %)
Split Node 0	75.04M	4.32	7.30
Split Node 1	100.04M	12.31	6.30
Split Node 2	200.04M	13.39	6.00
Split Node 3	100.04M	14.51	5.95
Split Node 4	37.54M	19.59	4.56
Split Node 5	12.54M	25.5	3.96
Split Node 6	3.95M	26.85	2.29
Split Node 7	15.67M	29.74	1.10
Split Node 8	0	36.07	0

Table 3 reports the latency breakdown for different partition stages and shows how the split point S balances local computation and network transmission. Because MobileViT is lightweight, a small increase in client-side computation is often acceptable if it leads to a large reduction in transmitted data. For example, when the split point moves from 3 to 4, the client computation time increases, but the data transfer volume is reduced by 50%. In bandwidth-limited settings,

Table 3. Analysis of Split Node Timing.

Split Node Set	Preprocessing Time(s)	Client Compute Time(s)	Client Transmission Time(s)	Client Receive Time(s)	Server Compute Time(s)	Total Inference Time(s)
Split Node 0	38.2	0	24.28	0.03	1.79	64.30
Split Node 1	38.1	2.18	35.81	0.04	1.70	77.83
Split Node 2	38.2	4.24	27.08	0.03	1.61	71.16
Split Node 3	38.1	7.37	26.25	0.03	1.59	73.34
Split Node 4	38.2	10.43	13.53	0.04	1.33	63.53
Split Node 5	38.2	13.42	5.59	0.03	0.82	58.06
Split Node 6	38.2	16.49	3.18	0.03	0.28	58.18
Split Node 7	38.3	17.33	6.41	0.03	0.13	62.20
Split Node 8	38.1	29.3	0	0	0	67.4

this reduction in communication time is more important than the extra local computation, and the total inference time decreases.

The experimental results reveal a global minimum in total inference latency. At partition index 5, the communication overhead is reduced by 80%, which offsets an additional 13.42 s of client processing. Compared with the baseline that performs full offloading (no splitting), this configuration achieves a 9.7% reduction in total latency. This result confirms the benefit of choosing the split point in a careful and informed way.

However, not all partition choices improve performance. Some MobileViT blocks increase the channel dimension and produce larger feature maps. At split nodes 1, 2, and 3, this leads to an expansion of intermediate feature size and, in turn, higher communication latency. These partition points are therefore counterproductive and highlight the need for topology-aware selection strategies that consider the internal structure of the model.

In addition to latency reduction, the proposed framework also enables server-side load balancing. As the split point moves deeper into the network and more layers are executed on the client, the computational burden on the server decreases. This property is especially useful in high-concurrency, multi-tenant scenarios, where the server must sustain a high overall throughput.

5   Conclusion

This study proposes a partitioned inference scheme that integrates the Mobile-ViT backbone into the YOLOv10 framework. The goal is to address bandwidth saturation in conventional client–server inference setups. By carefully splitting the model, we balance local computation on the client and transmission latency over the network under varying channel conditions. Our experiments show that data transmission is the main source of latency. The lightweight design of Mobile-ViT makes it suitable for execution on edge devices. The extra computation on the client is small compared with the large savings in communication cost. The analysis also highlights the importance of topology-aware partition selection.

Well-chosen split points can significantly reduce latency, while naive partitioning can increase intermediate feature sizes and degrade performance. The proposed offloading scheme distributes computation between client and server. This distribution improves scalability in high-concurrency scenarios where the server must serve many clients at the same time. In future work, we plan to extend this approach to other lightweight backbones and to study its behavior under time-varying and stochastic network conditions, in order to improve the robustness and flexibility of deployment.

Acknowledgment. This work is supported by the Joint Lab. on Networked AI Edge Computing Fudan University-Changan.

References

1. Bochkovskiy, A., Wang, C.Y., Liao, H.Y.M.: Yolov4: optimal speed and accuracy of object detection. arXiv preprint arXiv:2004.10934 (2020)
2. Carion, N., Massa, F., Synnaeve, G., Usunier, N., Kirillov, A., Zagoruyko, S.: End-to-end object detection with transformers. In: European Conference on Computer Vision (ECCV), pp. 213–229. Springer (2020)
3. Dosovitskiy, A., et al.: An image is worth 16x16 words: transformers for image recognition at scale. arXiv preprint arXiv:2010.11929 (2020)
4. Gao, Y., Kim, T., Wu, X., Suganthan, P.N.: End-to-end evaluation of federated learning and split learning for internet of things. arXiv preprint arXiv:2003.13376 (2020)
5. Girshick, R.: Fast R-CNN. In: Proceedings of the IEEE International Conference on Computer Vision (ICCV), pp. 1440–1448 (2015)
6. Girshick, R., Donahue, J., Darrell, T., Malik, J.: Rich feature hierarchies for accurate object detection and semantic segmentation. In: Proceedings of the IEEE Conference on Computer Vision and Pattern Recognition (CVPR), pp. 580–587 (2014)
7. Gupta, O., Raskar, R.: Distributed learning of deep neural network over multiple agents. J. Netw. Comput. Appl. **116**, 1–8 (2018)
8. Howard, A.G., et al.: Mobilenets: efficient convolutional neural networks for mobile vision applications. arXiv preprint arXiv:1704.04861 (2017)
9. Lin, T.Y., et al.: Microsoft COCO: common objects in context. In: European Conference on Computer Vision (ECCV), pp. 740–755. Springer (2014)
10. Liu, W., et al.: SSD: Single shot multibox detector. In: European Conference on Computer Vision (ECCV), pp. 21–37. Springer (2016)
11. Liu, Z., et al.: Swin transformer: hierarchical vision transformer using shifted windows. In: Proceedings of the IEEE/CVF International Conference on Computer Vision (ICCV), pp. 10012–10022 (2021)
12. Mehta, S., Rastegari, M.: Mobilevit: light-weight, general-purpose, and mobile-friendly vision transformer. arXiv preprint arXiv:2110.02178 (2021)
13. Peng, Y., et al.: D-FINE: redefine regression task in DETRs as fine-grained distribution refinement. arXiv preprint arXiv:2410.13842 (2024)
14. Poirot, M.G., et al.: Split learning for collaborative deep learning in healthcare. arXiv preprint arXiv:1912.12115 (2019)

15. Redmon, J., Divvala, S., Girshick, R., Farhadi, A.: You only look once: unified, real-time object detection. In: Proceedings of the IEEE Conference on Computer Vision and Pattern Recognition (CVPR), pp. 779–788 (2016)
16. Redmon, J., Farhadi, A.: YOLO9000: better, faster, stronger. In: Proceedings of the IEEE Conference on Computer Vision and Pattern Recognition (CVPR), pp. 7263–7271 (2017)
17. Ren, S., He, K., Girshick, R., Sun, J.: Faster R-CNN: towards real-time object detection with region proposal networks. In: Advances in Neural Information Processing Systems (NeurIPS), pp. 91–99 (2015)
18. Song, L., Hu, X., Zhang, G., Spachos, P., Plataniotis, K.N., Wu, H.: Networking systems of AI: on the convergence of computing and communications. IEEE Internet Things J. 9(20), 20352–20381 (2022)
19. Vaswani, A., et al.: Attention is all you need. In: Advances in Neural Information Processing Systems (NeurIPS) (2017)
20. Vepakomma, P., Gupta, O., Swedish, T., Raskar, R.: Split learning for health: distributed deep learning without sharing raw patient data. arXiv preprint arXiv:1812.00564 (2018)
21. Wang, A., Zhang, J., Li, X., Chen, Y.: Yolov10: real-time end-to-end object detection. arXiv preprint arXiv:2405.14458 (2024)
22. Wu, H., et al.: Cvt: introducing convolutions to vision transformers. In: Proceedings of the IEEE/CVF International Conference on Computer Vision (ICCV), pp. 22–31 (2021)

Unleashing the Potential of Transformers: An Efficient Inference Framework with Split Learning

Bobo Ju[1,2], Zengwen Li[2(✉)], Sudong Jiang[2], Maolin Liu[2], Yang Liu[1],
Jing Liu[1,3], Zhe Li[4], Peng Sun[3(✉)], and Liang Song[1(✉)]

[1] Academy for Engineering and Technology, Fudan University, Shanghai, China
`bbju21@m.fudan.edu.cn`, `{yang_liu20,jingliu19,songl}@fudan.edu.cn`
[2] Chongqing Changan Automobile Co., Ltd., Chongqing, China
`{lizw,jiangsd,liuml}@changan.com.cn`
[3] Division of Natural and Applied Sciences, Duke Kunshan University,
Suzhou, China
`peng.sun568@duke.edu`
[4] School of Civil Engineering, Qing Dao City University, Qingdao, China

Abstract. Although split learning has been widely applied to simpler models such as CNNs, its use in Transformer-based architectures remains underexplored. This study introduces Split-LLM and Split-ViT, two architectures that support efficient computation sharing for Transformer-based inference between mobile devices and cloud servers. By selecting optimal split points inside the models, the proposed method reduces both network congestion and computational load compared with conventional schemes that send raw data directly from the device to the cloud. Experiments show that Split-LLM improves the average inference speed per sample by about 40.5% over non-split baselines, and this advantage grows as the data volume increases. Split-ViT also achieves better performance in image classification. With an appropriate split, the inference time per image is reduced by 6.7% relative to direct cloud offloading. In addition, the method improves GPU load balancing, making better use of edge-side computation while easing the workload on cloud GPUs.

Keywords: Large Language Models · Vision Transformer · Split Learning

1 Introduction

Deep learning has advanced rapidly in recent years. Transformer-based architectures, such as the Vision Transformer (ViT) [4] and Large Language Models (LLMs) [22], have achieved major breakthroughs in their fields. ViT is now a core model in computer vision and performs well on image classification and object detection. It divides an image into fixed-size patches, arranges these patches as a sequence, and feeds the sequence into a Transformer to capture global context.

Z. Lin et al. (Eds.): INSAI 2025, CCIS 2894, pp. 71–84, 2026.
https://doi.org/10.1007/978-981-95-9299-9_6

This design requires substantial computational resources and large-scale training data, which makes deployment expensive, especially on resource-constrained devices. LLMs, including BERT and GPT, set strong benchmarks in natural language processing but rely on very large parameter counts and thus demand heavy computation. Cloud-based deployment can provide the required resources but introduces extra monetary cost and network latency. These limitations reduce the accessibility of such models and degrade the overall user experience.

Split Learning [19] is a paradigm designed to address the computational challenges of deep learning. It partitions a model into multiple segments and executes part of the computation on local devices, instead of running the entire model on a central server [10]. This architecture reduces the server workload and lowers network bandwidth usage. It also improves data privacy by avoiding large-scale transmission of raw inputs. Existing work mainly studies Split Learning on simple CNNs; its use in Transformer architectures such as ViTs and LLMs is still at an early stage [21]. Key questions on partition points and cross-node coordination remain open.

This study examines how Split Learning supports distributed inference for LLM and ViT models. The goal is to reduce network congestion and computational cost in cloud-based inference [9]. We partition the model across multiple nodes to lower latency and improve scalability. We analyze ViT and LLM architectures to identify suitable partition points, design a Split Learning framework with partition and assignment rules, and run experiments under realistic settings to measure efficiency and resource usage. The approach aims to offer a more cost-effective solution for large-scale applications, reducing resource consumption and operational cost while supporting broader deployment of ViT and LLM models.

2   Related Works

2.1   Large Language Models

LLMs evolved from sequence models such as RNNs and LSTMs, which struggle with long-range dependencies, gradient issues, and limited parallelism. The Transformer model proposed by Vaswani et al. [23] uses self-attention to enable efficient parallel computation and better long-range modeling. It has become the basis of modern LLMs such as BERT and GPT, which achieve state-of-the-art performance in text understanding and generation and are widely used in practice [2,25]. Their scale has grown rapidly; for example, GPT-3 has 175 billion parameters [5], which increases computation and storage cost and often requires expensive cloud infrastructure, leading to network congestion and latency.

To reduce these costs, researchers use model compression methods such as pruning, quantization, and sparsification, as well as knowledge distillation [24, 26]. These techniques lower model size and computational complexity and help LLMs run in resource-constrained settings. However, they do not fully solve the problem of efficient cloud resource usage. Latency and operational cost remain major obstacles for large-scale deployment.

2.2   Vision Transformer Models

Vision Transformers (ViTs) play a similar role in vision as LLMs do in language. Early vision systems relied on CNNs such as ResNet and DenseNet, which achieved strong results but had limits in modeling long-range dependencies and global context [6,13–16]. ViT applies the Transformer architecture to images by splitting an image into patches, treating them as a sequence, and feeding this sequence into a Transformer [3]. This design captures global information and often outperforms CNNs on large datasets, while improving training and inference efficiency [7]. However, ViT has high computational cost and many parameters. Methods such as pruning, quantization, and sparsification help reduce these costs but still make efficient deployment in strict edge environments challenging [11,17].

2.3   Split Learning

Split Learning splits a deep model across multiple nodes to reduce computation and communication on the central server. It was first used with CNNs, where shallow layers run on edge devices and deeper layers run in the cloud [7,8]. In medical imaging, for example, the device performs local feature extraction and sends only feature representations to the cloud, which protects sensitive data and lowers bandwidth usage [7]. This framework is also suitable for intelligent devices, because edge computing can offload part of the workload from centralized servers.

For Transformer models such as ViTs and LLMs, Split Learning is less explored. Their data flow and gradient dependencies are more complex, which makes split-point selection and cross-node coordination harder [8]. At the same time, self-attention can support efficient information exchange under a proper partition strategy. In this work, we design split strategies and communication schemes that balance model structure, hardware resources, and communication cost, and we propose Split-LLM and Split-ViT architectures. By segmenting Transformer networks, we enable flexible computation sharing between edge and cloud, which improves responsiveness and scalability and supports cost-effective deployment in resource-constrained and real-time scenarios.

3   Methods

3.1   Split-Policy

Our split policy (Algorithm 1) is a distributed training scheme that divides the model into two parts: an edge model ($\mathcal{M}_1$) and a cloud model ($\mathcal{M}_2$). The edge model runs on local devices and performs the initial computation, such as feature extraction, using local data. The cloud model then receives the intermediate outputs from the edge side and carries out more complex tasks, such as classification or regression. This division makes better use of available resources: simple, low-cost operations are executed on the edge, while computationally intensive processing is handled by the cloud.

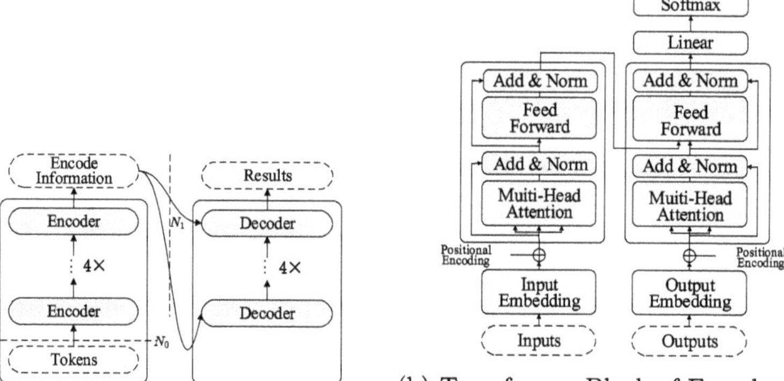

(a) Split-LLM Main Architecture.

(b) Transformer Block of Encoder and Decoder.

Fig. 1. Split-LLM Model Architecture (N_0, N_1 are alternative split nodes).

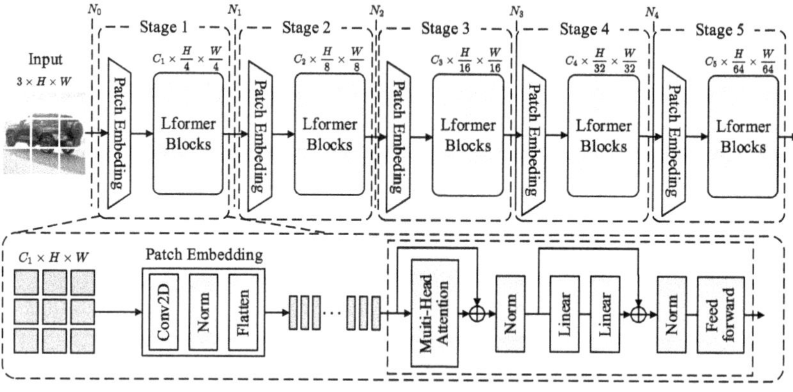

Fig. 2. Split-ViT Model Architecture (N_0, N_1,N_2, N_3, N_4 are alternative split nodes).

During training, the input data first passes through the edge model, which extracts features and sends them to the cloud model. The two parts are updated with their own optimizers, $\mathcal{O}_1$ for the edge model and $\mathcal{O}_2$ for the cloud model. However, the overall loss is computed only from the output of the cloud model using the loss function $\mathcal{L}$. Gradients are backpropagated through both the edge and cloud components, and the model parameters are updated accordingly. We record the total loss L_{total} in each epoch and compute the average loss L_{avg} to monitor training stability and convergence.

The best-performing model configurations are saved according to the observed loss values. We denote by L_1^{best} and L_2^{best} the lowest loss values achieved by the edge model and the cloud model, respectively. Whenever the current loss improves on these values, the corresponding model parameters are stored. This procedure ensures that training preserves the most effective versions of both models and helps the distributed learning process converge efficiently while maintaining strong performance on the edge and cloud components.

Algorithm 1. Transformer-based Model Partition Algorithm

1: **Input:**
2:    $\mathcal{M}_1, \mathcal{M}_2$: Models being trained (e.g., Edge and Cloud models)
3:    $\mathcal{D}_{train}$: Training dataset
4:    $\mathcal{D}_{val}$: Validation dataset (optional)
5:    $\mathcal{O}_1, \mathcal{O}_2$: Optimizers for the models
6:    $\mathcal{L}$: Loss function (e.g., DiceLoss, CrossEntropy)
7:    E: Total number of epochs
8:    $\mathcal{D}$: Hardware device (e.g., CPU or GPU)
9:    L_{total}: Accumulated loss for the epoch
10:    L_{avg}: Average loss per epoch
11:    L_1^{best}, L_2^{best}: Best loss values tracked to save the best model
12: **Initialize:**
13: $L_1^{best} \leftarrow \infty,\ L_2^{best} \leftarrow \infty$
14: **for** $e = 1$ **to** E **do**
15:     **for** batch in $\mathcal{D}_{train}$ **do**
16:         **Input:** batch (X, Y)
17:         $X, Y \leftarrow$ move to device
18:         **Forward pass:**
19:         $Z_1 \leftarrow \mathcal{M}_1(X),\ Z_2 \leftarrow \mathcal{M}_2(Z_1)$
20:         **Loss Calculation:**
21:         $L \leftarrow \mathcal{L}(Z_2, Y)$
22:         **Backward pass:**
23:         $\mathcal{O}_1.\text{zero\_grad}(),\ \mathcal{O}_2.\text{zero\_grad}()$
24:         $L.\text{backward}()$
25:         $\mathcal{O}_1.\text{step}(),\ \mathcal{O}_2.\text{step}()$
26:         **Log results:**
27:         $L_{total} \leftarrow L_{total} + L$
28:     **end for**
29:     $L_{avg} \leftarrow L_{total}/\text{len}(\mathcal{D}_{train})$
30:     **Validation (optional):**
31:     **if** $\mathcal{D}_{val}$ exists **then**
32:         $A \leftarrow \text{accuracy}(\mathcal{M}_1, \mathcal{M}_2, \mathcal{D}_{val})$
33:     **end if**
34:     **Save best model:**
35:     **if** $L_{avg} < L_1^{best}$ **then**
36:         $L_1^{best} \leftarrow L_{avg}$
37:         Save $\mathcal{M}_1$ weights
38:     **end if**
39:     **if** $L_{avg} < L_2^{best}$ **then**
40:         $L_2^{best} \leftarrow L_{avg}$
41:         Save $\mathcal{M}_2$ weights
42:     **end if**
43: **end for**

3.2 Split-LLM

The Split-LLM model (as shown in Fig. 1a) is a deep learning model based on the Transformer architecture, primarily designed for sequence-to-sequence tasks such as NLP. The model consists of twelve main components: six encoders and six decoders. It incorporates multi-head attention mechanisms, multilayer perceptrons (feedforward), and positional encodings to effectively process information from the input sequence.

Figure 1b illustrates that the core of the Split-LLM encoder and decoder lies in the multi-head self-attention mechanism, which captures the relationships between different positions in the input sequence through multiple independent attention heads. The multi-head attention mechanism divides the input features into multiple subspaces, allowing parallel computation of attention scores across different subspaces. Specifically, given the query, key, and value of the input sequence, the model obtains representations for multiple heads through linear transformations and computes the attention weights using the following equation:

$$\text{Atten}(Q, K, V) = \text{softmax}\left(\frac{QK^T}{\sqrt{d_k}}\right) V \tag{1}$$

Q denotes the query, K denotes the key, V denotes the value, and d_k is the dimension of the key. This design allows Split-LLM to capture information in different representation spaces and improves its feature extraction ability.

After the multi-head self-attention layer, the Split-LLM model also employs a feedforward neural network, consisting of two fully connected layers. The feedforward network further processes the output from the attention layer to enhance the model's ability to learn non-linear features. The output of the feedforward network can be represented by the following equation:

$$\text{FFN}(x) = W_2 \cdot \text{ReLU}\left(W_1 \cdot x\right) \tag{2}$$

W_1 and W_2 are the weight matrices, and x is the input feature.

The encoder portion of Split-LLM is composed of a stack of multiple Transformer blocks. A multi-head attention layer and a feedforward network layer are included in each Transformer block. The input to the encoder is represented by the sum of word embeddings and position embeddings, ensuring that the Split-LLM can obtain the relative positions of words in the input sequence. The output of the encoder is passed to the decoder, forming the final sequence representation. The main structure of the encoder is as follows:

$$\begin{aligned} \text{Enc}(x) = \ &\text{LNorm}(x + \text{Atten}(x, x, x)) \\ &+ \text{FFN}(\text{LNorm}(x + \text{Atten}(x, x, x))) \end{aligned} \tag{3}$$

The decoder is designed similarly to the encoder, but it additionally takes into account the previous outputs (the target sequence) to generate the new output sequence. The decoder's input is also encoded through word embeddings and position embeddings. During the decoding process, the Split-LLM first processes the target sequence through a multi-head attention mechanism, then uses the output of encoder as keys and values, forming an "encoder-decoder" structure. The output of the decoder is mapped to the size of the target vocabulary through a fully connected layer, ultimately generating the predicted target sequence. The main structure of the decoder is as follows:

$$\begin{aligned} \mathrm{Dec}(y, enc_{\mathrm{out}}) = {} & \mathrm{LNorm}(y + \mathrm{Atten}(y, y, y)) \\ & + \mathrm{Former}(enc_{\mathrm{out}}, enc_{\mathrm{out}}, y) \end{aligned} \tag{4}$$

In the decoding process, to ensure that the model can only access previous outputs, Split-LLM introduces a masking mechanism. The target mask, implemented through a triangular matrix, ensures that future time steps do not influence the prediction of the current time step. Additionally, the source mask prevents the model from attending to the padded portions of the input sequence.

3.3   Split-ViT

The Split-ViT model (shown in Fig. 2) is a deep learning architecture that combines CNNs with Transformer modules to improve performance on image processing tasks. Its core component is a Transformer block that uses multi-head self-attention and a feed-forward network to capture long-range dependencies in the input features. The structure can be written as

$$\begin{aligned} \mathrm{Lformer}(x) = {} & \mathrm{LNorm}(x + \mathrm{Atten}(x)) \\ & + \mathrm{LNorm}(x + \mathrm{FFN}(x)) \end{aligned} \tag{5}$$

where x is the input, Atten is the output of the self-attention mechanism, and FFN is the feed-forward network.

First, the input passes through the self-attention module, and the result is combined with the original input through a residual connection and layer normalization. The output is then processed by a feed-forward network, again with residual and normalization operations, which strengthens the model's representation ability. In Split-ViT, each Stage block combines convolution layers with Lformer blocks. The convolution layers preserve local spatial information. The self-attention in the Lformer blocks captures richer global context. In this way, the model maintains local details and learns global features at the same time, which improves its effectiveness on complex image understanding tasks.

The Split-ViT architecture has two parts: an edge model and a cloud model. The edge model contains Stage 1, and the cloud model contains Stages 2–5. The edge model targets resource-limited edge devices. It uses one Stage block with max-pooling layers. These layers extract features step by step and reduce the spatial resolution of the feature maps. This design improves computational efficiency. The edge model reduces computational burden while maintaining a certain level of feature expressiveness, making it well-suited for operation on resource-constrained devices. On the other hand, the cloud model is optimized for high-computational-power environments and includes four Stage blocks to accommodate more complex feature extraction needs. The cloud model has a more sophisticated structure, capable of handling higher-dimensional feature information. The final output of the model is processed through a fully connected layer for classification, providing the final prediction results.

4   Experiments

Table 1. Comparison of Accuracy between Split-LLM, Split-ViT, and Classical Methods.

Methods	IMDB	20 Newsgroups	MNIST	CIFAR-10
LSTM	82.63%	76.16%	–	–
Split-LLM(Ours)	94.74%	88.93%	–	–
CNN	–	–	98.65%	78.66%
Split-ViT(Ours)	–	–	98.93%	87.46%

Table 2. Split-LLM Computation Cost (GFLOPs) and Parameters (Million) for IMDB and 20 Newsgroups Datasets.

Dataset	Src Vocab Size	Trg Vocab Size	Seq Len	Batch Size	Computation Cost	Parameters
IMDB	25,000	25,000	256	2	7.2	13.93
20 Newsgroups	90,000	90,000	512	2	31.3	30.64

Table 3. Split-ViT Computation Cost (GFLOPs) and Parameters (Million) for Cifar-10 and MNIST Datasets

Dataset	Computation Cost	Parameters
Cifar-10	1.40	1.63
MNIST	0.92	1.63

4.1   Datasets

We evaluated the performance of Split-LLM and Split-ViT using two datasets. Below are the descriptions of these datasets:

Table 4. Comparison of Inference Time for Split-LLM at Different Split Nodes.

Split	End	Trans ↑	Trans ↓	Cloud	Total
N_0	0	0.008226408	0.000122842	0.008754204	0.017103454
N_1	0.003313456	0.002787186	0.000462682	0.005613069	0.012176393

Note: Time unit (second), Trans ↑ and Trans ↓ unit (second).

Table 5. Comparison of Split-ViT Inference Time at Different Split Nodes.

Split	End	Trans ↑	Trans ↓	Cloud	Total
N_0	0	0.004138257	0.000124820	0.004301528	0.008564604
N_1	0.001130059	0.002689876	0.000756082	0.003447325	0.008023342
N_2	0.001590051	0.002454692	0.001394229	0.003002621	0.008441592
N_3	0.002362175	0.004183492	0.004732442	0.002193109	0.013471217
N_4	0.003160061	0.009371821	0.011535370	0.001448523	0.025515775

Note: Time unit (second), Trans ↑ and Trans ↓ unit (second).

- **IMDB Dataset** [18]: A sentiment analysis dataset with 50,000 movie reviews (25k train, 25k test), labeled as positive or negative. Widely used for benchmarking sentiment classification tasks.
- **20 Newsgroups Dataset** [20]: Contains 18,000 documents from 20 newsgroups across topics like tech, sports, and politics. Used in text classification, topic modeling, and clustering.
- **MNIST Dataset** [1]: Includes 70,000 28×28 grayscale images of digits (0–9), with 60k for training and 10k for testing. A standard benchmark for classification and CNN models.
- **CIFAR-10 Dataset** [12]: Comprises 60,000 32×32 RGB images across 10 classes (e.g., airplane, cat), split into 50k training and 10k test images. Commonly used in image classification and CNN benchmarking.

4.2 Experimental Setups

- **Experimental Setup:** The experimental setup consists of three main components: a mobile device (laptop with Intel Core i7-10750H CPU @ 2.60 GHz,

Table 6. Resource Consumption of Split-LLM Inference at Different Split Nodes.

Split	End					Cloud				
	CPU	GPU	Mem	Net ↑	Net ↓	CPU	GPU	Mem	Net ↑	Net ↓
N_0	6.34	22.93	66.61	226023.20	5224.20	55.81	6.17	37.21	12381.50	264416.42
N_1	12.64	26.31	68.82	6618788.73	140086.13	55.07	6.13	37.19	156216.67	7092818.50

Note: CPU, GPU, Mem unit (%), Net ↑ and Net ↓ unit (bytes/s).

Table 7. Resource Consumption of Split-ViT Inference at Different Split Nodes.

Split	End					Cloud				
	CPU	GPU	Mem	Net ↑	Net ↓	CPU	GPU	Mem	Net ↑	Net ↓
N_0	6.55	4.71	42.24	6209070.81	1640369.38	13.53	9.44	42.44	146631.06	6690076.67
N_1	7.66	31.98	55.48	10145146.81	218259.68	11.99	9.07	42.11	233237.27	10618503.20
N_2	6.17	32.71	56.06	18012320.00	374948.39	13.65	9.17	42.36	411064.76	18956352.53
N_3	6.25	32.67	56.34	21414500.40	439487.07	9.15	8.99	42.21	475568.86	22545123.76
N_4	5.22	32.74	56.00	21857710.65	458386.92	6.56	8.99	42.22	483873.64	22838810.47

Note: CPU, GPU, Mem unit (%), Net ↑ and Net ↓ unit (bytes/s).

16 GB RAM, GTX1650-4G GPU, 5G Wi-Fi support, running Windows 10), a cloud device (GPU server with Intel Core i9-10850K CPU @ 3.60 GHz, 32 GB RAM, RTX-3090 GPU, LAN network interface, running Ubuntu 18.04), and a local area network router (supporting 2.4G Wi-Fi with speeds up to 300 Mbps, 5G Wi-Fi with speeds up to 867 Mbps, antennas with 2.4G/5G gain of 5dBi and 6dBi respectively, and a 10/100M self-adaptive LAN/WAN port).

- **Split-LLM Training Strategy:** We conducted text classification experiments using the IMDB movie review and 20 Newsgroups datasets to train the Split-LLM model. For IMDB, data preprocessing involved tokenization, vocabulary construction, and padding/truncating sentences to 20 tokens. The batch size was 32, training lasted 1000 epochs with the Adam optimizer (learning rate 1e–4) and cross-entropy loss. Model parameters were saved to 'imdb_client.pth' and 'imdb_server.pth' when average loss improved. For the 20 Newsgroups experiment, similar preprocessing steps were followed, with consistent batch size, epochs, optimizer, and loss monitoring. Best model parameters were saved after 1000 epochs to '20newsgroups_client.pth' and '20newsgroups_server.pth'. Both experiments followed consistent data processing and parameter configurations to ensure effective model saving for evaluation.

- **Split-ViT Training Strategy:** This study uses the Split-ViT architecture, comprising an edge model and a cloud model. The Edge model has 3 input channels, 16 output channels, and uses a multi-head self-attention mechanism with 4 heads and a feedforward layer dimension of 64. The Cloud model has 4 stages, starting with 32 input channels and using 4 heads and a feedforward layer dimension of 128 in the first block, followed by 8 heads and 256 dimensions in the last three blocks. Both models use the SGD optimizer (learning rate 0.01, momentum 0.9). During training, the Edge model performs feature extraction, and the Cloud model handles classification. The negative log-likelihood loss is used. In Experiment 1 (MNIST dataset), the models are trained for 40 epochs with 1 input channel. Experiment 2 (CIFAR-10 dataset) uses 3 input channels and also trains for 40 epochs. Both experiments use a batch size of 64, demonstrating Split-ViT's adaptability for classification tasks.

In all the aforementioned training processes, we employed a centralized training approach, utilizing a single RTX-3090 GPU to train the edge and cloud sub-models for both Split-LLM and Split-ViT. During deployment, the edge sub-model is deployed on a laptop, while the cloud sub-model is deployed on the RTX-3090. Joint task inference is then carried out via a socket network.

4.3   Experimental Analysis

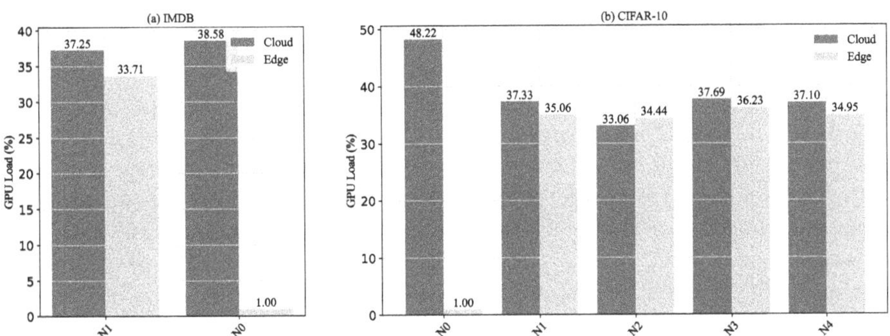

Fig. 3. Comparison of GPU Load Under Different Split Nodes at Inference Stage.

Table 2 shows that, although the overall model architectures are the same, Split-LLM exhibits clear differences in computational load and parameter usage on the IMDB and 20 Newsgroups datasets. This variation mainly comes from changes in vocabulary size and input sequence length. The size of the embedding layer grows with the vocabulary, while the complexity of the attention mechanism increases roughly with the square of the sequence length. We measure FLOPs and parameter counts using Thop, which is well suited for profiling language models. These computational demands make it difficult to run large-scale inference entirely on edge devices. To address this issue, we adopt a split strategy. Lighter, shallower layers are placed on the edge to maintain responsiveness, while deeper and more expensive layers are executed in the cloud. This design balances latency and resource consumption. In contrast, Table 3 shows that Split-ViT maintains a nearly constant parameter count of about 1.63 million on both CIFAR-10 and MNIST. The GFLOPs vary only slightly, which is mainly due to differences in input complexity between the two datasets. These results were derived using PtFlops, a widely used tool for estimating FLOPs in vision models. The findings highlight Split-ViT's structural consistency and lightweight nature, making it well-suited for modular deployment scenarios. Early-stage processing can comfortably run on the edge device, while the heavier self-attention computations are handled in the cloud, enabling smooth and efficient collaboration between edge and cloud in real-time vision applications.

The primary objective of this study is to evaluate the efficiency of distributed inference after the Split-LLM and Split-ViT models are partitioned. Therefore, while model accuracy is not our main performance metric, we also compare our proposed Split-LLM and Split-ViT models with some classic models. Specifically, we compare the encoder-decoder-based Split-LLM with a two-layer LSTM neural network on the IMDB and 20 Newsgroups datasets. Meanwhile, we compare Split-ViT with a ten-layer CNN model composed of convolutional layers on the MNIST and CIFAR-10 datasets. Table 1 present the superior performance of Split-LLM and Split-ViT on these datasets[1].

We conducted an ablation study focusing on the time efficiency of distributed inference after the Split-LLM and Split-ViT models are partitioned. For Split-LLM, we primarily compared the encoder-decoder split inference with the non-split model (i.e., where data is transmitted from the client to the cloud for inference). In Table 4, N_0 represents the non-split model, while N_1 indicates the encoder-decoder split inference method. Table 4 records the average inference time for 10,000 randomly selected samples from the IMDB dataset (including both edge-side and cloud-side inference time, as well as data transmission and reception times between the client and the cloud). It can be observed that the encoder-decoder split inference method is approximately 40.5% faster than the non-split model in terms of total average inference time per data point. This advantage increases significantly as the volume of inference data grows.

In the ablation study for Split-ViT, we investigated the impact of splitting the five ViT modules into partition nodes and compared these with the non-split model. Table 5 records the average inference time for 10,000 randomly selected images from the CIFAR-10 dataset, where N_0 represents the non-split model, and the partitioned inference methods for the five ViT modules are represented as N_i with different split locations[2]. It can be seen that the split at N_1 is optimal, with N_1 and N_2 providing inference speeds that are approximately 6.7% and 1.5% faster, respectively, compared to the non-split model. This advantage also increases as the number of inference images grows. Additionally, Table 5 demonstrates the impact of different partition node selections N_i on inference time. Notably, the total inference time for node N_4 is approximately 3.25 times that of node N_1.

Additionally, we examined the resource consumption during distributed inference for Split-LLM, Split-ViT, and their non-split models. Table 6 and Table 7 present comparisons of CPU usage, GPU memory consumption, RAM usage,

---

[1] **End:** Represents the inference time of the terminal mobile device or edge device; **Cloud:** Represents the inference time of the cloud server device; **Trans ↑:** Represents the data transmission time (upload); **Trans ↓:** Represents the data reception time (download); **Total:** Represents the total runtime during the inference phase.

[2] **CPU:** Central Processing Unit utilization; **GPU:** Graphics Processing Unit utilization; **Mem:** Memory utilization; **Net ↑:** Represents the data transmission rate (upload); **Net ↓:** Represents the data reception rate (download).

and data transmission requirements under different partition nodes. It is evident that the primary impact of the different split configurations is on the volume of upstream and downstream data transmission. As shown in Fig. 3, compared to the non-split model, the split inference process leverages edge-side computational resources effectively, significantly reducing the load on the cloud-side GPU. This approach also ensures that other computational tasks on the edge side are not affected during inference.

5   Conclusion

While Split Learning has been applied to simpler CNN models, its use with Transformer architectures such as ViTs and LLMs is still limited. In this work, we propose two split schemes for Transformer models, Split-LLM and Split-ViT, and study how to perform efficient split computation between mobile devices and the cloud. Our goal is to support distributed inference while reducing network congestion and resource usage through careful model partitioning and task allocation. Despite the structure of Transformers, our results show that Split Learning still works well for them. The key is to choose good split points that keep a balance between computation and communication. As Split Learning continues to develop, combining it with Transformers may provide efficient solutions for computer vision, NLP, intelligent devices, and large-scale data processing. This integration can also make AI systems more flexible and easier to adapt to different tasks.

Acknowledgments. This work is supported by the Joint Lab. on Networked AI Edge Computing Fudan University-Changan.

Disclosure of Interests. The authors have no conflicts of interest to declare that are relevant to the content of this article.

References

1. Cohen, G., Afshar, S., Tapson, J., Van Schaik, A.: Emnist: extending mnist to handwritten letters. In: 2017 International Joint Conference on Neural Networks (IJCNN), pp. 2921–2926. IEEE (2017)
2. Devlin, J., Chang, M.W., Lee, K., Toutanova, K.: Bert: bidirectional encoder representations from transformers. arXiv preprint arXiv:1810.04805 (2018)
3. Dosovitskiy, A.: An image is worth 16x16 words: transformers for image recognition at scale. arXiv preprint arXiv:2010.11929 (2020)
4. Dubey, S.R., Singh, S.K.: Transformer-based generative adversarial networks in computer vision: a comprehensive survey. IEEE Trans. Artif. Intell. (2024)
5. Floridi, L., Chiriatti, M.: Gpt-3: its nature, scope, limits, and consequences. Mind. Mach. **30**, 681–694 (2020)
6. Huang, G., Liu, Z., Van Der Maaten, L., Weinberger, K.Q.: Densely connected convolutional networks. In: Proceedings of the IEEE Conference on Computer Vision and Pattern Recognition, pp. 4700–4708 (2017)

7. Ju, B., Liu, Y., Hu, X., Zhao, D., Jiang, L.: A novel cell contour-based instance segmentation model and its applications in her2 breast cancer discrimination. Biomed. Signal Process. Control **85**, 104941 (2023)

8. Ju, B., Liu, Y., Liu, J., Sun, P., Song, L.: Cnn-dag-editor: a convolutional neural network offloading analyzer with multi-objective dynamic adaptive resource competitive swarm optimization. Computer Networks, p. 111374 (2025)

9. Ju, B., Liu, Y., Song, L., Gan, G., Li, Z., Jiang, L.: A high-reliability edge-side mobile terminal shared computing architecture based on task triple-stage full-cycle monitoring. IEEE Internet Things J. **10**(22), 20149–20161 (2023)

10. Ju, B., et al.: Open service for networking systems of ai: a case study in adaptation optimization. In: 2024 IEEE 10th World Forum on Internet of Things (WF-IoT), pp. 1–6. IEEE (2024)

11. Khan, S., Naseer, M., Hayat, M., Zamir, S.W., Khan, F.S., Shah, M.: Transformers in vision: a survey. ACM Comput. Surv. (CSUR) **54**(10s), 1–41 (2022)

12. Krizhevsky, A., Hinton, G., et al.: Learning multiple layers of features from tiny images (2009)

13. Li, D., Liu, Y., Song, L.: Adaptive weighted losses with distribution approximation for efficient consistency-based semi-supervised learning. IEEE Trans. Circuits Syst. Video Technol. **32**(11), 7832–7842 (2022)

14. Liu, J., Liu, Y., Zhu, W., Zhu, X., Song, L.: Distributional and spatial-temporal robust representation learning for transportation activity recognition. Pattern Recogn. **140**, 109568 (2023)

15. Liu, Y., et al.: Amp-net: appearance-motion prototype network assisted automatic video anomaly detection system. IEEE Trans. Ind. Inf. (2023)

16. Liu, Y., et al.: Generalized video anomaly event detection: systematic taxonomy and comparison of deep models. ACM Comput. Surv. **56**(7), 1–38 (2024)

17. Liu, Y., et al.: A survey of visual transformers. IEEE Trans. Neural Netw. Learn. Syst. (2023)

18. Maas, A., Daly, R.E., Pham, P.T., Huang, D., Ng, A.Y., Potts, C.: Learning word vectors for sentiment analysis. In: Proceedings of the 49th Annual Meeting of the Association for Computational Linguistics: Human Language Technologies, pp. 142–150 (2011)

19. Matsubara, Y., Levorato, M., Restuccia, F.: Split computing and early exiting for deep learning applications: survey and research challenges. ACM Comput. Surv. **55**(5), 1–30 (2022)

20. Mitchell, T.: Twenty newsgroups data set. UCI Machine Learning Repository (1999)

21. Poirot, M.G., Vepakomma, P., Chang, K., Kalpathy-Cramer, J., Gupta, R., Raskar, R.: Split learning for collaborative deep learning in healthcare. arXiv preprint arXiv:1912.12115 (2019)

22. Teng, L., Liu, Y., Liu, J., Song, L.: End-cloud collaboration framework for advanced ai customer service in e-commerce. arXiv preprint arXiv:2410.07122 (2024)

23. Vaswani, A.: Attention is all you need. In: Advances in Neural Information Processing Systems (2017)

24. Wan, Z., et al.: Efficient large language models: a survey. arXiv preprint arXiv:2312.03863 (2023)

25. Yenduri, G., et al.: Gpt (generative pre-trained transformer)–a comprehensive review on enabling technologies, potential applications, emerging challenges, and future directions. IEEE Access (2024)

26. Zhou, Z., et al.: A survey on efficient inference for large language models. arXiv preprint arXiv:2404.14294 (2024)

Communication and Edge Computing

CSI-Free Holographic Beamforming Enabled by Recordable and Reconfigurable Metasurface

Jinzhe Wang[1], Qinghua Guo[2], and Xiaojun Yuan[1(✉)]

[1] National Key Laboratory of Wireless Communications, University of Electronic Science and Technology of China, Chengdu, China
`wangjinzhe@std.uestc.edu.cn`, `xjyuan@uestc.edu.cn`
[2] School of ECTE, University of Wollongong, Wollongong, NSW 2522, Australia
`qguo@uow.edu.au`

Abstract. Holographic beamforming is rapidly emerging as a pivotal architecture for next-generation wireless network design. However, despite its promising capabilities, current implementation methods—especially those utilizing reconfigurable holographic surfaces (RHSs)—face a critical limitation: they rely heavily on accurate channel state information (CSI). This dependency creates a significant operational bottleneck, largely due to the excessive pilot overhead necessary to estimate channels in large-scale antenna arrays. To overcome this challenge, we propose a novel hardware framework termed the recordable and reconfigurable metasurface (RRM). This architecture effectively eliminates the requirement for explicit CSI acquisition by leveraging a holographic recording technique. During the uplink phase, power sensors embedded within the RRM measure the intensity of the interference pattern resulting from the superposition of incident user signals and a local reference wave. Because this recorded pattern inherently captures the necessary spatial phase data of the incoming waves, it allows for the direct calculation of holographic beamforming weights, bypassing resource-heavy channel estimation procedures. Through comprehensive mutual information analysis, we verify that the proposed CSI-free RRM system delivers performance on par with an RHS system utilizing perfect CSI, while simultaneously offering significant reductions in both signaling overhead and computational complexity.

Keywords: Hologram principle · reconfigurable holographic surfaces (RHS) · beamforming · metasurface · mutual information

1   Introduction

As the telecommunications sector advances towards the sixth-generation (6G) era, there is a growing necessity for systems that can sustain ubiquitous connectivity alongside ultra-high data rates. Achieving these high-performance targets, however, entails overcoming strict limitations regarding integration density,

Z. Lin et al. (Eds.): INSAI 2025, CCIS 2894, pp. 87–99, 2026.
https://doi.org/10.1007/978-981-95-9299-9_7

energy efficiency, and hardware costs. Although massive multiple-input multiple-output (MIMO) technologies offer a route to high capacity via extensive antenna arrays, conventional phased-array architectures face severe scalability issues. In particular, their dependence on intricate and costly phase-shifting networks—which require numerous high-precision phase shifters and power amplifiers—makes large-scale deployment economically unviable for dense 6G networks [12,18,22].

To address these hardware constraints, metamaterial-based surfaces have risen as a promising alternative. By designing subwavelength meta-atoms to control electromagnetic wavefronts, reconfigurable metasurfaces provide programmable apertures with drastically lower hardware complexity. The reconfigurable intelligent surface (RIS) is a notable example, consisting of passive reflective elements that modulate propagation environments without active radio frequency (RF) chains [19,20]. However, a key restriction of standard RISs is their passive nature, which generally prevents them from functioning as standalone transceivers.

In contrast, reconfigurable holographic surfaces (RHSs) apply optical holography principles to the RF domain, facilitating active beam steering via precise electromagnetic surface control [9]. Evolving from innovations like holographic artificial impedance surfaces [15], contemporary RHS designs utilize mechanisms such as PIN diodes or liquid crystals (LCs) to achieve dynamic reconfigurability [11,21]. Given their benefits—such as active radiation capabilities, cost-efficiency, and lightweight profiles—RHSs are considered a vital component of 6G infrastructure. Consequently, industry leaders like Kymeta [16] and Pivotal Commware [13] are actively developing commercial prototypes.

Holographic beamforming utilizing RHSs has become a focal point of research. Various studies have suggested strategies for performance optimization [6,7], resulting in advanced multi-user schemes like holographic-pattern division multiple access (HDMA) [5]. HDMA maps signals to superimposed holographic patterns and has been investigated in contexts such as Low Earth Orbit (LEO) satellite communications [4]. Additionally, the practical viability of RHSs has been confirmed through communication platform validations and prototype testing [3]. Despite this progress, a major hurdle persists: optimizing RHS-based beamformers generally requires precise channel state information (CSI). Due to the vast number of discrete elements or the continuous aperture of an RHS, CSI acquisition involves estimating a massive array of channel coefficients. This process results in prohibitive computational costs and pilot overhead, which scale poorly as the array size increases [2,10,23].

In this work, we present the recordable and reconfigurable metasurface (RRM) and outline a new communication framework based on the recording and reconstruction stages of optical holography. We term this approach "holographic communication." It should be noted that, in this paper, this term refers to electromagnetic-wave holography rather than 3D holographic imaging [8]. The core structural difference between the RRM and standard RHS lies in the embedding of a power recording module within the surface. This module detects the interference intensity between a local reference wave and received signals. The captured interference power is then used to compute weights for downlink holographic beamforming. We evaluate the mutual information of the RRM system, showing that it matches the performance of an RHS system with perfect CSI, thereby providing a highly efficient solution for future wireless networks.

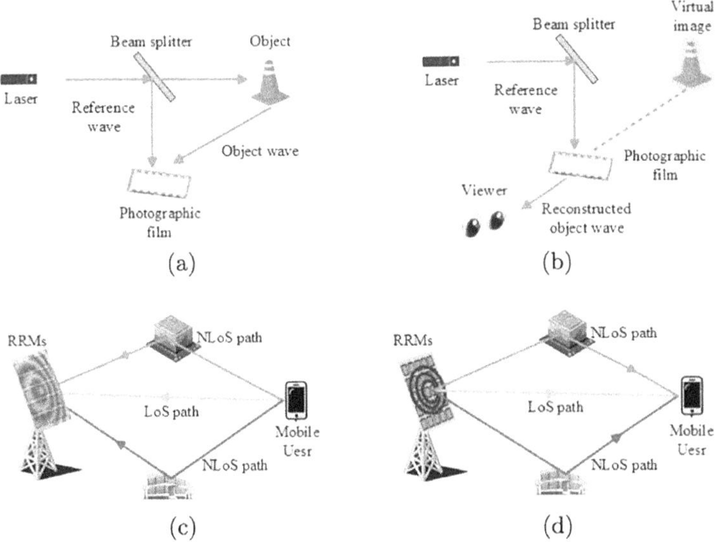

Fig. 1. Schematic comparison of optical and EM holography principles: (a) Optical recording phase; (b) Optical reconstruction phase; (c) RRM-based recording process; (d) RRM-based reconstruction process.

2   Optical Holography: The Foundation of EM Holographic Communication Theory

Here, we outline the essential mechanisms of optical holography, covering both the reconstruction and recording phases. These concepts form the theoretical basis for our proposed electromagnetic (EM) holography framework and the RRM design.

Optical holography is a method used to create 3D images by exploiting light diffraction and interference physics. By employing coherent light sources such as lasers, the system records wavefronts scattered by an object. This mechanism embeds both phase and intensity data within an interference pattern—known as a hologram—which is preserved on a photosensitive layer, as illustrated in Fig. 1(a). In the reconstruction phase shown in Fig. 1(b), the recorded hologram is illuminated by a reference wave to restore the original wavefronts, thereby generating a realistic 3D image complete with depth cues.

As illustrated in Fig. 1(a), the optical configuration typically uses a laser to produce a reference wave, split into two beams. One beam directly hits the recording medium at position $\boldsymbol{r}$, given by:

$$R(\boldsymbol{r}) = A_R e^{j\phi_R(\boldsymbol{r})}, \tag{1}$$

where A_R and $\phi_R(\boldsymbol{r})$ denote the reference wave's amplitude and phase, respectively. The second beam illuminates the target, creating the reflected object wave:

$$O(\boldsymbol{r}) = A_O e^{j\phi_O(\boldsymbol{r})}, \tag{2}$$

with A_O and $\phi_O(\boldsymbol{r})$ representing the object wave parameters. When these waves intersect at the recording medium, their superposition creates an interference pattern (hologram), expressed as:

$$\begin{aligned}
W(\boldsymbol{r}) &= |O(\boldsymbol{r}) + R(\boldsymbol{r})|^2 \\
&= |O(\boldsymbol{r})|^2 + |R(\boldsymbol{r})|^2 + R^*(\boldsymbol{r})O(\boldsymbol{r}) + O^*(\boldsymbol{r})R(\boldsymbol{r}),
\end{aligned} \tag{3}$$

where the cross terms effectively capture the phase differences between the waves, preserving the full wave information needed for reconstruction. During reconstruction, applying the original reference wave to the hologram produces the reconstructed field:

$$\begin{aligned}
A_{\text{rec}}(\boldsymbol{r}) &= W(\boldsymbol{r})R(\boldsymbol{r}) \\
&= |O|^2 R + |R|^2 R + O|R|^2 + O^* R^2,
\end{aligned} \tag{4}$$

In this equation, the third term $(O|R|^2)$ is proportional to the original object wave O, indicating successful reconstruction, while the remaining terms represent conjugate distortions or reference-aligned waves that are spatially separated.

These optical principles have motivated the creation of reference wave-based EM holographic communications, like the RHS. However, standard RHS implementations require explicit CSI, creating a heavy estimation burden. We solve this with the RRM, which physically executes both the recording (Fig. 1(c)) and beamforming reconstruction (Fig. 1(d)) processes. Crucially, recording occurs during uplink transmission, removing the need for explicit CSI acquisition via pilots. As shown later, our RRM-based method offers performance approaching that of an RHS with perfect CSI.

3 EM Holography Based on RRMs

This section details the RRM-based holographic beamforming framework, distinguishing its implementation and hardware structure from conventional RHS approaches. As shown in Fig. 2, the RRM utilizes leaky-wave antenna (LWA) architecture, consisting of substrates, feeds, and metamaterial radiation elements. Unlike RHSs, the proposed method integrates the full electromagnetic holography cycle—encompassing recording and reconstruction—into the wireless beamforming operation. The key structural difference is the inclusion of a

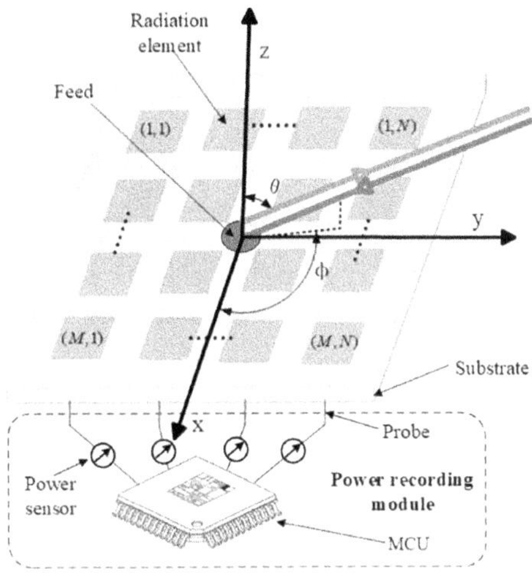

Fig. 2. Detailed hardware architecture of the proposed RRM.

dedicated power sensor with each RRM radiation element. These sensors measure the intensity of the interference pattern created by the interaction between incoming user signals and the reference wave during the recording phase. Specifically, the power sensors use miniaturized probes to detect power distribution in the standing waves resulting from the superposition of incident signals and the reference wave [14].

3.1 Interference Power Recording

As illustrated in Fig. 3(a), a reference wave travels across the surface, interfering with user signals to produce the holographic pattern seen in Fig. 3(b). The integrated sensors measure this interference intensity. The mathematical formulation of this process is detailed below.

Consider an RRM with $M \times N$ elements, and a feed at the geometric center. At the (m, n)-th element, the reference wave is defined as:

$$E_r(m, n) = A_r e^{jk_r d_r(m,n)}, \tag{5}$$

where A_r is the amplitude and k_r is the wavenumber in the substrate. The distance $d_r(m, n)$ from the feed to the element is given by:

$$d_r(m, n) = \sqrt{\left[d_x\left(m - \frac{M+1}{2}\right)\right]^2 + \left[d_y\left(n - \frac{N+1}{2}\right)\right]^2}, \tag{6}$$

where d_x and d_y denote element spacing along the x and y axes. The composite object wave reaching (m, n) from N_p distinct directions $\{(\theta_p, \phi_p)\}$ is expressed

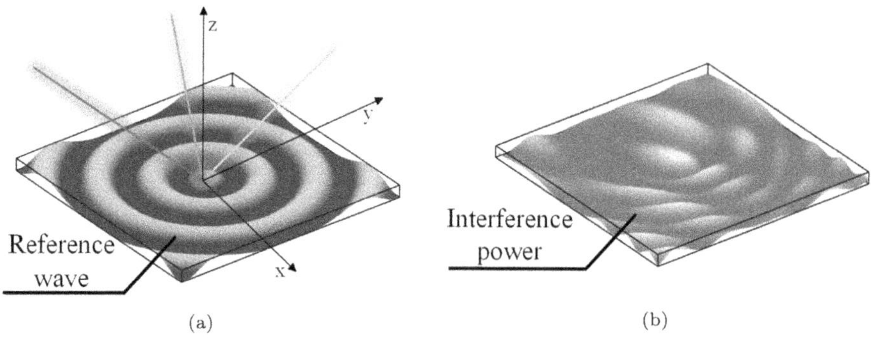

Fig. 3. Visualization of electromagnetic interference: (a) Wave interaction process; (b) Resultant power distribution map on the RRM.

as:

$$E_o(m, n) = \sum_{p=1}^{N_p} A_p \exp\left[j\left(k_f d_o^p(m, n) + \varphi_o^p\right)\right], \tag{7}$$

where A_p and φ_o^p are the amplitude and initial phase of the p-th wave. The distance $d_o^p(m, n)$ is defined as:

$$d_o^p(m, n) = d_x(m - 1)\sin\theta_p\cos\phi_p + d_y(n - 1)\sin\theta_p\sin\phi_p. \tag{8}$$

The interference field, arising from the combination of object and reference waves, is represented as:

$$E_c(m, n) = E_o(m, n) + E_r(m, n). \tag{9}$$

We note that the interference power detected by sensors at each element holds vital information for holographic beamforming. The elements of the interference power matrix $\boldsymbol{W}$ are:

$$\begin{aligned} W(m, n) &= E_c(m, n)E_c^*(m, n) \\ &= |E_o(m, n)|^2 + |E_r(m, n)|^2 + E_o(m, n)E_r^*(m, n) + E_o^*(m, n)E_r(m, n). \end{aligned} \tag{10}$$

3.2   Holographic Beamforming

Analogous to RHS methodologies, RRMs use amplitude control instead of phase shifting to create holographic patterns. The output power of the RRM's leaky-wave antennas is controlled by the hologram, allowing beamforming via spatially varying power distributions when excited by the reference wave. The main challenge is determining the holographic weights needed to transmit beams in directions opposite to the incoming object waves.

Referring to Fig. 2, we define the system geometry using a Cartesian framework centered at the origin, where the RRM lies within the x-y plane and the

z-axis is normal to the surface. Consequently, the entries of the interference power matrix $\boldsymbol{W} \in \mathbb{R}^{M \times N}$ map directly to the respective antenna elements. Assuming plane waves, electromagnetic waves moving in opposite directions share identical elevation and azimuth angles.

We derive the relation for reverse-propagating EM waves. In free space, a plane wave's electric field is:

$$E(\boldsymbol{r}) = A_0 e^{\mathrm{j}\boldsymbol{k} \cdot \boldsymbol{r}}, \tag{11}$$

where A_0 is amplitude, $\boldsymbol{k}$ is the wave vector, and $\boldsymbol{r}$ is the position vector. Thus, reversing the propagation direction reverses the wave vector. The reverse electric field propagates along $-\boldsymbol{k}$, yielding the conjugate relationship:

$$E^*(\boldsymbol{r}) = A_0 e^{-\mathrm{j}\boldsymbol{k} \cdot \boldsymbol{r}}. \tag{12}$$

This confirms that reconstructing the object wave requires the conjugate term $E_o^*(m, n)$.

Definition 1. *For $\boldsymbol{W} \in \mathbb{C}^{M \times N}$, the reindexed matrix $\boldsymbol{W}'$ is defined as $W'(m, n) = W(M - m + 1, N - n + 1)$ for $m = 1, \ldots, M$ and $n = 1, \ldots, N$.*

As shown in Fig. 2, this operation represents a $180°$ rotation around the z-axis. Applying this to $\boldsymbol{W}$ yields the holographic weight matrix $\boldsymbol{W}'$ for the intended beam directions. Using $\boldsymbol{W}'$, the RRM generates a reconstructed object wave as:

$$\begin{aligned}
E_h(m, n) &= E_r(m, n) W'(m, n) \\
&= A_c E_r(m, n) + |E_r(m, n)|^2 E_o^*(m, n) \\
&\quad + \sum_{i=1}^{N_p} \sum_{j=1}^{N_p} E_o^i(m, n) \left[E_o^j(m, n) \right]^* E_r(m, n) \\
&\quad + E_o(m, n) \left[E_r(m, n) \right]^2, i \neq j,
\end{aligned} \tag{13a}$$

$$\begin{aligned}
A_c &= |E_r(m, n)|^2 + \sum_{p=1}^{N_p} |E_o^p(m, n)|^2 \\
&= A_r^2 + \sum_{p=1}^{N_p} A_p^2,
\end{aligned} \tag{13b}$$

where $|E_r(m, n)|^2 E_o^*(m, n)$ represents the component propagating opposite to the incident object wave.

Directly applying $\boldsymbol{W}'$ is inefficient due to unwanted reconstruction terms. Only $|E_r(m, n)|^2 E_o^*(m, n)$ contributes constructively, while others create sidelobes. Terms vary in amplitude dependence: the second and fourth scale with $|E_r|^2$, while the third scales linearly. Using larger reference wave amplitudes lowers the third term's relative contribution but boosts the first term. To improve efficiency, we mitigate the constant term by subtracting an optimal bias b:

$$W_h(m, n) = \rho \left(W'(m, n) - b \right). \tag{14}$$

Setting $b = |E_r|^2$ effectively neutralizes the dominant constant term A_c. Since incoming wave energy is unknown, b can alternatively be the average of elements in $\boldsymbol{W'}$. The factor ρ normalizes weights to $[0, 1]$. Negative values after subtraction are clamped to zero.

3.3   Comparison with RHS-Based Holographic Frameworks

Unlike the RRM method, RHS-based schemes lack a physical recording mechanism. They assume availability of perfect CSI and beamforming directions at the transmitter, allowing direct computation of the hologram term:

$$W_{int}(m, n) = E_d(m, n)E_r^*(m, n), \tag{15}$$

where $E_d(m, n) = A_d e^{-jk_f d_o^0(m,n)}$ sets the desired direction (θ_0, ϕ_0). This approach avoids sidelobe-causing terms but requires prior object wave knowledge. The resulting holographic pattern radiating in (θ_0, ϕ_0) is:

$$E_t(m, n) = E_d(m, n)\left|E_r(m, n)\right|^2. \tag{16}$$

While RHS calculates complex weights for phase alignment, physical realization requires positive real-valued constraints. Following [7], the normalized holographic weight is:

$$\begin{aligned} M(m, n) &= \frac{\mathrm{Re}\left[W_{int}(m, n)\right] + 1}{2} \\ &= \frac{1}{2} + \frac{1}{4}E_r(m, n)E_d^*(m, n) + \frac{1}{4}E_r^*(m, n)E_d(m, n). \end{aligned} \tag{17}$$

This amplitude control adjusts radiation intensity but inevitably introduces interference terms. Table 1 summarizes the operational comparison between RHS and RRM frameworks.

Table 1. Operational comparison between RHS and RRM frameworks.

Attribute	RHS	RRM
Hardware Components	Feed, Substrate, Antennas	Feed, Substrate, Antennas, Power sensors
Core Mechanism	Computing holographic weights based on CSI	Recording of interference patterns & Matrix reindexing
Channel Requirement	CSI required	No CSI needed
Computational Load	High	Low
Implementation Overhead	Pilot-dependent	Zero pilot overhead

3.4   RRM-Based Holographic Communication Model

We examine a time-division multiple-access (TDMA) system shown in Fig. 2, with a single-antenna user and an $M \times N$ RRM. In RRM-based holographic communication, downlink beamforming utilizes information recorded during the uplink. Thus, we assume the channel satisfies reciprocity and varies slowly. Since reciprocity derives from the Rayleigh-Carson reciprocity theorem, we assume transmission medium and scatterer properties are symmetric for uplink and downlink [17]. Using holographic techniques based on uplink recordings allows precise beamforming without CSI reliance.

Let s be the downlink signal. The signal y received by the user is:

$$y = \boldsymbol{hm}s + \boldsymbol{z}, \tag{18}$$

where $\boldsymbol{h} \in \mathbb{C}^{1 \times MN}$ is the complex channel gain vector from RRM to user, $\boldsymbol{m}$ is an $MN \times 1$ vector with elements $\left\{ \boldsymbol{W}_h(m, n) \cdot e^{-\mathrm{j}\boldsymbol{ks \cdot r}_{m,n}} \right\}$, $e^{-\mathrm{j}\boldsymbol{ks \cdot r}_{m,n}}$ is the reference wave phase, and $z \sim \mathcal{CN}(0, \sigma^2)$ is additive white Gaussian noise (AWGN). The mutual information is thus:

$$I(s, y) = \log_2 \left(1 + \frac{|\boldsymbol{hm}|^2}{\sigma^2} \right). \tag{19}$$

4   Simulation Results

This section evaluates the efficacy of the proposed RRM-based holographic communication technique. The propagation environment includes one line-of-sight (LOS) path and four non-line-of-sight (NLOS) paths between the RRM and the user. Simulations adhere to standard 3GPP recommendations [1]. We utilize a carrier frequency of $f_c = 30$ GHz, with a free-space wavenumber of $k_f = 2\pi f_c/c$, and an internal RRM wavenumber of $k_s = \sqrt{3}\,k_f$, where c is the speed of light. Element spacings for both RHS and RRM in x and y directions (d_x, d_y) are set to half a wavelength. The transmit power is fixed at $P_T = 1$ W for both systems. We compare the proposed RRM scheme against an RHS-based benchmark possessing perfect CSI (see Sect. 3.3).

First, we analyze beamforming results derived from recording-based holographic weights. The RRM is set as a 32×32 aperture. Incident multipath angles are assumed to be $(15°, 100°)$, $(30°, 60°)$, $(40°, 35°)$, $(45°, 45°)$ and $(45°, 140°)$. Figure 4 displays the normalized radiation patterns. In Fig. 4(a), the constant-offset is ignored ($b = 0$ in (14)), while in Fig. 4(b), we subtract the mean of $\boldsymbol{W}'$ and clamp negative values to zero. The results confirm that the RRM's main lobes align well with true path directions, demonstrating effective beamforming without explicit CSI. Furthermore, subtracting the constant term significantly lowers sidelobes, enhancing performance over uncorrected weights.

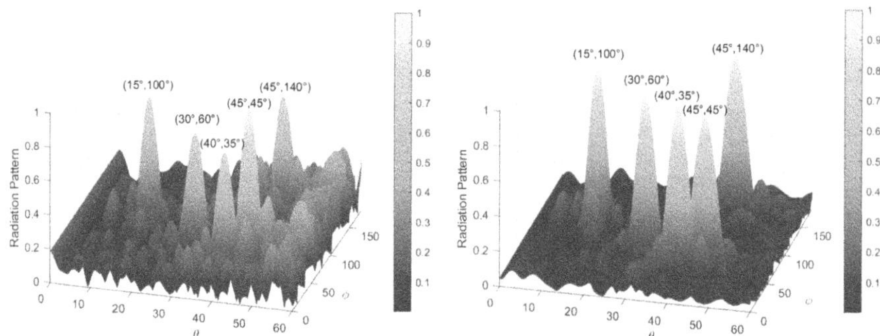

(a) RRM beam pattern without constant term correction.

(b) RRM beam pattern with constant term correction.

Fig. 4. Comparison of radiation patterns produced by the RRM.

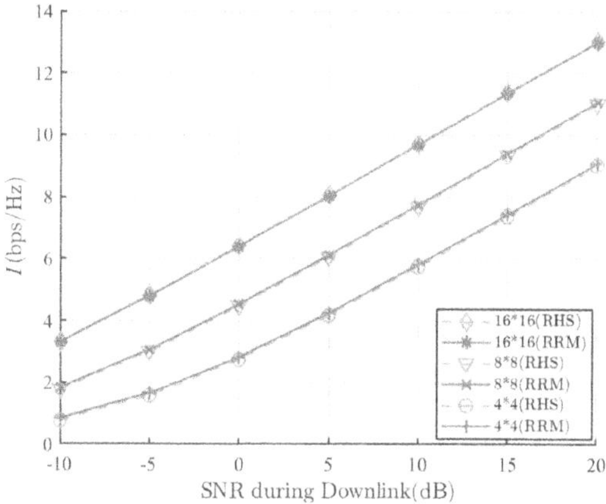

Fig. 5. Analysis of mutual information vs. SNR for varying RRM aperture sizes.

Figure 5 shows mutual information versus SNR for RRM aperture sizes of 4×4, 8×8, and 16×16. The RHS benchmark assumes perfect CSI, while the RRM recording stage uses an SNR of 10 dB. The data shows mutual information increasing with aperture size and SNR: larger arrays produce narrower beams and better power concentration, boosting spectral efficiency. For smaller arrays, constant term removal offers a distinct gain, potentially exceeding RHS performance; as aperture size increases, RRM performance converges with the RHS. Notably, even with noisy recording, the RRM achieves mutual information levels comparable to an RHS with perfect CSI.

5 Conclusions

In this paper, we proposed a novel electromagnetic holographic communication method utilizing RRMs. This scheme integrates both holographic beamforming and recording processes. By employing RRMs for recording, the interference power between reference waveforms and user waveforms is captured, allowing direct calculation of holographic beamforming weights. This approach avoids the difficult requirement for explicit channel estimation. Our analysis confirms that the RRM scheme attains performance comparable to RHS schemes with perfect CSI, offering a robust and efficient alternative for next-generation wireless communications.

References

1. 3GPP: Study on channel model for frequencies from 0.5 to 100 GHz (release 14). Tr 38.901, 3rd Generation Partnership Project (3GPP), Sophia Antipolis Cedex, France (2018)
2. Abood, T., Hburi, I., Khazaal, H.F.: Massive MIMO: an overview, recent challenges, and future research directions. In: 2021 International Conference on Advance of Sustainable Engineering and its Application (ICASEA), pp. 43–48 (2021). https://doi.org/10.1109/ICASEA53739.2021.9733081
3. Deng, R., et al.: Reconfigurable holographic surfaces for ultra-massive MIMO in 6G: practical design, optimization and implementation. IEEE J. Sel. Areas Commun. **41**(8), 2367–2379 (2023)
4. Deng, R., Di, B., Zhang, H., Poor, H.V., Song, L.: Holographic MIMO for LEO satellite communications aided by reconfigurable holographic surfaces. IEEE J. Sel. Areas Commun. **40**(10), 3071–3085 (2022). https://doi.org/10.1109/JSAC.2022.3196110
5. Deng, R., Di, B., Zhang, H., Song, L.: HDMA: holographic-pattern division multiple access. IEEE J. Sel. Areas Commun. **40**(4), 1317–1332 (2022). https://doi.org/10.1109/JSAC.2022.3143221
6. Deng, R., Di, B., Zhang, H., Tan, Y., Song, L.: Reconfigurable holographic surface: holographic beamforming for metasurface-aided wireless communications. IEEE Trans. Veh. Technol. **70**(6), 6255–6259 (2021). https://doi.org/10.1109/TVT.2021.3079465
7. Deng, R., Di, B., Zhang, H., Tan, Y., Song, L.: Reconfigurable holographic surface-enabled multi-user wireless communications: amplitude-controlled holographic beamforming. IEEE Trans. Wireless Commun. **21**(8), 6003–6017 (2022). https://doi.org/10.1109/TWC.2022.3144992
8. Ericsson Technology Review: Enabling holographic communication with 5G technology (2024). https://www.ericsson.com/en/reports-and-papers/ericsson-technology-review
9. Farhat, N.: Holographically steered millimeter wave antennas. IEEE Trans. Antennas Propag. **28**(4), 476–480 (1980). https://doi.org/10.1109/TAP.1980.1142359

10. Huang, C., Xu, J., Xu, W., You, X., Yuen, C., Chen, Y.: Low-complexity channel estimation for extremely large-scale MIMO in near field. IEEE Wirel. Commun. Lett. **13**(3), 671–675 (2024). https://doi.org/10.1109/LWC.2023.3339653
11. Johnson, M.C., Brunton, S.L., Kundtz, N.B., Kutz, J.N.: Sidelobe canceling for reconfigurable holographic metamaterial antenna. IEEE Trans. Antennas Propag. **63**(4), 1881–1886 (2015). https://doi.org/10.1109/TAP.2015.2399937
12. Letaief, K.B., Chen, W., Shi, Y., Zhang, J., Zhang, Y.J.A.: The roadmap to 6G: AI empowered wireless networks. IEEE Commun. Mag. **57**(8), 84–90 (2019). https://doi.org/10.1109/MCOM.2019.1900271
13. Pivotal Commware: Holographic beamforming and phased arrays (2019). https://pivotalcommware.com/wp-content/uploads/2019/10/HBF-vs-APA-White-Paper-2019.pdf
14. Samuel, A.: An oscillographic method of presenting impedances on the reflection-coefficient plane. Proc. IRE **35**(11), 1279–1283 (1947). https://doi.org/10.1109/JRPROC.1947.233570
15. Sievenpiper, D., Colburn, J., Fong, B., Ottusch, J., Visher, J.: Holographic artificial impedance surfaces for conformal antennas. In: 2005 IEEE Antennas and Propagation Society International Symposium, vol. 1B, pp. 256–259 (2005). https://doi.org/10.1109/APS.2005.1551536
16. Stevenson, R., Sazegar, M., Bily, A., Johnson, M., Kundtz, N.: Metamaterial surface antenna technology: commercialization through diffractive metamaterials and liquid crystal display manufacturing. In: 2016 10th International Congress on Advanced Electromagnetic Materials in Microwaves and Optics (METAMATERIALS), pp. 349–351 (2016). https://doi.org/10.1109/MetaMaterials.2016.7746395
17. Tang, W., et al.: On channel reciprocity in reconfigurable intelligent surface assisted wireless networks. IEEE Wirel. Commun. **28**(6), 94–101 (2021). https://doi.org/10.1109/MWC.001.2100136
18. Wang, D., Zhang, Y., Wei, H., You, X., Gao, X., Wang, J.: An overview of transmission theory and techniques of large-scale antenna systems for 5G wireless communications. Sci. China Inf. Sci. **59**(8), 081301 (2016). https://doi.org/10.1007/s11432-016-0278-5
19. Xing, Z., Wang, R., Yuan, X.: Joint active and passive beamforming design for reconfigurable intelligent surface enabled integrated sensing and communication. IEEE Trans. Commun. **71**(4), 2457–2474 (2023). https://doi.org/10.1109/TCOMM.2023.3244246
20. Yuan, X., Zhang, Y.J.A., Shi, Y., Yan, W., Liu, H.: Reconfigurable-intelligent-surface empowered wireless communications: challenges and opportunities. IEEE Wirel. Commun. **28**(2), 136–143 (2021). https://doi.org/10.1109/MWC.001.2000256
21. Yurduseven, O., Marks, D., Fromenteze, T., Smith, D.: Dynamically reconfigurable holographic metasurface aperture for a mills-cross monochromatic microwave camera. Optics Express **26**, 5281–5291 (2018). https://doi.org/10.1364/OE.26.005281

22. Zhang, Z., et al.: 6G wireless networks: vision, requirements, architecture, and key technologies. IEEE Veh. Technol. Mag. **14**(3), 28–41 (2019). https://doi.org/10.1109/MVT.2019.2921208
23. Zheng, K., Zhao, L., Mei, J., Shao, B., Xiang, W., Hanzo, L.: Survey of large-scale MIMO systems. IEEE Commun. Surv. Tutorials **17**(3), 1738–1760 (2015). https://doi.org/10.1109/COMST.2015.2425294

COSMOS: A Distributed Multi-Granularity Recognition Framework for Earth Observation Applications in Satellite Edge Computing Networks

Wei Li, Shuai Yu$^{(\boxtimes)}$, and Xu Chen

School of Computer Science and Engineering, Sun Yat-sen University, Guangzhou 510006, China
`liwei395@mail2.sysu.edu.cn`, `{yushuai,chenxu35}@mail.sysu.edu.cn`

Abstract. Advances in Earth observation have led to a deluge of Ultra-High Resolution (UHR) satellite imagery, overwhelming limited downlink bandwidth, while on-orbit processing is a critical solution. However, UHR object detection on a single resource-constrained satellite faces prohibitive computational costs and poor accuracy. To address this, we propose a distributed multi-granularity recognition framework, which we term COSMOS (COllaborative Satellite Multi-granularity Object Sensing). It first employs lightweight, on-orbit coarse-grained screening to efficiently find Regions of Interest (ROIs). Subsequently, high-resolution ROI data is offloaded to more resourceful edge computing satellites for precise, fine-grained analysis. The complex offloading decisions are solved using a QMIX-based multi-agent reinforcement learning algorithm. Experiments on a hardware-in-the-loop testbed emulating a heterogeneous satellite constellation demonstrate that our COSMOS framework outperforms a slice-and-detect baseline (SAHI) with a centralized DQN scheduler by over 14% in average completion time. Furthermore, this holistic design significantly reduces data transmission volume and maintains high fairness and reliability, proving its practical viability for future on-orbit processing systems.

Keywords: Satellite Edge Computing · Task Offloading · Multi-Agent Reinforcement Learning · Hardware Testbed

1 Introduction

Advances in Earth observation have created a data deluge, with satellite data volumes far exceeding limited downlink bandwidth, creating a significant bottleneck for timely data analysis [1]. On-orbit processing, or satellite edge computing [2], is a critical solution that enables rapid, localized data analysis by shifting computation from ground-based centers to the satellites themselves, significantly reducing communication latency and bandwidth consumption. This

Z. Lin et al. (Eds.): INSAI 2025, CCIS 2894, pp. 100–112, 2026.
https://doi.org/10.1007/978-981-95-9299-9_8

paradigm is crucial for transforming raw data into actionable insights directly in orbit, enhancing the timeliness of mission-critical applications [3]. However, a core task, i.e., object detection in Ultra-High Resolution (UHR) imagery presents a dilemma. Resizing large images (e.g., 3000×3000 pixels) for standard detectors (e.g., 640×640 for YOLO [4]) severely degrades small object detection, while direct on-orbit processing of raw UHR images is computationally infeasible.

Unlike "slice-and-detect" methods such as SAHI [5] that risk object fragmentation and redundant computation on background-only patches, our framework circumvents this by first analyzing a globally downsampled image. This ensures object integrity and guides high-resolution processing to pertinent areas only. It leverages a heterogeneous satellite constellation through a multi-granularity processing pipeline: it first performs rapid, coarse-grained screening on a resource-constrained observation satellite to find Regions of Interest (ROIs), then offloads only these high-resolution ROI data blocks to more powerful "intelligent" satellites for precise, fine-grained analysis. This hierarchical approach significantly outperforms traditional methods by reducing on-orbit processing time and data transmission volume while preserving the accuracy of fine-grained analysis.

The main contributions of this paper are summarized as follows:

1. We propose COSMOS, a novel distributed multi-granularity collaborative object recognition framework that effectively resolves the conflict between accuracy and efficiency when processing UHR remote sensing imagery on resource-constrained satellites. In end-to-end evaluations on a physical hardware testbed, our framework reduces total processing time by over 14% compared to a strong, slice-and-detect baseline (SAHI).
2. We formulate the resolution selection for coarse-grained screening as a constrained optimization problem, proposing a lightweight on-orbit procedure to solve it by maximizing an efficiency score that balances performance and resource costs.
3. We introduce a QMIX-based [15] multi-agent reinforcement learning method to solve the decentralized task offloading problem. Results from our hardware prototype show it achieves superior efficiency and fairness, outperforming centralized DQN-based scheduling while maintaining near-constant decision overhead, which is critical for system scalability.

2   Related Work

2.1   On-orbit Object Detection for UHR Imagery

On-orbit processing has evolved from simple data handling [6] to deploying lightweight Convolutional Neural Networks (CNNs) for tasks like scene classification [7] and real-time detection on CubeSats [8]. These advancements enable direct data analysis on satellites, reducing downlink pressure. For processing Ultra-High Resolution (UHR) imagery on the ground, "slice-and-detect" strategies are common. Frameworks like SAHI [5] and techniques incorporating background filtering [9] have been developed to manage large images by dividing

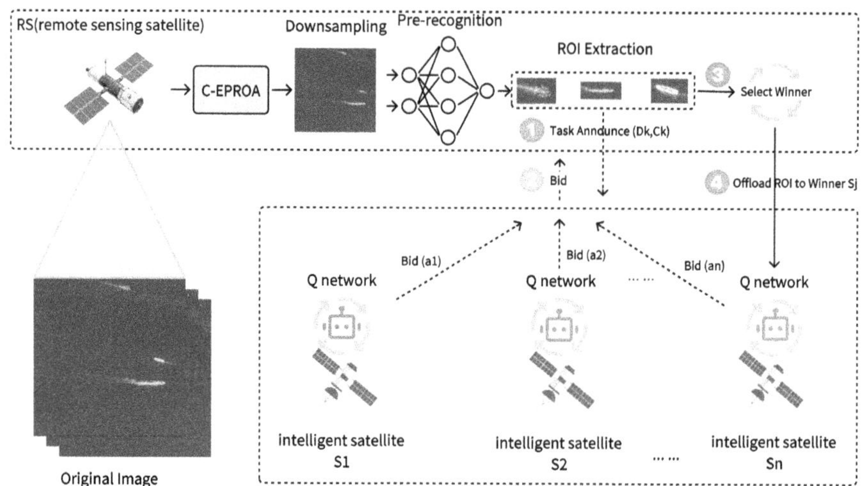

Fig. 1. System architecture and collaborative workflow of the COSMOS framework.

them into smaller, processable patches, aiming to handle the high resolution while mitigating the computational burden.

2.2 MARL for Task Offloading in Satellite Networks

Task offloading in satellite edge computing is a complex problem, characterized by highly dynamic network topologies and long propagation delays [10]. To address this, various methods have been investigated. Traditional optimization techniques [11] and centralized Deep Reinforcement Learning (DRL) approaches [12,13] have been explored for resource allocation and scheduling. More recently, Multi-Agent Reinforcement Learning (MARL) has emerged as a promising paradigm for enabling decentralized decision-making in these dynamic environments [14]. The "Centralized Training with Decentralized Execution" (CTDE) framework, exemplified by algorithms like QMIX [15], is particularly suitable, as it allows for complex joint policies to be learned offline and executed distributively with low on-orbit overhead. Such MARL approaches have been applied to task allocation in various satellite and hybrid network scenarios [16].

2.3 Discussion on Existing Solutions

In summary, previous research has generally addressed either on-orbit object detection or task offloading in isolation, creating a significant research gap. On one hand, existing on-orbit detection methods often focus on low-resolution imagery [7,8], failing to address the unique challenges of UHR scenes. Standard "slice-and-detect" strategies [5,9], if directly migrated to orbit, suffer from critical drawbacks such as object fragmentation and high computational overhead from processing redundant background patches.

Concurrently, in the domain of task offloading, centralized approaches using traditional optimization [11] or DRL [12,13] face significant scalability bottlenecks and single-point-of-failure risks in large, dynamic satellite constellations. While MARL offers a path to decentralized decision-making [14,16], existing work rarely tailors the offloading strategy to the specific characteristics of a computer vision pipeline, such as a multi-granularity workflow.

Our work, COSMOS, bridges this gap by proposing an integrated, end-to-end framework. It couples an intelligent, multi-granularity recognition pipeline that overcomes the limitations of traditional UHR image processing with a scalable, MARL-based distributed offloading strategy specifically designed for this vision workflow. This holistic approach is tailored for collaborative object recognition in large-scale satellite networks.

3   System Architecture and Problem Formulation

To effectively balance on-board resource limitations with high-precision recognition demands, we designed the COSMOS framework. The key notation used throughout the paper is summarized in Table 1.

Table 1. Summary of Key Notation.

Symbol	Description
RS, IS	Remote Sensing Satellite, Intelligent Satellite
$\mathcal{N} = \{S_1, \ldots, S_N\}$	The set of Intelligent Satellites (IS)
N	Total number of Intelligent Satellites, $N = |\mathcal{N}|$
T_k	The k-th computation task (an ROI)
D_k, C_k	Data size and computational complexity of task T_k
P_j	Processing capability of intelligent satellite S_j
$B_j(t), L_j(t)$	Transmission rate and propagation delay for S_j at t
T_{finish}	Total completion time for a single task
JFI	Jain's Fairness Index for load balancing
$\mathcal{M}, \mathcal{R}$	Sets of candidate models and resolutions
$F1_{\text{min}}, T_{\text{max}}$	Minimum F1-score and maximum latency constraints
E	Efficiency Score, defined as $F1/T_{\text{total}}$
$\mathcal{S}, \mathcal{A}_i, \mathcal{O}_i$	Global state, action, and observation space for agent i
a_i, o_i	A specific action (bid) and local observation for agent i
$r(s, \mathbf{a})$	Shared global reward for joint action $\mathbf{a}$ in state s

3.1 Proposed COSMOS Framework

The system architecture consists of a remote sensing satellite (RS) and a set of intelligent satellites (IS), denoted by $\mathcal{N}$. As shown in Fig. 1, the RS captures a UHR image, then performs downsampling and coarse-grained screening to identify ROIs. These high-resolution ROI data are subsequently offloaded via inter-satellite links to the IS constellation for fine-grained analysis. This process is divided into two synergistic levels:

- **Coarse-grained Screening:** Executed on the resource-constrained RS, this level uses a lightweight model (e.g., YOLOv5s) on a downsampled UHR image to rapidly identify potential ROIs. The optimal resolution is determined by an on-orbit optimization procedure (Sect. 4.2) to efficiently find ROIs without heavy computational costs.
- **Fine-grained Analysis:** Performed on the resource-rich IS, this level focuses on precision. Full-resolution image patches corresponding to the ROI coordinates are cropped from the original UHR image and transmitted to a selected IS for accurate classification. The offloading workflow involves four steps: (1) task announcement by RS, (2) bid submission by IS, (3) winner selection by RS, and (4) ROI offloading.

3.2 Collaborative Offloading Problem Formulation

The process of offloading ROI data from the RS to the IS is critical. We formulate this mathematically.

- **System Architecture and Models:** The system comprises one RS and the set $\mathcal{N}$ of IS . The inter-satellite links are time-varying, characterized by visibility $V_j(t)$, propagation delay $L_j(t)$, and transmission rate $B_j(t)$. A task T_k is defined by its data size D_k and complexity C_k, while each satellite S_j has a processing capability P_j.
- **Problem Formulation and Objective:** Let a binary variable $x_{kj} = 1$ if task T_k is offloaded to satellite S_j, and 0 otherwise. The task completion time is given by:

$$T_{\text{finish}}(k,j,t) = \frac{D_k}{B_j(t)} + L_j(t) + \frac{C_k}{P_j} \tag{1}$$

Our objective is to minimize a weighted cost of average completion time and unfairness (1 - JFI), where JFI is the Jain's Fairness Index [17].

$$\min \mathbb{E}\left[w_{\text{time}} \left(\frac{1}{|\mathcal{T}|} \sum_{k,j} x_{kj} T_{\text{finish}} \right) + w_{\text{fair}}(1 - \text{JFI}(\mathbf{Load})) \right] \tag{2}$$

Finding the optimal policy for this centralized objective is intractable in large and dynamic satellite edge computing networks. We therefore reformulate it for a scalable, distributed solution.

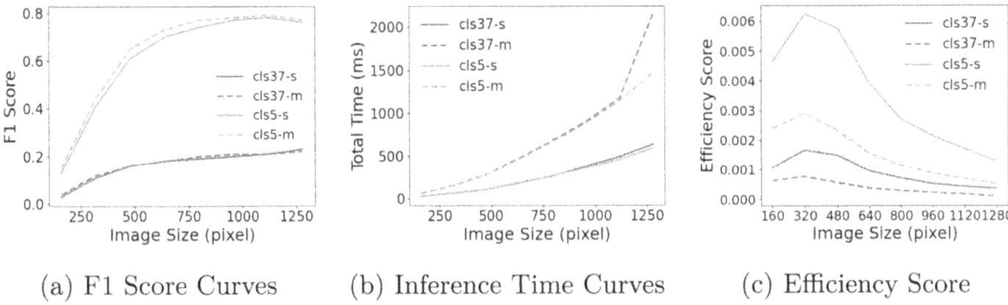

(a) F1 Score Curves   (b) Inference Time Curves   (c) Efficiency Score

Fig. 2. Motivation for multi-granularity design. The 5-class coarse-grained task shows superior (a) F1 score and (b) inference time scaling compared to the 37-class task. (c) This results in a significantly higher overall efficiency score (F1/Time), validating the coarse-to-fine approach.

4 Algorithm Design

4.1 Motivation for the Multi-Granularity Design

To validate our multi-granularity design, preliminary experiments on a Jetson Nano platform highlight the trade-offs between accuracy and efficiency (Fig. 2). While a lightweight model struggles with a fine-grained 37-class task, it performs effectively on a 5-class coarse-grained task. The 5-class task is far more efficient, and its inference time scales better with image size than the impractical 37-class task (Fig. 2a–b). This provides a strong empirical basis for our "coarse-to-fine" decomposition. Based on our experimental data, the peak efficiency score (F1/Time) for the 5-class coarse-grained task (0.0062 at 320 px) is over 3.6 times higher than the peak efficiency for the 37-class fine-grained task (0.0017 at 320 px), quantitatively justifying the proposed hierarchical approach (Fig. 2c).

4.2 On-orbit Processing Workflow

To systematically manage the on-orbit workflow, we designed an integrated process detailed in Algorithm 1. The workflow consists of two main stages: (1) **Resolution Selection for Coarse-Grained Screening**, performed on the RS satellite, and (2) **MARL-based Distributed Task Offloading**, a collaborative process between the RS and IS agents.

In the first stage, the RS selects the optimal input resolution by addressing a trade-off between accuracy and processing time, as illustrated in Fig. 2c. We quantify this with an Efficiency Score, E. The algorithm systematically finds the model-resolution pair that maximizes this score, subject to minimum performance ($F1_{\min}$) and maximum latency ($T_{\max}$) constraints, using pre-calibrated performance data stored on-orbit.

In the second stage, for each ROI identified, a distributed offloading process is initiated. This process, based on our MARL solution, uses a lightweight auction mechanism to efficiently assign the task to the most suitable IS, as will be further detailed in Sect. 4.3.

Algorithm 1 COSMOS: On-Orbit Collaborative Recognition Workflow

---

Part 1: On-board Resolution Selection (on RS Satellite)
Input: Candidate models $\mathcal{M}$, resolutions $\mathcal{R}$, thresholds $F1_{\min}, T_{\max}$.
Output: Optimal pair $(M_{\mathrm{opt}}, R_{\mathrm{opt}})$ for coarse-grained screening.
 1: Initialize $(M_{\mathrm{opt}}, R_{\mathrm{opt}}, E_{\max}) \leftarrow (\mathrm{null}, \mathrm{null}, -\infty)$
 2: **for** each pair $(M, R) \in \mathcal{M} \times \mathcal{R}$ **do**
 3:     **if** $F1(M, R) \geq F1_{\min}$ **and** $T_{\mathrm{total}}(M, R) \leq T_{\max}$ **then**
 4:         $E \leftarrow F1(M, R)/T_{\mathrm{total}}(M, R)$
 5:         **if** $E > E_{\max}$ **then**
 6:             $(M_{\mathrm{opt}}, R_{\mathrm{opt}}, E_{\max}) \leftarrow (M, R, E)$
 7:         **end if**
 8:     **end if**
 9: **end for**
10: Perform screening with $(M_{\mathrm{opt}}, R_{\mathrm{opt}})$ to get ROI tasks $\mathcal{T}$.

Part 2: Distributed ROI Offloading (RS-IS Collaboration)
Input: New ROI task $T_k(D_k, C_k) \in \mathcal{T}$; Set of IS $\mathcal{N}$; Pre-trained local networks $Q_i(\theta_i^*)$
    for each $S_i \in \mathcal{N}$.
Output: The ID of the winning satellite j^*.
11: RS broadcasts task announcement (D_k, C_k) to all agents in $\mathcal{N}$.
12: **for all** agent $S_i \in \mathcal{N}$ **in parallel do**
13:     Agent S_i acquires local observation $o_i(t)$.
14:     Agent S_i computes its bid a_i using its policy from $Q_i(\theta_i^*)$.
15:     $a_i \leftarrow \frac{D_k}{B_i(t)} + L_i(t) + \frac{C_k}{P_i}$
16:     Agent S_i transmits its bid a_i back to the RS satellite.
17: **end for**
18: RS satellite selects winner j^* with minimum bid: $j^* \leftarrow \arg\min_i(a_i)$.
19: RS offloads task T_k to the winning satellite S_{j^*}.
20: **return** j^*

4.3   MARL-Based Distributed Task Offloading

To solve the dynamic task offloading problem, we propose a distributed MARL solution.

Dec-POMDP Formulation. We model the system as a Decentralized Partially Observable Markov Decision Process (Dec-POMDP), formally defined by the tuple $\langle \mathcal{S}, \mathcal{N}, \{\mathcal{A}_i\}, P, \{\mathcal{O}_i\}, R \rangle$:

- **Global State $\mathcal{S}$ and Agents $\mathcal{N}$:** The global state $\mathcal{S}$ includes all task queues, resource states, and inter-satellite link qualities, which is not fully observable by any single agent. The set of intelligent satellites $\mathcal{N}$ act as cooperative agents.
- **Individual Action & Observation Spaces $\mathcal{A}_i, \mathcal{O}_i$:** For a new task, each agent S_i receives a local observation o_i and bids its estimated completion time $a_i \in \mathcal{A}_i$. The RS selects the agent with the lowest bid.
- **Shared Reward Function R:** As a cooperative task, all agents share a global reward r that aligns with the objective in Eq. (2). After a task is

assigned to winner j^*, the reward is:

$$r(s, \mathbf{a}) = -w_{\text{time}} \cdot a_{j^*} - w_{\text{fair}} \cdot (1 - \text{JFI}(\mathbf{Load}_{\text{new}})) \tag{3}$$

where a_{j^*} is the winning bid. This guides agents toward minimizing completion time and balancing load.

Solution Method: QMIX-Based Cooperative Reinforcement Learning. We employ the QMIX algorithm [15] to solve this Dec-POMDP. We chose QMIX because its "Centralized Training with Decentralized Execution" (CTDE) paradigm is ideal for our scenario, allowing for complex offline training while demanding minimal on-orbit computation. The on-orbit execution, detailed in Algorithm 1, Part 2, follows a distributed auction mechanism. After the RS broadcasts a new task, each IS agent independently computes a bid based on its local state and pre-trained policy. The RS then simply selects the winner with the minimum bid. This ensures a scalable decision process with minimal overhead.

5   Experimental Design and Evaluation

To rigorously evaluate the COSMOS framework and validate its performance in a realistic, resource-constrained environment, we made a hardware-in-the-loop testbed. This setup emulates the key characteristics of our proposed satellite edge computing network.

5.1   Hardware Testbed Setup

Our testbed consists of five NVIDIA Jetson devices interconnected via a Gigabit Ethernet switch: one Jetson Nano and four Jetson AGX Orin.

Remote Sensing Satellite (RS) Emulation. The Jetson Nano, with its modest computational capability, represents the resource-constrained remote sensing satellite. It is tasked with executing the first stage of the COSMOS pipeline: performing lightweight, coarse-grained screening on downsampled imagery using a YOLOv5-s model.

Intelligent Satellite (IS) Constellation Emulation. The four Jetson AGX Orin, each equipped with a powerful Ampere-architecture GPU, represent the constellation of intelligent satellites. These nodes possess superior processing power suitable for the second stage: performing precise, fine-grained analysis on the received ROIs using a more complex YOLOv5-m model. We vary the number of active Orin nodes ($N \in \{1, 2, 3, 4\}$) to evaluate system scalability.

Inter-Satellite Link (ISL) Simulation and Task. The devices are connected through a network switch, and we use the `tc` traffic control utility to shape the bandwidth, simulating a stable inter-satellite link rate of approximately 100 MB/s. The end-to-end task involves processing a 3000×3000 pixel high-resolution remote sensing image, for which the RS node first downsamples to 750×750. The identified ROIs, which constitute 20%-40% of the original image data, are then offloaded to the IS constellation.

5.2 Baselines and Evaluation Metrics

We compare the performance of our COSMOS framework against a "slice-and-detect" baseline, SAHI [5], which we adapted for our distributed satellite environment.

Baseline: SAHI-Based Distributed Framework. The SAHI framework slices the entire high-resolution image into smaller patches for processing. We apply several distributed scheduling strategies to offload these patches to the IS constellation:

1. **SAHI-Random:** Patches are offloaded to IS nodes selected randomly.
2. **SAHI-Round-Robin:** Patches are allocated to IS nodes in a fixed, cyclical order.
3. **SAHI-DQN:** A single omniscient DQN [19] agent makes centralized offloading decisions for each patch to minimize overall latency, serving as a strong performance benchmark.

Proposed Method: COSMOS. Our proposed framework, which integrates coarse-grained screening on the RS node with MARL-based (QMIX) intelligent ROI offloading to the IS constellation.

Evaluation Metrics. We evaluate the systems using three key metrics: (1) **Average Completion Time (ms)** for system efficiency; (2) **Jain's Fairness Index (JFI)** [17] for load balancing (1 is best); and (3) **Task Completion Rate (%)** for system reliability.

6 Results and Analysis

This section presents the evaluation of our framework. We first revisit the learning dynamics that justify our choice of the QMIX algorithm, and then analyze the end-to-end performance of COSMOS against the baselines on our hardware testbed.

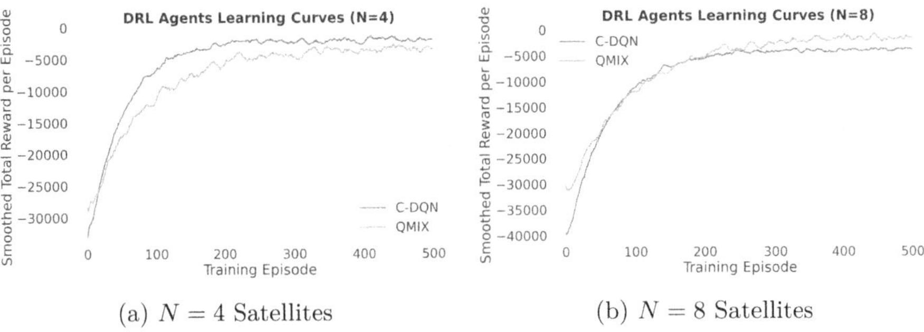

(a) $N = 4$ Satellites   (b) $N = 8$ Satellites

Fig. 3. Learning curves for QMIX and C-DQN from simulation. At $N = 4$, C-DQN achieves a higher reward. At $N = 8$, the growing state-action space challenges the centralized agent, allowing QMIX to converge to a better policy, justifying its selection for scalable systems.

6.1 Learning Dynamics and Policy Quality

Figure 3 shows the learning curves for QMIX and the centralized C-DQN from our initial simulations. In smaller constellations ($N = 4$, Fig. 3a), C-DQN leverages its global view for a higher reward. However, this advantage vanishes at larger scales ($N = 8$, Fig. 3b). Here, QMIX converges to a superior policy as the centralized C-DQN grapples with the curse of dimensionality. This confirms that our choice of a decentralized MARL approach is critical for ensuring scalability in large satellite networks.

6.2 End-to-End Performance on Hardware Testbed

We conducted end-to-end experiments on our hardware testbed, scaling the number of IS nodes (Jetson Orins) from $N = 1$ to 4. The results are presented in Fig. 4.

Efficiency Analysis. As shown in Fig. 4a, COSMOS consistently achieves the lowest average completion time across all constellation sizes. At $N = 4$, COSMOS completes the entire recognition task in approximately **60 ms**. This is **14% faster** than the strongest baseline, SAHI-DQN ($\approx$70ms), and over **25% faster** than SAHI-Round-Robin ($\approx$80ms). The performance gain stems from our fundamental coarse-to-fine design. By first identifying ROIs on the RS node, COSMOS drastically reduces the data volume for transmission and the computational workload for the powerful IS nodes, avoiding the redundant processing of background patches inherent to the SAHI method.

Fairness and Load Balancing. Figure 4b illustrates the load-balancing performance. While SAHI-Round-Robin achieves perfect fairness (JFI = 1.0) by its deterministic nature, it does so at the cost of efficiency. COSMOS maintains an

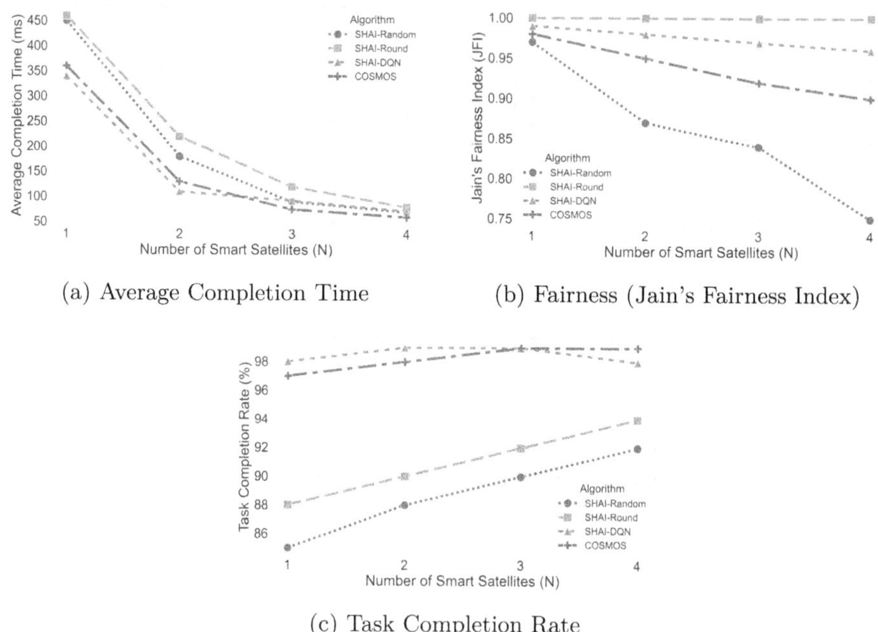

(a) Average Completion Time

(b) Fairness (Jain's Fairness Index)

(c) Task Completion Rate

Fig. 4. End-to-end performance evaluation on the hardware testbed as the number of intelligent satellites (N) increases. COSMOS consistently demonstrates superior efficiency, fairness, and reliability.

excellent JFI, stabilizing around **0.90** at $N = 4$. This is a dramatic improvement over the purely stochastic SAHI-Random (JFI$\approx$0.75) and demonstrates the effectiveness of the QMIX agent's learned cooperative policy, which implicitly balances the load to maximize shared rewards.

Reliability and Robustness. System reliability, measured by task completion rate, is shown in Fig. 4c. Both COSMOS and SAHI-DQN achieve the highest rates, consistently performing above **96%**. This highlights the benefit of intelligent scheduling; by actively managing resources and preventing node overloads, both methods minimize task failures. In contrast, the simpler SAHI-Random and SAHI-Round-Robin strategies are less adaptive, leading to a higher probability of task drops.

In summary, the hardware-based evaluation confirms the practical viability and superior performance of the COSMOS framework. Its holistic design, which couples an efficient multi-granularity vision pipeline with a scalable decentralized offloading intelligence, delivers substantial gains in processing speed, fairness, and reliability.

6.3   Discussion and Limitations

Our results, validated on a physical testbed, reveal the practical benefits of COSMOS. While centralized DRL (SAHI-DQN) offers strong performance, our

QMIX-based decentralized approach is competitive in efficiency while offering superior architectural scalability with near-zero decision overhead. This makes our framework a robust and future-proof solution for large-scale satellite collaboration.

We acknowledge, however, that our testbed emulates the satellite environment using terrestrial hardware and networking. While we controlled for key parameters like computational heterogeneity and link bandwidth, a true on-orbit deployment would face additional challenges such as propagation delays and potential link instability. Future work could involve validating COSMOS in a more sophisticated network simulation environment or on radiation-hardened hardware proxies to further assess its real-world operational performance.

7   Conclusion

This paper addressed the challenges of on-orbit UHR image processing by proposing an innovative multi-granularity collaborative framework, COSMOS. By combining lightweight on-orbit screening with MARL-based intelligent offloading of high-value ROIs, our framework effectively resolves the performance bottleneck of single-satellite processing. We solved the dynamic satellite task offloading problem, modeled as a Dec-POMDP, with QMIX, achieving distributed, efficient, and fair resource scheduling with constant decision latency, making it highly scalable. Our experiments on a hardware-in-the-loop testbed, emulating a heterogeneous satellite constellation, validate the framework's superiority in efficiency, fairness, and scalability, culminating in a significant end-to-end performance gain over state-of-the-art slice-and-detect methods.

Acknowledgments. This work was supported in part by Guangdong S&T Programme (No. 2024B0101040007 and 2022B1515120002), in part by Guangdong Basic and Applied Basic Research Foundation (No. 2023B1515120058).

References

1. Su, H., et al.: A review of deep-learning-based super-resolution: from methods to applications. Pattern Recogn. 110935 (2024)
2. Zhang, X., et al.: Energy-efficient computation peer offloading in satellite edge computing networks. IEEE Trans. Mob. Comput. **23**(4), 3077–3091 (2023)
3. Qin, X., et al.: Service-aware resource orchestration in ultra-dense LEO satellite-terrestrial integrated 6G: a service function chain approach. IEEE Trans. Wirel. Commun. **22**(9), 6003–6017 (2023)
4. Redmon, J., et al.: You only look once: unified, real-time object detection. In: Proceedings of the IEEE Conference on Computer Vision and Patter Recognition (CVPR), pp. 779–788 (2016)
5. Hao, C., et al.: Slinet: slicing-aided learning for small object detection. IEEE Signal Process. Lett. (2024)

6. Gao, G., et al.: Onboard information fusion for multisatellite collaborative observation: summary, challenges, and perspectives. IEEE Geosci. Remote Sens. Mag. **11**(2), 40–59 (2023)

7. Cui, X., et al.: CNN-based on-board intelligent processing for remote sensing images interpretation. In: 2023 International Conference on Image Processing, Computer Vision and Machine Learning (ICICML), pp. 1171–1175. IEEE (2023)

8. Li, Z., et al.: On-board real-time pedestrian detection for micro unmanned aerial vehicles based on YOLO-v8. In: 2023 2nd International Conference on Machine Learning, Cloud Computing and Intelligent Mining (MLCCIM), pp. 250–255. IEEE (2023)

9. Zhang, C., et al.: CoF-Net: a progressive coarse-to-fine framework for object detection in remote-sensing imagery. IEEE Trans. Geosci. Remote Sens. **61**, 1–17 (2023)

10. Hassan, S., et al.: Satellite-based ITS data offloading & computation in 6G networks: a cooperative multi-agent proximal policy optimization DRL with attention approach. IEEE Trans. Mob. Comput. **23**(5), 4956–4974 (2023)

11. Qin, Z., et al.: Multi-agent reinforcement learning aided computation offloading in aerial computing for the internet-of-things. IEEE Trans. Serv. Comput. **16**(3), 1976–1986 (2022)

12. Jia, M., et al.: Deep multi-agent reinforcement learning for task offloading and resource allocation in satellite edge computing. IEEE Internet Things J. (2024)

13. Zhou, J., et al.: Latency-energy efficient task offloading in the satellite network-assisted edge computing via deep reinforcement learning. IEEE Trans. Mob. Comput. (2024)

14. Zhu, C., et al.: A survey of multi-agent deep reinforcement learning with communication. Auton. Agent. Multi-Agent Syst. **38**(1), 4 (2024)

15. Rashid, T., et al.: QMIX: monotonic value function factorisation for deep multi-agent reinforcement learning. In: Proceedings of the 35th International Conference on Machine Learning (ICML), pp. 4295–4304 (2018)

16. Wei, P., et al.: Joint mobility control and MEC offloading for hybrid satellite-terrestrial-network-enabled robots. IEEE Trans. Wirel. Commun. **22**(11), 8483–8497 (2023)

17. Jain, R.K., et al.: A quantitative measure of fairness and discrimination. East. Res. Lab. Digital Equip. Corp. Hudson, MA **21**(1), 2022–2023 (1984)

18. Braquet, M., et al.: Greedy decentralized auction-based task allocation for multi-agent systems. IFAC-PapersOnLine **54**(20), 675–680 (2021)

19. Mnih, V., Kavukcuoglu, K., Silver, D., et al.: Human-level control through deep reinforcement learning. Nature **518**(7540), 529–533 (2015)

20. Rhodes, B.: Skyfield: high precision research-grade positions for planets and earth satellites. Astrophysics Source Code Library (2019)

21. Hoots, F.R., Roehrich, R.L.: Spacetrack Report No. 3: Models for propagation of NORAD element sets. Office of Astrodynamics, Peterson AFB, CO (1980)

22. Kelso, T.S.: CelesTrak: The world's leading source for orbital data. https://celestrak.com/. Accessed 01 Jan 2024

23. Maxar Technologies: WorldView-3 Satellite Imagery Products. https://www.maxar.com/products/satellite-imagery. Accessed 01 Jan 2024

24. Sheetz, M.: SpaceX's Starlink internet service is transmitting more than 100 gigabits per second in orbit. CNBC (2023)

25. NASA Earth Observatory: Every Day is Earth Day with NASA's Open Data. https://earthobservatory.nasa.gov/blogs/fromthefield/2021/04/22/every-day-is-earth-day-with-nasas-open-data/. Accessed 01 Jan 2024

Bayesian Near-Field Multiuser Tracking via Non-stationary Reconfigurable Intelligent Surface

Zhimeng Liu, Boyu Teng, Yuxin Duan, and Xiaojun Yuan[✉]

National Key Laboratory of Wireless Communications, University of Electronic
Science and Technology of China, Chengdu, China
{zmliu,byteng,yxduan}@std.uestc.edu.cn, xjyuan@uestc.edu.cn

Abstract. Reconfigurable intelligent surface (RIS) has attracted enormous interest in future 6G systems. Due to its low cost, it can be made sufficiently large in scale for localization enhancement. When deploying a large RIS, users are often operating in the near field of the RIS and the channels exhibit spatial non-stationarity (SNS), posing new challenges for near-field user localization and tracking. In this paper, we develop a bi-level array partitioning strategy to flexibly characterize the spatial non-stationarity effect in user localization and tracking problem. Considering user mobility and the group sparsity of the channels between users and the RIS, we introduce Markov processes and establish a probabilistic transition model to characterize the user tracking process. Subsequently, we propose a novel Bayesian user tracking algorithm, termed bi-level array partitioning for Bayesian near-field tracking (BLAP-BNT), which jointly estimates users' positions and their visible region (VR). The simulation results show the effectiveness of our algorithm.

Keywords: User tracking · Reconfigurable intelligent surface ·
Near-field · Spatial non-stationarity

1 Introduction

Reconfigurable intelligent surface (RIS) is considered as one of the key technologies for future 6G wireless communications [1]. A RIS consists of passive reflective elements that can independently adjust the phase of the incident signal to dynamically control the propagation environment [5]. In addition to improving communication quality, RIS also enhances localization by providing supplementary links, thereby reducing dependence on LoS conditions. In a RIS-aided localization system, RIS typically acts as an auxiliary anchor that enables the estimation of intermediate parameters such as the angle of arrival (AoA) and time of arrival (ToA), which are then used to locate users. [11,15,17].

Owing to its low cost, a RIS can be densely deployed with thousands of elements. Such a large-scale array shifts the wireless operational regime into the electromagnetic near field. In this regime, the curvature of the wavefront can no longer be neglected, the received signals are characterized by spherical wavefronts whose curvature directly depends on the propagation distance. This near-field effect provides richer spatial information for localization. However, from the existing research on extra large MIMO systems [4,14], a user can usually "see" a RIS with a large array aperture, but the visibility may be limited to only part of the array rather than its entirety. The channels between the RIS and the users exhibit spatial non-stationarity (SNS). The subset of elements visible to the user forms the visible region (VR). Prior studies [7–9] usually ignore SNS, resulting in a mismatch between the theoretical channel model and practical propagation conditions, which can severely degrade localization performance or even lead to localization failure.

Consequently, researchers have recently turned their attention to investigating RIS-assisted localization systems under SNS conditions. Specifically, [6] assumes that the VR is a cluster of adjacent RIS elements and proposes a localization scheme that first identifies VR and then refines user positions. While element-level VR detection enables very high resolution, its computational complexity grows cubically with the number of elements. In [3], RIS is partitioned into multiple tiles, each assumed spatially stationary, and localization is performed based on the TDOA of each tile. To guarantee reliable positioning performance, the algorithm imposes a constraint that the tile count remain strictly below the available number of pilots. These studies highlight a fundamental challenge in RIS-assisted localization, i.e. identifying the VR at the element level is not practically feasible due to the prohibitive computational complexity and scalability issues. To address this, array partitioning is usually necessary. However, the granularity of partitioning significantly influences localization accuracy. Overly fine-grained partitioning reduces the BS's ability to distinguish contributions from different subarrays, whereas overly coarse partitioning may mismatch the assumed and actual VRs, failing to capture SNS. Thus, a careful trade-off between spatial resolution and signal resolvability is required when addressing SNS via array partitioning.

In this paper, we investigate the tracking problem for multiuser in a large RIS-assisted uplink system, taking into account the spatial non-stationary channels between users and the RIS in the near-field region. We adopt a novel array partitioning strategy to flexibly exploit the spatial correlation for user tracking and VR identification. Specifically, a coarse-grained partitioning is first applied to help estimate user locations, followed by a finer partitioning for more accurate VR recognition. Considering the temporal correlation of the tracking system and the spatial correlation due to smaller arrays, we use a prior model based on Markov processes to model the group sparsity of the channel. By exploiting the relationship between user positions and subarray channels, we construct a probabilistic formulation to investigate the tracking problem from a Bayesian perspective. Then, we develop an online message passing algorithm, termed the bi-level array partitioning for Bayesian near-field tracking algorithm (BLAP-BNT) to jointly estimate the user positions and visible region. Numerical results show that the proposed algorithm outperforms existing baselines in localization accuracy, and its VR identification accuracy approaches 100%.

2   System Model

2.1   Signal Model

We consider a RIS-assisted multiuser uplink tracking system consisting of K users, a base station (BS) equipped with a uniform planar array (UPA) of $N_B = N_{Bx} \times N_{By}$ antennas, and a RIS consisting of $N_R = N_{Rx} \times N_{Ry}$ reflecting elements arranged as a UPA, as illustrated in Fig. 1. The antenna and RIS element spacing is set as $d = \frac{\lambda}{2}$, where λ is the carrier wavelength. We assume links between the users and the BS are blocked, and both the users and the BS are located in the near-field region of the RIS, i.e., $R_N < r < R_F$, where R_N and R_F are the Fresnel and Fraunhofer distance, respectively [10]. The BS-RIS channel is assumed to exhibit multipath propagation and is perfectly known, while the user-RIS channels are spatially non-stationary.

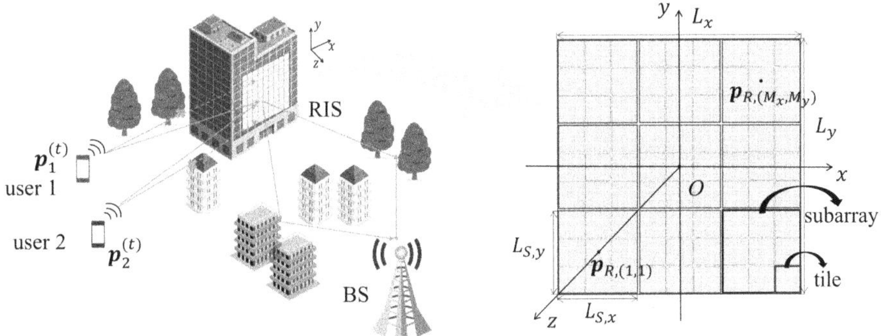

Fig. 1. System model. The left part shows the overall scenario of the tracking system, while the right part provides a magnified view of the RIS array.

Following the RIS partitioning strategy in [16], we divide the RIS array into $M = M_x \times M_y$ nonoverlapping subarrays to avoid the highly non-convex user position estimation problem. Each subarray consists of $N_S = N_{S,x} \times N_{S,y}$ elements. To better capture spatial non-stationarity, we divide each subarray further into $N = N_x \times N_y$ tiles. The total number of the tiles of the RIS is $N_t = MN$. We assume that the channel is spatially stationary for each tile of the RIS. Provided N_x and N_y large enough, the spatially non-stationary of the channel can be fully captured.

A 3D Cartesian coordinate system is established with the RIS center as the origin, and the x and y-axes aligned with the RIS edges. In the t-th time slot, the position of the k-th user is denoted by $\mathbf{p}_k^{(t)}$. Denote by $\mathbf{p}_{(u,v),(p,q)}$ the position of the (p,q)-th element in the (u,v)-th subarray, and the corresponding distance to user k at time t is $r^{(t)}_{(u,v),(p,q),k}$. For each subarray, we define the central element, indexed by $(\lceil \frac{N_{S,x}+1}{2} \rceil, \lceil \frac{N_{S,y}+1}{2} \rceil)$, as the reference. The distance between the k-th user and the reference element of the (u,v)-th subarray is $r^{(t)}_{(u,v),k}$ and the reference coefficient is represented as $h^{(t)}_{(u,v),ref,k} = \frac{\lambda}{4\pi r^{(t)}_{(u,v),k}} e^{-j\frac{2\pi}{\lambda} r^{(t)}_{(u,v),k}}$. The channel coefficient between the k-th user and the (u,v)-th subarray $\mathbf{h}^{(t)}_{(u,v),k}$ is given by

$$\tilde{\mathbf{H}}^{(t)}_{(u,v),k} = h^{(t)}_{(u,v),ref,k} \mathbf{B}_{(u,v)}(\mathbf{p}^{(t)}_k), \tag{1}$$

where the (p,q)-th item of $\mathbf{B}_{(u,v)}(\mathbf{p}^{(t)}_k)$ is given by

$$\left[\mathbf{B}_{(u,v)}(\mathbf{p}^{(t)}_k)\right]_{(p,q)} = \frac{r^{(t)}_{(u,v),k}}{r^{(t)}_{(u,v),(p,q),k}} e^{-j\frac{2\pi}{\lambda}\left(r^{(t)}_{(u,v),(p,q),k} - r^{(t)}_{(u,v),k}\right)}. \tag{2}$$

Based on the geometric relationships among the reference elements of different subarrays of the RIS, we obtain

$$\mathbf{h}^{(t)}_{ref,k} = h^{(t)}_{(\lceil \frac{M_x+1}{2} \rceil, \lceil \frac{M_y+1}{2} \rceil),ref,k} \mathbf{c}\left(\mathbf{p}^{(t)}_k\right), \tag{3}$$

where the entry in $\mathbf{c}\left(\mathbf{p}^{(t)}_k\right)$ corresponding to the m-th subarray is expressed as $\left[\mathbf{c}\left(\mathbf{p}^{(t)}_k\right)\right]_m = h^{(t)}_{(u,v),ref,k} / h^{(t)}_{(\lceil \frac{M_x+1}{2} \rceil, \lceil \frac{M_y+1}{2} \rceil),ref,k}$ with the index mapping from m to (u,v) given by $m = (v-1)M_x + u$.

We use a visibility indicator $\zeta^{(t)}_{m,n,k} \in \{0,1\}$ to indicate whether a LoS path from user k to the n-th tile of the m-th subarray exists. The corresponding channel is given by

$$\mathbf{H}^{(t)}_{m,n,k} = h^{(t)}_{(\lceil \frac{M_x+1}{2} \rceil, \lceil \frac{M_y+1}{2} \rceil),ref,k} \left[\mathbf{c}^{(t)}_k\right]_m \zeta^{(t)}_{m,n,k} \mathbf{B}_{m,n}(\mathbf{p}^{(t)}_k), \tag{4}$$

where $\mathbf{c}^{(t)}_k$ denote $\mathbf{c}\left(\mathbf{p}^{(t)}_k\right)$ for brevity, and $\mathbf{B}_{m,n}(\mathbf{p}^{(t)}_k)$ is the submatrix corresponding to the n-th block of $\mathbf{B}_{(u,v)}(\mathbf{p}^{(t)}_k)$.

The received signal in the t-th slot is given by

$$\begin{aligned}
\mathbf{y}^{(t)} &= \sum_{k=1}^{K}\sum_{m=1}^{M}\sum_{n=1}^{N} \mathbf{G}_{m,n} \mathbf{\Omega}^{(t)}_{m,n} \text{vec}\left(\mathbf{H}^{(t)}_{m,n,k}\right) x_k(t) + \mathbf{n}^{(t)} \\
&= \sum_{k=1}^{K}\sum_{m=1}^{M} \varrho^{(t)}_k \left[\mathbf{c}^{(t)}_k\right]_m \sum_{n=1}^{N} \mathbf{G}_{m,n} \mathbf{\Omega}^{(t)}_{m,n} \zeta^{(t)}_{m,n,k} \mathbf{b}_{m,n}(\mathbf{p}^{(t)}_k) \\
&\quad + \mathbf{n}^{(t)},
\end{aligned} \tag{5}$$

where $\varrho_k^{(t)} = h_{(\lceil \frac{M_x+1}{2} \rceil, \lceil \frac{M_y+1}{2} \rceil), ref, k}^{(t)} x_k(t)$ is the equivalent complex channel gain, $\mathbf{G}_{m,n}$ is the channel matrix from the n-th tile of the m-th subarray to the BS. $\boldsymbol{\Omega}_{m,n}^{(t)} = \mathrm{diag}(\boldsymbol{\omega}_{m,n}^{(t)})$ is the diagonal phase shift matrix with the phase shift vector $\boldsymbol{\omega}_{m,n}^{(t)}$, $\mathbf{n}^{(t)} \sim \mathcal{CN}(\mathbf{n}^{(t)}; \mathbf{0}, \boldsymbol{C}_n)$ and $\mathbf{b}_{m,n}(\mathbf{p}_k^{(t)}) = \mathrm{vec}(\mathbf{B}_{m,n}(\mathbf{p}_k^{(t)}))$. We define auxiliary variables

$$\boldsymbol{\rho}_k^{(t)} = \varrho_k^{(t)} \mathbf{c}_k^{(t)}, \quad \boldsymbol{\rho}^{(t)} = [(\boldsymbol{\rho}_1^{(t)})^\mathrm{T}, ..., (\boldsymbol{\rho}_K^{(t)})^\mathrm{T}]^\mathrm{T}, \tag{6a}$$

$$\boldsymbol{\zeta}_k^{(t)} = [\zeta_{1,1,k}^{(t)}, ..., \zeta_{1,N,k}^{(t)}, ..., \zeta_{M,1,k}^{(t)} ..., \zeta_{M,N,k}^{(t)}]^\mathrm{T},$$

$$\boldsymbol{\zeta}^{(t)} = [(\boldsymbol{\zeta}_1^{(t)})^\mathrm{T}, ..., (\boldsymbol{\zeta}_K^{(t)})^\mathrm{T}]^\mathrm{T}, \tag{6b}$$

where $\boldsymbol{\rho}_k^{(t)}$ denotes the equivalent complex channel gains for the user k and $\boldsymbol{\zeta}_k^{(t)}$ collects the visibility indicators of all tiles. We further define

$$\mathbf{A}_k^{(t)} = [\mathbf{G}_{1,1}\boldsymbol{\Omega}_{1,1}^{(t)}\mathbf{b}_{1,1}(\mathbf{p}_k^{(t)}), ..., \mathbf{G}_{M,N}\boldsymbol{\Omega}_{M,N}^{(t)}\mathbf{b}_{M,N}(\mathbf{p}_k^{(t)})],$$

$$\mathbf{A}^{(t)} = [\mathbf{A}_1^{(t)}, ..., \mathbf{A}_K^{(t)}]^\mathrm{T}, \tag{7a}$$

$$\boldsymbol{\alpha}^{(t)} = \mathbf{E}^{(t)}\mathbf{T}\boldsymbol{\rho}^{(t)}, \tag{7b}$$

where $\mathbf{E}^{(t)} = \mathrm{diag}\left(\boldsymbol{\zeta}^{(t)}\right)$ and $\mathbf{T} = \mathbf{I}_{KM} \otimes \mathbf{1}_{KN}$. A compact form of (5) is given by

$$\mathbf{y}^{(t)} = \mathbf{A}^{(t)}\boldsymbol{\alpha}^{(t)} + \mathbf{n}^{(t)}. \tag{8}$$

2.2   Probabilistic Problem Formulation

We adopt a Markov chain (MC) to characterize user movements in the tracking scenario [12]. For the k-th user, we have

$$p\left(\mathbf{p}_k^{(t)}|\mathbf{p}_k^{(t-1)}\right) = \mathcal{N}\left(\mathbf{p}_k^{(t)}; \mathbf{p}_k^{(t-1)}, \boldsymbol{C}_k\right), \tag{9}$$

where $\boldsymbol{C}_k = \mathrm{diag}\left([\sigma_{k,x}^2, \sigma_{k,y}^2, \sigma_{k,z}^2]\right)$. We define $\mathbf{p}^{(t)} = \left[(\mathbf{p}_1^{(t)})^\mathrm{T}, ..., (\mathbf{p}_K^{(t)})^\mathrm{T}\right]^\mathrm{T}$, $\boldsymbol{\varrho}^{(t)} = \left[\varrho_1^{(t)}, ..., \varrho_K^{(t)}\right]^\mathrm{T}$. From (6a), we obtain

$$p\left(\boldsymbol{\rho}^{(t)}|\mathbf{p}^{(t)}, \boldsymbol{\varrho}^{(t)}\right) = \prod_{k=1}^{K} \delta\left(\boldsymbol{\rho}_k^{(t)} - \varrho_k^{(t)}\mathbf{c}_k^{(t)}\right), \tag{10}$$

where $\delta(\cdot)$ is the Dirac delta function. From (7b), we obtain

$$p\left(\boldsymbol{\alpha}^{(t)}|\boldsymbol{\zeta}^{(t)}, \boldsymbol{\rho}^{(t)}\right) = \delta\left(\boldsymbol{\alpha}^{(t)} - \mathbf{E}^{(t)}\mathbf{T}\boldsymbol{\rho}^{(t)}\right). \tag{11}$$

Since all RIS tiles are densely packed, visibility indicators of neighboring tiles are correlated. Also, $\boldsymbol{\zeta}_k^{(1:T)}$ are generally correlated over time. The visibility indicators for the k-th user exhibit group sparsity across spatial and temporal domains.

The group sparsity can be modeled as a three dimensional Markov random field (MRF) and represented by the classical Ising model [18]. $p(\boldsymbol{\zeta}_k^{(t)}|\boldsymbol{\zeta}_k^{(t-1)})$ is expressed as

$$
\begin{aligned}
p(\boldsymbol{\zeta}_k^{(t)}|\boldsymbol{\zeta}_k^{(t-1)}) \propto \exp \Big(\sum_{s=1}^{N_t} \big(\frac{1}{2} \sum_{s_d \in \mathcal{D}_s} \beta_1 (2\zeta_{k,s_d}^{(t)} - 1) \\
+ \frac{1}{2}\beta_2 (2\zeta_{k,s}^{(t-1)} - 1) - \beta_3 \big) (2\zeta_{k,s}^{(t)} - 1) \Big)
\end{aligned}
\tag{12}
$$

where $\mathcal{D}_s$ is the neighbors of s. Since the visibility indicators of different users are independent, the overall conditional probability $p\left(\boldsymbol{\zeta}^{(t)}|\boldsymbol{\zeta}^{(t-1)}\right)$ can be factorized as the product of each user's conditional probability $p\left(\boldsymbol{\zeta}_k^{(t)}|\boldsymbol{\zeta}_k^{(t-1)}\right)$.

Based on the Gaussian observation model in (8), the likelyhood function in the t-th slot is given by

$$
p\left(\mathbf{y}^{(t)}|\mathbf{p}^{(t)}, \boldsymbol{\alpha}^{(t)}\right) = \mathcal{CN}\left(\mathbf{y}^{(t)}; \mathbf{A}^{(t)}\boldsymbol{\alpha}^{(t)}, \mathbf{C}_n\right),
\tag{13}
$$

where $\mathbf{p}^{(t)}$ is involved in $\mathbf{A}^{(t)}$ and $\boldsymbol{\alpha}^{(t)}$. we impose a complex Gaussian prior on $\varrho_k^{(t)}$ as $p(\varrho_k^{(t)}) = \mathcal{CN}\left(\varrho_k^{(t)}; 0, \tau_k^{\mathrm{pri}}\right)$.

In multiuser tracking, our objective is to design an online algorithm to estimate the position of each user $\mathbf{p}_k^{(t)}$ and the visibility indicators $\boldsymbol{\zeta}_k^{(t)}$ given the historically received signal $\mathbf{y}^{(1:t)}$. The well-known minimum mean-square error (MMSE) and maximum *a posteriori* (MAP) estimators are intractable in practice. In this paper, we provide a low-complexity yet near-optimal solution by following the message passing principle.

3   Proposed Algorithm

Given Eq. (8), if $\boldsymbol{\zeta}^{(t)}$ is assumed to be known, estimating $\mathbf{p}^{(t)}$ from $\mathbf{y}^{(t)}$ corresponds to a general near-field localization problem. On the other hand, if $\mathbf{p}^{(t)}$ is known, (8) reduces to a standard compressed sensing model, where $\mathbf{A}^{(t)}$ serves as a known sensing matrix and the sparse vector $\boldsymbol{\alpha}^{(t)}$ is determined by $\boldsymbol{\zeta}^{(t)}$ and $\boldsymbol{\varrho}^{(t)}$. As shown in Fig. 2, the position tracking module and visibility tracking module are introduced to illustrate the BLAP-BNT algorithm.

3.1   Position Tracking Module

In position tracking module, we replace the visibility vector $\boldsymbol{\zeta}^{(t)}$ with its estimate $\hat{\boldsymbol{\zeta}}^{(t)}$ obtained from the visibility tracking module. Accordingly, the model in Eq. (8) can be reformulated as

$$
\mathbf{y}^{(t)} = \mathbf{R}^{(t)}\boldsymbol{\rho}^{(t)} + \mathbf{n}^{(t)},
\tag{14}
$$

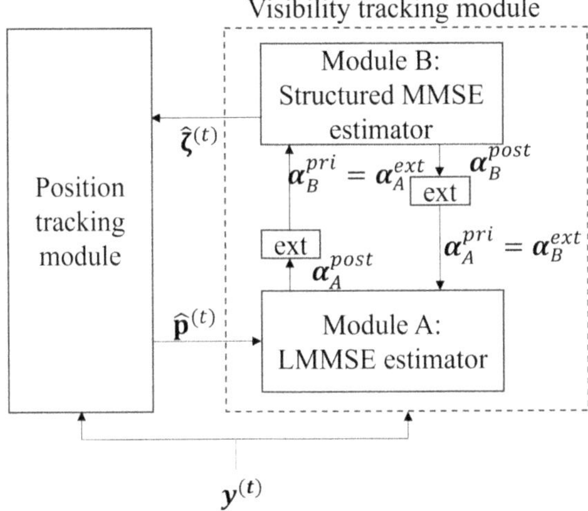

Fig. 2. Framework of the BLAP-BNT algorithm and message flows between different modules.

where $\mathbf{R}^{(t)} = \mathbf{A}^{(t)}\hat{\mathbf{E}}^{(t)}\mathbf{T}$ with $\hat{\mathbf{E}}^{(t)}$ obtained by substituting $\boldsymbol{\zeta}^{(t)} = \hat{\boldsymbol{\zeta}}^{(t)}$ into $\mathbf{E}^{(t)}$. Both $\mathbf{R}^{(t)}$ and $\boldsymbol{\rho}^{(t)}$ are functions of the user positions $\mathbf{p}^{(t)}$. Following the APLE-LM algorithm proposed in [13], a gradient ascent method is applied to these two functions to obtain a Gaussian distribution over the user positions at the t-th time slot, denoted as $\mathcal{N}(\mathbf{p}^{(t)}; \boldsymbol{\mu}_{\mathbf{p}^{(t)}}, \boldsymbol{C}_{\mathbf{p}^{(t)}})$.

This distribution is then combined with the prior information to yield the final position estimate

$$\mathcal{N}(\mathbf{p}^{(t)}; \boldsymbol{\mu}_{\mathbf{p}^{(t)}}^{ext}, \boldsymbol{C}_{\mathbf{p}^{(t)}}^{ext}) \propto \mathcal{N}(\mathbf{p}^{(t)}; \boldsymbol{\mu}_{\mathbf{p}^{(t)}}^{pri}, \boldsymbol{C}_{\mathbf{p}^{(t)}}^{pri}) \\ \times \mathcal{N}(\mathbf{p}^{(t)}; \boldsymbol{\mu}_{\mathbf{p}^{(t)}}, \boldsymbol{C}_{\mathbf{p}^{(t)}}),$$
(15)

with mean $\boldsymbol{\mu}_{\mathbf{p}^{(t)}}^{ext}$ and covariance $\boldsymbol{C}_{\mathbf{p}^{(t)}}^{ext}$ given by

$$\boldsymbol{C}_{\mathbf{p}^{(t)}}^{ext} = \left((\boldsymbol{C}_{\mathbf{p}^{(t)}}^{pri})^{-1} + \boldsymbol{C}_{\mathbf{p}^{(t)}}^{-1} \right)^{-1},$$
(16a)

$$\boldsymbol{\mu}_{\mathbf{p}^{(t)}}^{ext} = \boldsymbol{C}_{\mathbf{p}^{(t)}}^{ext} \left(\boldsymbol{C}_{\mathbf{p}^{(t)}}^{-1} \boldsymbol{\mu}_{\mathbf{p}^{(t)}} + (\boldsymbol{C}_{\mathbf{p}^{(t)}}^{pri})^{-1} \boldsymbol{\mu}_{\mathbf{p}^{(t)}}^{pri} \right),$$
(16b)

where the prior information $\mathcal{N}(\mathbf{p}^{(t)}; \boldsymbol{\mu}_{\mathbf{p}^{(t)}}^{pri}, \boldsymbol{C}_{\mathbf{p}^{(t)}}^{pri})$ is obtained from the previous slot using (9) with $\boldsymbol{\mu}_{\mathbf{p}^{(t)}}^{pri} = \boldsymbol{\mu}_{\mathbf{p}^{(t-1)}}^{ext}$ and $\boldsymbol{C}_{\mathbf{p}^{(t)}}^{pri} = \boldsymbol{C}_{\mathbf{p}^{(t-1)}}^{ext} + \boldsymbol{C}_q$, where $\boldsymbol{C}_q = \mathrm{blkdiag}(\boldsymbol{C}_1, ... \boldsymbol{C}_K)$. The initial distribution of the users' location is modeled as a non-informative Gaussian distribution with zero mean and a relatively large variance ν^{pri}, i.e., $\boldsymbol{\mu}_{\mathbf{p}^{(0)}}^{ext} = \mathbf{0}$, and $\boldsymbol{C}_{\mathbf{p}^{(0)}}^{ext} = \nu^{\mathrm{pri}}\mathbf{I}_{3K}$.

3.2 Visibility Tracking Module

In visibility tracking module, we replace $\mathbf{p}^{(t)}$ in $\mathbf{A}^{(t)}$ with its estimate $\hat{\mathbf{p}}^{(t)} = \boldsymbol{\mu}_{\mathbf{p}^{(t)}}^{ext}$ obtained from the position tracking module. $\hat{\mathbf{A}}^{(t)}$ is the known sensing matrix for the compressed sensing model $\mathbf{y}^{(t)} = \hat{\mathbf{A}}^{(t)}\boldsymbol{\alpha}^{(t)} + \mathbf{n}^{(t)}$. To further simplify the model, We ignore the correlations among the elements in vectors $\boldsymbol{\alpha}^{(t)}$ and $\boldsymbol{\rho}^{(t)}$, and rewrite the conditional probability in (11) as

$$p\left(\boldsymbol{\alpha}^{(t)} \mid \boldsymbol{\zeta}^{(t)}, \boldsymbol{\rho}^{(t)}\right) = \prod_{k=1}^{K} \prod_{s=1}^{N_t} \left(\delta\left(\zeta_{k,s}^{(t)} - 1\right) \delta\left(\alpha_{k,s}^{(t)} - \rho_{k,s}^{(t)}\right) \right.$$
$$\left. + \delta\left(\zeta_{k,s}^{(t)}\right) \delta\left(\alpha_{k,s}^{(t)}\right) \right). \tag{17}$$

Since the equivalent channel gain magnitudes of different subarrays for the same user are similar, we can approximate the distribution of $\rho_{k,s}^{(t)}$ as $\mathcal{CN}\left(\rho_{k,s}^{(t)}; 0, \tau_k^{\mathrm{pri}}\right)$. Then each element of $\boldsymbol{\alpha}^{(t)}$ has a Bernoulli–Gaussian distribution expressed as

$$p(\alpha_{k,s}^{(t)} | \zeta_{k,s}^{(t)}) = \delta(\zeta_{k,s}^{(t)} - 1)\mathcal{CN}(\alpha_{k,s}^{(t)}; 0, \tau_k^{\mathrm{pri}}) + \delta(\zeta_{k,s}^{(t)})\delta(\alpha_{k,s}^{(t)}). \tag{18}$$

Inspired by [2], we utilize Turbo massage passing for compressed sensing module. As shown in Fig. 2, the visibility tracking module is divided into two modules A and B. Module A is a linear minimum mean-square error estimator(LMMSE), which is used to handle (13) when $\mathbf{p}^{(t)}$ is knwon

$$v_{post,A}^{(t)} = -\mathrm{Tr}\left((\hat{\mathbf{A}}^{(t)})^{\mathrm{H}} \left(v_{pri,A}^{(t)}\hat{\mathbf{A}}^{(t)}(\hat{\mathbf{A}}^{(t)})^{\mathrm{H}} + \boldsymbol{C}_n\right)^{-1} \hat{\mathbf{A}}^{(t)}\right) \tag{19a}$$

$$\times \frac{(v_{pri,A}^{(t)})^2}{KMN} + v_{pri,A}^{(t)}, \tag{19b}$$

$$\boldsymbol{\alpha}_{post,A}^{(t)} = \boldsymbol{\alpha}_{pri,A}^{(t)} + (\hat{\mathbf{A}}^{(t)})^{\mathrm{H}}\left(v_{pri,A}^{(t)}\hat{\mathbf{A}}^{(t)}(\hat{\mathbf{A}}^{(t)})^{\mathrm{H}} + \boldsymbol{C}_n\right)^{-1}$$
$$\times \left(\mathbf{y}^{(t)} - \hat{\mathbf{A}}^{(t)}\boldsymbol{\alpha}_{pri,A}^{(t)}\right) v_{pri,A}^{(t)}. \tag{19c}$$

Module B is a minimum mean square error (MMSE) estimator, which is used to handle (18) and the massage passing in MRF. For the s-item of $\boldsymbol{\zeta}_k^{(t)}$, the massage passing into MRF is expressed as

$$\Delta_{\zeta_{k,s}^{(t)}}^{in} \propto \lambda_{\zeta_{k,s}^{(t)}}^{in} \delta\left(\zeta_{k,s}^{(t)} - 1\right) + \left(1 - \lambda_{\zeta_{k,s}^{(t)}}^{in}\right) \delta\left(\zeta_{k,s}^{(t)}\right), \tag{20}$$

where $\lambda_{k,s}^{(t)}$ is calculated by

$$\lambda_{\zeta_{k,s}^{(t)}}^{in} = 1 + \frac{\mathcal{CN}\left(0; [\boldsymbol{\alpha}_{pri,B}^{(t)}]_{k,s}, v_{pri,B}^{(t)}\right)}{\mathcal{CN}\left(0; -[\boldsymbol{\alpha}_{pri,B}^{(t)}]_{k,s}, \tau_k^{\mathrm{pri}} + v_{pri,B}^{(t)}\right)}. \tag{21}$$

The message passing within the MRF and the massage passing out MRF $\Delta_{\zeta_{k,s}^{(t)}}^{out} \propto \lambda_{\zeta_{k,s}^{(t)}}^{out} \delta\left(\zeta_{k,s}^{(t)} - 1\right) + \left(1 - \lambda_{\zeta_{k,s}^{(t)}}^{out}\right) \delta\left(\zeta_{k,s}^{(t)}\right)$ is calculated following [18].

The message from $p\left(\alpha_{k,s}^{(t)}|\zeta_{k,s}^{(t)}\right)$ to $\alpha_{k,s}^{(t)}$ is calculated by

$$\Delta_{\alpha_{k,s}^{(t)}} = \lambda_{\zeta_{k,s}^{(t)}}^{out}\mathcal{CN}(\alpha_{k,s}^{(t)};0,\tau_k^{\mathrm{pri}}) + (1-\lambda_{\zeta_{k,s}^{(t)}}^{out})\delta(\alpha_{k,s}^{(t)}) \tag{22}$$

Then $v_{post,B}^{(t)}$ and $[\alpha_{post,B}^{(t)}]_{k,s}$ are obtained by

$$[\alpha_{post,B}^{(t)}]_{k,s} = \int_{\alpha_{k,s}^{(t)}} \alpha_{k,s}^{(t)}p(\alpha_{k,s}^{(t)}|\boldsymbol{\alpha}_{pri,B}^{(t)}), \tag{23a}$$

$$v_{post,B}^{(t)} = \frac{1}{KN_t}\sum_{k=1}^{K}\sum_{s=1}^{N_t}\int_{\alpha_{k,s}^{(t)}} |\alpha_{k,s}^{(t)} - \mathrm{E}(\alpha_{k,s}^{(t)}|\boldsymbol{\alpha}_{pri,B}^{(t)})|^2$$
$$\times p(\alpha_{k,s}^{(t)}|\boldsymbol{\alpha}_{pri,B}^{(t)}), \tag{23b}$$

where $p(\alpha_{k,s}^{(t)}|\boldsymbol{\alpha}_{pri,B}^{(t)}) = \frac{1}{C}\Delta_{\alpha_{k,s}^{(t)}}\mathcal{CN}(\alpha_{k,s}^{(t)};[\boldsymbol{\alpha}_{pri,B}^{(t)}]_{k,s},v_{pri,B}^{(t)})$ with C is normalization factor. The output of visibility tracking module is the approximation $\hat{\boldsymbol{\zeta}}^{(t)}$ with $[\hat{\boldsymbol{\zeta}}^{(t)}]_s$ given by

$$[\hat{\boldsymbol{\zeta}}^{(t)}]_{k,s} = \begin{cases} 1, & \lambda_{\zeta_{k,s}^{(t)}}^{out} > 0.5; \\ 0, & \lambda_{\zeta_{k,s}^{(t)}}^{out} < 0.5. \end{cases} \tag{24}$$

3.3   Overall Algorithm

Our BLAP-BNT algorithm is summarized in Algorithm 1. The algorithm initializes $\mathbf{p}^{(t)}$ with the previous estimate $\hat{\mathbf{p}}^{(t-1)}$, and then iteratively updates $\mathbf{p}^{(t)}$ and $\boldsymbol{\zeta}^{(t)}$ until the stopping criterion is met. The visibility tracking module adopts Turbo message passing, we can iteratively update this module independently to obtain a more accurate estimate of the visibility indicator $\boldsymbol{\zeta}^{(t)}$ and reduce the number of iterations of overall algorithm. The complexity of APLE-LM is $\mathcal{O}(n_1 N_B N_R)$, where n_1 is the number of iterations in gradient ascend. Therefore, the overall complexity of the proposed algorithm is $\mathcal{O}\left(n_2(N_B^3 + n_1 N_B N_R)\right)$, where n_2 is the number of iterations.

4   Numerical Results

This section provides numerical results using the parameters summarized in Table 1, unless otherwise specified. We set $M_x = M_y = 6, N_x = N_y = 2$. The user mobility model is set as $\boldsymbol{C}_k = 0.03\mathbf{I}$ for $k = 1,2$. The binary SNS states are sampled via a Gibbs process from the Ising model. The total number of tracking time slots is set by $T = 100$. We evaluate the algorithm performance by the RMSE of user position and the accuracy of VR averaging from 10 independently generated trajectories.

Algorithm 1. BLAP-BNT algorithm

Input: $\mathbf{y}^{(t)}$, C_n, $\mathbf{H}_{BR}$, $\boldsymbol{\Omega}^{(t)}$, $\{\tau_k^{\mathrm{pri}}\}_{k=1}^K$.

1: **Initialization:** $\hat{\mathbf{p}}^{(t)} = \hat{\mathbf{p}}^{(t-1)}$.

2: **repeat**

3:     % LMMSE estimator:

4:     Update $v_{post,A}^{(t)}$ and $\boldsymbol{\alpha}_{post,A}^{(t)}$ by (19).

5:     $v_{pri,B}^{(t)} = v_{ext,A}^{(t)} = \left(\dfrac{1}{v_{post,A}^{(t)}} - \dfrac{1}{v_{pri,A}^{(t)}}\right)^{-1}$.

6:     $\boldsymbol{\alpha}_{pri,B}^{(t)} = \boldsymbol{\alpha}_{ext,A}^{(t)} = v_{pri,B}^{(t)}\left(\dfrac{\boldsymbol{\alpha}_{post,A}^{(t)}}{v_A^{post}} - \dfrac{\boldsymbol{\alpha}_{pri,A}^{(t)}}{v_A^{pri}}\right)$.

7:     % Structured MMSE estimator:

8:     **for all** $k = 1, ..., K$ **do**

9:         **for all** $s = 1, ..., N_t$ **do**

10:             Update $\Delta_{\zeta_{k,s}^{(t)}}^{in}$ by (20).

11:             Update $\Delta_{\zeta_{k,s}^{(t)}}^{out}$ according to [18].

12:             Update $\Delta_{\alpha_{k,s}^{(t)}}$ by (22).

13:         **end for**

14:     **end for**

15:     $v_{post,B}^{(t)}$ and $\boldsymbol{\alpha}_{post,B}^{(t)}$ by (23).

16:     $v_{pri,A}^{(t)} = v_{ext,B}^{(t)} = \left(\dfrac{1}{v_{post,B}^{(t)}} - \dfrac{1}{v_{pri,B}^{(t)}}\right)^{-1}$.

17:     $\boldsymbol{\alpha}_{pri,A}^{(t)} = \boldsymbol{\alpha}_{ext,B}^{(t)} = v_{pri,A}^{(t)}\left(\dfrac{\boldsymbol{\alpha}_{post,B}^{(t)}}{v_B^{post}} - \dfrac{\boldsymbol{\alpha}_{pri,B}^{(t)}}{v_B^{pri}}\right)$.

18:     Update $\hat{\boldsymbol{\zeta}}^{(t)}$ by (24).

19:     % Position tracking module:

20:     Update $\mathcal{N}(\mathbf{p}^{(t)}; \boldsymbol{\mu}_{\mathbf{p}^{(t)}}, C_{\mathbf{p}^{(t)}})$ by APLE-LM algorithm in [13].

21:     Update $\mathcal{N}(\mathbf{p}^{(t)}; \boldsymbol{\mu}_{\mathbf{p}^{(t)}}^{ext}, C_{\mathbf{p}^{(t)}}^{ext})$ by (16).

22: **until** the stopping criterion is met.

Output: $\hat{\boldsymbol{\zeta}}^{(t)}$ and $\hat{\mathbf{p}} = \boldsymbol{\mu}_{\mathbf{p}^{(t)}}^{ext}$.

For comparison, we introduce two baselines. For the first baseline, we extend APLE-LM algorithm in [13] to tracking scenarios via a large RIS. The analog beamforming matrix is equivalent to the product of the RIS-BS channel matrix and the RIS reflection matrix. The initialization of the user position is replaced by the position estimate obtained in the previous time slot. The second algorithm is gradient ascend (GA), which estimates the user positions sequentially assumed VR known. For $1 \leq k \leq K$, $\hat{\mathbf{p}}_k^{(t)}$ is obtained by applying the GA method to find a local maximum of the objective function

$$-(\mathbf{y}_{\mathrm{res}}^{(t)} - \hat{\varrho}_k^{(t)} \mathbf{A}_k^{(t)} \mathbf{E}_k^{(t)} \mathbf{Tc}_k^{(t)})^{\mathrm{H}} C_n^{-1} (\mathbf{y}_{\mathrm{res}}^{(t)} - \hat{\varrho}_k^{(t)} \mathbf{A}_k^{(t)} \mathbf{E}_k^{(t)} \mathbf{Tc}_k^{(t)}) \qquad (25)$$

where $\hat{\varrho}_k^{(t)} = \dfrac{(\mathbf{A}_k^{(t)} \mathbf{E}_k^{(t)} \mathbf{Tc}_k^{(t)})^{\mathrm{H}} C_n^{-1} \mathbf{y}_{\mathrm{res}}^{(t)}}{(\mathbf{A}_k^{(t)} \mathbf{E}_k^{(t)} \mathbf{Tc}_k^{(t)})^{\mathrm{H}} C_n^{-1} (\mathbf{A}_k^{(t)} \mathbf{E}_k^{(t)} \mathbf{Tc}_k^{(t)})}$. The residual signal $\mathbf{y}_{\mathrm{res}}^{(t)}$ is subsequently updated by removing the contribution associated with user k. The start point of iterations is $\hat{\mathbf{p}}_k^{(t-1)}$. We also plot a genie bound as a baseline, which is obtained by performing BLAP-BNT algrithm assuming VR known. We fol-

Table 1. System Parameters

Parameter	Symbol	Value
Carrier frequency	f	6 GHz
Wavelength	λ	0.05 m
Number of RIS elements	$N_{Rx} \times N_{Ry}$	60 × 60
Number of BS antennas	$N_{Bx} \times N_{By}$	16 × 10
Number of users	K	2
RIS-UE distance range	$[r_{\min}, r_{\max}]$	[5 m,10 m]

low the Bayesian Cramèr Rao bound(BCRB) to yield a performance LB of the position tracking problem.

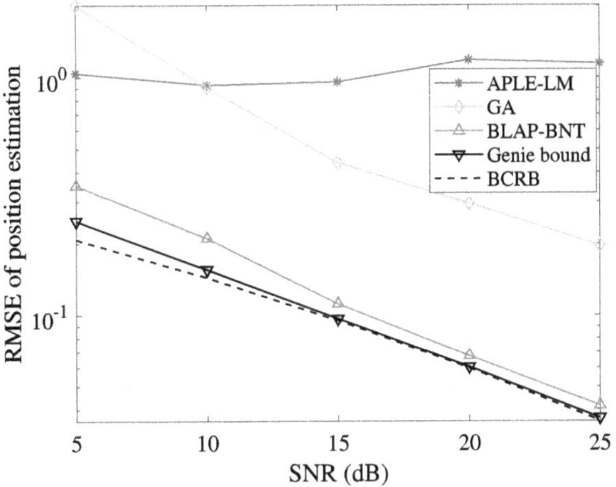

Fig. 3. The user tracking performance of the BLAP-BNT algorithm in comparison with the baselines v.s. received SNR

Figure 3 shows the tracking performance of the algorithm as received SNR. The baseline scheme APLE-LM does not account for the spatial non-stationarity of the channel, resulting in a mismatch between the channel model and the actual conditions. GA is highly dependent on the quality of initialization, which can lead to suboptimal localization performance despite of assuming VR is knwon. Under the assumption of known VR and considering only the localization problem, the genie bound of our algorithm is closely approaches the BCRB. However, since our algorithm cannot guarantee perfect accuracy in VR recognition, the actual tracking error is larger than its lower bound but smaller than other baseline.

Figure 4 illustrates the impact of different array partitioning strategies. When the RIS is only partitioned once, the subarray size is too large, the spatial non-

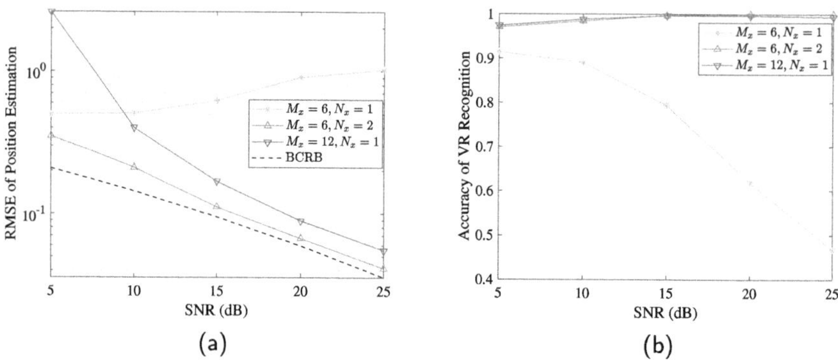

Fig. 4. The BLAP-BNT tracking performance v.s. received SNR with different partitioning, $M_x = M_y, N_x = N_y$. (a) users' position estimation error; (b) accuracy of VR recognition.

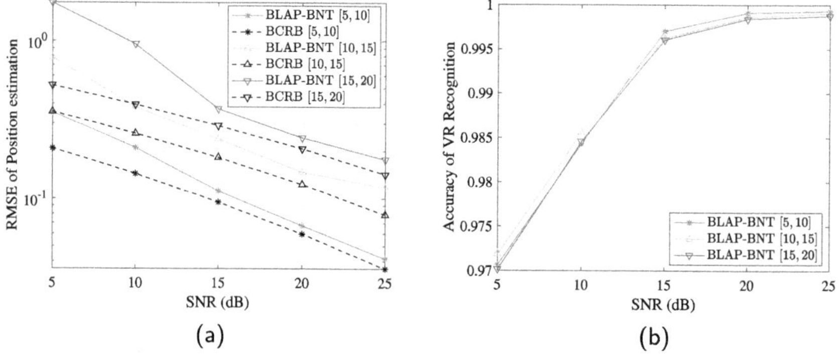

Fig. 5. The BLAP-BNT tracking performance v.s. received SNR with varying $[r_{min}, r_{max}]$. (a) the users' positions estimation error; (b) the accuracy of VR recognition.

stationary characteristics of the channel cannot be well captured, and the mismatch of the model to the actual channel will lead to a large estimation error. The $M_x = M_y = 12, N_x = N_y = 1$ partitioning strategy shows degraded position estimation performance compared with the $M_x = M_y = 6, N_x = N_y = 2$ strategy, despite both providing the same VR resolution. The BLAP-BNT algorithm is also evaluated for users distributed over different distance ranges, with $[r_{min}, r_{max}]$ between the RIS and the users. We set $[r_{min}, r_{max}]$ to $[5, 10]$, $[10, 15]$, and $[15, 20]$. As shown in Fig. 5(a), the estimation erorr increases with increasing distance. In contrast, VR recognition remains above 97% and is largely insensitive to the distance range, as illustrated in Fig. 5(b). Furthermore, VR recognition accuracy gradually approaches 100% as the SNR increases.

5   Conclusion

This paper addresses the problem of near-field multiuser tracking. To capture the spatial non-stationarity, a bi-level array partitioning strategy is first introduced, and a probabilistic model is constructed that accounts for both the spatial and temporal group sparsity of the near-field channel. We then developed an online message passing algorithm to estimate the position and VR of users. Numerical simulations demonstrate the proposed BLAP-BNT algorithm achieves higher localization precision than baseline methods, and its visibility recognition accuracy approaches 100%.

References

1. Basar, E., Di Renzo, M., De Rosny, J., Debbah, M., Alouini, M.S., Zhang, R.: Wireless communications through reconfigurable intelligent surfaces. IEEE Access **7**, 116753–116773 (2019)
2. Chen, L., Liu, A., Yuan, X.: Structured turbo compressed sensing for massive MIMO channel estimation using a Markov prior. IEEE Trans. Veh. Technol. **67**(5), 4635–4639 (2017)
3. Dardari, D., Decarli, N., Guerra, A., Guidi, F.: LOS/NLOS near-field localization with a large reconfigurable intelligent surface. IEEE Trans. Wireless Commun. **21**(6), 4282–4294 (2021)
4. De Carvalho, E., Ali, A., Amiri, A., Angjelichinoski, M., Heath, R.W.: Non-stationarities in extra-large-scale massive MIMO. IEEE Wirel. Commun. **27**(4), 74–80 (2020)
5. Di Renzo, M., Zappone, A., Debbah, M., Alouini, M.S., Yuen, C., De Rosny, J., Tretyakov, S.: Smart radio environments empowered by reconfigurable intelligent surfaces: How it works, state of research, and the road ahead. IEEE J. Sel. Areas Commun. **38**(11), 2450–2525 (2020)
6. Han, Y., Jin, S., Wen, C.K., Quek, T.Q.: Localization and channel reconstruction for extra large RIS-assisted massive MIMO systems. IEEE J. Sel. Top. Sig. Process. **16**(5), 1011–1025 (2022)
7. Pan, Y., Pan, C., Jin, S., Wang, J.: Joint channel estimation and localization in the near field of RIS enabled mmWave/subTHz communications. arXiv preprint arXiv:2208.11343 (2022)
8. Ramezani, P., Kosasih, A., Björnson, E.: An efficient modified MUSIC algorithm for RIS-assisted near-field localization. arXiv preprint arXiv:2409.14152 (2024)
9. Rinchi, O., Elzanaty, A., Alouini, M.S.: Compressive near-field localization for multipath RIS-aided environments. IEEE Commun. Lett. **26**(6), 1268–1272 (2022)
10. Selvan, K.T., Janaswamy, R.: Fraunhofer and Fresnel distances: unified derivation for aperture antennas. IEEE Antennas Propag. Mag. **59**(4), 12–15 (2017)
11. Teng, B., Yuan, X., Wang, R.: Variational bayesian multiuser tracking for reconfigurable intelligent surface-aided MIMO-OFDM systems. IEEE J. Sel. Areas Commun. **41**(12), 3752–3767 (2023)
12. Teng, B., Yuan, X., Wang, R., Jin, S.: Bayesian user localization and tracking for reconfigurable intelligent surface aided MIMO systems. IEEE J. Sel. Top. Sig. Process. **16**(5), 1040–1054 (2022)

13. Teng, B., Yuan, X., Wang, R., Liang, Y.C., Huang, X.: Near-field multiuser localization based on extremely large antenna array with limited rf chains. IEEE Trans. Wirel. Commun. 1–1 (2025). https://doi.org/10.1109/TWC.2025.3578399
14. Wang, J., Wang, C.X., Huang, J., Wang, H., Gao, X.: A general 3D space-time-frequency non-stationary THz channel model for 6G ultra-massive MIMO wireless communication systems. IEEE J. Sel. Areas Commun. **39**(6), 1576–1589 (2021)
15. Wymeersch, H., He, J., Denis, B., Clemente, A., Juntti, M.: Radio localization and mapping with reconfigurable intelligent surfaces. arXiv preprint arXiv:1912.09401 (2019)
16. Yuan, X., Zhang, M., Zheng, Y., Teng, B., Jiang, W.: Scalable near-field localization based on partitioned large-scale antenna array. IEEE Trans. Wireless Commun. **24**(3), 2203–2217 (2025)
17. Zhang, H., Zhang, H., Di, B., Bian, K., Han, Z., Song, L.: Metalocalization: reconfigurable intelligent surface aided multi-user wireless indoor localization. IEEE Trans. Wireless Commun. **20**(12), 7743–7757 (2021)
18. Zhang, M., Yuan, X., He, Z.Q.: Variance state propagation for structured sparse Bayesian learning. IEEE Trans. Signal Process. **68**, 2386–2400 (2020)

DHRA: DQN Based Deterministic Heterogeneous Resource Allocation for Multi-user Holographic Conferencing

Xu Huang[1], Xia Gong[2], Jia Chen[1,3(✉)], Shang Liu[1], Dongsheng Qian[1], Wentao Cui[1], and Weichao Li[1]

[1] Beijing Jiaotong University, Beijing, China
{21111024,chenjia,22115009,23115049,24115017,25115046}@bjtu.edu.cn
[2] China Telecom Corporation Limited, Guangzhou, China
gongxia@chinatelecom.cn
[3] Peng Cheng Laboratory, Shenzhen, China

Abstract. Holographic-type communication (HTC) services, such as multi-user holographic conferencing, have emerged as a promising direction for future immersive communication. However, point cloud, a mainstream format in HTC, is characterized by its large and fluctuating data size, which poses a challenge to ultra-low latency transmission. In this paper, we propose a DQN-based deterministic heterogeneous resource allocation system for multi-user holographic conferencing (DHRA). The DHRA system introduces a Point Cloud Shaper (PCS) and a Hierarchical Queuing and Forwarding (HQF) mechanism to extract core structural points from dynamically fluctuating point cloud frames and ensure their deterministic transmission. Furthermore, a heterogeneous resource scheduling model and a Multi-user Resource Scheduling Algorithm (MRSA) are designed to maximize user access. Experimental results demonstrate that the DHRA prototype can support multi-user holographic conferencing with 2 speakers and 3 audience members while maintaining a display frame rate of over 20 FPS. Additionally, MRSA achieves an 87% scheduling success rate with 100 users, outperforming baseline algorithms by a maximum of 27.9%.

Keywords: Holographic-type communication · Heterogeneous resource allocation · Deterministic Network

1 Introduction

With the rapid advancement of Virtual Reality (VR), Augmented Reality (AR), and the Metaverse, Holographic-Type Communication (HTC) applications, such as multi-user conferencing, have emerged as an emerging trend in future communication technologies [1]. In traditional multi-user conferencing, the size of

Z. Lin et al. (Eds.): INSAI 2025, CCIS 2894, pp. 127–137, 2026.
https://doi.org/10.1007/978-981-95-9299-9_10

captured video frames remains fixed once the resolution is set. In contrast, holographic conferencing employs point cloud data, which features significantly larger and highly fluctuating data sizes. This dynamic fluctuation stems from the nature of point cloud representation: in a 3D point cloud model, each point is defined by a six-tuple (x, y, z, r, g, b) representing spatial coordinates and color information, and this format enables a full 6 Degrees of Freedom (6DoF) experience [2]. However, as users or scenes move dynamically, the number of points required to represent the scene changes dynamically, making it challenging to transmit point cloud data with ultra-low latency.

Given the enormous data volume involved in multi-user holographic conferencing, some researchers have attempted to reduce data size through compression or transcoding methods. For instance, studies such as [3,4] utilize Point Cloud Compression (PCC) techniques [5,6], while [7] employs deep neural networks or large language models (LLMs) to generate 3D models from 2D images or textual prompts. These approaches highlight that point cloud data transmission not only relies on network performance but also demands substantial computational processing. Therefore, to better evaluate both Quality of Service (QoS) and Quality of Experience (QoE), the Motion-to-Photon (MTP) latency metric has been introduced, which measures the delay from the movement of a tracked object to its corresponding rendering on the display [8]. MTP latency encompasses computing, storage, and network transmission delays, and a satisfactory user experience can only be achieved when MTP latency is both bounded and ultra-low [8].

Time-Sensitive Networking (TSN) and Deterministic Networking (DetNet) are currently the dominant approaches for providing deterministic transmission with ultra-low bounded latency. However, existing traffic shaping mechanisms in TSN and DetNet primarily target time-triggered streams, where packets typically exhibit stable and small sizes. Therefore, existing mechanisms in TSN and DetNet are not suitable for deterministic transmission in holographic conferencing [9,10]. In summary, to guarantee bounded ultra-low Motion-to-Photon (MTP) latency in multi-user holographic conferencing, two major challenges must be addressed. On one hand, the massive and highly volatile data size of point clouds introduces unpredictable jitter, resulting in uncertain MTP latency. On the other hand, heterogeneous resources—including computing, network, and storage—must be efficiently allocated for each user to ensure the bounded MTP latency. To tackle these challenges, we propose DHRA, a DQN-based deterministic heterogeneous resource allocation system designed for multi-user holographic conferencing. The main contributions of this work are summarized as follows:

- We propose a Point Cloud Shaper (PCS) to classify points into core structural and surface detail parts, along with a Hierarchical Queuing and Forwarding (HQF) mechanism that provides hierarchical latency guarantees to mitigate dynamic data fluctuation.
- We formulate scheduling constraints and a computation-network-storage resource trading model for multi-user holographic conferencing, and further

propose the MRSA algorithm to maximize user access under given resource constraints.
- Experimental results show that the prototype system supports 2 speakers and 3 audiences with over 20 frames per second (FPS), while MRSA achieves an 87% scheduling success rate with 100 users.

The rest of this paper is structured as follows: Sect. 2 provides an overview of related work. Section 3 presents the design of the DHRA system. Section 4 introduces the scheduling constraints and describes the MRSA algorithm. Section 5 discusses the experimental results. Finally, Sect. 6 concludes the paper.

2 Related Work

Current multi-user holographic conferencing systems primarily adopt either direct streaming or transcoding approaches. Systems based on direct streaming typically utilize compression algorithms, such as Draco, V-PCC, or G-PCC [5,6], in conjunction with streaming algorithms deployed at the edge to transmit point cloud data efficiently. For instance, Han et al. [3] proposed ViVo, which reduces bandwidth consumption by determining video content according to the viewer's perceptual context (how, what, and where). Lee et al. [4] proposed Groot, which supports real-time transmission and decoding on mobile devices while enabling continuous on-demand view adaptation. Systems based on transcoding leverage AI or LLMs to generate 3D models on the audience side without directly transmitting large-volume point cloud data. For example, Huang et al. [11] implemented a preliminary prototype of an AI-driven holographic video communication system for immersive services. In our previous work, DT-CNST [12] was proposed to handle the deterministic transmission of point cloud frames within the FOV. However, none of these existing works focus on deterministic transmission for multi-user data streams with bounded MTP latency. In this paper, we propose DHRA and MRSA, which not only ensure bounded ultra-low latency but also realize deterministic resource allocation.

3 The DHRA System

3.1 The Introduction of DHRA System

The DHRA system outlines the complete processing pipeline for multi-user holographic conferencing, as illustrated in Fig. 1. The workflow of DHRA system is as follows:

- Step 1: Users at the capture side generate point cloud frames at a fixed FPS rate. Due to object motion, the data size of each point cloud frame varies dynamically.
- Step 2: An edge computing device processes each point cloud frame by separating the points into a core structural part and a surface detail part.

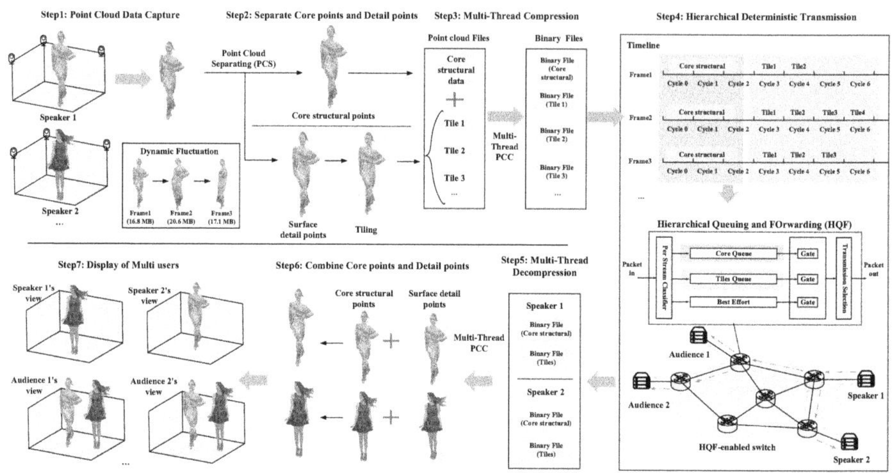

Fig. 1. The architecture of DHRA system.

- Step 3: The core structural points are compressed into a single file. The surface detail points are partitioned into multiple tiles, each compressed into a separate binary file.
- Step 4: The core structural points and surface detail tiles are transmitted through different queues and time slots via HQF.
- Step 5: On the audience side, an edge computing device receives data streams from multiple speakers and decompresses the binary files using a multi-threaded point cloud decompression algorithm.
- Step 6: After decompression, the core structural points and surface detail points from each user are merged into a complete point cloud.
- Step 7: The reconstructed point cloud is rendered on each user's display.

The point cloud frames are captured using 3D cameras such as the Intel RealSense or Microsoft Kinect. Therefore, once the captured FPS is set, the point cloud frames can be considered periodic, with a period of $1/captured\ FPS$. This periodic interval is defined as one Hypercycle. Within each Hypercycle, the timeline is divided into equal-duration time slots referred to as Cycles, labeled from $Cycle_1$ to $Cycle_N$, where N is equal to $Hypercycle/Cycle$.

3.2   The Details of PCS

Consider a sequence of frames frm_1 to frm_N captured from user u_i. Due to object motion, these frames exhibit varying data volumes. PCS is designed to guarantee deterministic transmission of the core structural part of each frame, rather than the entire frame. The number of core structural points in each frame is maintained constant and is defined as follows:

$$\forall \{frm_1, \ldots, frm_N\} \in u_i :$$
$$Num_{cs}^{u_i} = \gamma \times \max_{j \in [1,N]} \{Num_{frm_j}\}, \tag{1}$$

where γ denotes a sampling factor determined by the user's visual quality requirements.

Once the number of core structural points is determined, the data size of these points can be calculated by:

$$Size_{cs}^{u_i} = Num_{cs}^{u_i} \times 28Byte + Size_{file\ head},\tag{2}$$

where each point in the PLY format occupies 28 bytes and $Size_{file\ head}$ is a constant value of 334 bytes.

Therefore, the number of cycles for user u_i is given by:

$$Num_{cycle}^{u_i} = \left\lceil \frac{Size_{cs}^{u_i}}{BW \times Cycle} \right\rceil,\tag{3}$$

where the BW is bandwidth and $Cycle$ denotes the one cycle size. After the PCS extracts the core structural points, the remaining points are classified as surface detail points.

3.3   The Details of HQF

Each speaker can determine the required number of stable cycles for transmitting core structural data through the PCS. Based on the routing of streams, HQF-enabled switches reserve specific cycles for core structural data, ensuring deterministic transmission with bounded MTP latency. The remaining cycles within a Hypercycle are allocated for transmitting tiles of surface detail data and other best-effort traffic in the network.

Therefore, the worst-case end-to-end (E2E) transmission latency for the core structural data of user u_i can be derived based on the number of hops and the data size of the core structural data:

$$\forall U_{sw_n} = \{u_1, u_2, \ldots, u_N\}, R_{u_i} = \{sw_{src}, \ldots, sw_{dst}\} :$$

$$\begin{aligned}
L_{e2e}^{u_i} = \sum_{sw_n \in R_{u_i}} \Bigg((\sum_{u_j \in U_{sw_n}} Num_{cycle}^{u_j} - Num_{cycle}^{u_i}) \times Cycle \\
+ Cycle \Bigg) + Num_{cycle}^{u_i} \times Cycle
\end{aligned}\tag{4}$$

where U_{sw_n} denotes the set of user streams passing through switch sw_n, and R_{u_i} represents the routing path of user u_i.

4   The Scheduling Model and Algorithm

4.1   The Model of Scheduling Constraints

The heterogeneous resource trading model is designed to dynamically balance computation, network, and storage resources in multi-user holographic conferencing. Meanwhile, since the MTP latency must be constrained to an ultra-low bounded value, several constraints must be satisfied during resource scheduling.

C1: Computational Latency Constraint

The computational latency encompasses data separation, compression, decompression, and recombination. To minimize MTP latency, the data separation and recombination algorithms are implemented in C++ for high performance, which can be expressed as:

$$L_{dp}^{u_i} = \tau \times Num_{cycle}^{u_i} \tag{5}$$

where τ represents the time required to process a volume of point cloud data equivalent to $BW \times Cycle$.

The PCC algorithm employed in this work is based on Draco for both compression and decompression. The corresponding compression and decompression time for user u_i can be expressed as:

$$\begin{aligned}
L_{comp.}^{u_i} &= Draco(N_{\text{thread}}, \alpha, Size_{cs}^{u_i}) \\
L_{decp.}^{u_i} &= Dedraco(N_{\text{thread}}, Size_{cs}^{u_i})
\end{aligned} \tag{6}$$

where the function $Draco(N_{\text{thread}}, \alpha, Size)$ denotes the time required to compress point cloud data of size $Size$ using N_{thread} threads and a compression ratio α, while $Dedraco(N_{\text{thread}}, Size)$ represents the decompression time for the same data size using N_{thread} threads.

Therefore, the computational latency for core structural data can be expressed as:

$$L_{com}^{u_i} = L_{dp}^{u_i} + L_{comp.}^{u_i} + L_{decp.}^{u_i} \tag{7}$$

C2: Storage and Network Latency Constraint

The combined storage and network latency can be represented by the end-to-end transmission latency. Based on Eq. (4), their sum must satisfy:

$$L_{net} + L_{sto} = L_{e2e}^{u_i} \leq Hypercycle \tag{8}$$

This ensures that the total latency remains within the duration of one Hypercycle, thereby preserving deterministic transmission without stream conflict.

C3: MTP Latency Constraint

The MTP latency comprises the computational latency, storage latency, and network latency, and can be expressed as:

$$L_{MTP}^{u_i} = L_{dp}^{u_i} + L_{comp.}^{u_i} + L_{e2e}^{u_i} + L_{decp.}^{u_i} \tag{9}$$

This total latency must be rigorously bounded to meet the ultra-low latency requirement essential for real-time holographic conferencing.

C4: Heterogeneous Resources Trading Constraint

The resource allocation in multi-user holographic conferencing involves coordinated trading of computational, storage, and network resources. These resources must be dynamically balanced through two key parameters: Compression ratio α and Sampling factor γ. Higher α increases computational load but reduces network/storage demands. Higher γ expands core structural data size, increasing network/storage requirements for user u_i while limiting resources available to others.

Based on constraints C1-C4, the optimal values of α and γ maximize system capacity while satisfying the bounded MTP latency constraints. Therefore, the optimization problem can be formulated as:

$$\max_{A,Y} \frac{N(A,Y)}{|N_U|}$$

$$\text{subject to:}$$

$$A = \left[\alpha_1, \alpha_2, \ldots, \alpha_{|N_U|}\right]$$
$$Y = \left[\gamma_1, \gamma_2, \ldots, \gamma_{|N_U|}\right] \tag{10}$$
$$\bigcup L_{MTP}^{u \in N(A,Y)} \leq L_{MTP}^{max}$$

where $N(A,Y)$ denotes the maximum number of admissible users, N_U denotes the total number of potential users, and $L_{\max}$ is the upper bounded MTP latency required for conferencing.

4.2   The MRSA Algorithm

Algorithm 1. The MRSA algorithm

Input: Empty replay buffer D, Initial network parameters θ and θ', Target network replacement frequency N_-, Replay buffer maximum size N_r, Training batch size N_b.

Output: Optimal Scheduled Result $N(A,Y)$.

1: **for** *episode* $e \in \{1, 2, \ldots, M\}$ **do**
2:     Initialize state s;
3:     **for** *step* $t \in \{0, 1, \ldots, K\}$ **do**
4:         Sample action $a_t = [(\alpha_1, \gamma_1), \ldots, (\alpha_{N_U}, \gamma_{N_U})]$;
5:         Observe reward r_t and transmit to next state s_{t+1};
6:         Update the result $N(A,Y)$.
7:         Store the tuple $(s_t, a_t, r_t, s_{t+1}, done)$ into D;
8:         Replace the oldest tuple if $|D| > N_r$;
9:         Sample a minibatch of N_b tuples from D;
10:         Update target network $\theta' \leftarrow \theta$ every N_- steps;
11:     **end for**
12: **end for**
13: **return** Optimal Scheduled Result $N(A,Y)$.

The MRSA algorithm employs a Deep Q-Network (DQN) to solve the optimization problem, as outlined in Algorithm 1. The algorithm executes M episodes. Each episode initializes the state of heterogeneous resources (lines 1–3) and interacts with the environment over K steps. At each step, an action a_t, containing (α, γ) for all users, is sampled from the Q-network. The environment then returns a reward and a new state. Based on the reward, the result $N(A, Y)$ is recorded (lines 4–6). Once the replay buffer exceeds size N_r, it is updated. Every N_- steps, a minibatch is sampled from the buffer to update the Q-network (lines 7–10). After M episodes, the optimal result $N(A, Y)$ is returned.

5   Evaluation

5.1   Experiment Setup

We acquire multi-user point cloud data using an array of Intel RealSense D455 cameras. The simulation environment is implemented in OMNeT++. The baseline system is configured with a maximum of 5 access users, comprising 2 speakers and 3 audiences. Specifically, user 1 (U1) and user 2 (U2) act as speakers that both transmit and receive point cloud data, while users 3, 4, and 5 (U3, U4, U5) serve as audiences only. The connections are configured as follows: $U1 \leftrightarrow sw1 \leftrightarrow sw2 \leftrightarrow \{U3, U4, U5\}$, $U1 \leftrightarrow sw1 \leftrightarrow sw3 \leftrightarrow U2$, and $U2 \leftrightarrow sw3 \leftrightarrow sw2 \leftrightarrow \{U3, U4, U5\}$. The network bandwidth is set to 1 Gbps. A cycle size of 1 ms is used, and point cloud frames are generated at intervals of 50 ms.

Meanwhile, to evaluate the scalability and performance of the MRSA algorithm, the simulation is extended to include 100 users (as audiences) and a larger network topology comprising 31 switches in a fat-tree configuration. For comparative analysis, a Q-learning algorithm and a Greedy algorithm are employed as benchmarks.

5.2   Experiment Result

Figure 2 illustrates the MTP latency among different users. In $U1 \rightarrow \{U2, U3, U4, U5\}$, both the separation and encoding time remain consistent, as these operations are performed at the edge computing device of $U1$. Regarding transmission, the path $U1 \rightarrow U2$ allows direct data forwarding without storage latency. Similarly, for $U1 \rightarrow \{U3, U4, U5\}$, since all three users receive the same data from $U1$, the transmission latency is identical and also incurs no storage latency. However, slight variations arise during decompression, data combination, and rendering due to differences in user devices' processing capabilities. Additionally, the MTP latency for $U2 \rightarrow U1$ is measured. Because $U2$ utilizes greater computational resources for data separation, both encoding and transmission latencies are reduced, resulting in the lowest overall MTP latency compared to paths from $U1$ to other users. As shown in Fig. 2, the maximum MTP latency between any two users is 40.7 ms, which remains below the 50 ms interval between point cloud frame generations. This result indicates that the DHRA system can effectively support multi-user holographic conferencing with 2 speakers and 3 audiences while sustaining a display frame rate of over 20 FPS.

Moreover, we compare the scheduling rate of our proposed algorithm, MRSA, against the Q-learning and Greedy algorithms under the same constraints and

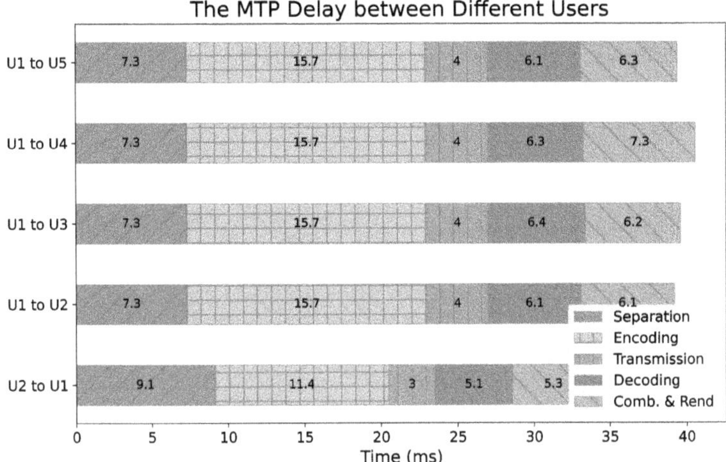

Fig. 2. The MTP latency between different users.

objective function. The results are presented in Fig. 3. As the number of audiences increases, the scheduling rate decreases due to limitations in heterogeneous resources. When fewer than 30 users are present, all can access the network and participate in the conference. However, as the number increases to 40, some users lose connectivity as the MTP latency exceeds the upper threshold. Both the Greedy and Q-learning algorithms demonstrate effective scheduling performance when the user count remains below 50. Beyond this point, their scheduling capabilities deteriorate. In contrast, our proposed MRSA algorithm employs a DQN-based approach that is better adapted to large-scale user scenarios. Consequently, it consistently outperforms the other two methods. With 100 users, MRSA achieves a scheduling rate of 87%, outperforming the comparison algorithms by 27.9% and 20.8%, respectively.

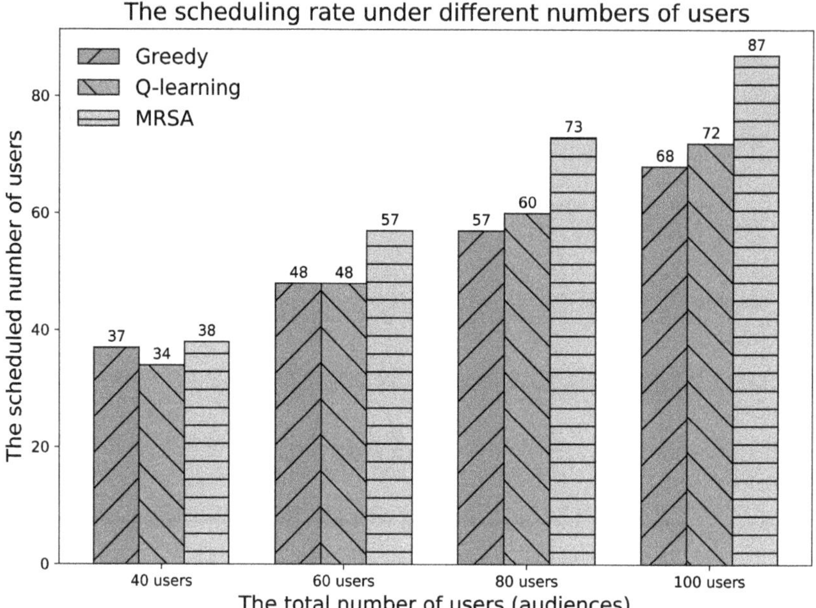

Fig. 3. Comparison of scheduling rate under different numbers of users.

6   Conclusion

This paper presents DHRA system, a DQN-based deterministic heterogeneous resource allocation system for multi-user holographic conferencing. The proposed system incorporates a PCS mechanism that decomposes volumetric data into core structural points and surface detail points, effectively mitigating the impact of dynamic volatility of point cloud frames. Furthermore, the HQF mechanism introduced to provide differentiated latency guarantees: core structural points are allocated deterministic transmission under strict priority, while surface detail points are transmitted utilizing residual bandwidth without interfering with core traffic. To address multi-user resource allocation, a MRSA algorithm is developed based on constraints and a heterogeneous resource trading model. Experimental evaluation demonstrates that DHRA system supports conferencing with 2 speakers and 3 audiences at a sustained rate of 20 FPS. Moreover, MRSA achieves a scheduling success rate of 87% under 100 users, outperforming baseline algorithms by 27.9% and 20.8%, respectively.

Acknowledgment. This work is supported by the National Key R&D Program of China (No. 2023YFB2904400), the Xiongan New Area Science and Technology Innovation Project (No. W25I00020), Nature and Science Foundation of China (No. 62394321, 62072030, 92167204).

References

1. Wang, Y., et al.: A survey on metaverse: fundamentals, security, and privacy. IEEE Commun. Surv. Tutorials **25**(1), 319–352 (2023)
2. Bourke, P.: Data formats: 3D, audio, image (2024). https://paulbourke.net/dataformats/
3. Han, B., Liu, Y., Qian, F.: Vivo: visibility-aware mobile volumetric video streaming. In: Proceedings of the 26th Annual International Conference on Mobile Computing and Networking, ser. MobiCom 2020. Association for Computing Machinery, New York, NY, USA (2020). https://doi.org/10.1145/3372224.3380888
4. Lee, K., Yi, J., Lee, Y., Choi, S., Kim, Y.M.: GROOT: a real-time streaming system of high-fidelity volumetric videos. In: Proceedings of the 26th Annual International Conference on Mobile Computing and Networking, ser. MobiCom 2020. Association for Computing Machinery, New York, NY, USA (2020). https://doi.org/10.1145/3372224.3419214
5. "Draco," Google (2022). https://github.com/google/draco
6. Yang, M., Luo, Z., Hu, M., Chen, M., Wu, D.: A comparative measurement study of point cloud-based volumetric video codecs. IEEE Trans. Broadcast. **69**(3), 715–726 (2023)
7. Mildenhall, B., Srinivasan, P.P., Tancik, M., Barron, J.T., Ramamoorthi, R., Ng, R.: NeRF: representing scenes as neural radiance fields for view synthesis. Commun. ACM **65**(1), 99–106 (2021). https://doi.org/10.1145/3503250
8. Zhao, J., Allison, R.S., Vinnikov, M., Jennings, S.: Estimating the motion-to-photon latency in head mounted displays. IEEE Virtual Reality (VR) **2017**, 313–314 (2017)
9. Finn, N.: Introduction to time-sensitive networking. IEEE Commun. Stand. Mag. **2**(2), 22–28 (2018)
10. Nasrallah, A., et al.: Ultra-low latency (ULL) networks: the IEEE TSN and IETF DetNet standards and related 5G ULL research. IEEE Commun. Sur. Tutorials **21**(1), 88–145 (2019)
11. Huang, Y., Zhu, Y., Qiao, X., Su, X., Dustdar, S., Zhang, P.: Toward holographic video communications: a promising AI-driven solution. IEEE Commun. Mag. **60**(11), 82–88 (2022)
12. Huang, X., et al.: DT-CNST: deterministic transmission based on computing-network-storage resources tradeoff for real-time holographic-type communication. IEEE Trans. Netw. Sci. Eng. (2025). https://doi.org/10.1109/TNSE.2025.3573287

A Docker Container-Based Dynamic Allocation System for Computational Resources

Ruijie Yao[1], Maolin Liu[2], Sudong Jiang[2], Kun Yang[1], BoBo Ju[1], Zengwen Li[2(✉)], and Liang Song[1(✉)]

[1] Academy for Engineering and Technology, Fudan University, Shanghai 200433, China
{yaorj20,kunyang20,songl}@fudan.edu.cn, bbju21@m.fudan.edu.cn
[2] Chongqing Changan Automobile Co., Ltd., Chongqing 401133, China
{liuml,jiangsd,lizw}@changan.com.cn

Abstract. As data scale and computation demand increase, traditional centralized computing are facing several challenges. Distributed computing and edge computing in particular handle those problems by extending computation to the network edge, allowing faster data processing and instant responses. A centralized platform is important for efficient task scheduling, resource allocation and system stability. In this study, we propose a Docker container-based dynamic resource allocation system designed to communicate between server and multiple clients. The system enables task transmission and real-time resource monitoring across clients. A dynamic allocation algorithm is applied to computation tasks such as model training and inference. The performance is evaluated by three metrics. Experiments show that the algorithm significantly reduces task latency, improves resource utilization, and achieves a more balanced load distribution. The findings highlight the potential for further development and application of dynamic resource allocation algorithms in computation platforms.

Keywords: Dynamic resource allocation · Docker container · Edge computing

1 Introduction

As computing needs grow, tasks get larger. Old centralized computing often hits limits and slowdowns. Distributed computing is one way to solve this. It splits big data and big tasks across many nodes, like in cloud and edge systems. Edge computing puts compute and data processing near the data source. This gives faster response and better real-time response. It also decrease network delay and reduces network traffic. It can improve system performance.

Z. Lin et al. (Eds.): INSAI 2025, CCIS 2894, pp. 138–152, 2026.
https://doi.org/10.1007/978-981-95-9299-9_11

For example, in car-to-mobile device collaboration, intelligent vehicles gather data through sensors and cameras, requiring instant processing to meet low-latency demands. Remote servers and large computation nodes often introduce significant transmission and queuing delays, while the vehicle's onboard computational capacity is limited. A distributed system can address this by offloading a portion of computational tasks to nearby mobile devices—such as laptops and phones connected to the vehicle—thereby alleviating the vehicle's computational load and improving overall system efficiency. Moreover, by means of the wireless communication between mobile devices and the vehicle, real-time data transmission and interface are enabled, allowing cars acquire and process information faster and improve the stability and security of the autonomous driving system.

To fully and securely utilize the surplus computational resources of computing devices, it is essential to leverage container virtualization technology. Virtualization is one of the key technologies in distributed and cloud computing; most cloud-based systems are built on virtualization [1]. Docker is a container-based virtualization technology used for developing various types of multi-cloud distributed systems. It divides the resource of a physical server into multiple virtual instances, also allowing for isolated resource management, where multiple applications can run simultaneously on the same physical device. The flexibility allows systems to dynamically adjust resource allocation based on workload differences, enhancing scalability and performance. While Docker is mostly focused on software development, it pays less attention to resource control in container-based environments.

In addition to virtualization, edge computing requires a robust computing platform. A centralized platform is needed to receive and allocate tasks to multiple nodes, as well as to manage resources. The platform should be able to effectively schedule and allocate tasks, ensuring completion in time, and provide unified management of resources, such as resource scheduling and load balancing. Consequently, the computing platform is critical to edge computing, which encourages the advancement and application of edge computing technologies.

Edge computing can meet today's computing needs, but large distributed platforms struggle with resource management. Heterogeneity in node hardware (e.g., CPU/memory capabilities) and network latency make effective resource allocation difficult. Task scheduling, load balancing, and data transmission further limit system performance.

This paper proposes a Docker based platform for heterogeneous automotive devices, composed of a server and clients. Each client (one per container) monitors real-time resource status, receives tasks, executes them and returns results after completion. On the other hand, the server collects resource data, stores it in Redis, pre-allocates containers, assigns tasks with parameters, dynamically adjusts container resources using an allocation algorithm, and aggregates results. Compared with Kubernetes, the platform is lighter and easier to deploy.

We conducted experiments with multiple scenarios to evaluate resource utilization rate, average execution latency, and task completion count over time. Results show that a scheduling algorithm with dynamic allocation handles high-concurrency workloads better than static strategies, which can respond faster and complete more tasks, even when available resources fluctuate.

The structure of the remaining sections of the paper is as follows: Sect. 2 will explain the technical background and current research related to the system. Section 3 will elaborate on the specific design and implementation of the system. Section 4 will detail the experimental methodology. Section 5 will present the experimental results and corresponding analysis. Finally, Sect. 6 will summarize and outline future work.

2   Related Work

2.1   Docker Container

As said in the introduction, virtualization provides a platform that can run various services on different operating systems in the cloud. It enables the existence of multiple virtual machines on a single physical machine. The demand for low-cost virtualization technologies is rapidly increasing. Among lightweight virtualization technologies, Docker stands out as an open-source platform. This technology enables developers and system administrators to build, create, and run applications using the Docker engine [2].

The client component of this system is written in Python and is primarily responsible for implementing specific functions or services. The server is deployed on the Windows Subsystem for Linux (WSL2) platform with Docker on a Windows operating system. WSL2 provides support for a Linux environment, enabling lightweight and convenient Docker container operation on Windows without the need to build a full virtual machine containing an entire operating system, thus significantly reducing resource requirements and waste. After configuring the project files, the client builds an image file with the required dependencies and configurations through Docker. After setting the configurations, multiple containers can be launched simultaneously, where each one can offer various services or functions. The server then retrieves resource information for each container, through its built-in commands. The methodology is simple and benefits fast deployment and management of the system.

2.2   Redis Database

Redis, developed by Salvatore Sanfilippo, is a highly advanced and open-source key-value storage system and is one of the fastest in-memory databases. Redis supports high read and write options. Unlike other NoSQL databases, Redis is also a data structure server, as it offers a wide range of data structures for key storage. These keys can contain strings, hashes, lists, sets, and sorted sets [3].

Moreover, the system is written in Python, which integrates well with Redis. Redis-py provides a simple yet powerful interface for communication and data manipulation between programs and the database, enabling fast and efficient data management and processing. Given Redis's speed and flexibility as a key-value storage system, coupled with Python's high adaptability, Redis is a reliable solution for managing the large volumes of data involved in real-time access to resource information from multiple clients.

2.3   Dynamic Allocation Strategy

Currently, most resource allocation algorithms are static and heuristic, such as the Min-Min algorithm [4] and genetic algorithms [5].

The core idea of the Min-Min algorithm is to minimize task waiting time by prioritizing tasks with the shortest expected completion time. Although this approach may lead to load imbalance across certain resources, it aims to minimize overall task completion time. This algorithm is often used as a heuristic method for large-scale task scheduling problems and can deliver good performance under specific conditions. Mocanu et al. designed a task scheduler on Hadoop using a genetic algorithm, where iterations of crossover, selection, and mutation operations on the task queue identify a queue combination with the maximum global average utilization, ensuring the shortest global execution time.

Another direction in algorithm research is auto-scaling algorithms [6]. These are service-level algorithms (SLAs) that adjust the number of computing instances according to predefined rules. The advantage of this approach is that it does not require pre-allocation; however, it also has limitations, such as the inability to share computational power between nodes, and it is unsuitable for certain computational tasks, as not all tasks can be arbitrarily split or remain independent. Overall, there are few algorithms available for fine-grained resource control of existing computing nodes. Additionally, many algorithms focus on task partitioning or addressing issues related to lower-level hardware, such as wireless communication and signal processing. For example, Bohge et al. proposed a dynamic resource allocation method in a wireless orthogonal frequency-division multiplexing system to optimize cross-layer strategies [7]. In summary, there are few existing algorithms focused on fine-grained resource control for computing nodes, and even fewer that explore dynamic resource allocation for computing units or virtual containers at the application layer.

D. Vengerov proposed a dynamic resource allocation system based on reinforcement learning and fuzzy rules, demonstrating stable performance improvements in Solaris 10 by dynamically migrating CPU and memory blocks to match randomly varying workloads in each resource partition, regardless of the presence or absence of resource migration costs [8]. Although machine learning algorithms show potential in resource prediction, they require extensive data for training and may introduce additional overhead during prediction.

However, the primary objective of this paper is not to develop algorithms but to design a system and validate its effectiveness. Therefore, a heuristic, lightweight strategy that is easy to deploy is a more suitable choice. The details of the strategy will be elaborated in the next section.

2.4 Kubernetes

Kubernetes, commonly known as K8s, is an open-source container orchestration system used for automating software deployment, scaling, and management. Kubernetes defines a series of modular components in its design structure to provide mechanisms that collectively support the deployment, maintenance, and scaling of applications. The components in Kubernetes are designed to be loosely coupled and extensible, enabling it to handle diverse workloads. Scalability is largely provided by the Kubernetes API, which is primarily used as an extension interface for internal components and the containers running on Kubernetes. Kubernetes follows a master-slave architecture, with its components divided into those managing individual nodes and those forming the control plane.

Recent research has advanced resource allocation and scheduling in Kubernetes, especially for elastic scaling and automation. Haibin Yuan's group proposed a time-series–based adaptive auto-scaling method that uses predictive scaling to reduce latency, stabilize service quality, and shorten cold starts [9]. Soongsil University researchers developed a traffic-prediction hybrid auto-scaling approach for Knative serverless edge computing, using Kubernetes operators and custom resources to adjust resources and concurrency; experiments showed better utilization and smooth Knative integration [10]. In conclusion, these studies emphasize the adaptive scaling for fluctuating workloads efficiently.

Despite Kubernetes' scalability and ecosystem, it undoubtedly has a steep learning curve to set up and considerable resource cost for beginners or simple deployments in particular. Complex configurations, continued maintenance and difficult troubleshooting across multiple components can make it feel overqualified, while scaling up increases security management demands.

To address these limitations, the proposed system streamlines configuration and operations to reduce the learning barrier and day-to-day overhead, meanwhile optimizing for smaller applications to lower resource usage. It also implements monitoring and log management to improve usability and support extension of containerized clusters.

3 System Design

The communication flow between the server and client are illustrated in Fig. 1. The following sections will provide a detailed explanation for each component.

The server primarily consists of two threads: information processing and dynamic allocation algorithms, with the specific workflow outlined as follows:

First, the server needs to acquire resource information from the containers and store this information in a Redis database. This resource information includes CPU usage, memory usage, and other metrics, which are essential for subsequent dynamic resource adjustment and monitoring.

Second, the server is responsible for constructing pre-allocated Docker containers. Based on the system's requirements and algorithmic rules, the server will configure a certain number of Docker containers for quick deployment and use in advance.

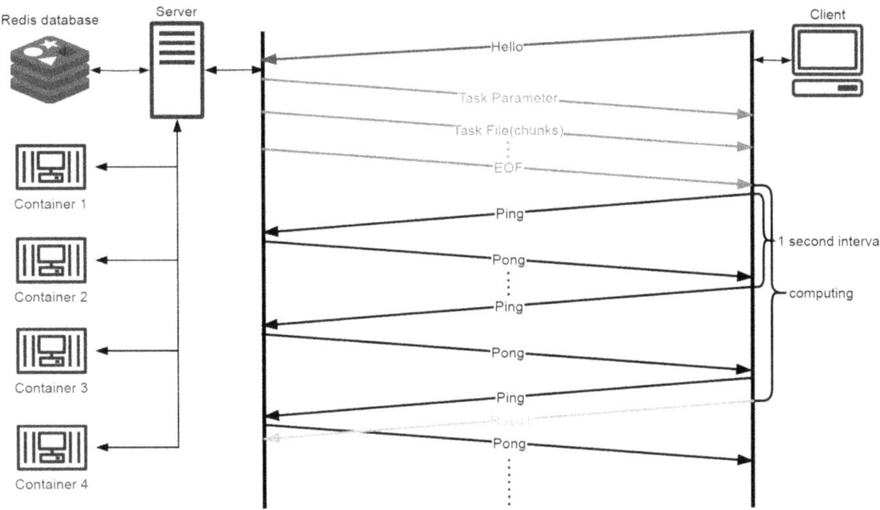

Fig. 1. System Design Diagram

Next, the server sends different tasks and parameter settings to various clients. Through communication with the clients, the server can transmit task files to the appropriate clients according to system needs for computation and processing.

Additionally, the server dynamically adjusts the resource allocation of the containers based on the dynamic allocation algorithm. By monitoring the system's operational status and resource utilization, the server can dynamically modify resource distribution to enhance system efficiency and optimize performance.

Finally, the server receives the computation results and integrates them for storage. Once the client completes the computational tasks and sends the results, the server will receive messages containing the result types and store the corresponding computation results and timing information in the system for subsequent data analysis and processing.

3.1   Data Processing

The server communicates with the containers using user datagram protocol (UDP) sockets, which is more suitable for this system compared to the transmission control protocol (TCP). UDP offers advantages such as connection-less communication, faster transmission speeds, and higher real-time performance. With only an 8-byte header, the connectionless nature results in lower network overhead. Given that the current system is relatively small and deployed within the same local area network, there are no strict requirements for the order of data transmission. In addition, UDP supports multicast and broadcast, ensuring the system's scalability.

Essentially, the server performs corresponding operations based on the prefixes of the received string messages, which can be categorized as follows:

"hello": This is a "handshake" message sent by the client. After receiving this message, the server acknowledges the client's ID, address, and port, and starts to send the task file in chunks.

"Ping": This message requests a reply from the server. The server then responds with "Ping" to the certain client, allowing it to calculate network delay, bandwidth, and other relevant information based on the time difference.

"delay": This message contains the current communication delay. The server then record the delay to the database. After processing the client information, the server uses Docker commands to read the container's CPU, total memory, current usage, and other metrics, which are then written to the Redis database along with the received delay.

"result": This message means the client has completed its task. The server then displays the computation results and time and stored them in the Redis database.

3.2 Pre-allocation and Parameter Configuration

By configuring the docker compose yml file, we can perform resource pre-allocation settings for each container in the system. In this file, we can specify key parameters, which are the image file used by each container, CPU limits, and memory constraints to ensure that the system can effectively utilize resources at runtime and meet the requirements of each container. Finally, we can start the container instance.

Additionally, we can further specify the hyperparameters for the tasks. These parameters include the input data for the task, algorithm parameter settings, and the output file save paths. By configuring these parameters properly, each container performs computations as expected and generates correct results.

3.3 Static Assignment Strategy

The system distributes computation tasks evenly across N nodes. Each node is allocated fixed computational resources. The task assignment strategies include three methods explained below:

Basic Assignment: Tasks are distributed in order and evenly among the nodes.

Random Assignment: Tasks are randomly assigned to the nodes.

Min-Min Algorithm: The current task is prioritized for assignment to the node that has previously completed tasks in the shortest total execution time.

By comparing these assignment strategies, we can know better about how different task distribution methods impact computation efficiency, thus providing a reference for optimizing task assignment and resource allocation.

3.4   Dynamic Allocation Strategy

We design an auto-scaling based algorithm to improve resource utilization efficiency in containerized environments. Containers operate as a process on the client host, where processes are competing to encroach on the resources the host has. So containers need to reduce resource usage if conflict happens. However, when host resource is again available, container will not automatically restore or to say, bounce back to its original resource level. This leads to monoatomic decrease in the resource a container can use.

To solve this problem, the proposed algorithm dynamically adjust its resource based on real-time host resource monitoring. As a result, containers scale up when resources are abundant and scale down adaptively under constrained conditions. It enhances overall efficiency and ensures system performance under dynamic load conditions.

3.5   Real-Time Retrieval of Client Information

The client information retrieved by the server is primarily divided into two parts: the latency messages sent by the client and the container resource information obtained through the Docker server. The latency messages have been discussed in the message processing section; here, we will detail the method for acquiring container resource information.

It is important to note that for virtualized containers, using the Python psutil library functions or reading CPU activity files within the container (such as cpuacct or cpu.stat) provides the CPU information of the physical host on which the container is running, rather than the information specific to the container itself. Therefore, using the built-in Docker command docker stats to obtain accurate container resource information is a preferable solution.

3.6   Redis Database

As shown in the Fig. 1, the server stores the real-time client information in key-value pairs in the previously created Redis database. This information is organized into three collections or lists: a set of currently online devices, the current resource information for each client, and the historical resource information for each client. It is important to note that the operation of writing information to the database should be performed using an asynchronous separate thread to avoid blocking communication between the socket and other clients.

3.7 Update Container Configurations

Using Python's built-in subprocess library to run the Docker command docker update allows for the updating of CPU and memory limits. The–cpus parameter can explicitly change the number of CPUs allocated to the client, and it conveniently accepts decimal values. It is also noteworthy that updating a container's configuration typically takes about 0.2 s. We do not consider the resource overhead and latency associated with configuration updates since the experiment scale is small. However, in scenarios that involves a large number of clients, it is necessary to reduce the frequency of allocations, increase the magnitude of each allocation, and minimize the resource overhead introduced by updating container configurations.

3.8 Client Functions

As illustrated in the flowchart, the client acts as a distributed computing node, with each client corresponding to a container that runs on a host. All hosts are connected to the server within the same local area network, communicating with the server through the TCP socket ports.

The client mainly implements four functions: providing real-time resource information for the container, receiving computation tasks, executing computation tasks with progress displayed, and returning computation results. The client first sends a "handshake" message to the server to inform its online status, after that it receives the tasks along with related parameters from the server.

The client then uses a dual-threading approach: one thread is responsible for executing the computation tasks using the given parameters and numbers of processes. The other thread is used to calculate latency information and send the results to the server. After all threads have completed their computation tasks, the client gathers the results and sends back to server. This design enables smooth task execution and prompt result transmission.

4 Experiments

4.1 Evaluation Metrics

This system is evaluated with three metrics:

Number of Completed Tasks: The total number of computation tasks executed within a specified time interval.

Computing Resource Utilization Rate: The utilization rate of available computing resources.

Average Execution Latency: The average completion latency of computation tasks.

The number of completed tasks means the total quantity of tasks executed by the client over a given time interval. The efficiency of computing resource utilization is calculated by the product of the number of CPU cores and the passed time, clearly reflecting the computing resources used by the system during task execution. Given that the sampling period is 1 s, the overall computing efficiency can be calculated using the following equation:

$$\eta = \frac{\sum_t C^t \cdot E^t}{\sum_t C^t} \tag{1}$$

where C represents the number of CPU cores, and E denotes the CPU utilization rate.

Application execution latency is the average duration from when the server receives each task results until it completes processing those results.

4.2   Experimental Setup

In this experiment, the system has a server and three clients, which were deployed on different hosts in a local network. We then pre-allocated resources for different clients to see the performance of various resource allocation algorithms across different tasks. Table 1 illustrates the detailed settings.

Table 1. Parameter Settings

Client	Cpu Cores	Memory(MB)	Operating System
client_1	5	1024	Windows 10 23H2
client_2	4	1024	macOS Sonoma 14.7
client_3	3	1024	Ubuntu 22.04

Parameter Settings Description:

Client: Different nodes used in the experiment, each configured with different computational resources to simulate diverse workload scenarios in real-world applications.

CPU Cores: The number of processor cores allocated to each client.

Memory: The amount of memory allocated to each client.

Operating System: The underlying operating system running on the client machine.

To observe the resource usage in different tasks, we chose a handwritten digit recognition task using the CIFAR-10 dataset, and then trained it with a Convolutional Neural Network (CNN). The model's training and inference phases are considered as two distinct tasks: inference phase and training plus inference one. Additionally, we simulate a dynamic resource environment where the total available resources fluctuate within a certain range, following a truncated normal distribution:

$$C^t \sim \mathcal{T}(N(C^0, 1), C^0 - 1, C^0 + 1) \tag{2}$$

where C represents the number of CPU cores, and E denotes the CPU utilization rate. Both static assignment and dynamic resource allocation strategies are applied in this environment.

Specifically, we compared four strategies. In the dynamic resource fluctuation environment described above, we first tested three static assignment strategies that do not incorporate auto-scaling, and found that the Min-Min strategy performed the best. Building upon this, we applied a dynamic strategy that combines the Min-Min static assignment with the auto-scaling algorithm we proposed, and compared its performance with the three static strategies. Through these configurations, the objectives of the experiment are to: (1) evaluate the performance of various resource allocation strategies under different client configurations; (2) examine the impact of CPU core count and memory configuration on task execution time and resource utilization; and (3) assess the scalability and performance stability of the system in a multi-client environment.

5   Results and Discussion

We developed a Docker-based interconnection platform for various vehicle heterogeneous devices, enabling communication between a server host and multiple client containers for task transmission and real-time resource information retrieval. Through the design of two scenarios and multiple evaluation metrics, and by applying a dynamic allocation algorithm in experiments, the results demonstrated significant advantages of the system. In inference tasks, the average execution time of the dynamic scheduling algorithm was 17.78 s, with a resource utilization rate of 87.31%, completing an average of 31.4 tasks within 3 min. In contrast, the average execution times for random and average assignment were 22.41 s (57.79% utilization) and 20.95 s (52.29% utilization), respectively. In the training and inference task scenario, the average execution time of the dynamic scheduling algorithm was 141.25 s, with a resource utilization rate of 88.64% and completing 12 tasks. Comparatively, the average execution times for random and average assignment were 292.99 s (50.13% utilization) and 294.30 s (53.04% utilization).

The table below shows the experimental results, which will be analyzed in detail (Table 2).

Table 2. Experiment Results

Inference Task (between 20 and 30 s)

metrics/ strategy	*Random*	*Average*	*Min-Min*	*Dynamic*
Average Execution Time(s)	22.41	20.95	23.01	17.78
Resource Utilization Rate	57.79%	52.29%	61.37%	87.31%
Number of tasks completed in 3 min	26.26	26.63	27.54	31.4
Training and Inference Task				
Average Execution Time(s)	292.99	294.3	298.15	141.25
Resource Utilization Rate	50.13%	53.04%	61.39%	88.64%
Number of tasks completed in 15 min	8.14	7.98	8.31	12.00

5.1   Performance of Four Strategies in Inference Tasks

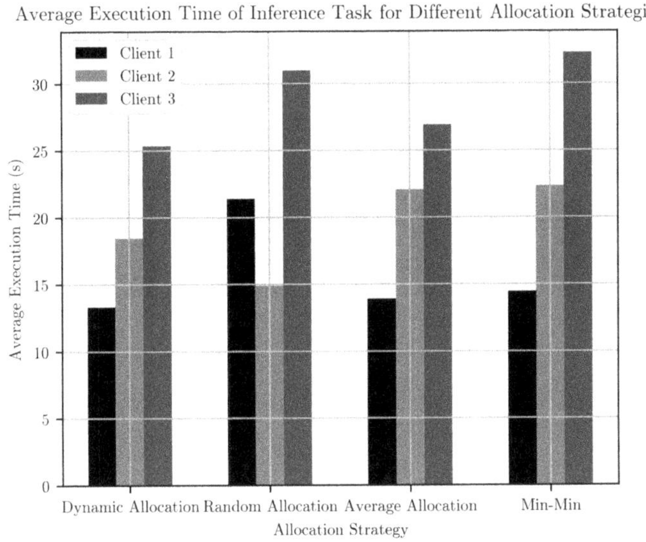

Fig. 2. Average Execution Time of Inference Task Comparison Across Clients for Different Allocation Strategies

Dynamic scheduling: The execution time distribution for Client 1 is relatively stable from 10.58 s to 16.74 s, meaning that the algorithm can balance execution times across different tasks. Client 2 has a longer execution time but overall it still demonstrates the effectiveness of dynamic scheduling when meeting varying workloads (Fig. 2).

Random assignment: Client 1 is much slower, about 15.9 s to 27.42 s. Client 2 and Client 3 also go up and down a lot. This means random choice can waste resources and make the load uneven.

Average assignment: Client 1 and Client 2 show lower execution times, indicating that this strategy can balance the workload and keep efficient at the same time. However, Client 3 got higher execution times, especially as task volumes increase, which may turn into bottlenecks.

For Min-Min assignment, the execution times for Client 1 and 2 are consistent, ranging from 13.35 s to 16.42 s and 22.5 s to 27.61 s, respectively, reflecting the effectiveness of the algorithm in prioritizing shorter tasks (Fig. 3).

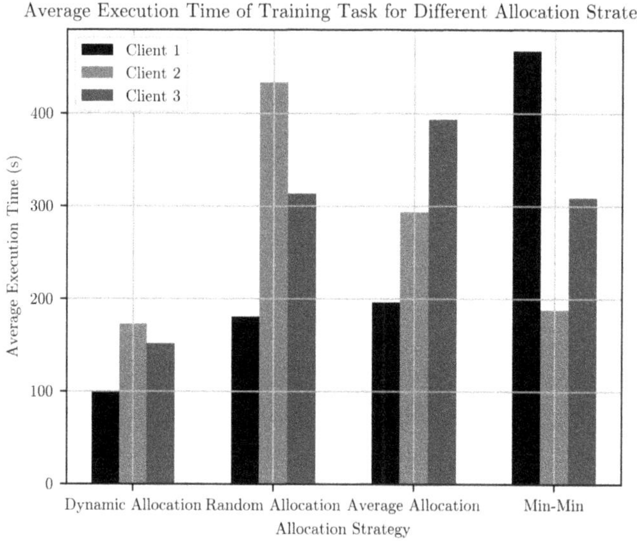

Fig. 3. Average Execution Time of Training Task Comparison Across Clients for Different Allocation Strategies

5.2   Performance of Four Strategies in Training Tasks

Dynamic Scheduling improves performance largely, we can see it from Client 1 with a minimum execution time of 48.97 s. All clients demonstrate a reasonable level of balance. This flexibility allows dynamic scheduling to maintain good resource utilization even with large-scale tasks.

Random Assignment: The task execution times fluctuate a lot, indicating that resource scheduling is not balanced.

Min-Min and Average Assignment: Client 1 shows higher execution times, suggesting that these strategies may be less flexible than dynamic scheduling under high-load conditions. However, for Clients 2 and 3, the task execution time distribution is better with the Min-Min strategy, despite the fact that overall performance is still worse than that of dynamic scheduling.

In all, dynamic scheduling exhibits high efficiency and stability in both inference and training tasks, effectively handling task scheduling under different load conditions. While the random assignment strategy is simple, it underperforms in both efficiency and resource utilization. The Min-Min and average assignment strategies can offer good performance in some cases, but when encountering with complex and high-load tasks, the advantages of dynamic scheduling are more obvious.

5.3   Summary of Results

The results shows clear differences in resource utilization across various strategies. The dynamic scheduling strategy has the highest resource utilization rates (87.31% and 88.64%). It shows its effectiveness when monitoring task loads and adjusting resource allocation to minimize idle time. The flexibility is crucial for handling tasks with load fluctuations.

Speaking of inference tasks, the dynamic scheduling algorithm is the fastest. For combined training and inference tasks, dynamic scheduling also showed high efficiency, with only 141.25 s, which means that it can better adapt to different task and ensure fast responsiveness.

Dynamic scheduling also finishes the most tasks in the same time, achieving an average of 31.4 tasks in inference and 12 tasks in training plus inference tasks. It shows the advantages of dynamic scheduling in handling high-concurrency tasks. This proves it handles many tasks at once better. It finds free resources fast and uses them properly, also when task numbers go up and down.

6   Conclusion

This study builds a distributed system for dynamic resource allocation. It uses Docker, Redis, and Python. A server talks with different client containers. It sends tasks and collects real-time resource information. We designed the model training and inference tasks, conducted experiments using different allocation algorithms and evaluated the results using three metrics. The results indicate that the algorithm significantly reduces computation latency, increases resource utilization efficiency, and balances system load. Those findings support further research and the application of dynamic allocation algorithms in computing platforms.

Acknowledgments. This work is supported by the Joint Lab. on Networked AI Edge Computing Fudan University-Changan.

Disclosure of Interests. The authors have no competing interests to declare that are relevant to the content of this article.

References

1. Naik, N.: Docker container-based big data processing system in multiple clouds for everyone. In: IEEE International Systems Engineering Symposium (ISSE), Vienna, Austria 2017, pp. 1–7 (2017)
2. Potdar, A.M., Narayan, D.G., Kengond, S., Mulla, M.M.: Performance evaluation of docker container and virtual machine. Procedia Comput. Sci. **171**, 1419–1428 (2020)
3. Srivastava, P.P., Goyal, S., Kumar, A.: Analysis of various NoSQL database. In: 2015 International Conference on Green Computing and Internet of Things (ICG-CIoT), Noida, India, pp. 539–544, October 2015
4. Etminani, K., Naghibzadeh, M.: A min-min max-min selective algorithm for grid task scheduling. In: 2007 3rd IEEE/IFIP International Conference in Central Asia on Internet, Tashkent, Uzbekistan, pp. 1–7, September 2007
5. Mocanu, E.M., Florea, M., Andreica, M.T., et al.: Cloud computing task scheduling based on genetic algorithm. In: 2012 IEEE International Systems Conference (SysCon), Vancouver, BC, Canada, pp. 1–6, March 2012
6. Mao, M., Li, J., Humphrey, M.: Cloud auto-scaling with deadline and budget constraints. In: 2010 11th IEEE/ACM International Conference on Grid Computing, Brussels, Belgium, pp. 41–48, October 2010
7. Bohge, M., Gross, J., Wolisz, A., Meyer, M.: Dynamic resource allocation in OFDM systems: an overview of cross-layer optimization principles and techniques. IEEE Netw. **21**(1), 53–59 (2007)
8. Vengerov, D.: A reinforcement learning approach to dynamic resource allocation. Eng. Appl. Artif. Intell. **20**(3), 383–390 (2007)
9. Yuan, H., Liao, S.: A time series-based approach to elastic Kubernetes scaling. Electronics **13**(285) (2024)
10. Tran, M.N., Kim, Y.: Optimized resource usage with hybrid auto-scaling system for Knative serverless edge computing. Future Gener. Comput. Syst. **152**, 304–316 (2024)

CmpV2X: Enabling Communication-efficient and Robust Cooperative Perception for Internet-of-Vehicles

Kun Yang[1], Maolin Liu[2], Sudong Jiang[2], Ruijie Yao[1], Bobo Ju[1], Zengwen Li[2(✉)], and Liang Song[1(✉)]

[1] Academy for Engineering & Technology, Fudan University, Shanghai, China
{kunyang20,yaorj20,songl}@fudan.edu.cn, bbju21@m.fudan.edu.cn
[2] Chongqing Changan Automobile Co., Ltd., Chongqing 401133, China
{liuml,jiangsd,lizw}@changan.com.cn

Abstract. As a promising multi-agent perception paradigm, feature-level cooperative perception has attracted widespread attention due to its enhancement of the perception capabilities of autonomous vehicles. However, existing solutions invariably ignore the heterogeneity in computational resources and local features among diverse agents, resulting in sub-optimal collaboration performance. In this paper, we propose CmpV2X, a communication-efficient and robust multi-agent perception system designed to address resource allocation and feature fusion challenges in dynamic Internet of Vehicles (IoV) scenarios. Specifically, we first introduce a resource-guided model selection method that dynamically select perception models according to the computational resources of agents to meet latency requirements. Second, we propose a three-stage communication scheme that leverages confidence maps to select agents for collaboration, enabling efficient communication based on data importance. Finally, an inter-agent domain adaptation and feature fusion module is presented to mitigate data heterogeneity among agents and achieve robust information aggregation. With existing cooperative perception datasets, we simulate dynamic IoV scenarios where agents adopt different perception models and exhibit varying computational resources. Extensive experiments demonstrate that CmpV2X significantly improves collaborative 3D object detection performance and improves average resource utilization compared to state-of-the-art methods.

Keywords: Internet of Vehicles · cooperative perception · resource scheduling · task offloading

1 Introduction

With the rapid development of vehicular communication technology, intelligent transportation systems (ITS) have emerged as a promising computational paradigm to enhance traffic efficiency [1–5]. However, these onboard ITS applications [6–11], such as vehicle-side large language models (LLM) and cooperative perception [12–16], require substantial computation resources and have strict latency demands. In this context, individual vehicles struggle to support such applications due to their limited computational and storage capacities. Although mobile cloud computing (MCC) has been proposed to alleviate the resource constraints of vehicle nodes by offloading computing tasks to cloud servers, transferring large amounts of data can result in significant transmission delays. Moreover, unstable network conditions can also affect the offloading effectiveness.

In such cases, vehicular edge computing (VEC) is employed to support onboard artificial intelligence applications. Specifically, autonomous vehicles on the road and road-side infrastructures are interconnected through vehicular communication channels like Vehicle-to-Everything (V2X), allowing vehicles to offload their computing tasks to other connected intelligent nodes to alleviate their resource shortages. Compared to the MCC paradigm, the VEC paradigm significantly reduces the communication distance to offloading nodes and fully utilizes the surrounding idle resources, thereby lowering communication latency and enhancing resource utilization efficiency.

In addition to the aforementioned progress, to meet the QoS requirements of AI applications and enhance resource utilization efficiency, the VEC computational paradigm still faces several challenges. Specifically, the main challenge is how to efficiently schedule computational and communication resources in a heterogeneous, interconnected vehicular network environment. To more specifically analyze the challenges faced by the VEC paradigm in the vehicular network environment, we select a representative multi-agent application, cooperative perception, as the supported onboard AI application. Specifically, in cooperative perception applications, vehicles enhance the perception range of individual vehicles and overcome occlusion issues by sharing their sensory data. Depending on the type of shared data, cooperative perception is divided into early, middle, and late perception fusion, where the transmitted data are raw sensor data, extracted intermediate Bird's Eye View (BEV) feature maps, and final detection results, respectively. We choose mid-fusion cooperative perception, which achieves a better performance-communication trade-off, as the application scenario.

In the process of using the VEC computational paradigm to support mid-fusion cooperative perception, we face three main challenges: data heterogeneity, resource heterogeneity, and model heterogeneity.

Data Heterogeneity. In cooperative perception, collaborating intelligent agent nodes are divided into ego agents and collaborators. Collaborators transmit their intermediate BEV features to the ego agent via V2X channels to enhance perception performance. During this process, due to the different spatial positions of collaborators, the quality of complementary perception data provided to the ego agent by each collaborator node varies significantly. Some nodes, which can supplement the perception data lacking in the ego agent, possess higher data quality, while others fail to provide sufficient performance gains. In this case, it is necessary to assess the quality of perception data provided by each node,

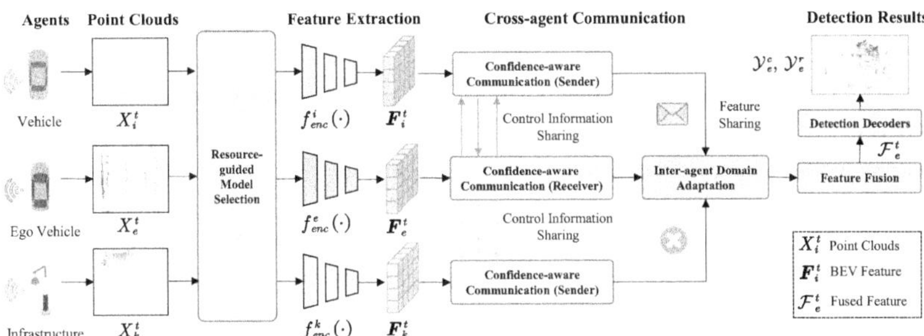

Fig. 1. Overall architecture of the proposed CmpV2X. Each agent i initially utilizes a Resource-guided Model Selection strategy to choose a local feature encoder to extract BEV features F_i^t. Subsequently, through the Confidence-aware Communication Scheme, collaborators and ego agent e exchange control information and prune redundant communication links. Upon receiving BEV features sent by collaborators, the ego agent employs the Inter-agent Domain Adaptation module to align feature resolutions and data distributions, and fuses the collaborator-shared features to output feature $\mathcal{F}_e^t$. Detection decoders then decode $\mathcal{F}_e^t$ into the final prediction results $\{\mathcal{Y}_e^c, \mathcal{Y}_e^r\}$.

thereby prioritizing the transmission of data with higher importance and stopping the transmission of low-quality data. This node selection mechanism based on data quality can efficiently utilize communication resources.

Resource Heterogeneity. At the resource level, different intelligent agent nodes (*e.g.*, autonomous vehicles and roadside infrastructure) often possess vastly different computing resources; some have powerful GPUs, while others can only use lower-end GPU chips. In this scenario, the processing time for different nodes to obtain BEV feature maps from raw perception data varies significantly. However, to meet the real-time requirements of autonomous driving, cooperative perception has strict latency demands, such as 100ms [13]. To address this, we propose selecting perception models with suitable resolutions based on the heterogeneous computational resources of the nodes, thereby adaptively adjusting the execution time of applications to meet latency requirements. This is because we find that by reducing the resolution of intermediate feature maps, the computational resource demand can be effectively lowered, thus shortening the application's execution time.

Model Heterogeneity. As mentioned, different intelligent agent nodes often use different perception models to obtain intermediate feature maps and transmit them to the ego agent for integrating perception information. In this process, the heterogeneous perception models cause significant domain differences in the resolution and data distribution of the intermediate feature maps. Existing feature fusion methods [17] invariably assume that different intelligent agent nodes use the same perception model to obtain intermediate feature maps, thus are not suitable for our heterogeneous interconnected vehicular network environment. Therefore, we need to design a domain adaptation component for heterogeneous perception among agents to unify the resolution of feature maps and bridge the data distribution of feature maps.

Inspired by the observations above, we design a communication-efficient and robust multi-agent perception system to address resource scheduling issues in scenarios involving interconnected heterogeneous devices. In brief, our design aims to address the three challenges outlined above to enhance the perception accuracy and resource utilization efficiency in cooperative perception applications. Specifically, **(i)** we propose a resource-guided model selection strategy based on the resources of intelligent agent nodes, ensuring that applications complete within a specified delay requirement through this adaptive model selection strategy. **(ii)** We utilize confidence maps provided by each agent to determine the importance of the agent's data. This confidence-aware communication scheme selects participating intelligent agent nodes and prunes redundant communication links, significantly enhancing communication efficiency. **(iii)** Subsequently, we demonstrate an Inter-agent Domain Adaptation (IDA) module to adapt collaborator features to ego domains and bridge domain gaps with an adversarial learning philosophy. A prior-guided feature resizer is used to align feature resolutions, and a domain aligner mitigates the data distribution discrepancies between features from distinct agents. The main contributions are as follows:

- We propose a communication-efficient and robust multi-agent perception system to resolve resource scheduling issues in heterogeneous scenarios. Through model and node selection strategies, our framework avoids excessive execution times and redundant transmissions, thereby significantly enhancing resource utilization efficiency while ensuring application execution.
- To address uneven data distribution among different intelligent agent nodes, we introduced the IDA module for domain adaptation between nodes. We first use prior information to align the resolution of different feature maps and employ a domain aligner to overcome domain discrepancies.
- To evaluate the performance of our framework and validate its effectiveness, we conducted extensive simulation tests and ablation experiments. We simulate a heterogeneous interconnected environment and utilize existing cooperative perception datasets to assess the accuracy of applications. Results demonstrate that our method achieves the state-of-the-art collaborative 3D object detection performance, while significantly enhancing resource utilization efficiency.

2   Related Work

As a promising application of the multi-agent system, cooperative perception aims to enhance perception capabilities by fusing visual information from nearby agents. The existing studies consist of three categories. (i) Early collaboration [18] where raw sensor data (*e.g.*, LiDAR point clouds, and RGB images) is transmitted. (ii) Intermediate collaboration [13,17,19] where feature maps are extracted from local sensor data and shared. (iii) Late collaboration [2] where agents transfer the prediction results of local observation. Recently, more mainstream works adopted the intermediate collaboration paradigm due to its advantages in balancing bandwidth consumption and detection accuracy. Specifically, F-Cooper [20] employs a maxout fusion strategy, and When2com [21] devises a three-phase handshake communication protocol. V2VNet [22] aggregates feature maps via a graph model, while Disconet [23] learns the fusion weights using a teacher-student network. Subsequently, V2X-ViT [13] derives a visual transformer to enhance the robustness of feature fusion to noises. CoBEVT [19] utilizes axial attention to aggregate sparse spatial information. Then, Where2comm [17] proposes a spatial filtering-based communication mechanism to save bandwidth. In addition, some approaches [24] explore flexible region partitioning under early collaboration, and many late collaboration methods [25] propose latency compensation and feature alignment methods to handle noises. Unlike the above intermediate collaboration efforts, we consider the domain gap between agents caused by sensor type and detector heterogeneity and design the corresponding domain adaptation module.

3   System Architecture and Problem Formulation

In this section, we will introduce the system architecture of CmpV2X presented in Fig. 1 and formulate the problems.

3.1   System Architecture

To balance detection accuracy and response latency in mult-agent perception, we adopt the feature-level intermediate collaboration paradigm [12] where each agent shares Bird's Eye View (BEV) features extracted from local sensor data via a V2X channel. Following existing literature [13], one of the connected on-road agents is identified as the ego agent to construct a communication graph, where nodes denote collaborators within the communication range, and edges represent direct V2X connections. In the initial phase of collaboration, the ego agent broadcasts its metadata, including pose and extrinsic, to synchronize the agents' coordinate system. Specifically, the collaborators obtain the transformation matrix based on the received metadata and project their point clouds to the ego coordinate system before feature extraction. Note that the latency caused by metadata transmission is negligible.

Then, as Fig. 1 shows, each agent adopts the resource-guided model selection strategy to select a local 3D detector and extract the BEV feature from the projected point clouds. Given the point cloud $\boldsymbol{X}_i^t$ of i-th agent under timestamp t, the corresponding feature is $\boldsymbol{F}_i^t = f_{enc}^i(\boldsymbol{X}_i^t) \in \mathbb{R}^{C_i \times H_i \times W_i}$, where $f_{enc}^i(\cdot)$ denote the 3D detector (*e.g.*, PointPillar [26], VoxelNet [27]), and C_i, H_i, W_i stand for the channel, height, and width, respectively. The subsequent collaboration process consists of the following two stages.

Cross-agent Communication. Firstly, the ego agent and collaborators exchange control information to allocate bandwidth through our proposed confidence-aware communication scheme. In this process, the ego agent collects the collaborators' confidence maps that express the features' spatial importance and selects the collaborators which can provide significant performance gains. After that, the ego agent directs the selected collaborators to transmit local features $\boldsymbol{F}_i^t$. Here, we consider a general V2X channel model where the transmission time is slotted, and each agent's bandwidth within a slot is constant.

Feature Fusion. Upon receiving the feature $\boldsymbol{F}_i^t$ from collaborators, the ego agent utilizes the inter-agent domain adaptation module to bridge the data distribution discrepancies between the ego and collaborator features. Afterward, the feature fusion module is employed to extract essential perceptual information from the shared features to obtain enhanced ego feature $\mathcal{F}_e^t$, which is decoded into the prediction results $\{\mathcal{Y}_e^c, \mathcal{Y}_e^r\}$ via the detection decoders.

3.2   Problem Formulation

In this paper, our primary goal is to develop a communication-efficient and noise-robust cooperative perception system to enhance the perception capability of the ego agent. As shown in Fig. 1, the proposed CmpV2X can accommodate diverse agents (*e.g.*, infrastructures, and CAVs) and heterogeneous 3D detectors, thus being more adaptable to real-world autonomous driving scenarios. Mathematically, consider a driving scenario with one ego agent e and N collaborators, let $\boldsymbol{F}_i^t$ and $\boldsymbol{Y}_i^t$ denote the BEV feature and the corresponding ground truth of i-th agent at timestamp t. Moreover, the real-time requirement (*i.e.*, maximum response latency) of the autonomous driving applications is set as T_{delay}, the time length of the V2X channel slot is T_{slot}, and the bandwidth of the ego agent at timestep t is B_e^t. Accordingly, to accomplish real-time multi-agent perception, the link capacity of the ego agent is constrained to $\boldsymbol{B}_e = (T_{slot} - T_1) * B_e^t$, where T_1 represents the latency consumed by feature extraction, control information sharing, and feature fusion. In this case, the objective of CmpV2X is to maximize the 3D detection precision of the ego agent under the communication budget $\boldsymbol{B}_e$, which is formulated as an optimization function of $\boldsymbol{B}_e$:

$$f(\boldsymbol{B}_e) = \arg\max_{\theta, \boldsymbol{F}_i} \sum_i^N \eth(\Psi_\theta(\boldsymbol{F}_e^t, \{\boldsymbol{F}_i^t\}_{i=1}^N), \boldsymbol{Y}_e), \tag{1}$$

$$\text{s.t.} \sum_i |\boldsymbol{F}_i^t| \leq \boldsymbol{B}_e, \tag{2}$$

where $\eth(\cdot, \cdot)$ denotes the 3D detection validation metric and $\Psi_\theta(\cdot)$ is a multi-agent perception system with θ as its learnable parameter. $\boldsymbol{F}_i^t$ denotes the feature transmitted from the i-th agent to the ego agent at timestamp t.

4   Methodology

This section presents the proposed CmpV2X, a communication-efficient and robust multi-agent perception system. As illustrated in Fig. 1, CmpV2X comprises three main modules: Resource-guided Model Selection (RMS), Confidence-aware Communication Scheme (CCS), and Inter-agent Domain Adaptation (IDA). Specifically, the RMS module adaptively selects perception models based on the dynamic computational resource status of nodes. The CCS component provides an efficient feature sharing mode and prunes redundant communication links between agents. Upon receiving BEV feature maps with varying resolutions, the IDA component bridges the domain gap between ego and collaborator features. The remainder of Sect. 4 provides a detailed introduction to these three critical components.

4.1 Resource-Guided Model Selection

In heterogeneous interconnected vehicular network scenarios, the execution time for different intelligent agent nodes to extract BEV features shows significant variation due to heterogeneous computational resources. However, cooperative perception applications have strict latency demands, requiring each node to extract BEV features within a specified time. In this context, we propose a resource-guided model selection (RMS) strategy that selects an appropriate perception model based on the node's computational resources and latency requirements.

The total application execution time includes the computation time to extract BEV features and the communication time to transmit these features to the ego agent. Assume each intelligent agent node has m perception models, with computational demands from D_1 to D_m FLOPs and corresponding resolutions for the BEV feature maps from R_1 to R_m. Within each cooperation cycle, we use the node's internal resource monitoring module to assess the current computational capability E_{exe}. For each perception model, the corresponding computation time is $\frac{D_m}{E_{exe}}$, recorded as T_1 to T_m. Subsequently, for a BEV feature map with resolution R_m, the total communication data volume is $\frac{R_m \times C \times 32}{8}$, where C represents the number of channels in the BEV feature map, 32 indicates the use of float32 data format, and 8 is the divisor because we use bytes as a metric. Thus, the communication time can be expressed as $\frac{R_m \times C \times 4}{B_e}$, where $\boldsymbol{B}_e$ represents the collaborator's communication bandwidth.

After obtaining the computation and communication times for each model, we calculate the total application execution time. Assuming the latency requirement for the autonomous driving application is set at T_{delay}, we select the model that satisfies the latency demand as the perception model for the current intelligent agent node. Since the node's computational and communication resources are dynamically changing, we perform the selection process described above before each collaboration cycle to choose the model that best meets the latency requirements. Overall, by predicting computation and communication times for perception models, we ensure that the cooperative perception application completes within the stipulated latency requirements.

Algorithm 1: Overall Workflow of the CCS Module

   Input   : Communication Budget $\boldsymbol{B}_e$, BEV Features
$$\{\boldsymbol{F}_i^t \in \mathbb{R}^{C_i \times H_i \times W_i} \mid i \in e, 1, ..., N\}$$

1 Ego agent e broadcast `Request` message;

2 # Each collaborator processes independently

3 for *each collaborator* $i = 1, 2, ..., N$ **do**

4 $S_i^t = \text{MaxPool}(f_{dec}^{i,c}(\boldsymbol{F}_i^t)) \in \mathbb{R}^{H_i \times W_i}$;

5   Transmit S_i^t to the ego agent;

6 # For ego agent

7 $S_e^t = \text{MaxPool}(f_{dec}^{e,c}(\boldsymbol{F}_e^t)) \in \mathbb{R}^{H_e \times W_e}$;

8 Get resized $\boldsymbol{S}_{all}^t = \{S_i^t \in \mathbb{R}^{H_e \times W_e} \mid i \in e, 1, ..., N\}$;

9 $\boldsymbol{C}_i^t \in \mathbb{R}^{H_e \times W_e} \leftarrow (1 - S_e^t) \odot S_i^t$;

10 Send resized $\boldsymbol{C}_i^t \in \mathbb{R}^{H_i \times W_i}$ to the collaborator i;

11 # Each collaborator processes independently

12 for *each collaborator* $i = 1, 2, ..., N$ **do**

13   Calculate the number of grids in $\boldsymbol{C}_i^t$ where the values exceed δ_{com};

14   Calculate the proportion p_i^t of effective grids;

15   Transmit $\boldsymbol{F}_i^t$ to the ego agent if $p_i^t > \delta_{grid}$;

4.2 Confidence-Aware Communication Scheme

Utilizing the spatial confidence maps that reflect the perception importance level provided by collaborators, the proposed Confidence-aware Communication Scheme (CCS) aims to eliminate redundancy between agents and guide collaborators to transmit important feature maps. Existing space-filtered communication mechanisms [17] explore how to eliminate redundant perception information of collaborators relative to the ego agent. However, due to redundancy caused by perception overlap areas among collaborators, existing methods still lead to additional bandwidth consumption. To further reduce communication bandwidth, the CCS module reassigns confidence maps based on spatial correlations between collaborators to filter out nodes that cannot provide sufficient perception gain. Through this confidence-aware agent selection strategy, we achieve efficient multi-agent communication.

As shown in Algorithm 1, the ego agent first broadcasts a request message to request the collaborators' confidence maps, which are used to describe the perception importance level of each grid in the feature map. In detail, existing lidar-based object detection methods utilize a decoder to obtain a classification map of dimensions $2 \times H_i \times W_i$, describing the probability that each grid encompasses a foreground object. This is followed by generating confidence maps of dimensions $H_i \times W_i$ through the channel-wise max pooling operation. It is important to note that different agent nodes, due to variations in their detectors, have feature map resolutions H_i and W_i. The confidence map S_i^t is then sent to the ego agent.

Similarly, the ego agent uses channel-wise max pooling operation to obtain the ego confidence map S_e^t. Subsequently, we synchronize the coordinate systems of each confidence map using the pose information sent by collaborators and unify the size of confidence maps using bilinear interpolation. For each collaborator's confidence map S_i^t, we calculate the communication map $\boldsymbol{C}_i^t$ as $(1-S_e^t)\odot S_i^t$, reflecting the importance of each spatial location's perception data for the ego agent. The higher the values in $\boldsymbol{C}_i^t$, the more important that area's perception data is to the ego agent. We then resize $\boldsymbol{C}_i^t$ back to its previous dimensions and send it back to collaborator i.

Upon receiving $\boldsymbol{C}_i^t$, collaborator i counts the number of grids in $\boldsymbol{C}_i^t$ with values exceeding a threshold δ_{com}. If the proportion of effective grids exceeds the threshold δ_{grid}, it is considered that the current collaborator has sufficient performance gain for the ego agent, and thus sends the local BEV features to the ego agent. Otherwise, the collaborator will stop feature transmission to avoid unnecessary bandwidth waste. In brief, we use the confidence map to assess the importance of each collaborator's perception data for the ego agent and prune unimportant communication links based on this importance. This confidence-aware communication strategy significantly enhances the execution efficiency of the application through node selection.

4.3   Inter-Agent Domain Adaptation

Considering that the received intermediate feature maps exhibit heterogeneity in data distribution and resolution, existing feature fusion methods [1,19] fail to effectively merge these BEV features to produce the final detection results. To address this, we propose an Inter-agent Domain Adaptation (IDA) strategy to align the resolutions of different BEV feature maps and bridge the domain differences between them.

We first use bilinear interpolation to align the received collaborators' BEV features to a resolution of $H_e \times W_e$. However, simple interpolation methods only consider a limited receptive field and neglect meaningful spatial information. We introduce a deformable attention-based feature resizing mechanism, which has a larger receptive field to capture global information and adaptively aggregates object information through learned offsets. Specifically, for the features of each grid, we use a linear layer to learn N_{off} relative offsets to obtain sampling points, encompassing object information semantically related to the current grid. Another linear layer is then used to learn the attention scores for each sampling point to adaptively distribute the sampling weights. Given the sampling points and their respective attention scores, we obtain the enhanced features for the current grid through an attention mechanism. Considering the sparse nature of deformable attention, our proposed method achieves global enhancement and efficient feature resizing in a computation-efficient manner.

Subsequently, we employ adversarial training, similar to [28], to bridge the domain distribution differences between different features. Specifically, we use

Table 1. Performance comparison on the V2XSet and OPV2V datasets. The detection results are reported in AP@0.5/0.7. CRU and TRU represent the utilization rates of computational resources and transmission resources, respectively.

Model	V2XSet		OPV2V		Resource Utilization Rate (%)	
	AP@0.5	AP@0.7	AP@0.5	AP@0.7	CRU	TRU
No Fusion	60.60	40.20	68.71	48.66	15.3	0
Late Fusion	62.39	47.95	74.24	58.78	56.7	32.0
Early Fusion	61.58	44.31	70.16	50.45	38.5	94.3
AttFuse-Random	72.16	54.63	74.86	56.30	64.7	68.1
AttFuse-Fixed	69.68	52.71	73.56	53.72	58.7	66.2
Where2comm-Random	78.47	63.15	80.22	68.35	75.8	82.4
Where2comm-Fixed	76.24	64.70	79.36	67.52	70.3	80.5
CoBEVT-Random	70.20	55.34	77.35	63.42	74.8	69.2
CoBEVT-Fixed	72.49	58.50	76.62	65.11	80.3	73.6
CmpV2X (Ours)	**82.63**	**67.25**	**83.74**	**72.35**	**86.5**	**88.3**

a domain classifier to determine whether the feature maps originate from the source domain or the target domain. A domain classifier, composed of two convolutional layers, outputs a score where 0 indicates that the feature comes from the source domain, and 1 indicates that it originates from the target domain. Since our goal is to bridge the features of different domains, we utilize a gradient reversal layer to facilitate adversarial training, making it difficult for the domain classifier to determine the domain of the features. This method of adversarial training effectively bridges the features from different data distributions. Finally, we employ the feature fusion mechanism [12] to merge the features of collaborators standardized to the same size and output the final perception results.

5   Experiments

5.1   Experiment Setup

Implementation Details. We employ five computing nodes with heterogeneous GPU resources, serving as one ego agent and four collaborators. To simulate the dynamic variability of GPU resources, we use a normal distribution with a mean of 50% and a standard deviation of 20%. This setup allows for the GPU resources available for use to range between 30% and 70% of the total GPU resources. We explore three distinct point cloud 3D perception models to simulate agent nodes utilizing different models, including PointPillar [26], VoxelNet [27], and SECOND [29]. The proposed models are implemented using the PyTorch toolbox [30], and these models are trained on four Nvidia 4090Ti GPUs using the Adam optimizer [31]. The training hyperparameters are aligned with [12].

Datasets. We conduct extensive experiments on the simulated datasets, V2XSet [13] and OPV2V [32], to validate the effectiveness of our proposed framework. Specifically, the V2XSet dataset includes 73 typical autonomous driving scenarios and 11,447 annotated frames of point clouds. The dataset is divided into training, validation, and test sets, containing 6,694, 1,920, and 2,833 frames, respectively. OPV2V [32] is a simulated dataset collected using the CARLA [33] and OpenCDA [34] frameworks. This dataset includes 11,464 annotated frames of point clouds, divided into training/validation and test sets with 6,764, 1,981, and 2,719 frames, respectively.

Compared Baselines. We set a baseline comparison method where the ego agent only considers its own perception data, referred to as No Fusion. We also employ late and early fusion for comparison, where the detection results and original sensor data are respectively sent to achieve cooperative perception. Moreover, we consider multiple state-of-the-art (SOTA) cooperative perception methods, including AttFuse [32], Where2comm [17], and CoBEVT [19]. AttFuse [32] utilizes per-location attention for feature fusion. Where2comm [17] employs a spatial filtering strategy. CoBEVT [19] designs a collaboration method based on axial attention. Given that we account for heterogeneous perception models and design the corresponding model selection strategy, we compare two model selection modes: fixed model and random selection, with the fixed model using the PointPillar [26] model. Considering that previous cooperative perception methods do not take into account the model selection process, we combine cooperative perception methods with two model selection strategies to establish comparative baseline methods, including AttFuse-Random, AttFuse-Fixed, Where2comm-Random, Where2comm-Fixed, CoBEVT-Random, and CoBEVT-Fixed.

Evaluation Metrics. Following [26], we use average precision with Intersection Over Union (IOU) thresholds of 0.5 and 0.7 as evaluation metrics to compare the detection performance of different methods. During the execution, if the application's execution time exceeds the latency requirement (100ms), we remove the perception data from the corresponding nodes. Consequently, the overall perception accuracy also reflects the completion rate of the cooperative perception task within the specified latency. Additionally, we consider the utilization rates of the computational resources of all computing nodes as well as the communication bandwidth utilization of the ego agent. Specifically, we measure the proportion of computational and communication resources used within the stipulated time against the total resources as an indicator of resource utilization efficiency. The utilization rates of computational resources and transmission resources are denoted as CRU and TRU, respectively.

5.2   Quantitative Evaluation

Detection Performance Comparison. Table 1 shows the perception performance of CmpV2X and the compared baseline models on the V2Xset [13] and OPV2V [32] datasets. As mentioned earlier, when a node fails to transmit the BEV features to the ego agent within the specified delay, we disregard the perception data from that node. Therefore, early fusion, which has longer data transmission times, suffers from lower perception performance due to failing to complete within the required time. Intuitively, the proposed method CmpV2X achieves SOTA detection performance on both datasets. There are two potential reasons. **(i)** CmpV2X uses model selection and three-stage communication strategies to avoid excessive task execution and data transmission times, ensuring that the cooperative perception tasks can be completed within the specified delay. **(ii)** The proposed IDA module effectively bridges the data distribution of the BEV features shared by collaborators, ensuring that the fused features can accurately perceive the surrounding driving environment.

Comparison of Resource Utilization. Similarly, as Table 1 shows, CmpV2X achieves the highest resource utilization, including both computation and communication resources, in the feature-level cooperative perception paradigm. Experimental results demonstrate that the proposed model selection method can dynamically adjust the perception model used based on the current node resources, thereby improving resource utilization and meeting the task's delay requirements. Meanwhile, the three-phase communication strategy uses confidence maps to reflect the perception data quality of different nodes, thereby enhancing communication resource utilization by pruning redundant communication links.

6   Conclusion

In conclusion, the CmpV2X system effectively addresses critical challenges in feature-level cooperative perception within the IoV scenarios. By integrating a resource-guided model selection method, a communication scheme based on confidence maps, and an inter-agent domain adaptation module, CmpV2X enhances both the efficiency and effectiveness of multi-agent perception. Our experiments in dynamic IoV scenarios demonstrate significant improvements in collaborative 3D object detection performance and resource utilization.

Acknowledgment. This work is supported by the Joint Lab. on Networked AI Edge Computing Fudan University-Changan.

References

1. Luo, G., Zhang, H., Yuan, Q., Li, J.: Complementarity-enhanced and redundancy-minimized collaboration network for multi-agent perception. In: Proc. ACM Int. Conf. Multimedia, pp. 3578–3586 (2022)

2. Shi, S., et al.: Vips: real-time perception fusion for infrastructure-assisted autonomous driving. In: Proc. Annu. Int. Conf. Mobile Comput. Netw., pp. 133–146 (2022)
3. Zhang, K., Li, R., Yu, Y., Luo, W., Li, C.: Deep dense multi-scale network for snow removal using semantic and depth priors. IEEE Trans. Image Process. **30**, 7419–7431 (2021)
4. Yuan, X., Kortylewski, A., Sun, Y., Yuille, A.: Robust instance segmentation through reasoning about multi-object occlusion. In: Proc. IEEE/CVF Conf. Comput. Vis. Pattern Recognit., pp. 11 141–11 150 (2021)
5. El Madawi, K., Rashed, H., El Sallab, A., Nasr, O., Kamel, H., Yogamani, S.: RGB and lidar fusion based 3d semantic segmentation for autonomous driving. In: Proc. IEEE. Intell. Transp. Syst. Conf., pp. 7–12 (2019)
6. Shi, X., et al.: A real-time semantic segmentation network for road scenes inspired from autoencoder. IEEE Trans. Circuits Syst. Video Technol. **34**(5), 3439–3450 (2024)
7. Ma, Z., Zheng, Z., Wei, J., Yang, Y., Shen, H.T.: Instance-dictionary learning for open-world object detection in autonomous driving scenarios. IEEE Trans. Circuits Syst. Video Technol. **34**(5), 3395–3408 (2024)
8. Tao, C., Cao, J., Wang, C., Zhang, Z., Gao, Z.: Pseudo-mono for monocular 3d object detection in autonomous driving. IEEE Trans. Circuits Syst. Video Technol. **33**(8), 3962–3975 (2023)
9. Yang, K., Sun, P., Lin, J., Boukerche, A., Song, L.: A novel distributed task scheduling framework for supporting vehicular edge intelligence. In: Proc. IEEE. Int. Conf. Distrib. Comput. Syst., pp. 972–982 (2022)
10. K. Yang, et al.: A novel efficient multi-view traffic-related object detection framework. In: Proc. IEEE Int. Conf. Acoust., Speech Signal Process., pp. 1–5 (2023)
11. Yang, K., Sun, P., Yang, D., Lin, J., Boukerche, A., Song, L.: A novel hierarchical distributed vehicular edge computing framework for supporting intelligent driving. Ad Hoc Netw. **153**, 103343 (2024)
12. Yang, K., et al.: Spatio-temporal domain awareness for multi-agent collaborative perception. In: Proc. IEEE Int. Conf. Comput. Vis., pp. 23 383–23 392 (2023)
13. Xu, R., Xiang, H., Tu, Z., Xia, X., Yang, M.-H., Ma, J.: V2x-vit: vehicle-to-everything cooperative perception with vision transformer. In: Proc. Eur. Conf. Comput. Vis. (2022)
14. Das, A., et al.: Tarmac: targeted multi-agent communication. In: Int. Conf. Mach. Learn., pp. 1538–1546 (2019)
15. Yang, D., et al.: How2comm: communication-efficient and collaboration-pragmatic multi-agent perception. Adv. Neural Inf. Process. Syst. **36** (2024)
16. Yang, K., Yang, D., Zhang, J., Wang, H., Sun, P., Song, L.: What2comm: towards communication-efficient collaborative perception via feature decoupling. In: Proceedings of the 31th ACM International Conference on Multimedia (ACM MM), pp. 7686–7695 (2023)
17. Hu, Y., Fang, S., Lei, Z., Zhong, Y., Chen, S.: Where2comm: communication-efficient collaborative perception via spatial confidence maps. Adv. Neural Inf. Process, Syst (2022)
18. Chen, Q., Tang, S., Yang, Q., Fu, S.: Cooper: cooperative perception for connected autonomous vehicles based on 3d point clouds. In: Proc. IEEE. Int. Conf. Distrib. Comput. Syst., pp. 514–524 (2019)
19. Xu, R., Tu, Z., Xiang, H., Shao, W., Zhou, B., Ma, J.: Cobevt: cooperative bird's eye view semantic segmentation with sparse transformers. In: Conf. Robot Learn. (2022)

20. Chen, Q., Ma, X., Tang, S., Guo, J., Yang, Q., Fu, S.: F-cooper: feature based cooperative perception for autonomous vehicle edge computing system using 3D point clouds. In: Proc. ACM Symp. Edge Comput., Arlington Virginia, pp. 88–100 (2019)
21. Liu, Y.-C., Tian, J., Glaser, N., Kira, Z.: When2com: multi-agent perception via communication graph grouping. In: Proc. IEEE/CVF Conf. Comput. Vis. Pattern Recognit., pp. 4106–4115 (2020)
22. Wang, T.-H., Manivasagam, S., Liang, M., Yang, B., Zeng, W., Urtasun, R.: V2vnet: vehicle-to-vehicle communication for joint perception and prediction. In: Proc. Eur. Conf. Comput. Vis., pp. 605–621 (2020)
23. Li, Y., Ren, S., Wu, P., Chen, S., Feng, C., Zhang, W.: Learning distilled collaboration graph for multi-agent perception. Adv. Neural Inf. Process. Syst. **34**, 29 541–29 552 (2021)
24. Qiu, H., Huang, P., Asavisanu, N., Liu, X., Psounis, K., Govindan, R.: Autocast: scalable infrastructure-less cooperative perception for distributed collaborative driving. arXiv preprint arXiv:2112.14947 (2021)
25. Rauch, A., Klanner, F., Rasshofer, R., Dietmayer, K.: Car2x-based perception in a high-level fusion architecture for cooperative perception systems. In: IEEE Intell. Vehicles Symp., pp. 270–275 (2012)
26. Lang, A.H., Vora, S., Caesar, H., Zhou, L., Yang, J., Beijbom, O.: Pointpillars: fast encoders for object detection from point clouds. In: Proc. IEEE/CVF Conf. Comput. Vis. Pattern Recognit., pp. 12 697–12 705 (2019)
27. Zhou, Y., Tuzel, O.: Voxelnet: end-to-end learning for point cloud based 3d object detection. In: Proceedings of the IEEE Conference on Computer Vision and Pattern Recognition, pp. 4490–4499 (2018)
28. Xu, R., Li, J., Dong, X., Yu, H., Ma, J.: Bridging the domain gap for multi-agent perception. In: Proc. IEEE Int. Conf. Robot. Autom., pp. 6035–6042. IEEE (2023)
29. Yan, Y., Mao, Y., Li, B.: Second: sparsely embedded convolutional detection. Sensors **18**(10), 3337 (2018)
30. Paszke, A., et al.: Pytorch: an imperative style, high-performance deep learning library. Adv. Neural Inf. Process. Syst. **32** (2019)
31. Kingma, D.P., Ba, J.: Adam: a method for stochastic optimization. In: Int. Conf. Learn. Represent. (2015)
32. Xu, R., Xiang, H., Xia, X., Han, X., Li, J., Ma, J.: Opv2v: an open benchmark dataset and fusion pipeline for perception with vehicle-to-vehicle communication. In: Proc. IEEE Int. Conf. Robot. Autom., pp. 2583–2589 (2022)
33. Dosovitskiy, A., Ros, G., Codevilla, F., Lopez, A., Koltun, V.: Carla: an open urban driving simulator. In: Conf. Robot Learn., pp. 1–16 (2017)
34. Xu, R., Guo, Y., Han, X., Xia, X., Xiang, H., Ma, J.: Opencda: an open cooperative driving automation framework integrated with co-simulation. In: Proc. IEEE Int. Intell. Transp. Syst. Conf., pp. 1155–1162. IEEE (2021)

EATSA: An MPTCP Scheduling Algorithm Based on Expected Arrival Time and Its Application in Bandwidth Compensation

Yuntian Shi[1], Sudong Jiang[2], Maolin Liu[2], Hao Chen[1], Zengwen Li[2(✉)], and Liang Song[1(✉)]

[1] Academy for Engineering and Technology, Fudan University, Shanghai 200433, China
{ytshi24,chen_h24}@m.fudan.edu.cn, songl@fudan.edu.cn
[2] Chongqing Changan Automobile Co., Ltd., Chongqing 401133, China
{jiangsd,liuml,lizw}@changan.com.cn

Abstract. The Internet of Vehicles (IoV) is developing rapidly, and user demands are increasing. Modern vehicular networks need high bandwidth, low latency, and stable links. A single network link often cannot meet these needs in complex mobile environments. The Multipath Transmission Control Protocol (MPTCP) can use multiple heterogeneous network links at the same time. It improves bandwidth utilization and communication robustness. In IoV heterogeneous networks, links still have very different bandwidths and delays. These differences reduce the performance of existing MPTCP scheduling algorithms. They cause low resource utilization and serious packet reordering. To solve these problems, this paper proposes the Expected Arrival Time-based Scheduling Algorithm (EATSA). EATSA analyzes the transmission characteristics of each link and estimates the expected arrival time of packets. It then allocates data to links based on these estimates and updates the allocation dynamically. This improves transmission efficiency and reduces packet reordering. We also design an intelligent bandwidth compensation framework based on MPTCP. The framework aggregates links from in-vehicle devices and user devices and adjusts bandwidth in real time. Experimental results show that EATSA improves network performance in complex heterogeneous environments and supports next-generation IoV communications.

Keywords: MPTCP · Internet of Vehicles · heterogeneous network environments · multipath data scheduling

1 Introduction

IoV technology is advancing fast, and people want more reliable connections. This demand consists of many different services, such as real-time navigation and V2X communication [1–6]. Traditional single-link architectures like 5G, Wi-Fi often have signal attenuation and network congestion. Multipath Transmission Control Protocol (MPTCP) [7] aggregates different networks to increase the bandwidth and improve stability. The performance of MPTCP is highly dependent on the data scheduling policy. Conventional algorithms like Minimum RTT algorithm emphasize latency. They don't perform so well in mobile environment with big differences between how much data can be carried at once, and when the data needs to be delivered. Resource utilization drops, and packets start getting reordered. So, IoV communication need new scheduling methods that fit the complicated and changing nature of them.

In the IoV context, vehicles face two main challenges. The first challenge is frequent network changes caused by high-speed movement. Second, different applications have diverse needs for latency and bandwidth. For example, high-definition video streaming needs high bandwidth. In contrast, autonomous driving tasks require low latency and high reliability [9,10]. These diverse needs place higher performance demands on MPTCP scheduling algorithms. In recent years, researchers have proposed several scheduling algorithms that focus on bandwidth and latency. However, most of them ignore the dynamic nature of subflows. They also overlook how the arrival order of packets affects transmission efficiency. How to achieve efficient data scheduling in complex IoV environments remains an urgent problem to solve.

This paper presents a solution to the problems described above. We propose a new algorithm for multipath data scheduling, called EATSA (Expected Arrival Time Scheduling Algorithm). The core idea of EATSA is to schedule data according to its expected arrival time. For each network path, EATSA considers several key factors, including queueing delay, transmission time, and propagation delay. The algorithm uses this info to guess when data sent on each link will get there. According to these estimated arrival times, it makes data dispatch decisions. And thus, the algorithm enhances the transmission efficiency and uses the available bandwidth more effectively. At the same time, it reduces the persistent risk of packet reordering. Besides the scheduling algorithm, we develop a bandwidth compensation framework. This framework is responsible for the network interface of vehicles and users' devices like smartphones. It gathers up all of these different resources and makes the total go up. Thus, it can enhance the quality of communication in tough IoV environments and give dependable connectivity to high-speed vehicles.

The main contributions of this paper include:

- Proposal of the EATSA Algorithm: We present an algorithm for multipath data scheduling, which is the EATSA algorithm. The algorithm calculates the expected arrival time for every subflow. Then it adjusts the distribution of data streams over many links. It can improve the transmission efficiency and bandwidth utilization, and reduce the packet reordering.
- Designing the Bandwidth Compensation Framework: This framework is based on MPTCP and combines network link resources from in-vehicle systems and users' own devices. It will do dynamic bandwidth compensation among them.

It can improve the communication stability and resource utilization of complex IoV scenarios, and can be used for effective vehicular communications.

2   Related Work

We provide a critical review of MPTCP data scheduling heuristics and multi-link aggregation schemes to evaluate the effectiveness of their flow allocations and resource optimization. We also study their limitation in heterogeneous environments. This analysis gives a theoretical basis for the following study.

2.1   MPTCP Data Scheduling Algorithm

Heuristic MPTCP scheduling algorithms use direct, empirical indicators such as RTT and the size of the congestion window to help determine a path. They also avoid the overhead of complicated environmental modeling. The classical strategies like MinRTT [8], Round Robin [11], and Redundant [12] are quite easy to implement. They don't handle heterogenous networks too well, leading to sub-optimal use of bandwidth as well as head-of-line blocking [13]. The BLEST algorithm [14] predicts the packet arrival time in advance and skips the subflow that might cause a packet to be blocked. This is a way to avoid the slow link and increase the throughput. DAPS [15] also reorganizes packet sequences to reduce out-of-order arrivals. As a result, it lowers receiver buffer occupancy and latency in complex environments.

Some applications need more specialized scheduling than general data transmission. Video streaming is a typical example and must handle high latency and throughput demands. Cross-layer architectures [16] address this need by matching the importance of application-layer data to the current transport-layer state. The ECF algorithm [17] computes expected completion times to avoid underuse of high-bandwidth paths. DEMS [18] and AEPS [19] refine subflow synchronization by partitioning data blocks and strictly managing sequence numbers. These designs promote simultaneous subflow completion and in-order delivery. However, these rule-based heuristics remain rigid. Under severe network fluctuations, they cannot balance multiple performance objectives well, and their performance degrades. This limitation reduces their applicability in highly dynamic environments.

2.2   Multi-link Aggregation

Traffic demand keeps growing. Single-link architectures cannot meet current bandwidth and reliability requirements. Multi-link aggregation combines several physical connections into one logical path with higher robustness. At the link layer, the Link Aggregation Control Protocol (LACP) [20] and Multi-Link PPP (MLPPP) [21] support physical link bundling. Their performance often degrades in heterogeneous environments. At the network layer, ECMP [22] at this level uses OSPF [23] and BGP [24] to distribute traffic. GRE tunnel aggregation [25] provides flexible virtualization. These mechanisms still lack fine-grained flow control. Transport-layer protocols like MPTCP create transparent subflows across the hybrid network to overcome this issue. SCTP [26] adds multi-homing redundancy. Multipath QUIC [27] can do low latency streaming, but the implementation is difficult.

Some situations demand a high degree of flexibility at the application level. Both VPN Bonding [28] and SD-WAN [29] use software-defined policies to optimize tunnels and QoS across the network. Linux Bonding [30] and dedicated hardware such as F5 and Citrix ADC [31] are used for load balancing data centers. Real-world deployment is still challenged. Large differences in bandwidth and latency among heterogenous links make the scheduling algorithms have a bigger load. Strict security requirements for distributed networks also raise the cost of the design. Furthermore, the demand for 5G systems is also ultra-low delay, making the operation even more difficult. As for future work, the focus will be on intelligent scheduling algorithm research, cross-layer optimization, and protocol standardization. These directions are important for making the most of multi-link aggregation.

3   Method

This part introduces the architecture of the intelligent bandwidth compensation system. It first introduces the operating principles of the EATSA algorithm. Then it describes how EATSA fits into a unified framework. Network interface management, real-time monitoring, and control of multipath transmission are carried out by the framework. In this way, it realizes reliable multi-link aggregation.

3.1   EATSA

EATSA is designed for MPTCP, and it aims to optimize the transmission latency and throughput simultaneously. It predicts arrival times for each path. And then, based on these forecasts, it chooses suitable transmission paths flexibly. This process helps make the whole system better.

In MPTCP architecture, data can be sent through many paths at a time. These paths might have very different amounts of space to move information, how long it takes to go along the path, and how crowded the path can get. That heterogeneity makes it difficult for resources to be used efficiently. EATSA uses a multi-step data scheduling strategy to take advantage of the different characteristics of these links.

First, the algorithm calculates the expected arrival time of each subflow, denoted as EAT_i. This value represents the total time required for a packet to travel from the sender to the receiver over subflow i. It consists of the queuing delay $T_{\mathrm{queue},i}$, the transmission time $T_{\mathrm{trans},i}$, and the propagation delay $T_{\mathrm{prop},i}$, and is defined as:

$$EAT_i = T_{\mathrm{queue},i} + T_{\mathrm{trans},i} + T_{\mathrm{prop},i} \tag{1}$$

1. The queuing delay $T_{\mathrm{queue},i}$: This term captures the time a packet spends waiting in the send queue before it can be transmitted. It is mainly affected by the congestion window and the amount of unacknowledged data. When the congestion window of subflow i is fully occupied, newly generated packets cannot be sent immediately and must wait in the queue. In this case, the queuing delay is given by:

$$T_{\mathrm{queue},i} = \frac{\max(U_i - \mathrm{cwnd}i \cdot MSS, 0)}{\mathrm{BW}i} \tag{2}$$

Here, U_i denotes the volume of unacknowledged data on subflow i (in bytes), while cwnd_i and MSS represent the congestion window size (in segments) and the Maximum Segment Size (in bytes), respectively. BW_i signifies the available bandwidth of subflow i (in bytes per second). The function $\max(\cdot, 0)$ is employed to strictly enforce the non-negativity of the calculated queuing delay.

2. The transmission time $T_{\mathrm{trans},i}$: This is the time it takes to send the packet. This time depends on two things. It depends on the size of the packet and the available speed of the subflow.We calculate it with the following formula:

$$T_{\mathrm{trans},i} = \frac{MSS}{\mathrm{BW}_i} \tag{3}$$

This formula indicates that the time required to send a packet of size MSS is equal to the packet size divided by the bandwidth.

3. The propagation delay $T_{\mathrm{prop},i}$: This is the time it takes for a signal to travel through the network. We can also call this the one-way travel delay of the subflow.It is hard to measure this one-way delay directly. So, we usually estimate it. We estimate the delay as half of the subflow's round-trip time (RTT_i).The formula is:

$$T_{\mathrm{prop},i} = \frac{RTT_i}{2} \tag{4}$$

where RTT_i is the round-trip time of subflow i, which can be measured using mechanisms such as TCP timestamp options. By performing the above calculations, the EATSA algorithm obtains the EAT_i for each subflow. The algorithm then selects the subflow with the minimum expected arrival time for data transmission:

$$i^* = \arg\min_i EAT_i \tag{5}$$

However, directly selecting the subflow with the minimum EAT_i may lead to packet reordering issues at the receiver, increasing the overhead of packet reassembly. To address this, the EATSA algorithm introduces a delay difference threshold Δ to control the range of candidate subflows. Specifically, the algorithm only considers subflows that satisfy the following condition:

$$EAT_i - EAT_{\min} \leq \Delta \tag{6}$$

where $EAT_{\min} = \min_i EAT_i$. By limiting the difference between EAT_i and the minimum expected arrival time, the algorithm avoids selecting subflows with excessively large EAT_i, thereby reducing the likelihood of packet reordering. The pseudocode of the EATSA algorithm is shown in Algorithm 1.

Algorithm 1. EATSA Scheduling Algorithm

1: **procedure** INITIALIZE EATSA
2:     Set Δ (Optional delay threshold for reordering)
3:     Initialize RTT, BW, CWND, MSS, U for all subflows
4: **end procedure**
5: **function** CALCULATE_EAT(subflow)
6:     $T_{\text{queue}} \leftarrow \frac{\max(U - \text{CWND} \cdot \text{MSS}, 0)}{\text{BW}}$
7:     $T_{\text{trans}} \leftarrow \frac{\text{MSS}}{\text{BW}}$
8:     $T_{\text{prop}} \leftarrow \frac{\text{RTT}}{2}$
9:     **return** $T_{\text{queue}} + T_{\text{trans}} + T_{\text{prop}}$
10: **end function**
11: **function** SCHEDULE_PACKET(subflows)
12:     $EAT_{\min} \leftarrow \infty$, $selected\_subflow \leftarrow$ None
13:     **for** each $subflow$ in $subflows$ **do**
14:         $EAT \leftarrow$ Calculate_EAT($subflow$)
15:         **if** $EAT < EAT_{\min}$ **then**
16:             $EAT_{\min} \leftarrow EAT$
17:             $selected\_subflow \leftarrow subflow$
18:         **end if**
19:     **end for**
20:     **if** $\Delta \neq$ None **then**
21:         Filter subflows with $EAT - EAT_{\min} \leq \Delta$
22:         Recompute $selected\_subflow$
23:     **end if**
24:     **return** $selected\_subflow$
25: **end function**
26: **procedure** SEND_DATA(subflows, packets)
27:     **for** each $packet$ in $packets$ **do**
28:         $subflow \leftarrow$ Schedule_Packet($subflows$)
29:         $subflow.\text{send}(packet)$
30:     **end for**
31: **end procedure**
32: **procedure** MAIN
33:     **while** True **do**
34:         Update RTT, BW, CWND, U for all subflows
35:         Send_Data(subflows, packets)
36:     **end while**
37: **end procedure**

3.2   Intelligent Bandwidth Compensation Framework

Intelligent bandwidth compensation is an application that enhances network transmission performance through multi-link aggregation technology. It integrates the bandwidth resources available from the car owner's mobile devices (which may include multiple devices) and the in-car system to form a larger log-ical communication link, thereby improving communication quality and band-width utilization. By dynamically aggregating heterogeneous network links such as 4G, 5G, and Wi-Fi, the system overcomes the bandwidth limitations of any single link. It provides users with a smoother network experience in scenarios such as high-definition video streaming, online navigation, and in-vehicle real-time communication. At the same time, intelligent scheduling and link redun-dancy enable efficient utilization of network resources and maintain communi-cation continuity, even in complex and time-varying network environments.

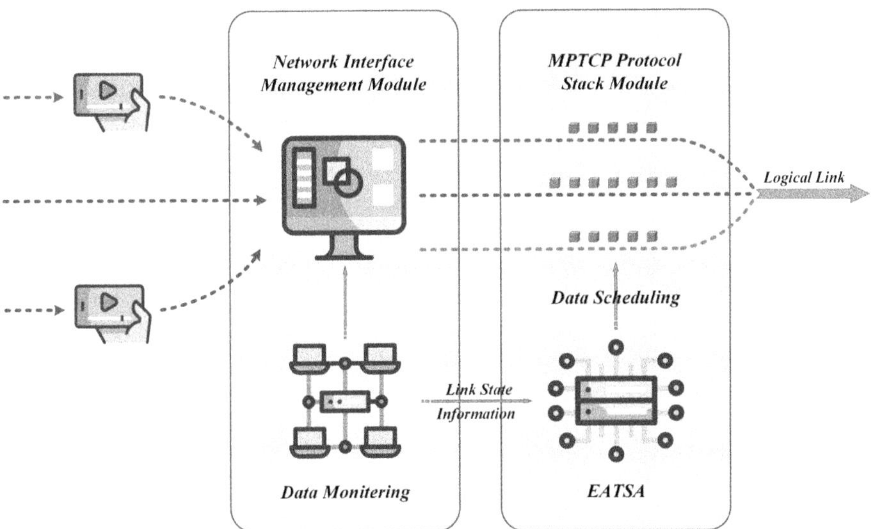

Fig. 1. Intelligent bandwidth compensation technology framework

As shown in Fig. 1, the intelligent bandwidth compensation architecture is built on the cooperation between the network interface management module and the MPTCP protocol stack module. The network interface management module forms the system's infrastructure. It dynamically organizes heterogeneous physi-cal links (e.g., 4G, 5G, and Wi-Fi) that connect user devices to the in-car system. Its embedded link state monitoring submodule continuously analyzes real-time metrics, including bandwidth, latency, and packet loss. Based on this teleme-try, the core MPTCP protocol stack module integrates the EATSA scheduler to merge these physical connections into a single logical high-bandwidth link. By giving priority to paths with the shortest expected arrival time, the system opti-mizes traffic allocation and supports fast failover, thereby significantly improving transmission stability.

Operationally, this architecture runs a closed-loop workflow that covers the entire process from link acquisition to adaptive data transmission. After connec-tivity is established, the EATSA scheduler uses real-time performance data to update the traffic allocation strategy. It splits the data into segments and sends them in parallel over the currently most efficient paths. At the receiver, these segments are reordered and reassembled into one continuous stream. The application layer thus sees a logical high-bandwidth connection. The system keeps recalibrating this process. When network conditions change, it adjusts path selection and flow distribution immediately. In this way, it maintains robust, low-latency communication in complex network environments.

4   Experiment

To comprehensively evaluate the performance of the EATSA data scheduling algorithm in different network environments, we carry out experiments under a variety of heterogeneous network conditions. To thoroughly analyze the advantages of EATSA, we select several classical scheduling algorithms, including Min-RTT, Selective [32], and Round Robin, as comparison baselines.

4.1   Experimental Environment

This experiment was conducted based on the MPTCP kernel module in the Linux system. The MPTCP module was installed in the Linux kernels of two laptops, with one serving as the sender and the other as the receiver. An MPTCP connection was established between the two ends, along with four transmission paths created for the experiment. The configurations of the two laptops are shown in Table 1. Since EATSA is implemented at the user layer of the Linux system, custom interface functions are required to enable interaction between EATSA and MPTCP.

Table 1. Configurations of laptops used in the experiment

Configuration	Sender	Receiver
CPU	Intel(R)i9-14900HX	Intel(R)i9-14900HX
Memory	16GB	16GB
Operating System	Ubuntu	Ubuntu
Programming Language	Python	Python

To simplify the experimental process and avoid repeated kernel modifications and compilations, the ProgMP (Programmable Multipath TCP) model [33] was introduced to handle the scheduling work between the two. ProgMP, as a programmable MPTCP packet scheduling model, facilitates the development and testing of MPTCP scheduling algorithms. This model abstracts the underlying implementation details of MPTCP and provides a set of high-level APIs, enabling users to design and implement their own scheduling strategies more flexibly and efficiently. It also allows the adaptation of these strategies to different network environments and application requirements. The setup of the experimental environment is shown in Fig. 2.

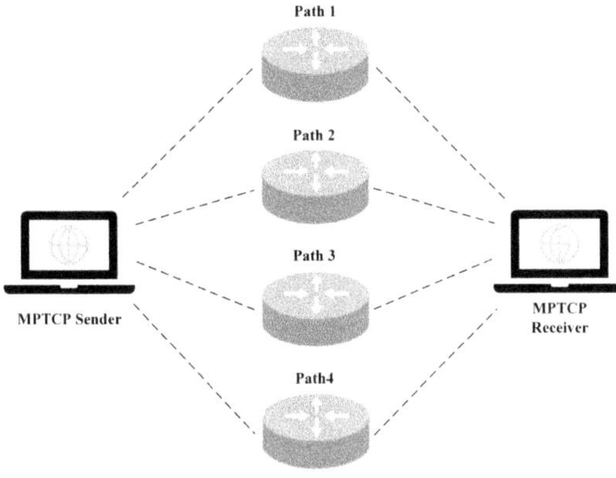

Fig. 2. Experimental environment setup

4.2   Experimental Setup

The experiment was conducted in a Linux environment supporting MPTCP, using the traffic control tool TC [34] to simulate asymmetric network conditions. The scenario was configured to resemble real-world network environments with asymmetric bandwidth. The file transfer size was uniformly set to 50 MB, and all algorithms were tested under the same conditions. The specific configuration of the experimental scenarios is shown in Table 2.

Table 2. Experimental Network Environment Configuration (Asymmetric Bandwidth)

Experimental Network Environment	Bandwidth of Each Path (Mbps)	Delay of Each Path (ms)	Packet Loss Rate of Each Path (%)
Environment 1	1 1 2 2	10 10 10 10	0 0 0 0
Environment 2	1 1 3 3	10 10 10 10	0 0 0 0
Environment 3	1 1 4 4	10 10 10 10	0 0 0 0
Environment 4	1 1 5 5	10 10 10 10	0 0 0 0

To facilitate the quantitative evaluation of the performance of different scheduling methods, three evaluation metrics were used in this experiment:

- Transmission time (s): The time taken to complete one MPTCP multipath file transfer.
- Transmission rate (kb/s): The amount of data transmitted via MPTCP multipath per unit of time.

- Bandwidth utilization (BU,%): The ratio of the MPTCP multipath transmission rate to the sum of the transmission rates of all paths. The calculation formula is as follows:

$$BU = \frac{\text{Transmission Rate}}{125 \sum_{i=1}^{n} \text{Bandwidth of Path } i} \times 100\% \tag{7}$$

In this experiment, five scheduling algorithms were selected as comparison groups. Four of them are based on heuristic rules: MinRTT, Round Robin, Active-RTT, and Selective, while the fifth is based on deep reinforcement learning: RLDS [35]. A brief introduction to Selective and RLDS, which are mentioned for the first time, is provided below:

- Selective: This algorithm selects the sending subflow based on the product of the RTT and congestion window of each subflow. A smaller RTT and congestion window product indicates lower latency, higher bandwidth utilization, and shorter data transmission completion time.
- RLDS: A data scheduling algorithm based on reinforcement learning, utilizing the DQN framework to adaptively select the optimal path for data transmission according to the sending window size of each path.

4.3   Experimental Results Analysis

The experimental results under different environments are shown in Tables 3, 4, 5, 6.

Table 3. Test Results for Asymmetric Bandwidth Environment 1

Data Scheduling Algorithm	Transmission Time (s)	Transmission Rate (kb/s)	Bandwidth Utilization (%)
MinRTT	78.93	635.84	84.78
Round Robin	117.38	427.56	57.01
ActiveRTT	75.59	662.15	88.29
Selective	79.21	633.59	84.48
RLDS	73.13	686.31	91.51
EATSA	72.81	689.29	91.90

Table 4. Test Results for Asymmetric Bandwidth Environment 2

Data Scheduling Algorithm	Transmission Time (s)	Transmission Rate (kb/s)	Bandwidth Utilization (%)
MinRTT	60.29	832.45	83.25
RR	114.86	436.95	43.70
ActiveRTT	58.41	859.23	85.92
Selective	60.90	824.06	82.41
RLDS	56.04	895.48	89.55
EATSA	55.76	900.05	90.01

Table 5. Test Results for Asymmetric Bandwidth Environment 3

Data Scheduling Algorithm	Transmission Time (s)	Transmission Rate (kb/s)	Bandwidth Utilization (%)
MinRTT	49.74	1008.95	80.72
RR	110.64	453.61	36.29
ActiveRTT	48.73	1029.84	82.39
Selective	51.60	972.68	77.81
RLDS	45.85	1094.56	87.56
EATSA	45.57	1101.31	88.11

Table 6. Test Results for Asymmetric Bandwidth Environment 4

Data Scheduling Algorithm	Transmission Time (s)	Transmission Rate (kb/s)	Bandwidth Utilization (%)
MinRTT	43.07	1165.36	77.69
RR	109.13	459.88	30.66
ActiveRTT	41.08	1221.57	81.44
Selective	43.84	1144.79	76.32
RLDS	39.70	1264.23	84.28
EATSA	39.35	1275.40	85.03

By analyzing the above experimental results, we can conclude that: EATSA demonstrated excellent performance under various asymmetric network conditions, outperforming other algorithms in terms of transmission time, transmission rate, and bandwidth utilization. At the same time, as the degree of bandwidth asymmetry increases, its advantages become more pronounced. Therefore, the EATSA algorithm is an excellent choice for efficient data transmission in complex network environments.

5 Conclusion

This paper addresses the demand for high-bandwidth, low-latency, and highly stable network connections in the Internet of Vehicles (IoV) by proposing an Expected Arrival Time-based Scheduling Algorithm (EATSA) and its intelligent bandwidth compensation framework. EATSA computes the expected arrival time of each link with high accuracy. It adjusts its scheduling strategies in real time to improve multi-link transmission efficiency and utilization rate and reduce the possibility of packet reordering. Based on the algorithm, the intelligent bandwidth compensation framework gathers links from vehicle systems and user devices and carries out dynamic bandwidth compensation. The framework meets various communication needs for IoV. The experimental results show that the EATSA scheme is more efficient, stable, and utilizes resources better than traditional scheduling schemes. It has a stronger adaptability and robustness in complex heterogeneous networks. The framework enables efficient bandwidth integration in practical IoV scenarios and provides stable network support for high-bandwidth, high-reliability applications such as real-time navigation, online entertainment, and autonomous driving.

The research presented in this paper offers an efficient solution for multipath data scheduling and bandwidth compensation in IoV but also has some limitations. For example, the algorithm's performance in extremely high-load network environments still requires further optimization. Additionally, the framework's compatibility with different network protocols warrants further investigation. Future work will focus on further optimizing the EATSA algorithm and extending the intelligent bandwidth compensation framework to larger-scale, multi-scenario IoV environments, providing more robust technical support for next-generation IoV communication.

Acknowledgments. This work is supported by the Joint Lab on Networked AI Edge Computing Fudan University-Changan.

Disclosure of Interests. The authors have no competing interests to declare that are relevant to the content of this article.

References

1. Song, L., Hu, X., Zhang, G., Spachos, P., Plataniotis, K.N., Wu, H.: Networking systems of AI: on the convergence of computing and communications. IEEE Internet Things J. **9**(20), 20352–20381 (2022)
2. Duan, W., Gu, J., Wen, M., Zhang, G., Ji, Y., Mumtaz, S.: Emerging technologies for 5G-IoV networks: applications, trends and opportunities. IEEE Netw. **34**(5), 283–289 (2020)
3. Tuyisenge, L., Ayaida, M., Tohme, S., Afilal, L.-E.: Network architectures in internet of vehicles (IoV): review, protocols analysis, challenges and issues. In: Skulimowski, A.M.J., Sheng, Z., Khemiri-Kallel, S., Cérin, C., Hsu, C.-H. (eds.) IOV 2018. LNCS, vol. 11253, pp. 3–13. Springer, Cham (2018). https://doi.org/10.1007/978-3-030-05081-8_1

4. Alouache, L., Nguyen, N., Aliouat, M., Chelouah, R.: Survey on IoV routing protocols: security and network architecture. Int. J. Commun. Syst. **32**(2), e3849 (2019)
5. Gyawali, S., Xu, S., Qian, Y., Hu, R.Q.: Challenges and solutions for cellular-based V2X communications. IEEE Commun. Surv. Tuts. **23**(1), 222–255 (2020)
6. Alnasser, A., Sun, H., Jiang, J.: Cyber security challenges and solutions for V2X communications: a survey. Comput. Netw. **151**, 52–67 (2019)
7. Barré, S., Paasch, C., Bonaventure, O.: Multipath TCP: from theory to practice. In: Proceedings Networking 2011: 10th International IFIP TC 6 Networking Conference, Valencia, Spain, pp. 444–457, May 2011
8. Paasch, C., Ferlin, S., Alay, Ö., Bonaventure, O.: Experimental evaluation of multipath TCP schedulers. In: Proceedings of the 2014 ACM SIGCOMM Workshop on Capacity Sharing Workshop, pp. 27–32 (2014)
9. Wu, J., Yuen, C., Wang, M., Chen, J.: Content-aware concurrent multipath transfer for high-definition video streaming over heterogeneous wireless networks. IEEE Trans. Parallel Distrib. Syst. **27**(3), 710–723 (2015)
10. Wang, J., Liu, J., Kato, N.: Networking and communications in autonomous driving: a survey. IEEE Commun. Surv. Tutorials **21**(2), 1243–1274 (2018)
11. Frommgen, A., Erbshäußer, T., Buchmann, A., Zimmermann, T., Wehrle, K.: ReMP TCP: low latency multipath TCP. In: 2016 IEEE International Conference on Communications (ICC), pp. 1–7 (2016)
12. Barré, S.: Implementation and assessment of modern host-based multipath solutions. Ph.D. dissertation, Catholic University of Louvain, Louvain-la-Neuve, Belgium (2011)
13. Kim, J., Oh, B.-H., Lee, J.: Receive buffer based path management for MPTCP in heterogeneous networks. In: 2017 IFIP/IEEE Symposium on Integrated Network and Service Management (IM), pp. 648–651 (2017)
14. Ferlin, S., Alay, Ö. Mehani, O., Boreli, R.: BLEST: blocking estimation-based MPTCP scheduler for heterogeneous networks. In: 2016 IFIP Networking Conference (IFIP Networking) and Workshops, pp. 431–439 (2016)
15. Kuhn, N., Lochin, E., Mifdaoui, A., Sarwar, G., Mehani, O., Boreli, R.: DAPS: intelligent delay-aware packet scheduling for multipath transport. In: 2014 IEEE International Conference on Communications (ICC), pp. 1222–1227 (2014)
16. Corbillon, X., Aparicio-Pardo, R., Kuhn, N., Texier, G., Simon, G.: Cross-layer scheduler for video streaming over MPTCP. In: Proceedings of the 7th International Conference on Multimedia Systems, pp. 1–12 (2016)
17. Lim, Y.-S., Nahum, E.M., Towsley, D., Gibbens, R.J.: ECF: an MPTCP path scheduler to manage heterogeneous paths. In: Proceedings of the 13th International Conference on Emerging Networking Experiments and Technologies, pp. 147–159 (2017)
18. Guo, Y.E., Nikravesh, A., Mao, Z.M., Qian, F., Sen, S.: DEMS: decoupled multipath scheduler for accelerating multipath transport. In: Proceedings of the 23rd Annual International Conference on Mobile Computing and Networking, pp. 477–479 (2017)
19. Chaturvedi, R.K., Chand, S.: An adaptive and efficient packet scheduler for multipath TCP. Iran. J. Sci. Technol. Trans. Electrical Eng. **45**, 349–365 (2021)
20. Irawati, I.D., Hadiyoso, S., Hariyani, Y.S.: Link aggregation control protocol on software defined network. Int. J. Electric. Comput. Eng. **7**(5), 2706 (2017)
21. Conant, G.E.: Multilink PPP: One big virtual WAN pipe. Data Commun. **24**(13), 85–89 (1995)

22. Zhang, H., Guo, X., Yan, J., Liu, B., Shuai, Q.: SDN-based ECMP algorithm for data center networks. In: Proceedings 2014 IEEE Computers, Communication IT Applications Conference, pp. 13–18 (2014)
23. Moy, J.T.: OSPF: Anatomy of an Internet Routing Protocol. Addison-Wesley Professional (1998)
24. Griffin, T.G., Wilfong, G.: An analysis of BGP convergence properties. ACM SIGCOMM Comput. Commun. Rev. **29**(4), 277–288 (1999)
25. Eskandar, A.A., Syed, M.R., Bahareh, Z.M.: Performance analysis of VoIP over GRE tunnel. Int. J. Comput. Netw. Inf. Secur. **7**(12), 1 (2015)
26. Stewart, R., Metz, C.: SCTP: new transport protocol for TCP/IP. IEEE Internet Comput. **5**(6), 64–69 (2001)
27. Viernickel, T., Froemmgen, A., Rizk, A., Koldehofe, B., Steinmetz, R.: Multipath QUIC: a deployable multipath transport protocol. In: Proceedings 2018 IEEE International Conference Communication (ICC), pp. 1–7 (2018)
28. Beritelli, F., La Corte, A., Lo Sciuto, G., Rametta, C., Scaglione, F.: Adaptive VPN bonding technique for enhancing dual-SIM mobile internet access. In: Proceedings SYSTEM, pp. 47–54 (2015)
29. Troia, S., Zorello, L.M.M., Maralit, A.J., Maier, G.: SD-WAN: an open-source implementation for enterprise networking services. In: Proceedings 2020 22nd International Conference on Transparent Optical Networks (ICTON), pp. 1–4 (2020)
30. Aust, S., Kim, J.-O., Davis, P., Yamaguchi, A., Obana, S.: Evaluation of Linux bonding features. In: Proceedings 2006 International Conference Communication Technology, pp. 1–6 (2006)
31. Moharir, M., et al.: A study and comparison of various types of load balancers. In: Proceedings 2020 5th IEEE International Conference on Advances and Innovations in Engineering (ICRAIE), pp. 1–7 (2020)
32. Moon, S.-M., Ebcioğlu, K.: Parallelizing nonnumerical code with selective scheduling and software pipelining. ACM Trans. Programm. Lang. Syst. (TOPLAS) **19**(6), 853–898 (1997)
33. Frömmgen, A., Koldehofe, B.: Programming application-defined multipath TCP schedulers. In: Proceedings 18th ACM/IFIP/USENIX Middleware Conference: Posters and Demos, pp. 13–14 (2017)
34. Stanic, M.P.: Tc–Traffic control. In: Linux QOS Control Tool (2001)
35. Luo, J., Su, X., Liu, B.: A reinforcement learning approach for multipath TCP data scheduling. In: Proceedings 2019 IEEE 9th Annual Computing and Communication Workshop and Conference (CCWC), pp. 0276–0280 (2019)

Supporting Dependent Task at Edge: A Computation-Communication-Cache Integrated Service Architecture

Yang Li[1], Guanhan Peng[1], Xiang Li[1], Shan Zhang[1,2],
Zhiyuan Wang[1,2], and Hongbin Luo[1,2(✉)]

[1] Beihang University, Beijing 100191, China
{younglee,xiaohan209,idealee,zhangshan18,zhiyuanwang,luohb}@buaa.edu.cn
[2] Zhongguancun Laboratory, Beijing, China

Abstract. In this paper, we propose a forwarding and processing mechanism based on the Information-Centric Networking (ICN) architecture that supports with dependent task requests. This mechanism enables multi-stage distributed decision-making, multi-node collaborative forwarding of dependent task requests, and distributed execution of dependent tasks at the edge. Furthermore, within the multi-stage distributed decision-making paradigm, we introduce an acceleration method based on parallelism between task decision-making and task execution. Additionally, the proposed mechanism incorporates an local state synchronization method for task decisions to reduce synchronization overhead. Finally, we build a prototype system to implement and evaluate the proposed forwarding and processing mechanism, verifying its functional correctness and demonstrating its performance advantages compared to both IP and ICN-based architectures.

Keywords: computing request · dependent task · forwarding · edge computing · distributed system

1 Introduction

The increasing adoption of smart end devices at the edge has spurred the emergence of numerous applications, such as augmented/virtual reality, smart transportation, and smart healthcare, which require rapid processing of substantial amounts of data within short time frames. This poses significant challenges to both network transmission capacity and computational capability [9]. Moreover, computational tasks generated by these applications often involve dependent subtasks that need to be executed across multiple servers. For example, a face recognition task based on video stream includes tasks such as video frame retrieval, image preprocessing, feature extraction, and recognition [4]. Recent algorithmic research demonstrates that by effectively orchestrating computing collaboration among multiple devices, computing efficiency at the edge can be

Z. Lin et al. (Eds.): INSAI 2025, CCIS 2894, pp. 181–194, 2026.
https://doi.org/10.1007/978-981-95-9299-9_14

improved by over 30% [6]. Investigating how to efficiently forward requests for dependent tasks at the edge can facilitate collaborative utilization of multiple computational resources, thereby reducing overall task execution time.

The traditional TCP/IP network architecture, originally designed for device connectivity, lacks awareness of computational resource states. The destination of computational requests depends on user choices. An intuitive solution involves introducing proxies at the application layer to manage computational resource information and recommend the best server resources for tasks [8]. However, this approach does not fundamentally alter the separation of routing and computation, can not achieve joint optimization of computation resource selection and transmission path. In conclusion, for edge computing scenarios where the edge server needs to be selected according to the status of the edge servers and network, we should redesign a new network architecture.

In contrast to the IP architecture, Information-Centric Networking (ICN) as a novel network architecture enables the integrated management of multi-dimensional forwarding information at the network layer, including link resource states and computational resource states, facilitating the optimization of both joint transmission and computational delays [5]. However, despite the ICN architecture's adeptness in routing and forwarding with coupling of transmission and computation, the current design enhancements for dynamic content within the ICN framework still only consider the request forwarding for single computational task [3]. There remains a multitude of demands to be met regarding how to forward computational requests for dependable tasks:

- **Distributed Control Plane:** In edge scenarios, the increasing number of device connections and the need for multidimensional information collection escalate centralized control overheads. There is a growing need for a decentralized control plane capable of gathering multidimensional resource information to support routing decisions for collaborative computing and transmission. In such scenarios, computational requests must move beyond the perspective of centralized control to consider how to handle packet forwarding and processing under a distributed control plane.
- **Distributed Task Execution:** In a distributed system, multiple nodes must collaboratively maintain task states to ensure the correct progression of overall task. Distributed systems face challenges such as state maintenance, state synchronization, and fault recovery to ensure robust operation.
- **Dependencies among Subtasks:** Managing dependencies among multiple tasks to ensure correct data transmission among nodes poses a new challenge.

To address these needs, we design and implement a forwarding and processing mechanism tailored for dependent task requests. Our contributions are as follows:

- Our mechanism supports multi-stage distributed decision-making for dependable task requests.
- Our mechanism facilitates distributed task execution, allowing simultaneous decision-making and task execution to advance overall task completion time.

- We introduces an local task decision state synchronization method to minimize communication overhead and support correct data transmission among nodes based on partial data dependency.

We construct a prototype system on multiple hosts to validate our system's capability in forwarding and processing dependable task requests. Experimental results demonstrate that our mechanism supports multi-stage distributed decision-making for computing requests, allows parallel decision-making and task execution, and facilitates correct data transmission among nodes based on data dependency.

In this paper, we first review existing work about computing request. Next, we detail the design of our forwarding and processing mechanism. We then describe the implementation of our prototype system and analyze experimental results. Finally, we conclude our work and analyze open issues.

2 Related Works

In this section, we summarize existing research on computing request forwarding, focusing particularly on enhanced approaches within IP and ICN frameworks.

2.1 Enhanced IP Approaches

Within current IP-based solutions for forwarding computational requests containing multiple tasks, Service Function Chain (SFC) often utilize IPv6 Segment Routing (SRv6). SRv6's programmability allows forwarding nodes to sequentially process data packets and execute network functions based on flow tables issued by controllers [7]. The specific forwarding mechanism involves intermediate nodes determining the next-hop address by inspecting segment information in the SRH header extension. However, traditional SFC, which rely on serial dependencies, may not effectively handle the typical Directed Acyclic Graph (DAG) representation of data dependencies in general edge computing tasks, and IP-based SRv6 cannot do the routing and forwarding that is coupled to the transmission and computation.

2.2 Enhanced ICN Approaches

ICedge [5] utilizes the RICE [2] method at the network layer to associate estimated application-level computation times with service names, influencing the forwarding of computational requests. Addressing the challenge of accurately estimating application computation times, Serving at the Edge [1] proposed a basic service session model by using the push mechanism based on the traditional ICN request-response model, with which not too many states need to be saved in the intermediate nodes or estimate the computing time. While these solutions achieve coupling of transmission and computing, they only consider scenarios where requests contain a single task. Exploring how to efficiently forward requests containing multiple tasks to locate multiple service providers remains an open research question.

3   System Design

In this section, we introduce a detailed exposition of the design of a forwarding and processing mechanism tailored for dependent task requests. Initially, we conduct an analysis of the entities present in edge scenarios, as well as the typical applications that exist within the edge. Subsequently, we delve into a step-by-step analysis of the task decision request forwarding, task deployment request forwarding, and task execution phases, examining which nodes require specific forwarding and processing of requests to meet the new demands of handling dependent tasks in edge computing. Based on this concrete analysis, we clarify the functional modules which our prototype system needs to possess and describe the specific design approach for these modules. Finally, we present a detailed use case of how the system handles dependent tasks.

3.1   Edge Computing Scenario

We consider that network nodes are classified into two categories: powerful edge servers and heterogeneous terminal devices such as various sensors, smartphones, and vehicle-mounted terminals.

Devices at the edge possess varying degrees of computational resources. It is assumed that these devices can acquire information about computational resources within a certain range and schedule tasks based on locally available information.

As an illustrative case, we take a road condition analysis application as an example, as shown in Fig. 1. Vehicles in motion on highways initially capture video footage of the surrounding road conditions. Subsequently, they segment the video into frame images and dispatch them to various nearby devices equipped with computational capabilities, such as other vehicles on the road or smart end devices. These devices are tasked with the distributed extraction of feature points. The vehicle itself is responsible for the reception and consolidation of a limited set of feature points for the purpose of target identification. Additionally, it transmits the captured video frames to a more distant edge server, which in turn aggregates comprehensive urban traffic condition data. This aggregated data is utilized to issue early warnings to vehicles approaching congested or accident-prone areas.

3.2   Specific Requirements Analysis

In this subsection, we conduct a detailed requirements analysis for forwarding dependent task requests. Specifically, the forwarding and processing workflow is divided into three stages: task decision request forwarding, computing request forwarding, and task execution, in that sequential order. Next, we will analyze the specific requirements of each stage in detail.

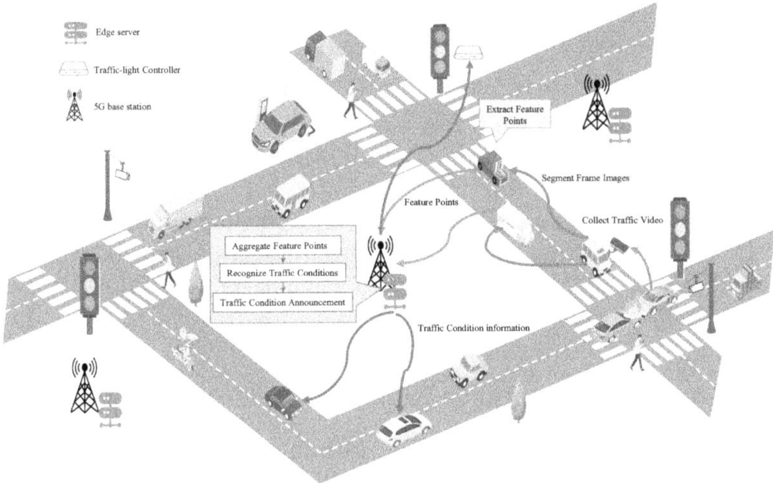

Fig. 1. Traffic Analysis Application Scenario.

(1) Phase of Task Decision Request Forwarding: End devices typically serve as initiators of computing requests. Considering the necessity for multiple nodes with decision-making capabilities to engage in multi-stage decision-making, comprehensive decision results are formed. We encapsulate information about multiple dependent sub-tasks within decision requests. Early-stage decision-making nodes are termed downstream decision nodes, responsible for making downstream decisions. Conversely, late-stage decision-making nodes are termed upstream decision nodes, responsible for upstream decisions. Downstream decision nodes forward incomplete decision results to upstream decision nodes. Each decision node must process decision requests and determine the destination address for forwarding to the next decision node.

(2) Phase of Computing Request Forwarding: After decision-making, we need to forward computing requests to target computing nodes. Computing nodes analyze decision result information stored in computing requests to determine which sub-tasks to deploy. However, due to the multi-stage nature of decision-making, we need to decide whether to parallelize the task decision phase with the computing request forwarding phase. The benefit of choosing serial execution is that all executing nodes maintain a unified task decision status without considering potential inconsistencies between nodes. The benefit of parallel execution is that it allows some tasks to be deployed and executed earlier, thereby shortening the overall task execution time. However, unlike serial execution, parallel execution may lead to inconsistent task decision statuses among multiple nodes. We need to analyze the impact of inconsistent task decision statuses on subsequent task deployment and execution. Additionally, due to data dependencies between nodes, it is essential to maintain a certain state on nodes to ensure correct transmission of task computation results.

(3) Phase of Task Execution: A prerequisite for starting task execution is that the required data and image data are ready. Therefore, it is necessary to ensure that data can be pulled and transmitted between nodes, and the intermediate results can be transmitted to the corresponding nodes. Given the variability in data arrival times required for task execution and data buffering is necessary. For task deployment and execution, management of the task carrier—containers—is also required.

3.3   Design of Key Functional Modules

After analyzing specific requirements, we identify the following functional modules that the prototype system needs:Packet Processing Module, Packet Forwarding Module, Data Buffer Module, Container Management Module, Task State Maintenance Module. Prototype system architecture is depicted in Fig. 2.

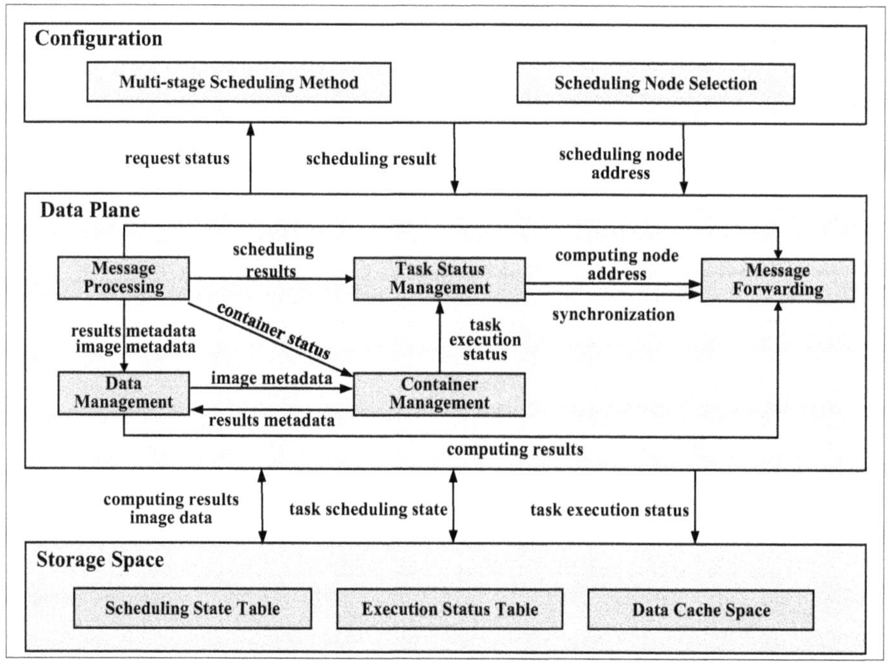

Fig. 2. Prototype System Architecture.

(1) Task State Management Module: The Task State Management Module is primarily responsible for managing the task-related states on a node, including task execution state and task decision state. The node senses external or internal events to modify both the task decision state and task execution state, thereby ensuring multi-node collaborative execution of dependable tasks. This approach guarantees that tasks are executed cohesively across multiple nodes. On the other hand, although we introduce a parallelization method for task decision-making and task execution to shorten the overall task completion time, this method also introduces inconsistencies in task states across multiple nodes. To address this issue, the Task State Management Module incorporates an local state synchronization method, which avoids excessive network overhead from synchronization messages while ensuring correct data transmission among nodes.

- **Task Decision States:**Task decision states capture the execution addresses of multiple dependent sub-tasks, while task execution states reflect the current phase of task execution. Task decision states are derived from the results of decision-making at the decision layer and maintained by computing nodes. These states include information on the execution addresses of dependent sub-tasks. Computing nodes use these states to verify addresses of nodes that they depend on before forwarding. Task decision states are divided into two stages: incomplete and complete. An incomplete state indicates that some sub-tasks lack specific execution addresses, whereas a complete state means that all sub-tasks have determined their execution addresses. Updates to task decision states occur only upon receiving new decision in formation.
- **Task Execution States:** Task execution states are created during task deployment based on specific task information and maintained by computing nodes. Task execution states have three dimensions: data dependency readiness, container image readiness, and task completion. A task can only begin once both data dependencies and container images are ready.
- **Parallelization Method for Task Decision-making and Task Execution:** The multi-stage distributed decision making model supports the Parallelization of the task decision phase and the task execution phase. In each decision stage, a portion of the sub-tasks from the Directed Acyclic Graph (DAG) is assigned to compute nodes, and it is necessary at this point to select suitable sub-tasks for early deployment and execution. The selected sub-task nodes must meet the following conditions:1)The sub-task node must belong to a sub-sequence of the DAG after topological sorting. The starting point of this sub-sequence should be the initial node of the chain formed after DAG topological sorting. 2) All sub-tasks within this sub-sequence must be bound to compute nodes. We select and deploy the eligible additional sub-tasks for early execution to maximize the reduction in the overall task completion time while avoiding resource waste caused by premature deployment.
- **Local Synchronization:** In the parallel method of task decision-making and task execution, multi-stage distributed decision-making can lead to inconsistencies in task decision states across different compute nodes. Such inconsistencies may result in incorrect data transmission between nodes, making state

synchronization necessary. Considering that the upstream decision results provide more comprehensive information, we initiate data requests from the upstream compute nodes that have deployed the tasks, directed towards the downstream compute nodes. Upon receiving the data request, the downstream compute nodes not only analyze whether to return the corresponding data but also modify their task decision state to align with the requesting node. This approach embeds the synchronization semantics within the data request itself, thereby reducing network overhead associated with synchronization.

(2) Packet Processing Module: The Packet Processing Module is primarily responsible for decapsulating incoming packets, parsing fields, and modifying node states. This Module is subdivided into four sub-modules: decision request packet processing, task computing packet processing, data request packet processing, and data packet processing.

– *Decision Request Packet Processing:* Decision nodes process received decision request packets, analyze the upstream decision results contained within, make new decisions based on this information and their own environmental data, and return confirmation packets prompting the previous decision node to delete timeout entries.
– *Computing Request Packet Processing:* Computing nodes process received computing request packets, store decision results to establish task decision states, and determine which tasks need to be deployed early.
– *Data Request Packet Processing:* Computing nodes process received data request packets, check if relevant computation results exist in their buffer, and return data packets if available. If not, they mark the buffer to notify when results become available.
– *Data Packet Processing:* Computing nodes process received data packets, integrate and store the data in relevant buffer spaces, and delete corresponding timeout entries for the data packets.

(3) Data Buffer Module: Provides cache spaces for data dependencies and container images required for task computations, as well as for storing results from these computations. Additionally, extra records are maintained in the cache spaces to indicate potential requesters of the cached data. When data in caches is updated or computation results are produced, the Task State Maintenance Module is notified to update the states.

3.4   Multi-stage Video Analysis Use Case at the Edge

Decision Node (DN) represents a node that has knowledge of the multidimensional resource state information within a certain network scope, such as a base station, an edge server, or a smart device with significant computing power.

Server (S) represents an intelligent terminal device equipped with certain computational resources, such as a smartphone, an in vehicle terminal, etc. DNx refers to DN number x, while Sx-y represents the y-th device within the network scope managed by DN number x. Figure 3 illustrates a typical case of dependent tasks at the edge, where DN1 and DN2 are decision nodes that have information of the local resources. Part (a) represents the process of task decision-making and task execution in the first stage, while part (b) represents the process of task decision-making and task execution in the second stage. DN1 maintains resource information for end devices S1-1 and S1-2, while DN2 maintains information for S2-1 and S2-2. Both DN1 and DN2 can perceive the specific computational resources within their domain. The execution nodes maintain task decision states based on computational requests to determine the data flow direction.

DNs can specify the exact execution server for each sub-task using their control module based on the local resource information they possess. However, due to the incompleteness of the information, it may only assign a portion of all sub-tasks and forward decision requests to other DNs for further decision-making. Initially, DN1 receives a forwarded request from the user describing the need to deploy the "video" sub-task, with the following three tasks yet to be assigned execution servers, as indicated in Phase(1). Accordingly, DN1 decides to assign "extraction(1)" to S1-1 and "extraction(2)" to S1-2, as indicated in Phase(2-1) and Phase(2-2). The "recognition" task remains without an assigned execution server, prompting DN1 to seek further decision-making from DN2 by forwarding the decision request, as indicated in Phase(2-3). Both S1-1 and S1-2, knowing that the user is deploying the video, request the "video result" from the user and start their respective computations upon receiving the data, as indicated in Phase(3-1) and Phase(3-2).

The task decision phase and the computation request phase occur in parallel. After making the first-stage decision immediately, DN1 forwards the computation requests for "extraction(1)" and "extraction(2)" to S1-1 and S1-2, respectively. Upon receiving these requests, S1-1 and S1-2 begin to deploy and simultaneously execute "extraction(1)" and "extraction(2)". After DN2 makes the second-stage decision, it immediately forwards the computation request for "recognition" to S2-2, as indicated in Phase(1). Upon receiving the request, S2-2 deploys "recognition" and sends data requests to S1-1 and S1-2 based on a more comprehensive upstream task decision state. S1-1 and S1-2 then forward their computational results to S2-2 after completing "extraction(1)" and "extraction(2)", as indicated in Phase(2-1) and Phase(2-2). Once all required data arrives, S2-2 begins the computation and returns the final computational result to the user, as indicated in Phase(3).

4   Performance Evaluation Using a Prototype

To validate the functionality of the data plane forwarding processing system for dependent tasks and to assess its performance, we constructed a prototype of a distributed edge computing environment. Within this prototype, we compared serial and parallel implementations of task decision-making and execution.

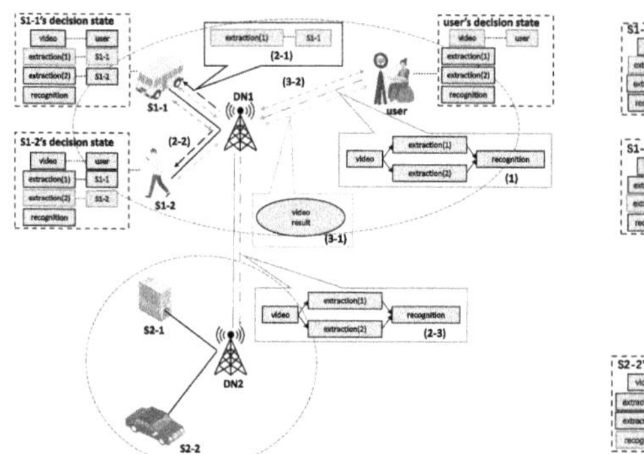

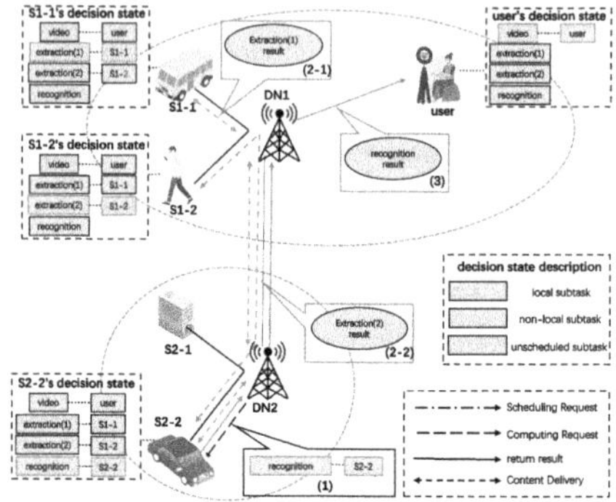

(a) Task Decision and Execution in the First Stage

(b) Task Decision and Execution in the Second Stage

Fig. 3. Multi-stage Video Analysis Use Case at the Edge.

4.1   Prototype Configuration

Our prototype system consists of six physical hosts interconnected via an optical switch. The hardware environment includes one server model ROG STRIX B760-G GAMING WIFI equipped with a 13th Gen Intel(R) Core(TM) i5-13600KF processor and a 4070ti graphics card, and an Intel X710 SFP+ network card with four 10GbE ports. The other five servers are model 10N9CTO1WW, each powered by an Intel(R) Core(TM) i7-6700 CPU@3.40GHz and an Intel X710 SFP+ network card with four 10GbE ports. Each machine uses version 22.04.3 LTS of Ubuntu as the operating system. The IP protocol is used for node communication, with the 4070ti-equipped machine's IP set to 192.168.50.11, and the others set from 192.168.50.12 to 192.168.50.16. The images of each subtask are pre-deployed on each machine, and the container image tool uses Docker version 20.10.8. The information and dependencies of these subtasks are stored in a JSON file on the user-designated physical node.

4.2   Experimental Parameter Settings

For the experiments, we use a Directed Acyclic Graph (DAG) form for dependent tasks, where each subtask is packaged into a container image stored on the physical machine's disk, deployed upon receiving a computation request. The DAG used in the experiment consists of seven interdependent sub-tasks, each implemented using mathematical functions to fulfill a scientific computation requirement. Specifically, the process begins with the generate function, which generates an initial value d1. The Split function then takes d1 and produces three different results: d2, d3, and d4. The Pow function processes d3 to perform an exponentiation operation, resulting in d5. The Divide function receives d5 and performs a division to produce d6. Next, the Add function takes d4 and d6 to perform an addition operation. The Sqrt function then takes d7 to calculate the square root, resulting in d8. Finally, the mul function takes d2 and d8 to perform a multiplication, producing the final result. Considering that the purpose of the experiment is to analyze the impact of decision time variation on task completion time, it is necessary to exclude overhead factors unrelated to decision and execution times. We measure the total time overhead associated with packet processing and container deployment, which is comparable to the actual task decision and execution times. This similarity is mainly due to the minimal computational load of each sub-task and the small volume of data transmitted between sub-tasks, resulting in relatively low time overhead for real function calculations and data transmission. To disregard the impact of any time not related to task decision-making and execution, we adjust the function computation and decision times to ensure that both the task decision time and task execution time exceeded the additional overhead by at least 100 times. The DAG form is shown in Fig. 4.

To assess the impact of distributed task decision-making on overall task execution, we conduct two sets of experiments: the first set examined the influence of decision-making duration in each phase on overall task runtime; the second set investigated the impact of decision results in each phase that allow for early task deployment on overall task runtime. The experiments are designed so that the task execution commence with the start of computation and conclude with the generation of results.

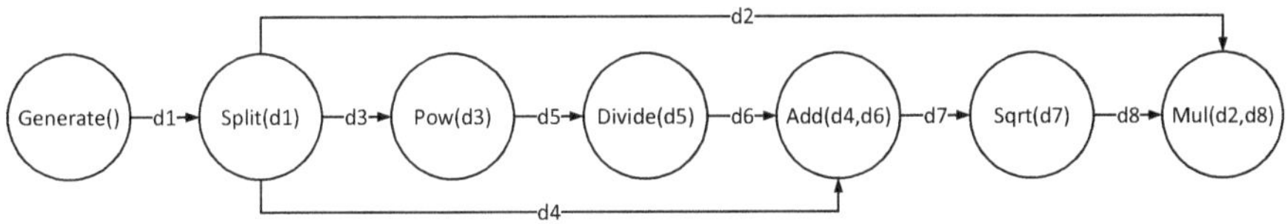

Fig. 4. DAG-Structured dependent Task.

4.3   Experiment Results Analysis

In the first set of experiments, we assume that the decision-making time for each task segment is the same, with each task execution time fixed at 20 milliseconds. We configure three decision phases to ensure that each phase's decisions allow some tasks to be deployed and executed earlier. The decision times for each segment are set to be $1/5$, $1/3$, $1/2$, and $1/1$ of the total task runtime to conduct four comparative experiments. These experiments are designed to compare the differences among the earliest completion time, parallel completion time, and serial completion time. The results are shown in Fig. 5. The data indicate that under different time ratios, the completion time for parallel execution is consistently earlier than that for serial execution, and as the ratio decreases, the completion time for parallel execution approaches the earliest possible completion time. In practice, under parallel execution, the task completion time is significantly later than the earliest completion time when the ratio is high, primarily due to the increased probability of delays in task deployment caused by waiting for decision results. To eliminate delays caused by waiting for decision results, it is essential to ensure that, when the final computing results under current decision stage are generated, the computing requests for the next phase have already been forwarded. However, meeting this requirement consistently is challenging.

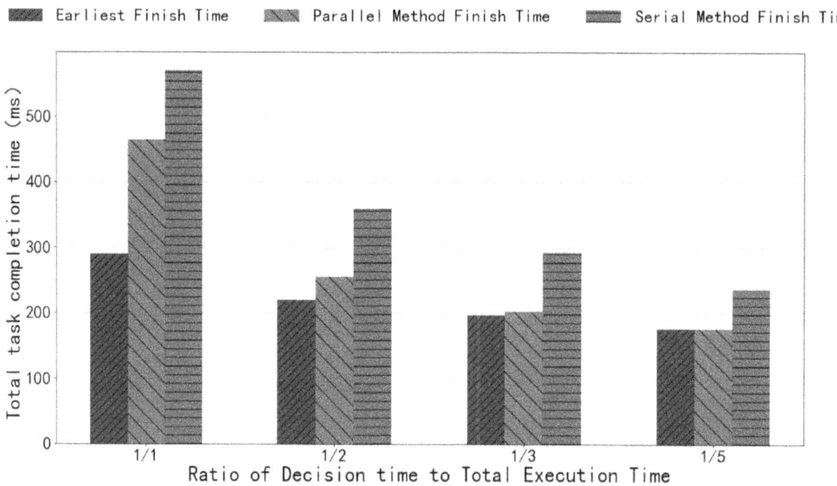

Fig. 5. Comparison of results under different ratios of decision times to total execution time.

In the second set of experiments, we divide the decision phases into three segments, with each phase's decision time set to 1/5 of the total task runtime. We conduct three experimental configurations. In the first configuration, partial task execution is allowed in every decision phase. In the second configuration, partial task execution is only permitted in the first phase of decision-making. The third configuration allows tasks to start execution only after the decision is made in the third phase. The results, as shown in Fig. 6, indicate that in the first configuration, the parallel execution time matches the optimal time due to the absence of additional waiting. In the second configuration, tasks begin execution only after decisions are made in the second phase, resulting in a completion time later than that of the first configuration. In the third configuration, tasks begin execution only after the third phase's decision, effectively rendering it equivalent to serial execution, and therefore, the completion time is the latest.

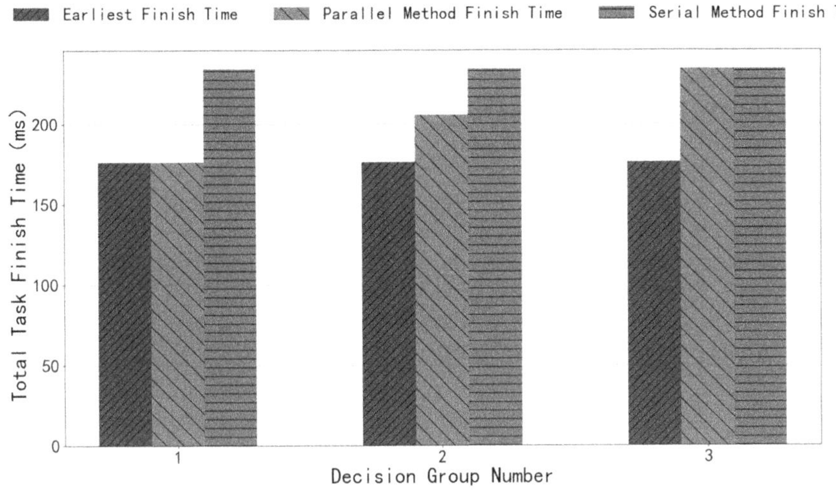

Fig. 6. Comparison of results under different distributed decision results.

5   Open Issues

In this section, we discuss potential directions for optimizing future forwarding system tailored for dependent task requests, focusing on task deployment timing and the spatio-temporal trade-offs of data caching.

5.1   Task Deployment Timing

In our current work, we assume that containers are pre-deployed and ready to receive data as it arrives. However, premature container deployment can lead to inefficient resource utilization, while deploying containers too late can delay the overall task completion time. Accurately estimating task deployment times is crucial to address this challenge.

5.2   Spatio-Temporal Trade-Offs in Data Buffering

Data caching involves a trade-off between limited storage resources and read/write speeds. Storing data in memory can accelerate read speeds but is constrained by available memory resources. Conversely, storing data on disk slows down read and write operations. We cannot indiscriminately utilize memory resources. Instead, we need to devise strategies that optimize the use of space and time information.

6   Conclusion

In this article, we design and implement a forwarding and processing mechanism tailored for dependable tasks, aimed at coordinating distributed computational resources and enhancing the efficiency of executing dependent tasks. Specifically, this mechanism adopts a parallel approach for task decision-making and execution to deploy and execute sub tasks at the earliest opportunity, thereby advancing the overall task completion time. The effectiveness and performance advantages of the proposed method were validated through a prototype system we develop.

Acknowledgment. This work was supported in part by the National Key R&D Program of China under Grant 2022YFB4501000, in part by the Nature Science Foundation of China under Grant 62422201, 62225201, U24B20128, 62271019, 62202021, in part by the Fundamental Research Funds for the Central Universities, China, and State Key Laboratory of Complex & Critical Software Environment.

References

1. Fan, Z., Yang, W., Wu, F., Cao, J., Shi, W.: Serving at the edge: an edge computing service architecture based on ICN. ACM Trans. Internet Technol. (TOIT) **22**(1), 1–27 (2021)
2. Król, M., Habak, K., Oran, D., Kutscher, D., Psaras, I.: RICE: remote method invocation in ICN. In: Proceedings of the 5th ACM Conference on Information-Centric Networking, pp. 1–11 (2018)
3. Li, X., et al.: HiCom: a Hyper-ICN architecture for computing power network in edge. IEEE Network (2025)
4. Mao, Y., You, C., Zhang, J., Huang, K., Letaief, K.B.: A survey on mobile edge computing: the communication perspective. IEEE Commun. Surv. Tutor. **19**(4), 2322–2358 (2017)
5. Mastorakis, S., Mtibaa, A., Lee, J., Misra, S.: Icedge: when edge computing meets information-centric networking. IEEE Internet Things J. **7**(5), 4203–4217 (2020)
6. Peng, Q., Wu, C., Xia, Y., Ma, Y., Wang, X., Jiang, N.: DoSRA: a decentralized approach to online edge task scheduling and resource allocation. IEEE Internet Things J. **9**(6), 4677–4692 (2021)
7. Santos, J., van der Hooft, J., Vega, M.T., Wauters, T., Volckaert, B., De Turck, F.: SRFog: a flexible architecture for virtual reality content delivery through fog computing and segment routing. In: 2021 IFIP/IEEE International Symposium on Integrated Network Management (IM), pp. 1038–1043. IEEE (2021)
8. Yang, Z., et al.: SkyPilot: an intercloud broker for sky computing. In: 20th USENIX Symposium on Networked Systems Design and Implementation (NSDI 23), pp. 437–455 (2023)
9. Yukun, S., et al.: Computing power network: a survey. China Commun. **21**(9), 109–145 (2024)

Behavior Modeling and Social Computing

OEL-AD: An Online Evolutive Learning Framework for Cross-Region Adaptive Autonomous Driving

Jiayue Jin[1,2], Lang Qian[1], Jingyu Zhang[1], Chuanyu Ju[1], and Liang Song[1,2(✉)]

[1] College of Intelligent Robotics and Advanced Manufacturing, Fudan University, Shanghai, China
`24110860008@m.fudan.edu.cn`
[2] Innovation Platform for Academicians of Hainan Province, Haikou, China
`songl@fudan.edu.cn`

Abstract. Autonomous driving models have achieved great progress in recent years, yet most existing approaches remain static, following a train-then-deploy paradigm that lacks the ability to adjust internal parameters when encountering new environments. This limitation is particularly critical in cross-region scenarios, which are common in real-world deployments in autonomous driving where differences in road layouts, traffic patterns, and environmental conditions introduce distribution shifts. In this paper, we argue for a paradigm shift towards Online Evolutive Learning (OEL), a learning paradigm designed to enable adaptive, online model optimization through the interaction and coordination of intelligent components in dynamic environments. We introduce OEL-AD, a novel framework that instantiates this paradigm for autonomous driving. Specifically, OEL-AD leverages trajectory uncertainty from the planning module to determine whether adaptive updates are necessary. When triggered, the framework uses discrepancies between predicted agent behaviors and subsequent observations as a self-supervised learning signal to refine perception and prediction modules, thereby indirectly improving planning accuracy and safety. Experiments on the nuScenes dataset with a cross-region split between Singapore and Boston demonstrate that OEL-AD consistently improves perception and prediction performance. This enhancement in perception and prediction consequently results in improved planning capabilities, thereby confirming the promise of online evolutive learning as a fundamental approach for building adaptive and robust autonomous driving systems.

Keywords: Autonomous Driving · Online Evolutive Learning · Cross-Region Distribution Shifts

1 Introduction

Autonomous driving has become one of the most influential research areas in artificial intelligence and robotics, supported by advances in perception, prediction, and planning algorithms, large-scale datasets, and increasingly powerful

Z. Lin et al. (Eds.): INSAI 2025, CCIS 2894, pp. 197–208, 2026.
https://doi.org/10.1007/978-981-95-9299-9_15

computing platforms. Recent progress has demonstrated a clear trend from modular pipelines toward more integrated end-to-end architectures [1]. End-to-end models are able to jointly optimize multiple tasks, benefiting from shared representations and improved coordination between modules, and have achieved strong results on curated datasets and established benchmarks.

Despite these achievements, most current methods follow a static train-then-deploy paradigm, in which models are optimized offline on fixed datasets and deployed as frozen systems. This paradigm assumes that training and deployment environments are drawn from similar distributions, an assumption that often does not hold in real-world conditions. Autonomous driving systems must operate in environments that are highly diverse and dynamic, influenced by regional differences, weather changes, and evolving traffic conditions. Under such circumstances, models trained in one environment frequently experience performance degradation when deployed in new contexts, highlighting the limitations of static pipelines.

Among them, cross-region generalization represents one of the most challenging and common scenarios in real-world autonomous driving. Variations between cities in terms of road topology, traffic density, and driving behavior create distribution shifts that are difficult to capture during offline training. Addressing such distribution shifts is crucial for building reliable and scalable autonomous driving systems. Existing approaches to domain adaptation [2–5] attempt to alleviate these issues through additional labeled data, domain-invariant representations, or adversarial learning strategies. While effective to some extent, these approaches are fundamentally constrained by their dependence on pre-defined training datasets and lack the ability to dynamically adapt during deployment [6]. Recent research on test-time adaptation [7–9] demonstrates the promise of updating models on-the-fly using unlabeled data; however, these methods typically focus on single-task perception, operate in isolation from downstream planning, limiting their long-term effectiveness for safety-critical applications.

To address these limitations, we argue for a paradigm shift to Online Evolutive Learning (OEL) [10], a learning paradigm that enables autonomous driving systems to refine internal representations and policies in real time through a closed-loop optimization process. Instead of treating perception, prediction, and planning as isolated stages, OEL promotes collaboration between modules, allowing the system to selectively update its components based on feedback from decision-making outcomes. By incorporating adaptation into the system's operational cycle, OEL reduces the dependence on curated training datasets and improves the ability to handle dynamic, open-world environments.

Building on this paradigm, we instantiate OEL in the autonomous driving domain by introducing the OEL-AD framework. OEL-AD uses an uncertainty-triggered adaptation mechanism, where the confidence of the system's planning outputs is used to determine when updates are necessary. An attention-guided module focuses adaptation efforts on the most influential agents in the driving scene, and a self-supervised optimization strategy based on temporal consistency adjusts perception and prediction models by comparing predicted trajectories with subsequent observations. This feedback-driven design enables the autonomous driving system to perform targeted adaptation without requiring additional labeled data, thus improving robustness.

We evaluate OEL-AD on the nuScenes dataset [11] under a challenging cross-region setting between Singapore and Boston. The experiments demonstrate that OEL-AD consistently improves perception and prediction performance, leading to better planning accuracy and enhanced safety under distribution shifts. The main contributions are as follows:

- We propose OEL-AD, a novel framework that instantiates the OEL paradigm in autonomous driving. Unlike conventional train-then-deploy approaches, OEL-AD enables models to perform online adaptation during deployment, effectively handling cross-region distribution shifts.
- We design an uncertainty-aware and attention-guided update mechanism that leverages trajectory uncertainty to selectively trigger model evolution. By focusing only on high-uncertainty and high-attention objects, OEL-AD performs efficient self-supervised updates to the perception and prediction modules without requiring additional human annotations.
- We conduct extensive cross-region evaluations on the nuScenes dataset, simulating realistic deployment scenarios where models are trained in one city and tested in another. Results demonstrate that OEL-AD consistently improves both perception and prediction accuracy under challenging domain shifts, leading to enhanced planning reliability and lower collision rates. These findings validate OEL-AD as a promising step towards adaptive autonomous driving systems.

2   Related Works

2.1   Autonomous Driving Models

Autonomous driving systems have evolved significantly, progressing from traditional modular architectures to modern end-to-end models. Traditional systems, which sequentially connect perception, prediction, and planning, offer strong interpretability and are easier to diagnose. Nevertheless, this pipeline design is prone to accumulating errors between sequential modules [1]. To mitigate this limitation, recent studies increasingly employ end-to-end solutions [12–17]. Such differentiability facilitates joint training across tasks, which enhances overall system performance. Our proposed framework is designed to be broadly compatible, supporting both traditional modular and modern end-to-end architectures. Furthermore, planning modules within these models have also advanced. Most contemporary planners generate multiple trajectories with corresponding probabilities to capture environmental uncertainty [15–17], offering greater robustness than earlier approaches that produced only a single deterministic trajectory [12–14]. Our work builds upon this capability. Concurrently, transformer-based designs have become prevalent in planning modules, utilizing attention mechanisms to enhance decision-making [18,19]. We capitalize on this common architectural feature by using the attention weights to identify the most influential objects for our self-supervised updates. Overall, OEL-AD is highly generalizable and supports the majority of contemporary autonomous driving models.

2.2 Cross-Region Adaptive Autonomous Driving Methods

While the majority of research in autonomous driving follows the paradigm of proposing novel architectures, training them on a designated training set, and validating on a test set, a growing body of work has begun to address the generalization and adaptation of models when facing distribution shifts especially the cross-region scenarios. One category of research leverages foundation models to create autonomous driving architectures [20]. These methods capitalize on the zero-shot generalization capabilities of large models, which can yield strong performance across a variety of environments. However, the large models themselves remain static; they may still produce decision-making errors when confronted with drastically changing environments, and the cost of adapting to each new domain is substantial. Domain adaptation (DA) techniques are also explored to address regional distribution shifts [2–5]. However, these approaches typically introduce additional training stages and rely on extra labeled data, which limits their efficiency in real-world deployment. A related category includes test-time adaptation (TTA) strategies [7–9,21,22]. Unlike the aforementioned approaches, the Online Evolutive Learning (OEL) method we propose is a lightweight framework that enables the model to evolve and adapt in real-time during deployment, offering a more efficient solution to handling distribution shifts.

2.3 Online Evolutive Learning

Online Evolutive Learning (OEL) is a learning paradigm designed to enable adaptive, online model optimization through the interaction and coordination of multiple intelligent components, such as perception, control, and generation, within dynamic environments [10]. OEL emphasizes real-time learning and adaptation based on agent-environment interaction and inter-agent collaboration. Several recent works have explored this direction for general multi-agent systems. For example, the Collaborative Normality Learning framework [23] proposes a structure for continual adaptation in multi-agent systems. Mutual Match (MM) [24] explores information consistency between agents for robust distributed learning. Additionally, Qian et al. [25] propose a bidirectional optimization framework that integrates supervised learning and reinforcement learning agents, enabling adaptation through coordinated sensing and control. While these works focus on OEL for general agents, our paper applies this paradigm specifically to the domain of autonomous driving. We enable the model itself to evolve online, using feedback to trigger adaptation and leveraging attention mechanisms to guide self-supervised updates to improve robustness against cross-region distribution shifts.

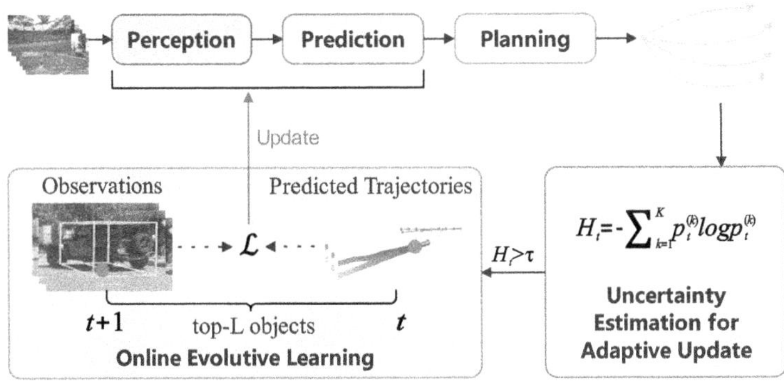

Fig. 1. Overview of OEL-AD. The framework maps raw observations to multi-trajectories, measures trajectory uncertainty, and triggers an online, self-supervised update when $H_t > \tau$. The selected objects provide next timestep supervisions to refine perception and prediction, thereby enhancing planning.

3   Method

We introduce our proposed OEL-AD framework in this section, which is built upon the Online Evolutive Learning (OEL) paradigm to enable adaptation in cross-region scenarios. The OEL-AD framework is presented in Fig. 1, providing a high-level overview of its core components and their interactions. OEL-AD integrates perception, prediction, and planning into a closed-loop system where trajectory uncertainty is used to determine the need for online updates, and self-supervised signals from future observations guide targeted adaptation.

3.1   Forward Inference

The forward inference phase is a necessary step during model deployment. Since our OEL-AD is based on the results of forward inference, we first describe this process for completeness, covering perception, prediction, and trajectory planning. During inference, the trained driving model directly transforms sensor observations into multiple candidate motion plans for the ego vehicle. Let o_t denote the raw sensor inputs at time step t. An encoder f_θ maps these observations into a latent representation of the scene:

$$z_t = f_\theta(o_t), \quad o_t \in \mathcal{O}, \ z_t \in \mathbb{R}^d, \tag{1}$$

where z_t encodes road context, dynamic agent states, and their potential future evolutions.

Based on this latent representation, the model implicitly integrates prediction of surrounding agents' behaviors through an internal transformation $h_\psi(z_t)$. The resulting predictive features are fused back into the latent representation, yielding

$$\tilde{z}_t = \Phi(z_t, h_\psi(z_t)), \tag{2}$$

where $\Phi(\cdot)$ denotes the fusion operation that enriches the scene representation with predictive information.

The planning head g_ϕ then generates a set of K candidate trajectories for the ego vehicle over a horizon of length H, together with a probability for each candidate:

$$(\hat{X}_t, \pi_t) = g_\phi(\tilde{z}_t),\tag{3}$$

$$\hat{X}_t = \left\{\hat{x}_t^{(k)}\right\}_{k=1}^{K}, \quad \hat{x}_t^{(k)} = \left\{\hat{\mathrm{pt}}_{t+1}^{(k)}, \hat{\mathrm{pt}}_{t+2}^{(k)}, \ldots, \hat{\mathrm{pt}}_{t+H}^{(k)}\right\},\tag{4}$$

$$\pi_t = \left\{\pi_t^{(k)}\right\}_{k=1}^{K}, \quad \pi_t^{(k)} \in [0,1], \quad \sum_{k=1}^{K}\pi_t^{(k)} = 1,\tag{5}$$

Thus, the overall inference process can be summarized as

$$(\hat{X}_t, \pi_t) = g_\phi\Big(\Phi\big(f_\theta(o_t), h_\psi(f_\theta(o_t))\big)\Big),\tag{6}$$

which describes the mapping from raw observations to a multi-trajectory output with associated probabilities.

3.2   Uncertainty Estimation for Adaptive Update

To determine whether an adaptive update is required, the system evaluates the uncertainty of the candidate planning trajectories. To be specifically, the planning module produces K trajectories with associated probability scores $\pi_t = \{\pi_t^{(1)}, \pi_t^{(2)}, \ldots, \pi_t^{(K)}\}$. These scores are first normalized through a softmax operation to obtain a valid probability distribution:

$$p_t^{(k)} = \frac{\exp(\pi_t^{(k)})}{\sum_{j=1}^{K}\exp(\pi_t^{(j)})}, \quad \sum_{k=1}^{K}p_t^{(k)} = 1.\tag{7}$$

The entropy of this distribution is then computed as

$$H_t = -\sum_{k=1}^{K}p_t^{(k)}\log p_t^{(k)},\tag{8}$$

which measures the degree of uncertainty in the model's trajectory selection.

A predefined threshold τ is used to decide whether the uncertainty level indicates potential distribution shift. If the entropy exceeds the threshold, the system triggers an adaptive update procedure:

$$H_t > \tau \quad \Rightarrow \quad \text{perform online evolutive learning},\tag{9}$$

otherwise the model continues inference without update:

$$H_t \leq \tau \quad \Rightarrow \quad \text{skip adaptive update}.\tag{10}$$

The threshold τ can be calibrated on a validation set by measuring the average entropy of planning outputs under in-distribution scenarios.

3.3   Online Evolutive Learning

When the entropy H_t of the trajectory distribution exceeds the threshold τ, the system activates the online evolutive learning procedure. The goal is to refine perception and prediction capabilities in order to enhance the planning performance under cross-region distribution shifts.

First, from the planning module, the ego vehicle's attention scores over surrounding objects are obtained. Let $\mathcal{A}_t$ denote the set of indices corresponding to the L highest-ranked agents, determined by their attention scores. For each selected object $i \in \mathcal{A}_t$, the prediction module provides a set of future trajectories $\hat{y}_t^{(i)} = \{\hat{\mathrm{pt}}_{t+1}^{(i)}, \hat{\mathrm{pt}}_{t+2}^{(i)}, \ldots, \hat{\mathrm{pt}}_{t+H}^{(i)}\}$. The trajectory point of interest is the immediate next-step prediction $\hat{\mathrm{pt}}_{t+1}^{(i)}$. At the next time step, the perception module provides an updated observation of object i, typically represented as a bounding box that includes position, size, orientation, and velocity. From this representation, the ground-truth center position of the object is extracted and denoted as $\mathrm{pt}_{t+1}^{(i)}$.

The prediction error is then measured as the discrepancy between the predicted and observed positions:

$$\mathcal{L}_t^{(i)} = \left\| \hat{\mathrm{pt}}_{t+1}^{(i)} - \mathrm{pt}_{t+1}^{(i)} \right\|_2^2, \quad i \in \mathcal{A}_t. \tag{11}$$

The overall online evolutive learning loss aggregates these errors across the attended objects:

$$\mathcal{L}_t = \frac{1}{|\mathcal{A}_t|} \sum_{i \in \mathcal{A}_t} \mathcal{L}_t^{(i)}. \tag{12}$$

Finally, this loss is used to update the parameters of both the perception module f_θ and the prediction module h_ψ:

$$\theta \leftarrow \theta - \eta \nabla_\theta \mathcal{L}_t, \quad \psi \leftarrow \psi - \eta \nabla_\psi \mathcal{L}_t, \tag{13}$$

where η is the learning rate. By continually refining these modules online, the system improves its ability to perceive dynamic agents and predict their future motions, which in turn enhances the reliability of the planning outputs. This procedure naturally forms a self-supervised online update loop, since the perception outputs at the next timestep serve as immediate supervision for the prediction errors. As a result, the model can adapt to unseen cross-region environments without requiring additional manual annotations.

4   Experiments

4.1   Experimental Setup

Datasets. We use the nuScenes dataset [11] to conduct experiments. It contains diverse traffic scenarios, including multiple agents such as vehicles, pedestrians, and cyclists, as well as rich sensor information from LiDAR, cameras, and radar. To evaluate the model's ability to handle cross-region distribution shifts, we split the dataset into two geographic regions, Singapore and Boston. One region is used for training and the other for testing, and vice versa.

Implementation Details. We adopt SparseDrive [17] as our base model and extend it with the proposed OEL-AD framework. During the training phase, we use four 24GB NVIDIA RTX 4090 GPUs. For the OEL stage, which is performed during inference when the uncertainty exceeds the threshold, we use one 24GB NVIDIA RTX 3090 GPU. We use a learning rate of 3×10^{-7} for online updates and select the top 35 attended objects ($L = 35$) for loss computation.

Evaluation Metrics. We evaluate the proposed framework across perception, prediction, and planning components using widely adopted metrics. For perception, we use nuScenes Detection Score (NDS) to evaluate the model performance. For prediction, following the standard motion prediction protocols, we adopt conventional metrics, including minADE (minimum Average Displacement Error), minFDE (minimum Final Displacement Error) and EPA (End-to-end Prediction Accuracy). For planning, we adopt commonly used L2 error and collision rate to evaluate the planning performance, aligning with SparseDrive [17]. Together, these metrics provide a comprehensive assessment of the system's ability to accurately perceive its surroundings, forecast future dynamics, and produce safe and reliable trajectories under cross-region distribution shifts.

Table 1. Cross-region planning results of four methods (UniAD [13], VAD [14], SparseDrive [17], OEL-AD). Metrics are reported for prediction horizons of 1s, 2s, and 3s. Lower L2 and Collision Rate values indicate better performance. OEL-AD consistently achieves the best overall results across both scenarios. Abbreviations: SG = Singapore, BOS = Boston.

Scenario	Methods	L2 (m)↓			Collision Rate (%)↓		
		1s	2s	3s	1s	2s	3s
SG → BOS	UniAD	0.4069	0.8403	1.9228	0.038	0.121	0.958
	VAD	0.4175	0.8621	2.2082	0.035	0.119	0.516
	SparseDrive	0.4057	0.8350	1.4294	0.034	0.117	0.459
	OEL-AD	**0.3904**	**0.8054**	**1.3645**	**0.032**	**0.117**	**0.377**
BOS → SG	UniAD	0.6017	1.1601	1.9652	0.055	0.256	0.836
	VAD	0.6019	1.1611	1.9970	0.061	0.258	0.978
	SparseDrive	0.6001	1.1567	1.8534	0.065	0.283	0.797
	OEL-AD	**0.5909**	**1.1429**	**1.8361**	**0.054**	**0.256**	**0.753**

4.2 Experimental Results

Results on Cross-Region Nuscenes Dataset. Tables 1 and 2 summarize the quantitative results of different methods on the cross-region nuScenes benchmark, where models are trained on one region (Singapore or Boston) and evaluated on the other to simulate distribution shifts. Across both transfer

Table 2. Cross-region perception (NDS) and prediction (minADE, minFDE, EPA) results of SparseDrive [17] and OEL-AD across SG → BOS and BOS → SG. Higher is better for NDS and EPA, while lower is better for minADE and minFDE. OEL-AD consistently achieves the best overall results across both scenarios. Abbreviations: SG = Singapore, BOS = Boston.

Scenario	Methods	Perception	Prediction		
		NDS↑	minADE↓	minFDE↓	EPA↑
SG → BOS	SparseDrive	0.2453	0.9669	1.4718	0.2820
	OEL-AD	**0.2454**	**0.9565**	**1.4596**	**0.2834**
BOS → **SG**	SparseDrive	0.2982	1.3696	2.3571	0.2641
	OEL-AD	**0.2993**	**1.3606**	**2.3561**	**0.2660**

directions (SG → BOS and BOS → SG), OEL-AD consistently outperforms prior approaches, including UniAD, VAD, and SparseDrive, in terms of perception, prediction, and planning metrics. For perception, OEL-AD achieves higher NDS scores than SparseDrive, indicating improved 3D object detection performance under cross-domain distribution shifts. In prediction, OEL-AD reduces both minADE and minFDE across all scenarios, while achieving higher EPA, demonstrating its ability to generate more accurate and reliable trajectory forecasts. In planning, OEL-AD achieves the lowest L2 trajectory error and collision rate at all prediction horizons (1s, 2s, and 3s). For instance, under the SG → BOS setting, OEL-AD reduces the 3s L2 error to 1.36 m compared to 1.43 m for SparseDrive, and lowers the 3s collision rate to 0.377%, the best among all methods. Similar trends are observed in the BOS → SG scenario, confirming that the benefits of OEL generalize across domains. These results validate that OEL-AD effectively leverages online self-supervised signals to adapt perception and prediction components in real time, leading to a closed-loop improvement in planning safety and accuracy. By dynamically adjusting to environment-specific characteristics such as traffic density, agent behavior, and scene geometry, OEL-AD demonstrates strong robustness and adaptability for cross-region autonomous driving deployment.

Qualitative Results. Figure 2 illustrates qualitative examples that demonstrate the adaptive capability of the proposed OEL-AD framework. These results are obtained by training the model on the Singapore subset and performing online evolutive learning on the Boston validation set. Compared to the baseline, OEL-AD more accurately detects distant objects, reflecting improved perception under cross-region distribution shifts. In addition, OEL-AD provides more precise predictions of surrounding agents' behaviors. For instance, in scenarios where nearby vehicles are stationary, OEL-AD correctly predicts minimal movement, whereas the baseline incorrectly forecasts significant motion trajectories for the same agents. This behavior highlights the ability of OEL-AD to

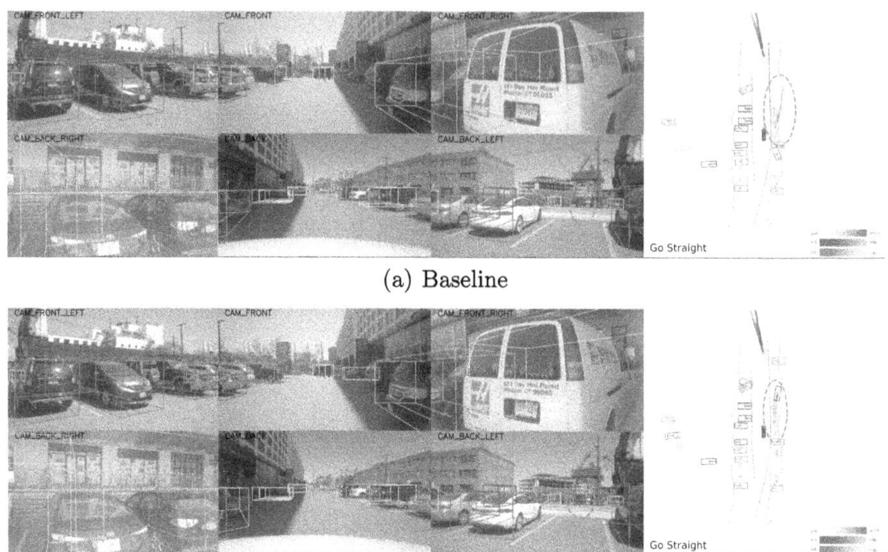

(a) Baseline

(b) OEL-AD

Fig. 2. Qualitative results. Compared to the baseline, OEL-AD achieves higher accuracy in detecting distant objects. Moreover, it demonstrates superior prediction accuracy for surrounding agents. In our experiments, the surrounding vehicles are stationary; OEL-AD correctly predicts minimal movement for these vehicles, whereas the baseline erroneously predicts significant motion trajectories for the same agents, which is clearly incorrect.

leverage online self-supervised signals to adjust predictions based on real-time observations, leading to more reliable and physically consistent outputs.

5 Conclusion

We introduced OEL-AD, an adaptive autonomous driving framework built on the OEL paradigm to achieve real-time adaptation under cross-region distribution shifts. Unlike conventional train-then-deploy approaches, OEL-AD continuously monitors trajectory-level uncertainty to determine when online updates are required and leverages discrepancies between predicted agent behaviors and subsequent observations as self-supervised signals to refine perception and prediction modules. This feedback-driven process enhances planning performance and safety by enabling the system to dynamically adjust its internal models without additional labeled data. Extensive experiments on the nuScenes dataset with a challenging cross-region split between Singapore and Boston show that OEL-AD consistently improves perception and prediction accuracy, leading to more reliable planning. These results demonstrate the effectiveness of integrating online optimization and self-supervised learning into a closed-loop system and highlight the potential of OEL as a foundation for building autonomous driving systems capable of operating robustly in diverse and evolving environments. Future research will focus on several directions. First, although OEL-AD successfully adapts to unseen environments, it does not explicitly address catastrophic forgetting. Incorporating continual learning techniques will be essential to ensure the retention of previously acquired knowledge. Second, this study focuses primarily on cross-region distribution shifts; we will extend the evaluation to a broader range of scenarios, including diverse weather conditions and large-scale datasets, to further validate the scalability and generality of the framework.

Acknowledgments. This work was supported by National Key Research and Development Program of China, Project No. 2024YFE0200700, Subject No. 2024YFE0200703. This work was also supported in part by the Specific Research Fund of the Innovation Platform for Academicians of Hainan Province under Grant YSPTZX202314, in part by the Shanghai Key Research Laboratory of NSAI and the Joint Laboratory on Networked AI Edge Computing, Fudan University-Changan.

References

1. Chen, L., Wu, P., Chitta, K., Jaeger, B., Geiger, A., Li, H.: End-to-end autonomous driving: challenges and frontiers. IEEE Trans. Pattern Anal. Mach. Intell. (2024)
2. Shan, Y., Lu, W.F., Chew, C.M.: Pixel and feature level based domain adaptation for object detection in autonomous driving. Neurocomputing **367**, 31–38 (2019)
3. Li, G., Ji, Z., Qu, X., Zhou, R., Cao, D.: Cross-domain object detection for autonomous driving: a stepwise domain adaptative yolo approach. IEEE Trans. Intell. Veh. **7**(3), 603–615 (2022)
4. Li, J., Xu, R., Ma, J., Zou, Q., Ma, J., Yu, H.: Domain adaptive object detection for autonomous driving under foggy weather. In: Proceedings of the IEEE/CVF Winter Conference on Applications of Computer Vision, pp. 612–622 (2023)
5. Yasarla, R., et al.: ROCA: robust cross-domain end-to-end autonomous driving. arXiv preprint arXiv:2506.10145 (2025)
6. Farahani, A., Voghoei, S., Rasheed, K., Arabnia, H.R.: A brief review of domain adaptation. In: Advances in Data Science and Information Engineering: Proceedings from ICDATA 2020 and IKE 2020, pp. 877–894 (2021)
7. Sun, Y., Wang, X., Liu, Z., Miller, J., Efros, A., Hardt, M.: Test-time training with self-supervision for generalization under distribution shifts. In: International Conference on Machine Learning, pp. 9229–9248. PMLR (2020)
8. Yuan, L., Xie, B., Li, S.: Robust test-time adaptation in dynamic scenarios. In: Proceedings of the IEEE/CVF Conference on Computer Vision and Pattern Recognition, pp. 15 922–15 932 (2023)
9. Segu, M., Schiele, B., Yu, F.: Darth: holistic test-time adaptation for multiple object tracking. In: Proceedings of the IEEE/CVF International Conference on Computer Vision, pp. 9717–9727 (2023)
10. Song, L., Hu, X., Zhang, G., Spachos, P., Plataniotis, K.N., Wu, H.: Networking systems of AI: on the convergence of computing and communications. IEEE Internet Things J. **9**(20), 20 352-20 381 (2022)

11. Caesar, H., et al.: nuscenes: a multimodal dataset for autonomous driving. In: Proceedings of the IEEE/CVF Conference on Computer Vision and Pattern Recognition, pp. 11 621–11 631 (2020)
12. Hu, S., Chen, L., Wu, P., Li, H., Yan, J., Tao, D.: St-p3: end-to-end vision-based autonomous driving via spatial-temporal feature learning. In: Avidan, S., Brostow, G., Cissé, M., Farinella, G.M., Hassner, T. (eds.) ECCV 2022. LNCS, vol. 13698, pp. 533–549. Springer, Cham (2022). https://doi.org/10.1007/978-3-031-19839-7_31
13. Hu, Y., et al.: Planning-oriented autonomous driving. In: Proceedings of the IEEE/CVF Conference on Computer Vision and Pattern Recognition, pp. 17 853–17 862 (2023)
14. Jiang, B., et al.: VAD: vectorized scene representation for efficient autonomous driving. In: Proceedings of the IEEE/CVF International Conference on Computer Vision, pp. 8340–8350 (2023)
15. Chen, S., et al.: Vadv2: end-to-end vectorized autonomous driving via probabilistic planning. arXiv preprint arXiv:2402.13243 (2024)
16. Li, Z., e al.: Hydra-MDP: end-to-end multimodal planning with multi-target hydra-distillation. arXiv preprint arXiv:2406.06978 (2024)
17. Sun, W., Lin, X., Shi, Y., Zhang, C., Wu, H., Zheng, S.: Sparsedrive: End-to-end autonomous driving via sparse scene representation. arXiv preprint arXiv:2405.19620 (2024)
18. Chitta, K., Prakash, A., Jaeger, B., Yu, Z., Renz, K., Geiger, A.: Transfuser: imitation with transformer-based sensor fusion for autonomous driving. IEEE Trans. Pattern Anal. Mach. Intell. **45**(11), 12 878-12 895 (2022)
19. Jia, X., You, J., Zhang, Z., Yan, J.: Drivetransformer: unified transformer for scalable end-to-end autonomous driving. arXiv preprint arXiv:2503.07656 (2025)
20. Pan, C., et al.: VLP: vision language planning for autonomous driving. In: Proceedings of the IEEE/CVF Conference on Computer Vision and Pattern Recognition, pp. 14 760–14 769 (2024)
21. Sima, C., et al.: Centaur: Robust end-to-end autonomous driving with test-time training. arXiv preprint arXiv:2503.11650 (2025)
22. Yang, H., Chen, Z., Zhang, F., Huang, Z., Luo, Y.: Codemerge: codebook-guided model merging for robust test-time adaptation in autonomous driving. arXiv preprint arXiv:2505.16524 (2025)
23. Liu, Y., Liu, J., Zhao, M., Li, S., Song, L.: Collaborative normality learning framework for weakly supervised video anomaly detection. IEEE Trans. Circuits Syst. II Express Briefs **69**(5), 2508–2512 (2022)
24. Li, D., Zhu, X., Song, L.: Mutual match for semi-supervised online evolutive learning. Appl. Intell. **53**(3), 3336–3350 (2023)
25. Qian, L., Sun, P., Wang, Y., Jin, J., Boukerche, A., Song, L.: A new online evolutive optimization method for driving agents. In: GLOBECOM 2024-2024 IEEE Global Communications Conference, pp. 2244–2249. IEEE (2024)

An Online Evolutive Framework for Cross-Subject EEG Emotion Recognition

Hanqi Wang[1]([✉]), Liang Song[1], Sunil Maharaj[2], Filip Paluncic[2], and Peng Sun[3]

[1] College of Intelligent Robotics and Advanced Manufacturing,
Fudan University, Shanghai, China
`wanghq21@m.fudan.edu.cn`
[2] Department of Electrical, Electronic and Computer Engineering,
University of Pretoria, Pretoria, South Africa
[3] Division of Natural and Applied Sciences, Duke Kunshan University,
Suzhou, China

Abstract. Electroencephalography (EEG)-based emotion recognition has attracted growing attention due to its potential in healthcare and human-computer interaction. A major challenge in this domain lies in the high inter-subject variability of EEG signals, which significantly limits the generalization of models across unseen subjects. To address this issue, we propose a novel self-supervised framework that leverages multiple candidate models, each specialized in extracting discriminative representations from EEG data. These models are trained with pretext tasks combining reconstruction and contrastive objectives to capture both temporal dynamics and frequency-domain patterns. During inference, an online selection mechanism adaptively identifies the most suitable model based on reconstruction loss, thereby improving robustness against data drift. Experiments on public EEG emotion recognition datasets demonstrate that the proposed framework achieves superior performance under the leave-one-subject-out (LOSO) protocol, outperforming existing self-supervised methods. The results highlight the effectiveness of dynamically leveraging heterogeneous model capabilities, offering a promising direction for calibration-free and generalizable EEG emotion recognition.

Keywords: EEG · Deep Learning · Emotion Recognition

1 Introduction

Affective state recognition is a core capability for intelligent, human - centered systems. It underpins applications in clinical monitoring, adaptive user interfaces, neurofeedback, and affective computing more broadly. Electroencephalography (EEG) is particularly attractive for affect recognition due to its direct link to neural activity and its high temporal resolution [1,4]. Compared with peripheral sensors, EEG can capture covert or rapid affective responses and thus

Z. Lin et al. (Eds.): INSAI 2025, CCIS 2894, pp. 209–217, 2026.
https://doi.org/10.1007/978-981-95-9299-9_16

enables applications where behavioral or physiological proxies are unreliable or unavailable [3,5,8].

Despite these advantages, EEG - based affect recognition faces several practical challenges [3,5,8]. EEG signals exhibit low signal - to - noise ratio, are nonstationary, and present pronounced inter - subject variability caused by differences in head geometry, electrode placement, baseline brain activity, and cognitive styles. Such variability undermines the generalization of models trained on a subset of subjects when applied to unseen participants, which in turn impedes translation to real - world systems.

Self - supervised learning (SSL) has emerged as a promising approach to learn robust representations from unlabeled EEG data, reducing reliance on scarce manual labels [3,7,8]. Typical SSL approaches define pretext tasks such as reconstruction, masked modeling, or contrastive instance discrimination to force the encoder to capture structure useful for downstream tasks. However, high inter - subject variability presents a critical obstacle: representations learned by a single SSL model are often biased toward the subjects seen during pretraining and may fail to generalize to subjects with different signal statistics. As a result, downstream emotion classifiers built upon such representations can suffer severe performance degradation in leave - one - subject - out (LOSO) evaluations or live deployments.

A common remedy is test - time calibration or adaptation, which updates model parameters using a small amount of target data prior to deployment or intermittently during operation. While effective in controlled settings, these strategies commonly require either access to a calibration set from the target subject or the willingness to pause deployment for parameter updates. In online streaming scenarios where decisions must be made with strict latency constraints, such requirements are impractical. Moreover, naive online adaptation without careful regularization risks overfitting to transient session artifacts, further compromising robustness.

To address these limitations, we propose an *online evolutionary self - supervision* framework that reframes cross - subject robustness as a lightweight selection problem among a pool of complementary SSL models. Each candidate model is trained offline using a reconstruction - based self - supervised objective, but candidates are designed to differ in input representation and architectural inductive biases so that their failure modes are complementary. During streaming inference, the system evaluates short EEG windows on all candidates and computes normalized reconstruction discrepancies. A compact selection mechanism then chooses either a single best model or a soft ensemble for downstream inference. This strategy avoids online parameter updates, reduces latency, mitigates catastrophic online overfitting, and provides interpretable diagnostics about which candidate is best suited for the current signal profile.

The main contributions of this work are summarized as follows:

1. We introduce an online evolutionary self - supervision framework that maintains a diverse pool of reconstruction - based SSL candidates and selects among them dynamically under streaming constraints.

2. We design complementary candidate models that emphasize distinct inductive biases (time - domain reconstruction, channel - frequency reconstruction, and masked segment reconstruction) and provide training objectives that preserve temporo - spectral and inter - channel information.
3. We develop lightweight discrepancy measures and online stabilization heuristics (smoothing, hysteresis, and anomaly handling) that enable low - latency, robust selection in real - time deployments.
4. We empirically evaluate the framework under LOSO and simulated streaming protocols on standard EEG emotion datasets and demonstrate improved cross - subject robustness against single - model SSL baselines and common test - time adaptation schemes.

2   Method

2.1   Overview and Notation

Let $\mathbf{X} \in \mathbb{R}^{C \times T}$ denote a short EEG segment with C channels and T time samples. The system maintains a pool of M candidate self-supervised models $\mathcal{M}mm = 1^M$. Each model produces a latent vector and a reconstruction:

$$\mathbf{z}_m = f_m^{\mathrm{enc}}(\mathbf{X}; \theta_m^{\mathrm{enc}}), \ \hat{\mathbf{X}}_m = f_m^{\mathrm{dec}}(\mathbf{z}_m; \theta^{\mathrm{dec}}m). \tag{1}$$

All algebraic expressions below consistently use proper LaTeX math delimiters and grouped subscripts/superscripts (e.g. dm, t not d_m, t) (Fig. 1).

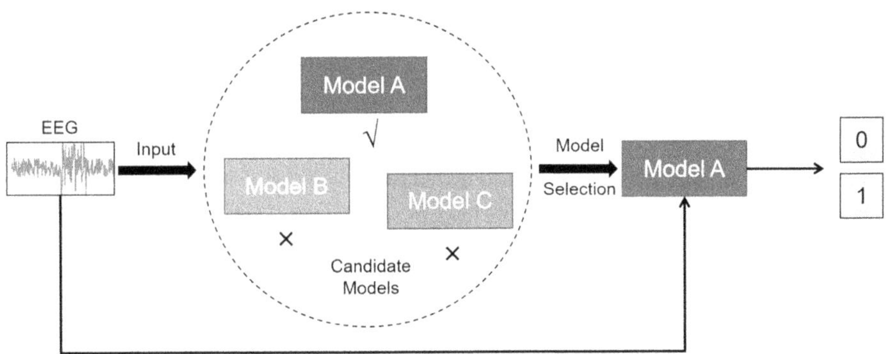

Fig. 1. The overall framework of the proposed method.

2.2   Candidate Models: Concrete Architectures and Formulas

Below we give concrete layer specifications, example hyperparameters, and exact loss formulas for three candidates. These choices are intentionally modest to allow real-time deployment on common hardware; they can be scaled if resources permit.

Model A: Temporal Convolutional Autoencoder (T-AE)

Architecture (Example Instantiation). Let the input have shape $C \times T$. Encoder blocks (index $l = 1, \ldots, L_e$):

- Block l: Conv1D with $N^{(l)}$ output channels, kernel size k_l, dilation δ_l, stride $s_l = 1$, followed by BatchNorm and LeakyReLU. Typical configuration:

$$N^{(1)} = 32, \; k_1 = 9, \; \delta_1 = 1; \quad N^{(2)} = 64, \; k_2 = 7, \; \delta_2 = 2;$$
$$N^{(3)} = 128, \; k_3 = 5, \; \delta_3 = 4.$$

- Global temporal average pooling across the time axis to obtain per-channel statistics, then a linear projection to latent dimension d (e.g. $d = 128$).

The decoder mirrors the encoder with ConvTranspose1D layers: use symmetric channel sizes and kernel sizes, optionally with nearest-neighbor upsampling followed by Conv1D to improve numerical stability.

Formally, the l-th encoder operation is

$$\mathbf{h}^{(l)} = \phi\left(\mathrm{BN}(\mathrm{Conv1D}(\mathbf{h}^{(l-1)}; N^{(l)}, k_l, \delta_l))\right), \tag{2}$$

with $\mathbf{h}^{(0)} = \mathbf{X}$. The latent vector is

$$\mathbf{z}_m = W_b, \mathrm{GAP}(\mathbf{h}^{(L_e)}) + b_b, \tag{3}$$

where $\mathrm{GAP}(\cdot)$ denotes global average pooling over time.

Receptive Field. The temporal receptive field R of the encoder is important for capturing slow oscillations. For stacked dilated convs with kernel sizes k_l and dilations δ_l and stride 1, the receptive field is:

$$R = 1 + \sum_{l=1}^{L_e} (k_l - 1), \delta_l. \tag{4}$$

Choose k_l, δ_l so that R covers the longest EEG rhythms of interest (e.g. to cover 0.5–4 s at sampling rate f_s, set $R \gtrsim 4f_s$).

Training Losses. We use a combination of time-domain MSE and spectral magnitude loss:

$$\mathcal{L}\mathrm{rec}^{(A)} = \frac{1}{CT}|\mathbf{X} - \hat{\mathbf{X}}|F^2, \tag{5}$$

$$\mathcal{L}\mathrm{spec}^{(A)} = \frac{1}{CF} \sum c = 1^C |, |\mathcal{F}\mathbf{X}c,:| - |\mathcal{F}\hat{\mathbf{X}}c,:|, |2^2, \tag{6}$$

where $\mathcal{F}\cdot$ is the discrete Fourier transform and F is the number of frequency bins. The combined loss is

$$\mathcal{L}A = \lambda\mathrm{rec}\mathcal{L}\mathrm{rec}^{(A)} + \lambda_{\mathrm{spec}}\mathcal{L}\mathrm{spec}^{(A)}. \tag{7}$$

Typical weights: $\lambda\mathrm{rec} = 1.0$, $\lambda_{\mathrm{spec}} = 0.1$.

Model B: Channel – Frequency Convolutional Autoencoder (CF-AE)

Preprocessing. Compute STFT per channel with window length N_{fft} and hop H: for channel c,

$$S_c = \mathcal{STFT}(\mathbf{X}c, :; N\text{fft}, H) \in \mathbb{C}^{F \times T'}, \tag{8}$$

and form the real-valued magnitude tensor $\mathbf{S} \in \mathbb{R}^{C \times F \times T'}$ via $\mathbf{S}_{c,f,t} = |S_c(f,t)|$.

Architecture (Example). Encoder blocks are 2D convolutions over channel and frequency axes (optionally time). Example pipeline:

- Conv2D: input $1 \times (C \times F)$ (tiled along time) $\rightarrow$ 16 filters of size (3×3), stride $(1, 1)$.
- Conv2D: 32 filters (3×3), followed by pooling over frequency axis to reduce $F \rightarrow F/2$.
- Conv2D: 64 filters (3×3), followed by flattening and linear projection to latent d.

Decoder reconstructs $\hat{\mathbf{S}}$ using ConvTranspose2D and then applies inverse STFT to obtain $\hat{\mathbf{X}}$ (overlap-add).

Training Losses. Spectral-domain reconstruction:

$$\mathcal{L}\text{rec}^{(B)} = \frac{1}{CFT'}|\mathbf{S} - \hat{\mathbf{S}}|F^2. \tag{9}$$

Band-power preservation across predefined bands $\mathcal{B}$ (e.g. theta, alpha, beta):

$$\mathcal{L}\text{bp}^{(B)} = \sum b \in \mathcal{B} \Big| P_b(\mathbf{S}) - P_b(\hat{\mathbf{S}}) \Big| 2^2, \tag{10}$$

where $P_b(\mathbf{S}) \in \mathbb{R}^C$ computes per-channel average power in band b. Final loss:

$$\mathcal{L}B = \lambda\text{rec}\mathcal{L}\text{rec}^{(B)} + \lambda_{\text{bp}}\mathcal{L}\text{bp}^{(B)}. \tag{11}$$

Typical weights: $\lambda\text{rec} = 1.0$, $\lambda_{\text{bp}} = 0.5$.

Model C: Masked Segment Reconstruction with Spatial Convolution (MSR-AE)

Masking Distribution. We sample masks that remove contiguous temporal segments and/or whole channels. Concretely, for each training sample we choose with probability p_{chan} to drop each channel independently and sample n_{gaps} temporal gaps where each gap length L is drawn from a geometric distribution with mean μ_L. The binary mask $\mathbf{M} \in 0, 1^{C \times T}$ has zeros at masked entries.

Architecture. Use residual spatial–temporal blocks that perform depthwise separable temporal convs followed by pointwise channel mixing:

- Temporal depthwise Conv1D ($k = 7$, dilation optionally >1) per channel, BN, Swish activation.
- Pointwise Conv1D (1×1) across channels to model inter-channel mixing, BN, Swish.
- Residual connection and stacking of L such blocks (e.g. $L = 6$).

The decoder takes the masked input concatenated with $\mathbf{M}$ (as an additional channel) and reconstructs values at masked positions.

Training losses. Masked reconstruction loss (focused on masked entries):

$$\mathcal{L}_{\mathrm{mask}}^{(C)} = \frac{1}{|\mathbf{M}|_0} |\mathbf{M} \odot (\mathbf{X} - \hat{\mathbf{X}})|_F^2, \tag{12}$$

where $\odot$ denotes element-wise multiplication and $|\mathbf{M}|0$ is the number of masked elements. To encourage stable representations across maskings, we add a latent consistency loss: sample two masks $\mathbf{M}^{(1)}, \mathbf{M}^{(2)}$ and minimize

$$\mathcal{L}\mathrm{cons}^{(C)} = |\mathbf{z}m^{(1)} - \mathbf{z}m^{(2)}|2^2, \tag{13}$$

where $\mathbf{z}m^{(i)}$ is the encoder output under mask $\mathbf{M}^{(i)}$. The full loss is

$$\mathcal{L}C = \lambda\mathrm{mask}\mathcal{L}\mathrm{mask}^{(C)} + \lambda\mathrm{cons}\mathcal{L}\mathrm{cons}^{(C)}. \tag{14}$$

Typical weights: $\lambda\mathrm{mask} = 1.0$, $\lambda\mathrm{cons} = 0.1$.

Practical Hyperparameters and Deployment Notes

- Sample rate f_s: typical EEG datasets use $f_s \in 128, 256$Hz. Choose N_{fft} so that frequency resolution covers desired bands (e.g. $N_{\mathrm{fft}} = 256$ for 1 Hz resolution at 256 Hz sampling).
- Latent dimension d: 64–256 depending on model capacity and downstream classifier.
- Pool size M: 3–5 candidates balance coverage and runtime. Evaluate end-to-end latency (window stride) to meet application constraints.

2.3   Online Selection Mechanism

During the inference stage, the framework aims to select the most suitable candidate model from the pool described above in an online manner. Specifically, for an incoming EEG trial denoted as $\mathbf{X} \in \mathbb{R}^{C \times T}$, each candidate model $f_m(\cdot)$ with parameters θ_m produces a reconstructed output $\hat{\mathbf{X}}_m = f_m(\mathbf{X}; \theta_m)$, where

$m \in \{1, 2, 3\}$. The discrepancy between the original input and its reconstruction is quantified through a reconstruction loss function $\mathcal{L}_{rec}(\cdot)$:

$$\mathcal{L}_{rec}^{(m)} = \|\mathbf{X} - \hat{\mathbf{X}}_m\|_2^2. \tag{15}$$

The candidate model with the smallest reconstruction loss is regarded as the most appropriate for the current trial:

$$m^* = \arg \min_{m \in \{1,2,3\}} \mathcal{L}_{rec}^{(m)}. \tag{16}$$

Subsequently, the latent representation $\mathbf{z}_{m^*}$ extracted by the selected model is adopted as the feature for downstream decoding:

$$\mathbf{z}_{m^*} = f_{m^*}^{enc}(\mathbf{X}), \tag{17}$$

where $f_{m^*}^{enc}$ denotes the encoder part of the selected candidate. This online selection mechanism enables adaptive switching among models with different generalization capabilities, thereby mitigating the influence of inter-subject variability and data drift in real-world EEG applications.

3   Experiment

3.1   SEED Dataset

The SEED dataset is a widely used benchmark for EEG-based emotion recognition. It contains EEG recordings from 15 subjects, each participating in three separate sessions spaced by approximately one week. During each session, subjects watched 15 film clips designed to elicit three types of emotions: positive, neutral, and negative. The EEG signals were recorded using a 62-channel ESI NeuroScan system at a sampling rate of 1000 Hz, and then downsampled to 200 Hz. This dataset provides sufficient variability in both temporal and inter-subject dimensions, making it suitable for evaluating cross-subject generalization.

3.2   Evaluation Protocol

To assess the generalization ability of the proposed framework, we adopt the leave-one-subject-out (LOSO) cross-validation protocol, which is the standard evaluation strategy on SEED. Specifically, in each round, the data of one subject are held out as the test set, while the data from the remaining subjects are used for training. This process is repeated until each subject has been used as the test set once. The final performance is reported as the mean accuracy and standard deviation over all subjects.

Table 1. Performance Comparison on SEED (LOSO Protocol)

Method	Accuracy (%)	Std (%)
KPCA [9]	61.28	14.62
TCA [9]	63.64	14.88
T-SVM [9]	72.53	14.00
TPT [9]	76.31	15.89
TSception [2]	73.00	11.00
DeepConvNet [6]	75.91	9.43
ShallowConvNet [6]	76.93	8.72
Proposed Framework	**77.29**	**8.61**

3.3   Results and Comparison

Table 1 summarizes the experimental results. We compare the proposed framework with several representative baseline methods, including traditional machine learning models with handcrafted features and recent deep learning approaches.

These results highlight several important insights into the behavior of self-supervised EEG models. First, the consistent improvements across different evaluation settings suggest that the proposed framework is not only effective under specific conditions but also exhibits strong adaptability to variations inherent in EEG data. This indicates that the framework can generalize more effectively across diverse subjects, a critical requirement for real-world applications. Second, the stability observed in the results implies that the approach mitigates the risk of performance fluctuations, which are often caused by individual differences in neural responses. Such robustness is particularly valuable in scenarios where reliability is essential, such as clinical and affective computing environments. Finally, the findings underline the broader significance of designing strategies that emphasize adaptability and collaboration, as they offer a promising direction toward addressing the long-standing challenge of inter-subject variability in EEG-based emotion recognition.

4   Conclusion

In this work, we proposed a novel online collaborative self-supervised framework for cross-subject EEG emotion recognition. Unlike conventional approaches that rely on a single pre-trained model, our method introduces multiple candidate models with differentiated generalization capabilities and an online selection mechanism to dynamically choose the most suitable model for unseen subjects. This design effectively addresses the challenge of inter-subject variability, which has long been a critical bottleneck in EEG-based affective computing.

Experimental results on the SEED dataset under the leave-one-subject-out (LOSO) protocol demonstrate that our approach achieves superior performance compared with state-of-the-art baselines, delivering higher average accuracy and more stable results across subjects. These findings confirm that online model collaboration and adaptive selection can substantially enhance the robustness and generalizability of self-supervised EEG emotion recognition frameworks.

Future research will extend this framework to larger datasets and more diverse affective states, as well as explore its potential integration into real-time human-computer interaction systems.

Acknowledgment. This work was supported by National Key Research and Development Program of China, Project No.2024YFE0200700, Subject No.2024YFE0200703. This work was also supported in part by the Specific Research Fund of the Innovation Platform for Academicians of Hainan Province under Grant YSPTZX202314, in part by the Shanghai Key Research Laboratory of NSAI and the Joint Laboratory on Networked AI Edge Computing, Fudan University-Changan.

References

1. Cimr, D., Fujita, H., Busovsky, D., Cimler, R.: Enhancing EEG signal analysis with geometry invariants for multichannel fusion. Inf. Fusion **102**, 102023 (2024)
2. Ding, Y., Robinson, N., Zhang, S., Zeng, Q., Guan, C.: Tsception: capturing temporal dynamics and spatial asymmetry from EEG for emotion recognition. IEEE Trans. Affect. Comput. **14**(3), 2238–2250 (2023)
3. Kan, H., Yu, J., Huang, J., Liu, Z., Wang, H., Zhou, H.: Self-supervised group meiosis contrastive learning for EEG-based emotion recognition. Appl. Intell. 1–19 (2023)
4. Qiu, S., et al.: A review on semi-supervised learning for EEG-based emotion recognition. Inf. Fusion **104**, 102190 (2024)
5. Rafiei, M.H., Gauthier, L.V., Adeli, H., Takabi, D.: Self-supervised learning for electroencephalography. IEEE Trans. Neural Netw. Learn. Syst. 1–15 (2022)
6. Schirrmeister, R.T., et al.: Deep learning with convolutional neural networks for EEG decoding and visualization. Hum. Brain Mapp. **38**(11), 5391–5420 (2017)
7. Shen, X., Liu, X., Hu, X., Zhang, D., Song, S.: Contrastive learning of subject-invariant EEG representations for cross-subject emotion recognition. IEEE Trans. Affective Comput. (2022)
8. Wang, X., Ma, Y., Cammon, J., Fang, F., Gao, Y., Zhang, Y.: Self-supervised EEG emotion recognition models based on CNN. IEEE Trans. Neural Syst. Rehabil. Eng. **31**, 1952–1962 (2023). https://doi.org/10.1109/TNSRE.2023.3263570
9. Zheng, W.L., Lu, B.L.: Personalizing EEG-based affective models with transfer learning. In: Proceedings of the Twenty-fifth International Joint Conference on Artificial Intelligence, pp. 2732–2738 (2016)

Intelligent Prediction Model for Key Group Propagation Based on Community Partition and Multiple Influences

Yunpeng Xiao[1]([✉]), Yan Tang[1], Wanjing Zhao[1], Haichuan Zhou[1], Rong Wang[1], and Guoyin Wang[2]

[1] School of Computer Science and Technology, Chongqing University of Posts and Telecommunications, Chongqing, China
{xiaoyp,wangrong1}@cqupt.edu.cn
[2] Chongqing Key Laboratory of Brain-Inspired Cognitive Computing and Educational Rehabilitation for Children with Special Needs, Chongqing Normal University, Chongqing, China
wanggy@cqnu.edu.cn

Abstract. Predicting the communication behavior of key groups in guiding topics plays an important role in aspects such as advertising marketing and rumor supervision. Against the backdrop of the rapid development of Large Language Models (LLMs), aiming at the problems of uncertain topic communication scale and diverse influence drivers in social networks, an intelligent prediction model for key group communication based on community division and multiple influences is proposed. First, starting from the breadth of the communication space, to address the uncertainty in the scale of topic dissemination, we propose the community intelligent detection MB-Link algorithm to segment different groups. This algorithm quantifies attributes such as the number and size of communities where different groups are located, so as to characterize the scale of communication. Additionally, leveraging the excellent graph processing capability of Graph Convolutional Networks (GCN), we construct node representations based on the breadth-oriented communication network. Second, in view of the differences between network structure information and text information, an LLM-driven ST2vec representation method is proposed. It extracts the influence of topic dissemination from two levels: user individuals and their friends, and quantifies various influencing factors to reconstruct the topological structure of topic dissemination. Meanwhile, this method combines the sentiment analysis capability of LLMs to determine users' emotional tendencies, thereby improving the accuracy of user behavior prediction. Finally, in response to the timeliness and dynamics of topic dissemination, time slicing is used to discretize the dissemination data. An intelligent prediction model for key group communication based on community division and ST2vec is proposed, which combines the CNN network to predict the behavior of key groups at the next dissemination moment. Experiments show that this model can not only effectively divide key groups in different communities, but also accurately predict group communication behaviors in topic networks based on complex influencing factors.

Keywords: social networks · community detection · representation learning · large language models

1 Introduction

With the in-depth development of big data and the Internet, social networks have evolved into a complex and dynamic information ecosystem. Various topics spread rapidly here, with true and false information intertwined, which can easily lead to the spread of rumors and trigger social panic and unrest. For example, false information such as "salt prevents radiation" or "salt causes cancer" after natural disasters once caused people to rush to buy salt and damaged the reputation of enterprises. It can be seen that if malicious messages are not curbed in time, they will have catastrophic consequences for individuals, society and even the country. Therefore, effectively predicting the spread trend of topics and gaining insight into user behaviors in advance are crucial for curbing malicious information, guiding the public, and creating a healthy social environment. Against this background, the rapid development of artificial intelligence technology has provided a powerful tool, which can conduct in-depth analysis and intelligent management of complex information flows in social networks. The in-depth integration of AI and social networks has spawned AI-driven social network research. Through machine learning and deep learning, it realizes intelligent insight and behavior prediction of large-scale, dynamic and heterogeneous social data, showing great potential in solving traditional challenges.

In recent years, research on predicting group communication behavior has mainly focused on three aspects: key individual users, network structure, and real-time information. Common methods include the classic SIR model, Support Vector Machine (SVM) in machine learning, as well as Convolutional Neural Network (CNN) and Recurrent Neural Network (RNN) in deep learning. However, considering the complexity of data in guiding topic networks and the diversity of key groups, the current models for predicting group communication behavior in guiding topic networks still have the following problems:

1. Uncertainty in the scale of topic dissemination. Community information reflects the breadth of topic dissemination in information spread. For example, the more communities there are, the wider the influence range of the topic is. If the factor of topic breadth can be taken into account, it will help improve the accuracy of predicting group communication behaviors.

2. Differences between network structure information and text information. Multiple influences drive the spread and diffusion of topics, forming a network of user interaction behavior relationships. How to quantify complex relationships using diverse influences and reconstruct the network topology is a major challenge. At the same time, there is the issue of how to integrate the text information involved in the dissemination process and utilize intelligent services to comprehensively predict dissemination behaviors.

3. Timeliness and dynamics of information dissemination. The popularity of information dissemination changes over time, and the forms and trends of

topic dissemination may show significant differences in different periods. Therefore, how to dynamically predict users' behaviors at the next moment based on temporal characteristics has become a task with certain challenges.

To address the above three major challenges, this paper subsequently proposes a key group communication prediction model based on community division and multiple influences. The main research contributions are as follows:

1. Construct an intelligent network segmentation community detection algorithm named MB-Link. In the breadth dissemination of topics, there are differences in the scale of the audience, and different groups also have varying community statuses in the network. By dividing the network into multiple communities, the characteristics of the communities where the groups are located can be extracted, and Graph Convolutional Networks (GCN) can be used to effectively represent the characteristics of key groups.

2. An LLM-driven S (Structure) T (Text) 2vec method is proposed to represent the structural network and text network of topics. This method, by incorporating the differences between structural information and text information, extracts the dissemination influence from both the user level and the friend level, quantifies various influencing factors, and reconstructs the topological structure of topic dissemination. Meanwhile, it leverages the text processing capability of LLMs to analyze emotional information and determine users' emotional tendencies, thereby improving the accuracy of user behavior prediction.

3. An intelligent prediction model for key group communication based on community division and ST2vec is constructed. Considering the timeliness and dynamic characteristics of topic dissemination, the topic dissemination data can be discretized through time slicing. Combined with Convolutional Neural Networks (CNN) to analyze the data characteristics of different time periods, the user behavior at the next moment of topic dissemination can be predicted.

2   Related Work

2.1   Information Propagation Prediction

In the dynamics of topic dissemination in social networks, the differentiated interaction behaviors among users often lead to the non-linear evolution of dissemination paths. Current research has constructed multi-dimensional prediction models by integrating network structure features and user behavior time-series data. Especially with the breakthrough progress in machine learning technology, researchers have combined Graph Convolutional Networks (GCN) with Long Short-Term Memory (LSTM) models, achieving significant improvements in the task of predicting dissemination scope. The following mainly elaborates on the key research results in the field of social network information dissemination prediction in recent years.

On one hand, there is a focus on analyzing the impact of the coupling mechanism between text semantic representation and node attribute features on information diffusion paths [1]. Such models adopt a multi-modal data fusion strategy, combine text semantic representation with users' historical interaction behaviors, construct embedded representations of heterogeneous network nodes, and use attention mechanisms to dynamically model the spatio-temporal dependencies in the dissemination process. Finally, they realize the probability prediction of topic dissemination behaviors based on deep learning frameworks. FIRDAUS et al. [2] revealed the dynamic interaction mechanism between users' information preferences and emotional states by constructing a sentiment polarity feature space under topic constraints and a multi-dimensional cognitive map of users, thus achieving the analysis of cross-modal dissemination decision-making mechanisms from semantic cognition to emotional drive. PANG et al. [3] optimized the joint distribution of topics and sentiments using a variational inference framework, effectively capturing the impact mechanism of semantic sparsity in short texts on sentiment representation. LI et al. [4] proposed a multi-view structure-temporal fusion framework (MISTR), which realizes social media rumor detection by jointly modeling the heterogeneous structural features and temporal dynamic evolution laws of the dissemination network. HOU et al. [5] put forward a multi-dimensional emotion prediction method that integrates users' social attributes and topic cognitive features, breaking through the representation bottleneck of traditional methods for implicit network expressions. When studying the ways of rumor dissemination, VARSHNEY et al. [6] conducted in-depth discussions on rumor texts and image-related content. LI et al. [7] extracted text features to analyze the emotions in microblogs posted by users with opposing opinions, and evaluated the effectiveness of rumor-refuting messages released on social media. WANG et al. [8] observed that network rumor information shows a credibility attenuation phenomenon during the dissemination cycle, and text mining technology based on sentiment polarity dictionaries can effectively identify the evolution of multi-dimensional emotional intensity in user comments. These studies usually consider network structure and text information in combination, being able to take both factors into account, but they lack an analysis of the opposition and unity between the complex driving forces of information dissemination.

On the other hand, there is research on information dissemination based on influence [9,10]. ZHAO et al. [11] proposed the IBPF model, which jointly decomposes forwarding data and tweet texts to quantitatively analyze complex influences. WU et al. [12] explored the implicit connections between users, and extracted personal-driven and friend-driven influencing factors based on the improved network topology to synthesize the overall social influence and predict the information dissemination situation based on social influence. LI et al. [13] proposed that different messages interact and influence each other during diffusion, mapping the uncertainty and polymorphism of topic dissemination to the dissemination space to predict the dissemination paths of dynamic messages. ZHOU et al. [14] took various social factors into account, such as users' interests, identities and emotions, and analyzed users' dissemination behaviors from different perspectives. LI et al. [15] pointed out that user behaviors on social network platforms are roughly divided into two types: consumption behaviors and social link behaviors, and designed the NJBP model to integrate the correlation between the two types of behaviors for further user behavior prediction. YAN et al. [16] mitigated the impact of short-term data on predicting development trends, introduced time-lag parameters, and proposed a grey model to predict the development trends of real events on microblogs. LI et al. [17] considered the inconsistency of users' cognitive states under the action of multiple influences, introduced information entropy to quantify the driving force of message forwarding, and took into account the differences in the amount of information forwarded by users' cognition to analyze the information dissemination trends.

2.2 AI-Driven Social Network Research

Large language models (LLMs) possess exceptional language understanding, generation, and manipulation capabilities, enabling them to handle various natural language processing tasks related to social networks. GAO et al. leveraged the strong human-like abilities of LLMs in perception, reasoning, and behavior to construct a social network simulation system, modeling interactive behaviors to observe the spread of information, attitudes, and emotions. ZHANG et al. integrated LLMs into agent-based modeling to simulate influence diffusion. It allows agents (representing users) to generate language-level, context-aware responses, thereby providing deeper insights into user interactions than traditional probabilistic models. DHIMAN et al. combined BERT's deep contextual understanding capability with GPT's generative capability to achieve robust fake news classification. GUR et al. proposed an LLM-enhanced agent-based influence diffusion model, along with a web-based visualization tool for simulating information dissemination in social networks. Despite their advanced capabilities, LLMs still face challenges in complex reasoning and are prone to generating factually inaccurate or meaningless information.

3 Problem Definition

3.1 Relevant Definitions

The main task of this paper is to predict the dissemination behavior of key groups in the guiding topic network. We will analyze the dissemination trends based on the multiple influencing factors that drive user behavior and the users' own historical data. The motivations that drive users to make decisions can be divided into individual psychological factors and friend influence factors, and the game or complementary relationship between these two will affect users' final decisions. The relevant attributes of the driving forces at the individual level and the friend level are defined as follows:

Definition 1: Individual Activeness $Act(v_i)$

The activity level of individual users in a topic network reflects, to a certain extent, their subjective willingness to participate in topic discussions and dissemination. The higher the individual's activity level, the greater the possibility of disseminating the topic. We can measure a user's activity level through their historical topic forwarding rate.

$$Act(v_i) = \frac{replyNum(v_i)}{allGetNum(v_i)} \tag{1}$$

where $replyNum(v_i)$ refers to the number of replies and forwards in the historical behaviors of v_i, while $allGetNum(v_i)$ represents the total number of all messages received. A higher historical topic forwarding rate indicates that the user is more active and has a stronger acceptance of new topics, thus being more likely to participate in the spread of topics.

Definition 2: Individual Influence $InfLevel(v_i)$

The propagation power of an individual user depends on the influence $InfLevel(v_i)$ of the user in the topic network. The SIR model can be relied on to calculate the influence score of a node, determine the value of $InfLevel(v_i)$, and then learn about the user's propagation power. Users with high propagation power are more sensitive to the perception of topics and will have a greater probability of participating in topic discussions.

Definition 3: Friend Group Influence $InfFriends(v_i)$

A user's behavior is influenced by the behaviors of surrounding friend nodes. For example, the more opinion leaders there are in the community where a node resides, the larger the influential group will be. In addition, the frequency of interactions between friends also affects the probability of a user participating in a topic. The influence of friends is calculated by Formula (2).

$$InfFriends(v_i) = \frac{leaderNum(v_i)}{allfriendsNum(v_i)} + \mu * Interaction \tag{2}$$

where $leaderNum(v_i)$ represents the number of opinion leaders among friends $allfriendsNum(v_i)$ represents the total number of all friends of user v_i, Interaction represents the interaction quantity between v_i and friends, and μ is the attenuation coefficient.

Definition 4: Friend Leadership in Topics $Leadership(v_i)$

Friends who exhibit leadership in topic discussions tend to influence others' willingness to participate. Leadership is quantified by the average level of responses (likes, retweets, comments) received by friends. The leadership score is defined as:

$$Leadership(v_i) = \alpha \cdot \overline{likeNum(v_i)} + \beta \cdot \overline{replyNum(v_i)} \\ + \gamma \cdot \overline{comNum(v_i)} \tag{3}$$

In the formula, $\overline{likeNum(v_i)}$ refers to the average number of likes obtained from the messages posted by user v_i within one month, $\overline{replyNum(v_i)}$ is the average number of forwards, and $\overline{comNum(v_i)}$ is the average number of comments. Since different interaction behaviors have different influence effects on topic dissemination, α, β and γ are introduced as weights to ensure the rationality of the calculation.

Definition 5: Friend Similarity $Sim(v_i, v_j)$

Friend similarity can be used to measure the similarity between users. The higher the degree of similarity between two users, the more likely their behavior trajectories are to be consistent. Here, we use the number of common friends and the number of messages jointly participated in by two users to measure friend similarity, as shown in Formula (4).

$$Sim(v_i, v_j) = \frac{ComFriends(v_i, v_j)}{Friends(v_i) + Friends(v_j)} + \frac{ComMessage(v_i, v_j)}{Message(v_i) + Message(v_j)} \tag{4}$$

In the formula, $ComFriends(v_i, v_j)$ represents the number of common friends between user v_i and user v_j; $Friends(v_i)$ denotes the total number of friends of user v_i, and $Friends(v_j)$ denotes the total number of friends of user v_j. $ComMessage(v_i, v_j)$ stands for the number of messages jointly participated in by user v_i and user v_j; $Message(v_i)$ represents the number of messages participated in by user v_i, and $Message(v_j)$ represents the number of messages participated in by user v_j.

3.2   Formal Problem Definition

The main task of the model constructed in this paper is to predict the behavior trajectory of key groups in the guiding topic network at the next moment. By integrating individual influence and friend influence to characterize multiple influences, the accuracy of prediction is improved, and the dissemination trend of the entire topic is grasped. To formalize the research problem, we define the guiding topic network at time T as $G^T = \{U^T, E\}$, where U^T is the set of user nodes in the network at time T, and E is the set of edges formed by user interactions in the network. Then, the set of individual attributes of users is extracted as $A = \{(v_i, a) | v_i \in G\}$, and the set of message texts of users is $M^T = \{(v_i, I) | v_i \in G\}$. First, the MB-Link algorithm is used to segment the network and assign values to the attributes of community user nodes; second, the weights of the edges in the topic network are reconstructed by combining the quantified multiple influences, so as to obtain the updated network structure representation. At the same time, text representation learning is used to analyze the user's message text set to obtain information representation; finally, the structural representation and text representation are concatenated to get the feature representation U^d, and time is discretized by time slicing to obtain the user behavior prediction result $B^{(t+1)}$ at time t+1. The problem definition formula is given by Formula (5).

$$\left. \begin{array}{l} G^T = \{U^T, E\} \\ A = \{(v_i, \alpha) \mid v_i \in G\} \\ MT = \{(v_i, I) \mid v_i \in G\} \end{array} \right\} \Rightarrow U^d \Rightarrow B^{t+1} \tag{5}$$

(1)Problem input

Based on the above introduction, the input of the model in this paper is defined as:

- The guiding topic network at time T, denoted as $G^T = \{U^T, E\}$, includes all users in the network and the edges formed by their interactions.
- The set of users' individual attributes is $A = \{(v_i, a) \mid v_i \in G\}$, where attribute a includes the previously defined activity level, communication power, and so on.
- The set of users' message texts is $MT = \{(v_i, I) \mid v_i \in G\}$, which contains the text content of messages disseminated by users.

(2)Problem output

Based on the above inputs and combined with the prediction model in this paper, the output can be obtained as:

- The user feature representation U^d is obtained by combining structural representation and text representation. Specifically, the weights of edges in the topic network are reconstructed through quantified multiple influences, and then the user feature representation is constructed by combining the reconstructed structural features with the text representation derived from Doc2vec analysis.
- The prediction result of users' dissemination behavior at the next moment is $B^{(t+1)}$. Based on the constructed user feature vectors, a key group dissemination prediction model is designed, which is based on community division and multiple influences. The final user behavior results are dichotomized into forwarding and non-forwarding. Specifically, $B^{(t+1)} = 0$ indicates that the user will not forward and will not participate in the dissemination of the topic; while $B^{(t+1)} = 1$ indicates that the user will forward and actively participate in the dissemination of the topic.

4   Model

This paper proposes an intelligent prediction model for key group communication based on community division and multiple influence. The main content is divided into three parts: community division, quantification of multiple influences, and communication behavior prediction. The overall framework diagram of the model is shown in Fig. 1. First, the MB-Link algorithm is used to intelligently divide the community structure, decompose the complex network, and assign values to user node attributes. Second, the driving effect of user behavior on influence is quantified from both the individual level and the friend level, the weights of network edges are reconstructed, and LLM is used to analyze users' emotional information. Finally, considering the timeliness of topic popularity, time slicing technology is adopted for discretization, and the convolutional neural network is combined to complete the final prediction of user communication behavior.

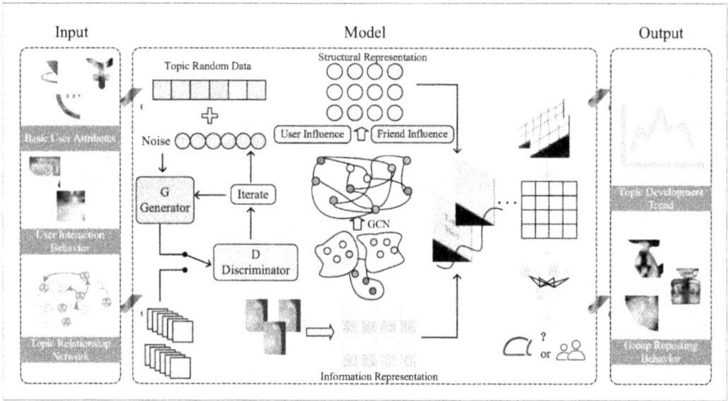

Fig. 1. Model diagram.

4.1   Community Partitioning

From the perspective of extensive dissemination, information in the guiding topic network spreads widely with an uncertain scale. As one of the structural features of the topic network, communities are characterized by close internal connections and sparse external connections. Social networks based on community division can undergo dimensionality reduction and local focusing, thereby improving the computational efficiency and prediction accuracy of subsequent dissemination behavior prediction. First, the topic network is divided into different community structures using a community division algorithm, through which attributes such as the structure, size, and quantity of the community where a node resides can be obtained. These attributes are attached to the user's node attributes, and then the characteristics of the community network are taken as node features. Graph Convolutional Network (GCN) is used to perform feature representation on user nodes in the topic network, which serves as the basis for the representation of user structural features. The schematic diagram is shown in Fig. 2.

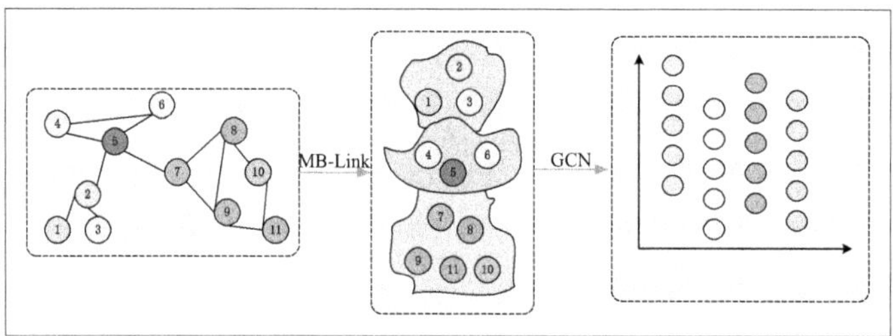

Fig. 2. Community division.

(1)Division of user groups

The breadth of propagation in a topic network is closely related to the information of the community to which users belong. Traditional methods for community division in social networks include the Louvain algorithm and modularity optimization algorithms. This paper argues that although connections between communities in a topic network are not as frequent as those within communities, some special user nodes in communities may maintain close connections with multiple communities. These nodes not only belong to multiple communities but also act as "bridges" between communities. Therefore, an improved MB-Link algorithm is proposed based on the classic Link community division algorithm [18], with the following process:

The classic Link algorithm is an edge-based division algorithm. It calculates the similarity between edges, such as topological overlap based on shared nodes, and performs hierarchical clustering on edges to form "link communities" with multi-scale structures, which can more naturally reveal overlapping community structures in the network. The MB-Link algorithm based on this is also an overlapping community detection algorithm that divides communities by aggregating edges. Its core idea is: identify overlapping nodes in the topic network, calculate the similarity between each adjacent edge of these nodes, sort them by similarity, merge edges with high similarity, and finally obtain a community structure based on edge division.

Analogous to the definition of edge similarity in the Link algorithm, this paper defines edge similarity as the interaction frequency between user nodes. Different weights are assigned according to different interaction counts. Obviously, the connection between users with more frequent interactions is closer than that between users with little interaction. For example, if two edges e_{ik} and e_{jk} share a node k, the similarity calculation formula for these two edges is shown in Formula (6).

$$S_{(e_{ik},e_{jk})} = \frac{1}{|n_{ik} - n_{jk}|} \cdot \frac{Common}{Number} \tag{6}$$

In the formula, n_{ik} represents the total number of all types of interaction behaviors between user node i and k, and n_{jk} represents the total number of all types of interaction behaviors between user node j and k. The absolute value of the difference between the two is taken, and the smaller this value is, the higher the similarity between the two nodes; $Common$ represents the intersection of the neighbor nodes of node i and node j, that is, the set of neighbor nodes they jointly have, and its definition formula is shown (7).

$$Common = n_{+}(i) \cap n_{+}(j) \tag{7}$$

Here, $n_{+}(i)$ refers to all neighbor nodes of node i, and similarly, $n_{+}(j)$ refers to all neighbor nodes of node j; the intersection of the two is taken. Corresponding to Common, Number represents the union of the neighbor nodes of node i

and node j, that is, all the neighbor nodes of the two nodes, and its definition formula is shown in Formula (8).

$$Number = n_+(i) \cup n_+(j) \tag{8}$$

To evaluate the quality of community division, this paper defines the division density Density as an indicator, whose value is positively correlated with the effectiveness of the division algorithm. Assuming that the total number of edges in the topic network is M, the total number of nodes is N, and the set of community structures divided by the algorithm is $C = \{C_1, C_2, \ldots, C_e\}$, the calculation formula of Density is shown in Formula (9).

$$Density = \frac{2}{M} \sum_e m_c \frac{m_c - (n_c - 1)}{(n_c - 2)(n_c - 1)} \tag{9}$$

In the formula, m_c represents the number of edges of a random community C_c, and n_c represents the number of nodes of a random community C_c.

(2)Representation of Community Nodes

After dividing into different communities, each community has distinct attributes, including characteristics such as the community's network structure, node attributes, and activity level. These diverse community features symbolize rich node representations. To more effectively utilize the features contained in different communities, this paper adopts the GCN model, taking factors such as the size of the community where a node resides, the number of communities, and the number of edges of the node itself as node attributes to reflect the node's influence on the topic within the scope of extensive propagation. Then, leveraging GCN's powerful graph data processing capability, the two important factors of the node's own features and the network structure it belongs to are fully integrated to obtain the node vector representation in the horizontal propagation space.

The breadth of propagation range of a user node is closely related to the community it belongs to. Therefore, we take the number of communities connected to the node, the community size, and the number of edges of the node itself as the node's attributes, so that the feature representation of a single user node can be obtained as $S_a = \{Num\_community, Num\_size, Num\_degree\}$. Then, the user feature matrix of the entire topic network is $X = N \times S_a$, where N is the total number of user nodes in the topic network.

This paper uses the GCN model for feature representation of community nodes, considering the interaction between the attributes of user nodes themselves and the network topology. This model can effectively mine the hidden information of nodes in different community structures. The input layer consists of the user feature matrix x, adjacency matrix A, and degree matrix D. The output of the GCN model is shown in Formula (10).

$$Z^{(n+1)} = f(H(n), A) = \sigma\left(\hat{A} H^{(n)} W^{(n)}\right) \tag{10}$$

In the formula, $H^{(0)} = X$, which is the original feature matrix of users. The input matrix $H^{(n)}$ of the next layer is the output matrix of the previous layer. The output result of the first layer is $Z^{(1)} = f(H^{(0)}, A) = \mathrm{ReLu}(\hat{A}XW^{(0)})$; $W^{(n)}$ is a shared parameter matrix; σ is a nonlinear activation function, such as the often - used softmax function, sigmoid function, etc.

$$\hat{A} = \tilde{D}^{-\frac{1}{2}}\tilde{A}\tilde{D}^{-\frac{1}{2}}X \tag{11}$$

Herein, $\tilde{D}$ represents the averaged processing of the degree matrix; $\tilde{A}$ is the adjacency matrix after normalization processing, which balances the influence degree among nodes, and $\tilde{A} = A + I$, where I is a diagonal matrix.

4.2 Feature Representation via ST2vec

In the guiding topic network, there are numerous influencing factors that drive the dissemination behavior of user groups. How to better integrate various influencing factors, combine the structural characteristics of the network and the information characteristics of the text, and deeply explore the essential attributes of users is an urgent problem to be solved in the current prediction of group dissemination behavior. To address this issue, this paper proposes a representation learning method called ST2vec. Based on multiple influences, this method integrates factors from both network structure and text features to construct a multi-dimensional user feature representation.

(1)Structural Representation

The magnitude of multiple influences directly affects users' further responsive behaviors after receiving information. For instance, under high influence, users may choose to forward or comment, and these behaviors are more conducive to the spread of topics; while under low influence, users are more likely to give likes or simply receive the information without taking any action. Therefore, how to quantify multiple influences can further help us predict the types of users' dissemination behaviors. To this end, we comprehensively quantify it from two aspects: user influence $PersonInf(v_i)$ and friend influence $FriendInf(v_i)$. User influence is mainly extracted from aspects such as an individual's psychological effects, preferences, and activity level. The specific user influence consists of individual activity and individual dissemination power, and its calculation formula is shown in Formula (12).

$$PersonInf(v_i) = Act(v_i) + Spread(v_i) \tag{12}$$

The friend influence, on the other hand, is constructed from three aspects: the influence of the friend group, the topic leadership of friends, and the similarity with friends, with the specific calculation formula as follows:

$$\begin{aligned} FriendInf(v_i) = {} & InfFriends(v_i) \\ & + Leadership(v_i) + Sim(v_i, v_j) \end{aligned} \tag{13}$$

Given that users' dissemination behaviors are influenced by both users' own influence and friends' influence, to ensure that the influence degrees of the two are balanced, a multiple linear regression algorithm is adopted to quantify the multiple influences $MultipleInf(v_i)$ of users' behaviors.

$$MultipleInf(v_i) = \rho_0 + \rho_1 \times PersonInf(v_i) \\ + \rho_2 \times FriendInf(v_i) \tag{14}$$

In the formula, ρ_0, ρ_1, and ρ_2 are partial regression coefficients obtained from the training of the multiple linear regression model. ρ_1 and ρ_2 are important parameters that characterize the significance of user influence and friend influence in driving their respective behaviors.

This paper explores quantifying the multiple influences that drive users' dissemination behaviors. We map these driving influences to the weights of one-way edges in the interaction network within the topic network, thereby reconstructing the overall structure of the interaction network. The greater the comprehensively considered multiple influences, the greater the weight of the interaction edges between users. We introduce the Node2vec algorithm to represent the structural characteristics of the topic network, which can more efficiently mine and reconstruct the hidden relationships between users. A schematic flow chart is shown in Fig. 3.

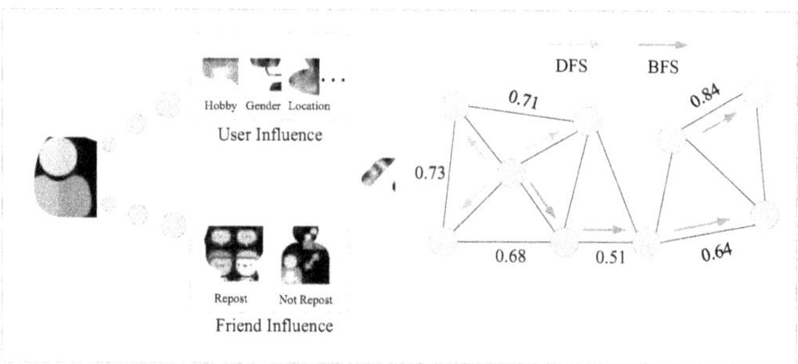

Fig. 3. ST2vec structure representation.

The reason for using Node2vec to reconstruct the network structure is that it combines two sampling methods: deep propagation and breadth propagation, which enables the final feature representation of nodes to have stronger expressive ability and can retain both the local and global characteristics of the network structure. Assuming that the current walking node is v_i and its neighbor node is v_k, the probability calculation formula for the next walking node being v_j is shown in Formula (15).

$$p(v_j \mid v_i) = \begin{cases} \dfrac{\alpha_{pq}(v_k, v_j)w(v_i, v_j)}{z}, & (v_i, v_k, v_j) \in G \\ 0, & \text{others} \end{cases} \tag{15}$$

In the formula, $\alpha_{pq}(v_k, v_j)$ is the bias coefficient that controls the direction of the random walk, $w(v_i, v_j)$ is the edge weight between node v_i and node v_j, and z is the normalization constant.

Finally, the obtained feature representation of the topic network structural feature vector is shown in Formula (16).

$$S = [s_1, s_2, s_3, \ldots, s_n] \tag{16}$$

In it, S is the matrix of all node vectors of the topic network, and s_n represents the n-th node vector.

(2) Textual Representation

In addition to extracting influence from network structural features, users' daily topic information also contains personal emotions or tendencies, which are important factors affecting users' behavior choices. Regarding how to extract emotional tendencies from the topic information posted or forwarded by users, traditional text feature representation methods face problems such as dimensionality explosion, data sparsity, and failure to consider word order. The text content feature representation method of the ST2vec algorithm combines two methods, TF-IDF and Doc2vec, and the overall flow diagram is shown in Fig. 4.

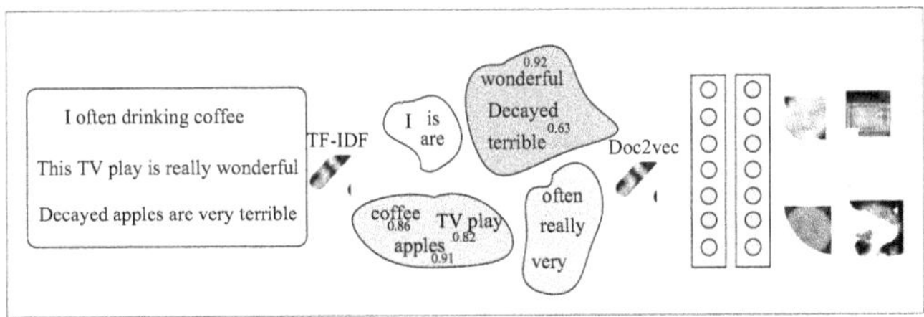

Fig. 4. ST2vec text representation.

We aggregate the text data posted or forwarded by users over a certain period of time to form a complete paragraph for each user. Then, we perform word segmentation on the paragraph, separating words with low semantic significance such as auxiliary words, stop words, and modal particles from candidate words that can reflect the topic content. We use the TF-IDF algorithm to represent the importance of effective words in the paragraph, thereby extracting high-quality keywords. The core of this method lies in the combination of term frequency and inverse document frequency, and the definition formula of term frequency is shown in Formula (17).

$$TF(t) = \frac{wordNum}{docAllWords} \tag{17}$$

In the formula, $TF(t)$ represents the importance of a certain word t in the current paragraph, and the importance is characterized by the proportion frequency of the word in the paragraph. wordNum denotes the number of occurrences of the word in the current paragraph, and docAllWords is the total number of words in the current paragraph. The definition formula of inverse document frequency is shown in (18). Wherein, $IDF(t)$ represents the importance and representativeness of a certain word t in all paragraphs. N denotes the total number of paragraphs, and $DF(t)$ refers to the number of paragraphs containing the word t.

$$IDF(t) = \ln \frac{1+N}{1+DF(t)} + 1 \tag{18}$$

After filtering words using the TF-IDF method, the weights of all candidate words can be obtained, and core words are determined based on these weights. Next, the Doc2Vec representation learning method is used to map the text information of the selected core words into feature vectors, so as to mine users' hobbies or interests, extract their emotional tendencies from them, and finally obtain the text information feature vectors of users as shown in Formula (19):

$$M = [v_1, v_2, \ldots, v_n] \tag{19}$$

In the formula, M represents the user interest vector matrix; n represents the number of users in the topic network.

In addition, we leverage the powerful semantic understanding and emotional reasoning capabilities of Large Language Models (LLMs) to perform direct sentiment analysis on users' text content, thereby obtaining more accurate and detailed representations of emotional tendencies. Specifically, after preliminary text preprocessing, users' text data is input into a pre-trained LLM. The LLM can capture complex relationships between words and contextual information, directly outputting the user's emotional intensity score s. Let $m_i = [v_i, s_i]$, then the new user interest vector matrix can be expressed as:

$$M = [m_1, m_2, \ldots, m_n] \tag{20}$$

4.3   Key Group Behavior Prediction Model

After the above work, we have successfully quantified the multiple influencing factors that drive user behavior and conducted feature representation from both network structure and text information. The task of this section is to use the topic network feature representation to complete the prediction of key group propagation behavior. Considering the evolving propagation trends of hot topics over time, we discretize time based on time slicing technology and combine convolutional neural networks (CNN) to complete the final group propagation behavior prediction, proposing a group behavior prediction model ST2vec-CNN based on time discretization and CNN. For the propagation behavior of key groups, we define it as a binary classification problem, i.e., reposting or not reposting, because reposting behavior has the greatest impact on the propagation trend of topics. Given the input topic feature vector at time t, the prediction result of the propagation behavior of key groups in the topic network at time $t+1$ can be output.

We concatenate the obtained network topology feature representation vector S and the text information sentiment feature representation vector M to obtain the fused feature vector matrix representation E, whose definition is shown in Formula (21).

$$E = S \oplus M = [e_1, e_2, \ldots, e_n] \tag{21}$$

Drawing on the structure of CNN, the prediction model mainly consists of three parts: a convolutional layer, a pooling layer, and a fully connected layer. First, the fused feature matrix is input into the convolutional layer, undergoes two layers of convolution operations, and then enters the fully connected layer to obtain a two-dimensional output for each user. The softmax function is used to perform binary classification on users, and the expression of the prediction result is shown in Formula (22).

$$B^{t+1} = \begin{cases} 1 & \text{if } P(y = 1 \mid v_i) > P(y = 0 \mid v_i) \\ 0 & \text{if } P(y = 1 \mid v_i) < P(y = 0 \mid v_i) \end{cases} \tag{22}$$

In this context, B^{t+1} represents the predicted user behavior result at time $t+1$. $B^{t+1} = 1$ indicates that the user will repost the topic information and participate in topic propagation; while $B^{t+1} = 0$ indicates that the user will not perform the reposting behavior and will not participate in the topic propagation.

4.4   Model Algorithm

The input of the guiding topic network key group propagation behavior prediction model is the topic network $G^T = \{U^T, E\}$, the user's individual attribute set $A = \{(v_i, a) \mid v_i \in G\}$, and the user's message text set $M^T = \{(v_i, I) \mid v_i \in G\}$. We comprehensively quantify the multiple influences driving users' propagation behaviors from two perspectives: user influence and friend influence, reconstruct the network structure of the topic network, use the ST2vec algorithm to represent the features of the network structure and text messages, and finally obtain the predicted results of users' propagation behaviors at time $t+1$. The specific model algorithm is shown in Table 1.

The complexity analysis of the model algorithm is as follows: The time complexity of the breadth propagation algorithm based on community division is $O(N^2)$, the time complexity of the ST2vec algorithm is $O(\log_2 N) + O(N^2)$, and the time complexity of the final CNN prediction model is $O(N^2)$. Therefore, the time complexity of the entire model is $O(\log_2 N) + O(N^2) + O(N^2) \sim O(N^2)$.

5   Experiments and Analysis

5.1   Experimental Setup

(1)Datasets

Two publicly available datasets are used in this study. The first is the Sina Weibo dataset [19], from which two trending topics are selected for experimentation: Topic A, "The viral popularity of Liu Genghong's fitness workouts," and Topic B, "The Paris Olympic Games." The second is the Facebook dataset [20], from which two additional hot topics are chosen: Topic C, "The lockdown of the U.S. Capitol," and Topic D, "Why Charlie Hebdo became a target of attack." The detailed statistical information for these topics is presented in Table 2.

(2)Baseline Methods

Table 1. Prediction algorithm of group behavior in leading topic network

Alg.	Prediction Algorithm of Key Group Propagation Behavior in Leading Topic Network
Input:	Leading topic network $G^T = \{U^T, E\}$ User attribute set: $A = \{(v_i, a) \| v_i \in G\}$ User text set: $MT = \{(v_i, I) \| v_i \in G\}$
Output:	$t + 1$ time propagation result: B^{t+1}
1.	Segment communities via Eq. (6)-(11) to get node representations;
2.	**For** each user v_i **do**
3.	Compute $Act(v_i)$ and $Spread(v_i)$ via Eq. (4-1);
4.	Compute $InfFriends(v_i)$, $Leadership(v_i)$, $Sim(v_i, v_j)$ via Eq. (4-2)-(4–4);
5.	Quantify user and friend multi-dimensional influence;
6.	Extract structure feature S via ST2vec (Eqs. 12, 13, 14, 15 and 16);
7.	Extract text feature M via ST2vec (Eqs. 17, 18 and 19);
8.	**End for**
9.	Fuse S and M as CNN input;
10.	**Repeat**
11.	Minimize cross entropy, update w and b;
12.	**Until** convergence;
13.	Train model to predict B^{t+1};
14.	**Return** B^{t+1}

Table 2. Statistical data of four groups of topics

Topic	#Users	#Followers	#Edges
Topic A	3,534	6,245	35,624
Topic B	6,247	8,541	45,788
Topic C	7,983	12,432	74,579
Topic D	3,436	4,247	15,467

To comprehensively compare the performance of our proposed model, we select the following four state-of-the-art baseline methods:

- HGNN-TD [21]: A method that integrates heterogeneous graph structures (user-post-topic) with temporal features. It models user interest evolution via dynamic edge weights and improves F1 scores in retweet prediction on Twitter and Weibo datasets.
- EAMM [22]: A multimodal emotion-aware model that fuses features from text (BERT), images (CLIP), and audio (Mel-spectrogram). It employs a cross-modal alignment loss to mitigate bias caused by modality inconsistency, thereby enhancing emotional expressiveness in social content.

- EURD [23]: A role-discovery framework that uses contrastive learning to classify users into roles (e.g., opinion leaders, disseminators, silent users). It leverages SHAP values to explain feature contributions and improve interpretability of dissemination predictions.
- HST-GCN [24]: A spatiotemporal graph convolutional network that decomposes information diffusion into global (city-level) and local (user-level) processes. It jointly models geographic distance and propagation delay to enhance prediction accuracy.

The evaluation metrics used for the dissemination behavior prediction model include accuracy, recall, F1-score, precision, and the ROC curve, which are employed to assess the overall performance of the prediction model.

5.2 Performance Analysis

The comparative experiments in this section are divided into two main parts: The first part evaluates the performance of the proposed ST2vec method in terms of network topology and textual content representation; the second part compares the performance of the proposed key group dissemination behavior prediction model with that of four baseline methods.

(1) Representation Learning Evaluation

To capture both the network structural features and user textual information within topic networks, this study proposes the ST2vec method for feature representation. To evaluate its contribution to the overall prediction model, we conduct comparative analyses from two perspectives: network topology representation and text content representation, using other representative embedding methods as baselines.

First, we compare the structural feature representation performance. A controlled experiment is conducted under identical model training parameters, using two classical methods—DeepWalk and Node2vec—as benchmarks. The comparison results are shown in Fig. 5. It is evident that across all four topics, the proposed ST2vec method consistently outperforms the other two in terms of performance metrics, indicating its significant effectiveness in enhancing prediction accuracy. The performance gap is especially notable on Topic A and Topic B, suggesting that users in the Weibo dataset are more susceptible to the effects of multi-dimensional influence.

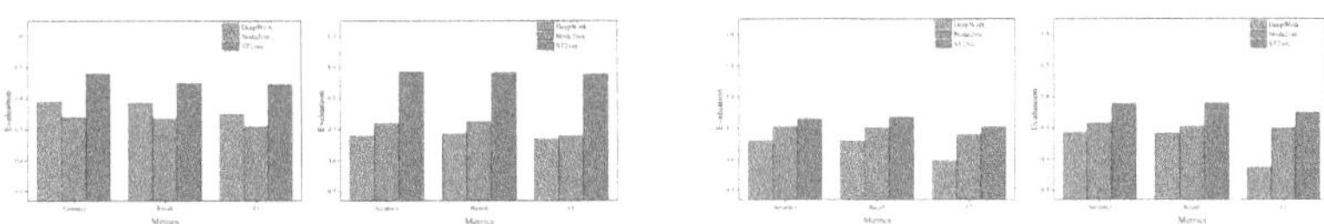

Fig. 5. Comparison of learning performance of topic structure feature representation.

Considering that the structural representation of the ST2vec method comprehensively considers the impact of multiple influences on users' propagation behaviors based on two aspects, namely user influence and friend influence, we reconstructed the network structure and assigned new edge weights. To demonstrate the necessity and effectiveness of taking multiple influences into account, we designed a set of controlled experiments. The experimental groups include: the topic network reconstructed with multiple influences + Node2vec representation (S), the topic network reconstructed only based on user influence + Node2vec representation (U), the topic network reconstructed only based on friend influence + Node2vec representation (F), and the unreconstructed topic network + Node2vec (O). We used the ROC curve as a comparison indicator, and the results are shown in Fig. 6. It can be seen from the figure that the method based on reconstructing with multiple influences has a significant advantage in effect compared with the other groups, further proving that comprehensively considering multiple influences is helpful for predicting users' propagation behaviors. In addition, the performance of the topic network reconstructed only considering user influence is better than that of the topic network reconstructed only considering friend influence. This indicates that in most cases, the dominant factor affecting users' propagation behaviors is still the autonomous emotional tendency. Although the influence of friends accounts for a certain proportion, it does not play a dominant role.

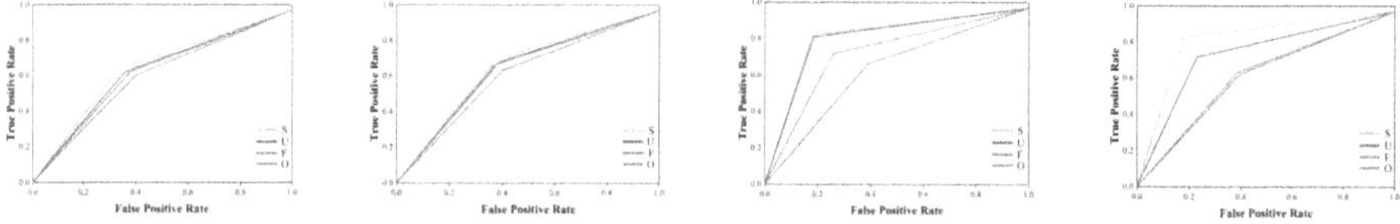

Fig. 6. Comparison of ROC curves of different methods.

On the other hand, we conducted comparative experiments on the representation of user text information. The ST2vec method characterizes users' emotional tendencies by extracting their hobbies or interests. In the comparative experiments, we selected two text representation learning methods, namely Doc2vec and Word2vec, and the experimental results are shown in Fig. 7. It can be seen that the performance of the four topics varies slightly, but overall, the ST2vec method performs slightly better than the other two methods. Among them, it achieves the best performance on Topic B, with an accuracy rate **12%** higher than that of Word2vec. The datasets of Topic A and Topic B generally perform better than those of Topic C and Topic D, which indicates that Topic A and Topic B contain more abundant effective text information, enabling the extraction of more key information representing users' emotional tendencies.

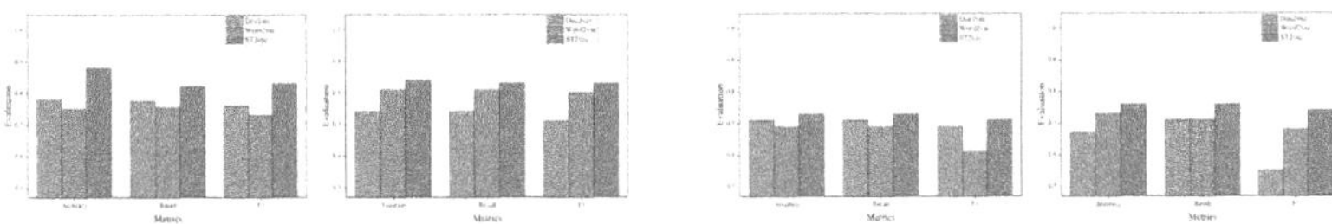

Fig. 7. Comparison of learning performance of topic text feature representation.

To further verify the rationality of combining structural feature representation and text feature representation, we conducted a controlled experiment, selecting different combinations for comparison. These combinations include Combination A (Node2vec + Word2vec), Combination B (Node2vec + Doc2vec), Combination C (DeepWalk + Word2vec), Combination D (DeepWalk + Doc2vec), as well as the ST2vec method itself. The performance comparison chart is shown in Fig. 8. It can be seen from the figure that on the datasets of Topic C and D, Combination B performs poorly, with the lowest accuracy rate of **69%**; while on the datasets of Topic A and B, Combination C has poor performance, with the lowest accuracy rate of **72%**. Overall, among the performances of the four topics, the performance of Combination A is close to that of ST2vec, and only in some indicators and topics, ST2vec is slightly better than Combination A. This indicates that the ST2vec method has certain significance in the reconstruction of network structure and the selection of key words in text information on the basis of Combination A.

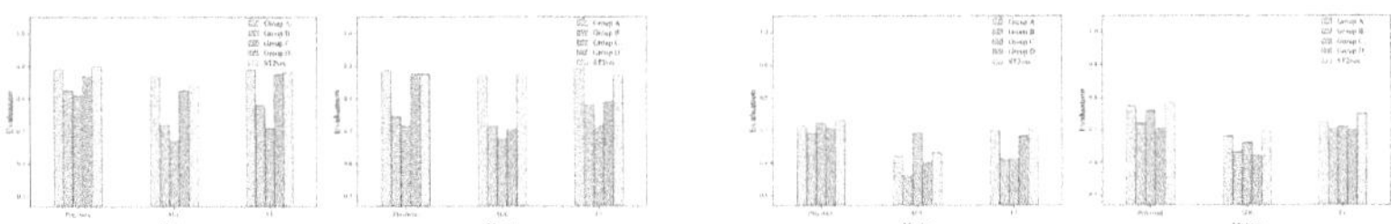

Fig. 8. Characteristic combination performance comparison.

(2) Comparison with Baseline Methods

In addition to the comparative experiments on representation learning methods, this section will conduct a performance comparison analysis between the four baseline methods mentioned in the previous section and the behavior prediction model, using multiple indicators as measurement parameters. The specific comparison results are shown in Tables 3 to 4, 5 and 6. Based on data analysis, it fully demonstrates the effectiveness of the proposed model in predicting user propagation behavior and verifies the correctness of the idea in this paper. Among the four different topics, the prediction model performs best on Topic A, with an accuracy rate of **89%**, which is **16%** higher than that of HGNN-TD; while its performance on Topic C is not satisfactory, with an accuracy rate of only **74%**. Overall, the performance of Topics A and B is better, while that of Topics C and D is relatively poor. This may be related to the rich text data in the Weibo dataset. Making full use of text information can more accurately grasp users' emotional tendencies. To sum up, the prediction model in this paper achieves the best effect.

Table 3. Topic A performance of different models

Method	ACC	AUC	F1
HGNN-TD	0.76	0.63	0.70
EAMM	0.89	0.86	0.89
EURD	0.77	0.66	0.72
HST-GCN	**0.90**	**0.89**	**0.90**
ST2vec-CNN	0.89	0.88	0.87

Table 4. Topic B performance of different models

Method	ACC	AUC	F1
HGNN-TD	0.73	0.66	0.72
EAMM	0.79	0.73	0.77
EURD	0.83	0.81	0.83
HST-GCN	0.86	0.83	0.86
ST2vec-CNN	**0.87**	**0.86**	**0.86**

Table 5. Topic C performance of different models

Method	ACC	AUC	F1
HGNN-TD	0.67	0.51	0.55
EAMM	0.72	0.61	0.68
EURD	0.68	0.52	0.57
HST-GCN	0.73	0.63	0.70
ST2vec-CNN	**0.74**	**0.65**	**0.71**

Table 6. Topic D performance of different models

Method	ACC	AUC	F1
HGNN-TD	0.73	0.65	0.71
EAMM	0.76	0.68	0.74
EURD	0.73	0.63	0.70
HST-GCN	0.69	0.56	0.61
ST2vec-CNN	**0.77**	**0.69**	**0.75**

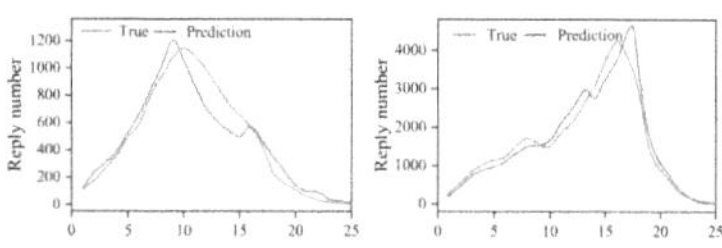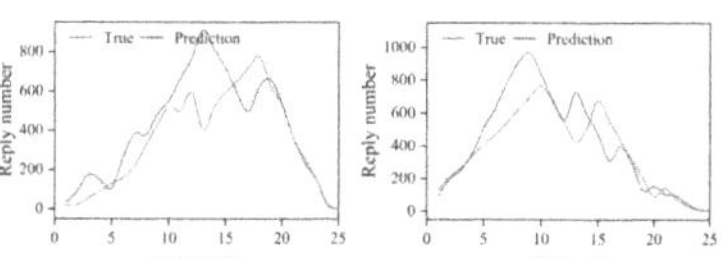

Fig. 9. Characteristic combination performance comparison.

Figure 9 shows the comparison between the future propagation trend predicted by the proposed model in the guided topic network and the real topic development trend. It can be seen that the number of user reposts predicted by the propagation behavior prediction model is basically consistent with the actual number of user reposts, and can well fit the real development trend of the topic. Among them, the fitting effect of Topic A and Topic B is particularly significant.

6   Conclusion

In response to the uncertainty of the propagation scale in guided topic networks and the multiple complex factors influencing users' propagation behaviors, this paper proposes an intelligent prediction model for key group propagation based on community division and multiple influences, which is used to dynamically predict the propagation behaviors of topic users at future moments. Firstly, aiming at the uncertainty of the breadth propagation scale of topics, the improved MB-Link algorithm is used for community division to obtain community node representations, which serve as the basis for user structural features. Secondly, considering the multiple influencing factors driving users' propagation behaviors, the influences are comprehensively quantified from two aspects: user influence and friend influence, and an LLM-driven ST2vec method is proposed to represent the topological structure features of the topic network and the text information features of user nodes respectively. Finally, considering the differences in topic popularity in different time periods, time slicing technology is used to discretize time, and a convolutional neural network (CNN) is adopted to complete the prediction of user propagation behaviors. In the controlled experiments on multiple topic datasets, the results show that the model has high prediction accuracy for the propagation behaviors of users in guided topic networks, indicating that the consideration based on multiple influences is effective, and it plays an important role in grasping the topic situation and controlling the spread of rumors.

Acknowledgments. This paper is partially supported by the National Natural Science Foundation of China (Grant No.62221005).

References

1. Wang, H., Yang, C., Shi, C.: Neural information diffusion prediction with topic-aware attention network. In: Proceedings of the 30th ACM International Conference on Information & Knowledge Management, New York, USA, 1899–1908 (2021)
2. Firdaus, S.N., Ding, C., Sadeghian, A.: Topic specific emotion detection for retweet prediction. Int. J. Mach. Learn. Cybern. **10**, 2071–2083 (2019)
3. Pang, J., Rao, Y., Xie, H., et al.: Fast supervised topic models for short text emotion detection. IEEE Trans. Cybern. **51**(2), 815–828 (2019)
4. Li, J., Bao, P., Shen, H., et al.: Mistr: a multiview structural-temporal learning frame-work for rumor detection. IEEE Trans. Big Data **8**(4), 1007–1019 (2021)
5. Hou, W., Li, Y., Liu, Y., et al.: Leveraging multidimensional features for policy opinion sentiment prediction. Inf. Sci. **610**, 215–234 (2022)
6. Varshney, D., Vishwakarma, D.K.: A review on rumour prediction and veracity assessment in online social network. Expert Syst. Appl. **168**, 114208 (2021)
7. LI Z, ZHANG Q, DU X, et al. Social media rumor refutation effectiveness: Evaluation, modelling and enhancement[J]. Inf. Process. Manage. **58**(1), 102420 (2021)
8. Wang, Z., Guo, Y.: Rumor events detection enhanced by encoding sentimental information into time series division and word representations. Neurocomputing **397**, 224–243 (2020)

9. Zhou, X., Wu, B., Jin, Q.: User role identification based on social behavior and networking analysis for information dissemination. Futur. Gener. Comput. Syst. **96**, 639648 (2019)
10. Cai, M., Luo, H., Meng, X., et al.: Influence of information attributes on information dissemination in public health emergencies. Humanities Soc. Sci. Commun. **9**(1), 1–22 (2022)
11. Zhao, W., Guan, Z., Huang, Y., et al.: Discerning influence patterns with beta-poisson factorization in microblogging environments. IEEE Trans. Knowl. Data Eng. **32**(6), 1092–1103 (2020)
12. Wu, X., Xiao, Y., Liang, X., et al.: A dynamic information dissemination model based on implicit link and social influence. IEEE Trans. Comput. Soc. Syst. **8**(2), 345–354 (2020)
13. Li, Q., Wang, Z., Wu, B., et al.: Competition and cooperation: Dynamical interplay diffusion between social topic multiple messages in multiplex networks. IEEE Trans. Comput. Soc. Syst. **6**(3), 467–478 (2019)
14. Zhou, X., Liang, W., Luo, Z., et al.: Periodic-aware intelligent prediction model for information diffusion in social networks. IEEE Trans. Netw. Sci. Eng. **8**(2), 894–904 (2021)
15. Li, J., Wu, L., Hong, R., et al.: A joint neural model for user behavior prediction on social networking platforms. ACM Trans. Intell. Syst. Technol. (TIST) **11**(6), 1–25 (2020)
16. Yan, S., Su, Q., Gong, Z., et al.: Fractional order time-delay multivariable discrete grey model for short-term online public opinion prediction. Expert Syst. Appl. **197**, 116691 (2022)
17. Li, Q., Xiang, T., Dai, T., et al.: An information dissemination model based on the rumor & antirumor & stimulate-rumor and tripartite cognitive game[J]. IEEE Trans. Cogn. Developmental Syst. **15**(2), 925–937 (2022)
18. Xiao, Y., Liao, Y., Li, Y., et al.: Reasoning over the air: a reasoning-based implicit semantic-aware communication framework. IEEE Trans. Wireless Commun. **23**(4), 3839–3855 (2023)
19. Liu, Z., Ma, Y.: A divide and agglomerate algorithm for community detection in social networks. Inf. Sci. **482**, 321–333 (2019)
20. Chin, W.Y., Loh, Y.X., seah, c.s., et al.: determinants of privacy Policy on social media site: comparison between Weibo and Facebook In: 2023 16th International Symposium on Computational Intelligence and Design (ISCID). IEEE, 139–142 (2023)
21. Ngomane, D.: An investigation of the effectiveness of using Twitter data for predicting South African protests with Graph Neural Networks (2024)
22. Chen, L., Zhou, X., Zhang, K., et al.: Multi-Modal emotion-aware retweet prediction with crossmodal alignment. IEEE Trans. Affect. Comput. **15**(2), 789–802 (2024)
23. Kim, J., Park, S., Lee, D., et al.: Explainable user role discovery and influence maximization in social networks. IEEE Trans. Knowl. Data Eng. **36**(1), 345358 (2024)
24. Kavitha, G., Veena, K.: Research on user behaviour prediction in social networks based on deep learning model. In: 2024 International Conference on Electronic Systems and Intelligent Computing (ICESIC). IEEE, 40–45 (2024)

Identify Neural Areas for Bilingual by Interpreting EEG-Based Deep Learning Models

Hanqi Wang[1]($\boxtimes$), Liang Song[1], Sunil Maharaj[2], Filip Paluncic[2], and Peng Sun[3]

[1] College of Intelligent Robotics and Advanced Manufacturing,
Fudan University, Shanghai, China
`21110860045@m.fudan.edu.cn`
[2] Department of Electrical, Electronic and Computer Engineering,
University of Pretoria, Pretoria, South Africa
[3] Division of Natural and Applied Sciences, Duke Kunshan University, Suzhou,
China

Abstract. Currently, the research on bilingualism is a challenging task. This topic has captured the attention of many researchers. Inspired by the robust performance of the deep learning model, we propose to reveal the underlying characteristics of brain activity in bilingual reading by interpreting how deep learning works. To support our proposal, we offer a saliency method using mask perturbation to interpret the deep learning model. Further, we design a class-oriented loss to elaborate on the difference between the two languages. In the experiment, we collect a bilingual reading EEG dataset and build multiple representative deep-learning models. Then, the proposed saliency method is applied to identify the neural areas corresponding to the salient channels. The revealed large overlap in neural areas between the two languages is consistent with existing conclusions in cognitive neuroscience. And there are also similarities in the views of different models, suggesting the existence of underlying cognitive patterns.

Keywords: Bilingualism · neural area identification · deep learning · interpreting deep learning model · EEG

1 Introduction

Bilingualism is the ability to acquire, store, and use more than one language [19]. Understanding bilingualism is important to reveal the cognitive process in both linguistic and non-linguistic cognitive domains [20]. Thus, there is a rising interest in exploring involved neural areas for bilingualism. Recently, the emergence of neuro-imaging technology help advance the field [19]. However, the high cost of neuro-imaging technology and its slow reaction to neuronal activity [4] still limit further progress in this area. Consequently, some researchers turn to develop the EEG-based methods [9,15] to uncover the underlying cognitive mechanism.

Z. Lin et al. (Eds.): INSAI 2025, CCIS 2894, pp. 241–250, 2026.
https://doi.org/10.1007/978-981-95-9299-9_18

Deep learning has shown capacity of understanding complex data in many areas. Recently, some works introduce it to investigate the bilingual problems based on the recorded bilingual EEG signals [1,8]. The performance suggests the convincing ability of deep learning to understand bilingual brain activities. This observation inspires us that interpreting how these strong deep learning models understand the bilingual EEG responses might help indicate the neural areas involved in this cognitive process. Specifically, an interpretation is expected to identify from which brain areas the signals with significant contributions to the output are collected. And then, those indicated areas are assumed to be involved in the process. The basic assumption is that the areas where the discriminative activities occur in the eyes of the deep model should correspond to the involved areas. As far as we know, our work is a pioneering attempt to explore the mechanism of bilingualism from this new perspective.

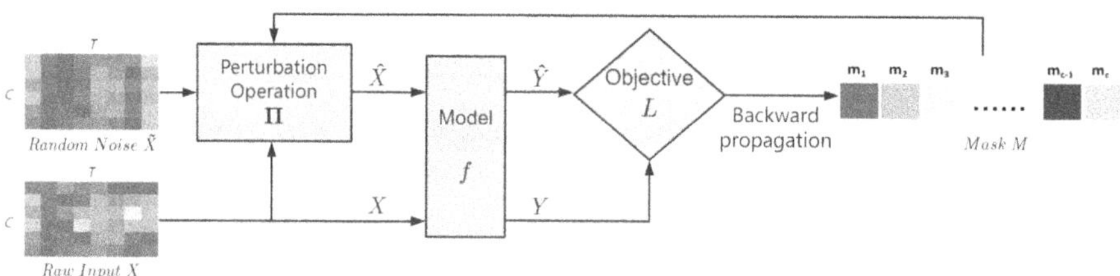

Fig. 1. Overview of the proposed saliency method. The perturbation operation Π takes the X, $\hat{X}$, and M as input to generate the perturbed input $\tilde{X}$. Both X and $\tilde{X}$ are fed into the deep learning model, issuing the output Y and $\tilde{Y}$. The loss L is set to measure the difference between Y and $\tilde{Y}$. And then, the backward propagation is introduced to optimize the M with the objective of minimizing the L.

The saliency map highlights the salient components in the input which influence the output [18,22], well-suited to our research. It has been commonly used as the interpreting method in the previous EEG-based deep learning works [5,11,14]. However, most of them adopt the gradient-based saliency map. As pointed in the previous works [7,21], this method shows a limited ability to capture the casual relationship between the input and output. Hence, it cannot be regared as an optimal method for our research. Besides, the existing methods of saliency maps mainly focus on generating element-wise estimates, while our research aims to investigate the saliency of each neural areas in the EEG records. Moreover, considering the need of bilingual research, the proposed interpreting method is required to reveal how brain respond to different languages respectively. Based on these considerations, it demands a more tailored interpreting method for our task.

In response to the issues, we propose a interpreting method specifically for investigating the neural areas involved in the bilingual cognitive process. Inspired by the [3,7], we develop our method based on the mask perturbation. In detail, we utilize mask to perform joint perturbation on all candidates and introduce the backward-propagation algorithm to enable an automatic search for the optimal mask. This mask perturbation based method can model the correlation and provide an accurate estimate [3,7,21]. And, it can also generalize to the input individually [3,7,21]. In addition, we propose a position-level mask to estimate the saliency of each electrode position. Compared with the element-wise masks, our method applies the perturbation on the whole EEG records from an electrode position. Thus, it generate the estimate for the candidate positions instead of the elements. Finally, we design a class-oriented loss considering the need of bilingualism research. When optimizing the mask, this loss can help users capture the characteristics of a specific language and enable the comparison between the first language (L1) and the second language (L2). In the experiment section, the proposed saliency method is tested through identifying the involved neural area for bilinguals. Considering the absence of the public datasets in this area, we conduct trials and construct a bilingual reading EEG dataset. We collect the extracranial EEG records from multiple bilingual subjects when they read in L1 and when they read in L2. Next, we train three representative EEG-based deep learning models, including EEGNet [10], ShallowConvNet [17], and DeepConvNet [17], on the collected data with the objective of L1 and L2 classification. Due to the lack of In order to we implement three experiments. In the first experiment, the neural overlap and the dissociation between L1 and L2 are investigated using the proposed class-oriented loss. We find a large overlap in neural area between L1 and L2. This result is consistent with the existing conclusions in cognitive neuroscience [12,19]. In the second experiment, we adopt the commonly used cross-entropy loss. We apply the proposed saliency method to localize the occurrence of discriminative activities for bilingual reading. The results from various models show a similarity with each other, suggesting the existence of underlying cognitive pattern. Meanwhile, we also implement an experiment to validate the effectiveness of the proposed saliency method. Our contributions can be summarized as follows.

- We propose a new perspective to investigate the cognitive mechanism of bilingualism. The mechanisms by which deep learning models respond to data are used to infer cognitive characteristics.
- We propose a saliency method to identify the bilingual neural areas. We adopt the mask perturbation based on joint perturbation and backward propagation. And we further propose a class-oriented loss to satisfy the interest in bilingualism research. This loss can help expose the salient components for a specific language.
- We collect EEG data from subjects and implement the neural area identification experiments. And we also implement experiment to validate the effectiveness of the proposed method.

2   Method

In this section, we describe our approach with regard to two parts, including perturbation operation and optimization. The whole structure of our method can be seen in Fig. 1. Notably, we want to emphasize that our method can easily transfer to other scenarios.

2.1 Perturbation Operation

Let $X \in R^{C \times T}$ denotes an normalized raw EEG input, where C is the number of channels, and T is the time length. Each channel reflects the activity of the corresponding brain region. We adopt a mask $M \in [0,1]^C$ to jointly perturb the signals in various channels. Note that the shape of the mask will adapt to the input size or the component of interest in other scenarios. For example, users can investigate the bands of interest by setting the mask size to the number of bands. The mask M dictates the perturbation operation Π, as described in (1):

$$\hat{X} = M \cdot X + (1 - M) \cdot \tilde{X}, \tag{1}$$

where $\hat{X}$ denotes the perturbed sample, and $\tilde{X}$ denotes a generated random noise conforming to the normal distribution. As can be seen in (1), the M controls the suppression or preservation for all the channels. If the i_{th} element m_i in the M is 1, the perturbation term would be eliminated. Otherwise, if the m_i is 0, the original signal would be replaced with the random noise.

This operation is designed considering the basic assumption of the perturbation-based saliency method. The output of the deep learning model is sensitive to the perturbation in the salient region and resistant to the perturbation in the non-salient region [2,3,6,7]. Based on this assumption, comparing the output using perturbed input and output using original input can reveal the saliency of the perturbed area. If only a small change occurs in the output, it implies that the mask preserves the original signals in the salient channels. Therefore, the elements in M can be regarded as an indicator of the salient channel. According to the (1), if m_i is close to 1, the i_{th} channel in the input is salient; otherwise, the i_{th} channel would be regarded as the opposite.

2.2 Optimization

For a given model f and an input X, the output $Y \in [0,1]^{1 \times 2}$ and perturbed output $\hat{Y} \in [0,1]^{1 \times 2}$ can be generated as described in (2).

$$Y = f(X), \hat{Y} = f(\hat{X}). \tag{2}$$

As we mentioned above, the mask needs to be optimized with the objective of minimizing the change in the issued output. Here, we formulate this problem as a machine learning problem. We set the mask M as a learnable vector. And then, we set a loss L measuring the difference between two outputs as the training objective. Finally, we introduce backward propagation to search for the optimal mask. This automatic learning approach makes the final result accurate and reasonable.

In order to deal with the bilingualism problem, we provide two kinds of L in this work. The first one is the proposed class-oriented loss. This loss only cares about the relevant components for a specific class. It is shown in (3).

$$L_i = (y_i - \hat{y}_i)^2, \tag{3}$$

where L_i denotes the class-oriented loss for the class i, y_i denotes the i_{th} element in the output Y, and $\hat{y}_i$ denotes the i_{th} element in the output $\hat{Y}$. The y_i and $\hat{y}_i$ imply the probability that the received EEG data belong to the reading process in the i_{th} language. In this scenario, the class-oriented loss instructs the optimization of the mask to identify those salient components of reading in language i.

$$L_c = -\sum y_i \log \hat{y}_i, \tag{4}$$

The second loss is the classification loss. This loss is supposed to instruct the mask to identify the salient components on which the decision boundary relies. Here, we adopt the commonly used cross-entropy loss shown in (4).

3 Experiment

3.1 Dataset Introduction and Experiment Settings

In this work, we collect an EEG dataset from 6 subjects. All the subjects are undergraduate students at Fudan University, aged 18 to 21. They are native Chinese speakers and proficient English speakers. During the trial, each subject reads Chinese and English articles separately. The extracranial EEG signals from 59 electrodes are recorded with a sampling 1000 Hz. The EEG records are then split into 2-second segments, with size 59×2000. Finally, we build three deep learning models with various scales, EEGNet, ShallowConvNet, and DeepConvNet. These models are representative works that proved powerful for general EEG analysis tasks. Following the cross-subject paradigm, the models are trained on all the collected data, with the objective of classifying Chinese and English.

The hyper-parameter settings of these models follow the default in the original papers. For the mask optimization, we set the learning rate as 0.01, the initial value of the mask as 0.9, the optimizer as Adam, and the training epoch as 100. All the experiments are implemented on a GTX2080Ti GPU.

3.2 Overlap and Dissociation Between L1 and L2 Readings in Neural Areas

Many previous works [19] are interested in the neural area overlap and dissociation underlying the L1 and L2 language processing. We use the proposed saliency method to investigate this problem in this experiment. We adopt the class-oriented loss in (3) to identify the salient channel for recognizing L1 and

L2, respectively. The electrode positions corresponding to the identified channels are expected to be where discriminative brain activities occur.

In order to score the saliency of the channels, we calculate the mask for each input in the dataset, and then we average the masks over all the inputs to get the score for each channel. Then, we select the top 8 salient channels using various models. The result is shown in Table 1.

Table 1. The corresponding electrode positions of the top 8 salient channels for L1 and L2. The dissociated electrode positions, which means they are not simultaneously identified as salient for both L1 and L2, are marked in **bold**.

Model	Language	9_{th}	8_{th}	7_{th}	6_{th}	5_{th}	4_{th}	3_{rd}	2_{nd}	1_{st}
EEGNet	L1	FC4	PO3	FC1	**FC6**	F4	PO4	Fpz	F6	Poz
	L2	PO3	**P4**	FC1	FC4	Fpz	F4	F6	PO4	Poz
ShallowConvNet	L1	FC2	CP5	**PO4**	P4	P6	FT7	Poz	P5	TP7
	L2	**T7**	FC2	CP5	Poz	P4	P6	FT7	P5	TP7
DeepConvNet	L1	FC6	TP8	O1	C2	F7	Pz	PO4	Fpz	Poz
	L2	FC6	TP8	O1	C2	F7	Pz	PO4	Fpz	Poz

As we can see, for each model, there is a significant overlap between L1 and L2 in the identified 8 electrode positions. This observation accords with the conclusion of the previous cognitive neuroscience studies [12,19]. And we also notice that the identified electrode positions are different from model to model. In the next subsection, we attempt to make an explanation for this point.

3.3 Salient Electrode Positions for Classification

In this subsection, we identify the salient channels for classification decision-making. We adopt the classification loss in (4). And we score the channels following the previous subsection. The corresponding electrode positions of the top 12 salient channels are marked with red color in Fig. 2.

As can be seen, the three results show a similarity in the distribution of identified electrodes. For example, all three results agree on the significance of the areas around electrode position POz, F8, and T8. Furthermore, all three results convey a clear left-right imbalance. The convergence of the results suggests the existence of an underlying rhythm in the cognitive process of bilingual reading. However, there are also differences among the various models, especially the discrepancy between the result of ShallowConvNet and the others. We observed a similar problem in the previous subsection as well. Here, we attempt to explain this observation. First, the EEG signal is featured by the low signal-to-noise ratio. The recorded EEG data is susceptible to interference by a variety of factors. It can influence the focus of the deep learning model. Second, the learning capacities of deep learning models are different. This capacity is related

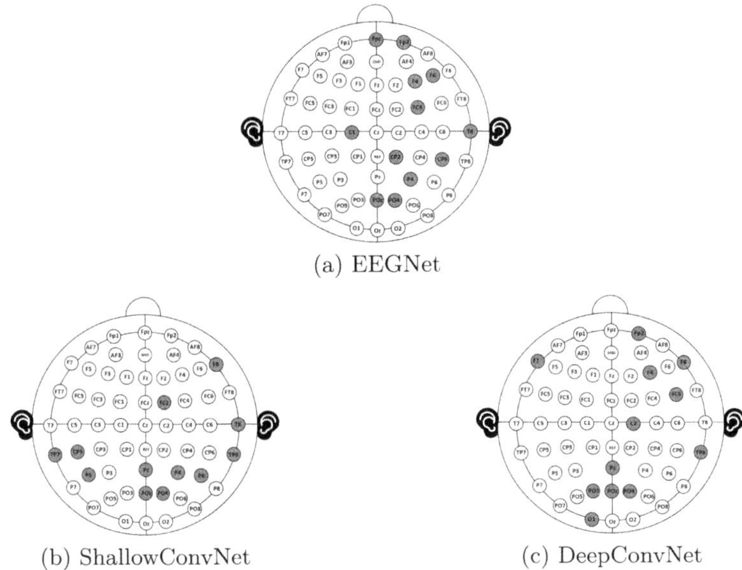

(a) EEGNet

(b) ShallowConvNet   (c) DeepConvNet

Fig. 2. The visualization of the top 12 salient electrode positions. The identified salient positions are marked with red color. (Color figure online)

to many factors, e.g., the scale of learnable parameters [13,16]. Thus, the existing difference is within the expectation. Particularly, the ShallowConvNet shows a relatively limited performance on the original data, as shown in Fig. 3 in the next subsection. It means that the capacity of this model is possibly insufficient compared with the others. Therefore, its result shows divergence from the other results.

3.4   Validate the Proposed Saliency Method

To support the observation revealed by the proposed saliency method, an examination of the proposed method is mandatory. In this subsection, we implement an experiment to examine whether the identified channels are truly salient. Our method is to remove the channels and observe the change in performance. If the identified channels are salient, the change in the performance should be significant. To make the comparison, we remove the top 12 salient channels and the bottom 12 salient channels. Following [5], we set the features in the removed channel to 0. The results are as presented in Fig. 3.

We can see that removing the top salient channels causes a more significant drop in accuracy than the bottom salient channels. This observation suggests that the identified channels are truly salient. Thus, our experiment validates the effectiveness of the proposed saliency method.

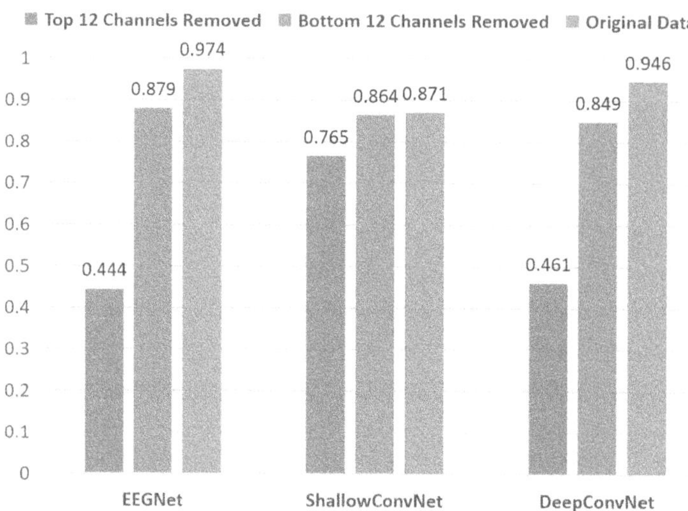

Fig. 3. The comparison of the change in performance. The accuracies of the three models using the top 12 salient channels removed data, the bottom 12 salient channels removed data, and the original data are shown in this figure.

4 Conclusion

The paper provide a new perspective to explore the bilingual brain mechanism. We propose to reveal bilingual neural areas by interpreting the deep learning model. Thus, a saliency method is proposed to identify the salient neural areas in the eyes of the model. We experiment our method on real data from bilingual subject. The outcomes show either consistency with the previous studies or similarity with the others.

However, we observe an apparent divergence of the results among the various models. A possible explanation is that the precision of the identified results is related to the learning capacity of the investigated deep learning model. In future works, a promising direction of improvement is developing a more powerful task-specific model and applying our method to it.

Acknowledgment. This work was supported by National Key Research and Development Program of China, Project No. 2024YFE0200700, Subject No. 2024YFE0200703. This work was also supported in part by the Specific Research Fund of the Innovation Platform for Academicians of Hainan Province under Grant YSPTZX202314, in part by the Shanghai Key Research Laboratory of NSAI and the Joint Laboratory on Networked AI Edge Computing, Fudan University-Changan.

References

1. Balaji, A., et al.: EEG-based classification of bilingual unspoken speech using ann. In: 2017 39th Annual International Conference of the IEEE Engineering in Medicine and Biology Society (EMBC), pp. 1022–1025. IEEE (2017)
2. Crabbé, J., Van Der Schaar, M.: Explaining time series predictions with dynamic masks. In: International Conference on Machine Learning, pp. 2166–2177. PMLR (2021)
3. Dabkowski, P., Gal, Y.: Real time image saliency for black box classifiers. Adv. Neural Inf. Process. Syst. **30** (2017)
4. Deco, G., Jirsa, V.K., McIntosh, A.R.: Emerging concepts for the dynamical organization of resting-state activity in the brain. Nat. Rev. Neurosci. **12**(1), 43–56 (2011)
5. Farahat, A., Reichert, C., Sweeney-Reed, C.M., Hinrichs, H.: Convolutional neural networks for decoding of covert attention focus and saliency maps for EEG feature visualization. J. Neural Eng. **16**(6), 066010 (2019)
6. Fong, R., Patrick, M., Vedaldi, A.: Understanding deep networks via extremal perturbations and smooth masks. In: Proceedings of the IEEE/CVF International Conference on Computer Vision, pp. 2950–2958 (2019)
7. Fong, R.C., Vedaldi, A.: Interpretable explanations of black boxes by meaningful perturbation. In: Proceedings of the IEEE International Conference on Computer Vision, pp. 3429–3437 (2017)
8. Goyal, A., Gupta, V., Kumar, M.: A deep learning-based bilingual Hindi and Punjabi named entity recognition system using enhanced word embeddings. Knowl.-Based Syst. **234**, 107601 (2021)
9. Grundy, J.G., Anderson, J.A., Bialystok, E.: Bilinguals have more complex EEG brain signals in occipital regions than monolinguals. Neuroimage **159**, 280–288 (2017)
10. Lawhern, V.J., Solon, A.J., Waytowich, N.R., Gordon, S.M., Hung, C.P., Lance, B.J.: EEGNet: a compact convolutional neural network for EEG-based brain-computer interfaces. J. Neural Eng. **15**(5), 056013 (2018)
11. Lin, P.J., et al.: CNN-based prognosis of BCI rehabilitation using EEG from first session BCI training. IEEE Trans. Neural Syst. Rehabil. Eng. **29**, 1936–1943 (2021)
12. Liu, H., Hu, Z., Guo, T., Peng, D.: Speaking words in two languages with one brain: neural overlap and dissociation. Brain Res. **1316**, 75–82 (2010)
13. Montufar, G.F., Pascanu, R., Cho, K., Bengio, Y.: On the number of linear regions of deep neural networks. Adv. Neural Inf. Process. Syst. **27** (2014)
14. Nahmias, D.O., Kontson, K.L.: Easy perturbation EEG algorithm for spectral importance (EASYPEASI) a simple method to identify important spectral features of EEG in deep learning models. In: Proceedings of the 26th ACM SIGKDD International Conference on Knowledge Discovery & Data Mining, pp. 2398–2406 (2020)
15. Petsche, H., Etlinger, S.C., Filz, O.: Brain electrical mechanisms of bilingual speech management: an initial investigation. Electroencephalogr. Clin. Neurophysiol. **86**(6), 385–394 (1993)
16. Poole, B., Lahiri, S., Raghu, M., Sohl-Dickstein, J., Ganguli, S.: Exponential expressivity in deep neural networks through transient chaos. Adv. Neural Inf. Process. Syst. **29** (2016)
17. Schirrmeister, R.T., et al.: Deep learning with convolutional neural networks for EEG decoding and visualization. Hum. Brain Mapp. **38**(11), 5391–5420 (2017)

18. Simonyan, K., Vedaldi, A., Zisserman, A.: Deep inside convolutional networks: visualising image classification models and saliency maps. arXiv preprint arXiv:1312.6034 (2013)
19. Sulpizio, S., Del Maschio, N., Fedeli, D., Abutalebi, J.: Bilingual language processing: a meta-analysis of functional neuroimaging studies. Neurosci. Biobehav. Rev. **108**, 834–853 (2020)
20. Tao, L., Wang, G., Zhu, M., Cai, Q.: Bilingualism and domain-general cognitive functions from a neural perspective: a systematic review. Neurosci. Biobehav. Rev. **125**, 264–295 (2021)
21. Wang, H., Zhu, X., Chen, T., Li, C., Song, L.: Rethinking saliency map: a context-aware perturbation method to explain EEG-based deep learning model. IEEE Trans. Biomed. Eng. (2022)
22. Zeiler, M.D., Fergus, R.: Visualizing and understanding convolutional networks. In: Fleet, D., Pajdla, T., Schiele, B., Tuytelaars, T. (eds.) ECCV 2014. LNCS, vol. 8689, pp. 818–833. Springer, Cham (2014). https://doi.org/10.1007/978-3-319-10590-1_53

Virtual Reality and Intelligent Application

Performance Analysis and Modeling of Monitoring Systems for Sustainable Agriculture

Abdulaziz M. Alawwad, Salman Khan$^{(\boxtimes)}$, and Salman A. AlQahtani

New Emerging Technologies and 5G Network and Beyond Research Chair, Department of Computer Engineering, College of Computer and Information Sciences, King Saud University, Riyadh, Saudi Arabia
salmanq@ksu.edu.sa

Abstract. This study focuses on evaluating the performance of monitoring systems designed to address challenges in sustainable agriculture, emphasizing resource management and timely decision-making. The proposed model employs a queuing network framework to analyze system performance, identify bottlenecks, and enhance monitoring processes. By assessing resource requirements, the system is designed to meet strict Service Level Agreement (SLA) standards, particularly concerning response times, which are critical for agricultural efficiency. To validate the proposed model, discrete event simulation is conducted using the Java Modeling Tool (JMT), replicating real-world agricultural scenarios. These simulations provide insights into the system's reliability, scalability, and operational effectiveness under varying conditions. This research aligns with environmental sustainability goals by enabling precise resource management and optimizing monitoring processes, which contribute to reduced waste and improved agricultural productivity. The model's comprehensive evaluation ensures it can effectively support decision-making in dynamic agricultural environments. By addressing critical operational challenges, this study provides a roadmap for developing robust and efficient monitoring systems tailored to sustainable agriculture. The findings offer valuable insights for future advancements in monitoring technologies, contributing to enhanced productivity while mitigating environmental impacts in the agricultural sector.

Keywords: Environmental Science · Environmental Risk · IoT · Mobile · Agriculture Computing

1 Introduction

The number of internet-connected devices has grown dramatically over the past decade, creating new challenges for delivering services within specified Quality of Service (QoS) requirements [1]. Use cases such as remote surgery, virtual reality, and augmented reality demand infrastructure capabilities beyond 4G, including ultra-low service delay and highly reliable connectivity. To meet these requirements, 3GPP introduced the 5G architecture [2], which relies on three main pillars: Enhanced Mobile Broadband (eMBB),

© The Author(s), under exclusive license to Springer Nature Singapore Pte Ltd. 2026
Z. Lin et al. (Eds.): INSAI 2025, CCIS 2894, pp. 253–265, 2026.
https://doi.org/10.1007/978-981-95-9299-9_19

Massive Machine Type Communication (mMTC), and Ultra-Reliable Low Latency Communication (URLLC) [3–5]. Forecasts indicate that the number of connected IoT devices worldwide will rise from 11.5 billion in 2022 to 25.44 billion by 2030 [6], serving industries like healthcare, where real-time data transmission and efficient power use are critical. According to Gartner, IoT service revenue is expected to reach 4.3 billion USD by 2024 and continue growing [7], highlighting IoT's importance. Consequently, studies increasingly focus on IoT applications across sectors such as healthcare, agriculture, and oil and gas [8].

Anas et al. [9] proposed an IoT Agriculture Monitoring System to improve farmers' acceptance of IoT, identifying four barriers: educational requirements [10, 11], lack of technical expertise, operational challenges, and high costs. Zafar et al. [12] addressed these by developing hardware sensors for humidity, rain, light, and temperature, but focused only on the Hardware (HW) layer, excluding the Network Infrastructure layer. Likewise, Phasinam et al. [15] proposed an automated irrigation system with soil moisture and humidity sensors, Raspberry Pi, cloud storage, machine learning, and a mobile app, covering the HW and Application layers but not the Network Infrastructure layer. In healthcare, Khaled et al. [16] analyzed IoT monitoring systems from a network perspective, incorporating NFV, MEC, Fog, and public/private clouds [17, 18]. Using queuing models, they evaluated system response time, resource requirements, and waiting time [19, 20]. MEC's role in 5G networks has been emphasized in [21–24], providing edge computing, ultra-low latency, improved QoS, network slicing, fast computing, and efficient resource utilization, thereby enhancing multi-domain service performance and flexibility.

Most of these studies focus on a specific layer within the IoT architecture, with a significant number covering the Application and Hardware (HW) layers. Unfortunately, the Network Infrastructure layer is often overlooked in these studies. For this reason, our study will concentrate on the Network Infrastructure layer within the agriculture industry, considering all necessary parameters. This work outlines IoT technology, the proposed IoT monitoring system, and simulation results, demonstrating the system's potential for real-world implementation.

2 IoT Technology Background

In this section, we explain the architecture of IoT technology and other emerging technologies, such as MEC, NFV, and network slicing. These technologies will be used to build our end-to-end IoT monitoring system.

2.1 IoT Architecture

According to the ITU, IoT architecture consists of four layers: Hardware, Network, IoT Platform, and Application Servers [25]. The Hardware layer, or transducer [26], includes sensors, which convert physical phenomena into electrical signals, and actuators, which convert electrical inputs into physical actions. The Network layer uses wired and wireless technologies, with this study focusing on wireless access technologies common in agriculture. As shown in Fig. 1 [8], wireless technologies are categorized by range: short-distance (<30 m), medium-distance (<100 m), and long-distance LPWA (>100 m).

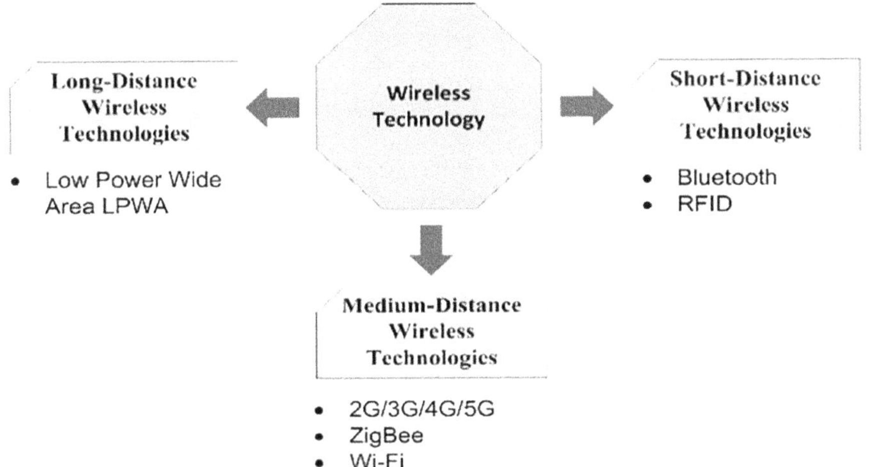

Fig. 1. The different types of wireless technologies.

The IoT platform comprises three main components [27]: Data Ingestion, Data Processing, and Data Storage. Data Ingestion captures messages, identifies their source, and classifies data types. Data Processing, the core of the platform, applies logic based on the IoT use case to perform actions. Data Storage allows storing and retrieving IoT data. Devices communicate with the platform, and applications exchange data with it [28]. Application servers provide user interaction via UI [29, 30], data analytics for interpretation, and visualization tools to represent data graphically.

2.2 Multi-access Edge Computing (MEC)

As explained earlier, data traffic has been increasing over recent years. One of the technologies introduced to address the new challenges is Multi-access Edge Computing (MEC) by ETSI. The MEC concept moves application hosting from centralized data centers (DC) to the network's edge, closer to the customer/end-user premises [31]. In other words, data plane processing will be closer to the end user. As a result, the delay of the service can be reduced, especially for delay-sensitive services. Therefore, the purpose of MEC is to improve the Quality of Experience (QoE) and Quality of Service (QoS), for instance, in Virtual Reality (VR) or Augmented Reality (AR) services, where delay plays a critical role in service delivery [32].

2.3 Network Function Virtualization (NFV)

The main goal of Network Function Virtualization is to virtualize network services such as routers, switches, and core mobile nodes. As a result, there will be no need for dedicated hardware for a specific network function [33]. However, several VMs will serve different network functions on the same hardware. Various advantages of NFV include hardware and maintenance costs, Easier management and operation, and reduced network power consumption.

2.4 Network Function Virtualization (NFV)

With the introduction of new services that come with 5G technology, the concept of One-Size-Fits-All is no longer applicable. For this reason, the slicing solution provides several logical networks, each with specific requirements, while sharing the same infrastructure [34].

3 Architecture & Model of the IoT Agriculture System

This section describes the architecture of our proposed IoT monitoring system in agriculture. It has two main sub-sections: the network model & assumption and the queuing model for the agriculture monitoring system.

3.1 Network Model & Assumption of the IoT Monitoring System

The agriculture monitoring system uses IoT devices—such as sensors, cameras, and trackers—connected via wired or wireless technologies (LPWA, 2G, 4G). Data is aggregated at a gateway with FIFO service and, as shown in Fig. 2, sent either to a private cloud for secure storage or via the Fog to the public cloud to reduce response time. Authorized users access the data through web or mobile applications.

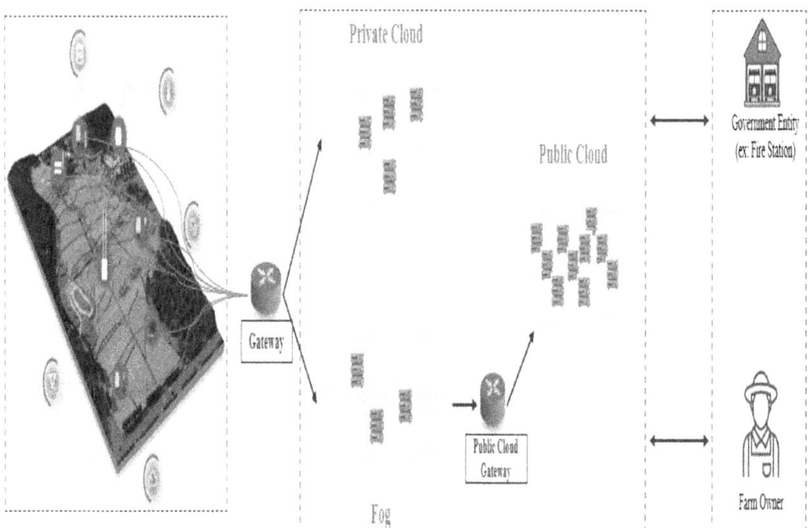

Fig. 2. The Architecture IoT agriculture monitoring system.

3.2 Queuing Model for the Agriculture Monitoring System

The agriculture monitoring system consists of four main components from the network perspective. Firstly, there are two gateways: the main gateway and the public cloud gateway. Secondly, the private cloud, considered an isolated network, offers more security. Thirdly, the Fog, an edge computing solution, provides better response times for time-sensitive applications. Lastly, the public cloud has more resources and capabilities than the others.

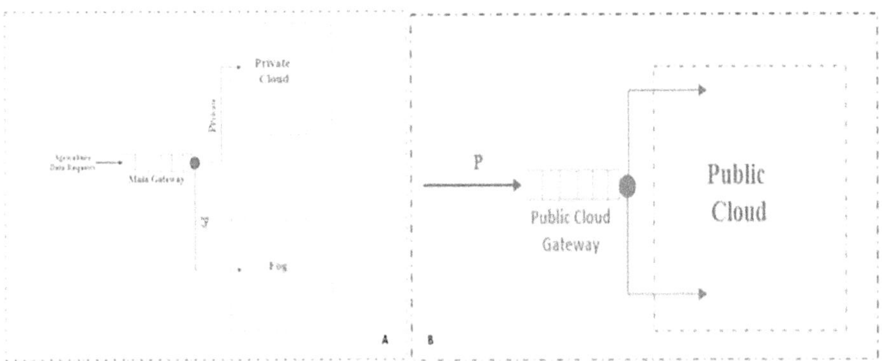

Fig. 3. The queuing model for the primary gateway (b) The queuing model for the public cloud gateway.

Main & Public Cloud Gateways Queuing Model

As mentioned earlier, all IoT data in the gateways will be processed using the same queuing discipline, FIFO (First In, First Out). Additionally, the waiting buffer for both gateways is considered infinite to prevent potential data loss of IoT data that might occur between the IoT devices and our proposed system. The proposed queuing model for both gateways is M/M/1. Moreover, they are Poisson distribution, and the service process is exponential time distribution with mean rates 1/ μGW and 1/μ_PublicG. Figure 3(a) shows the main gateway's queuing model, which connects the incoming IoT data with the private cloud and Fog. Also, the queuing model for the public cloud is described in Fig. 3(b) and connects the Fog with the public cloud.

Private Cloud Queuing Model

The private cloud is an isolated network with hardware fully dedicated to the owner. Also, it is more secure than the public cloud. The private cloud could be on the customer premises or provided as a co-located service by one of the regional operators, which will provide power and space for the requester. Since the private cloud has limited resources, there will be several processing nodes (R), multiple VMs in each processing node, and a finite waiting buffer. Based on that, we assume the queuing model for the private cloud is M/M/n/Z. Figure 4 illustrates the queuing model of the private cloud.

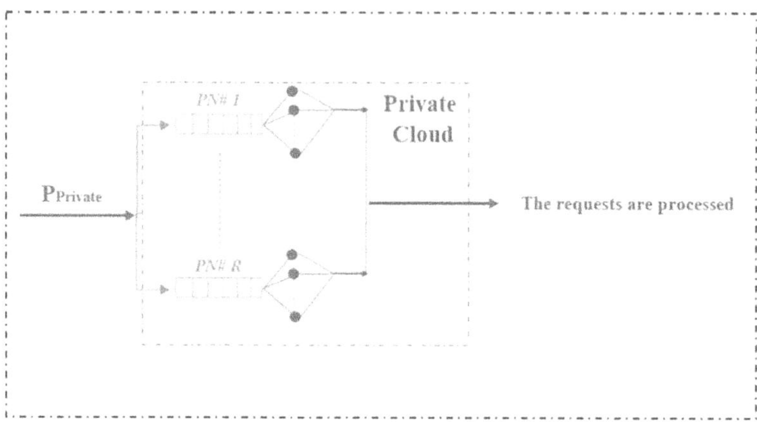

Fig. 4. The queuing model for the private cloud.

Fog Queuing Model

The Fog is a form of Multi-Access Edge Computing (MEC) technology. The primary advantage of the Fog is its ability to enhance the latency for time-sensitive applications by bringing the data plane closer to the end user. Given this, the Fog will have limited resources dedicated to specific types of applications. Additionally, the Fog comprises several processing nodes (F), each with a finite waiting buffer. Consequently, we assume that the queuing model for the Fog is M/M/1/A. Figure 5 illustrates the fog queuing model.

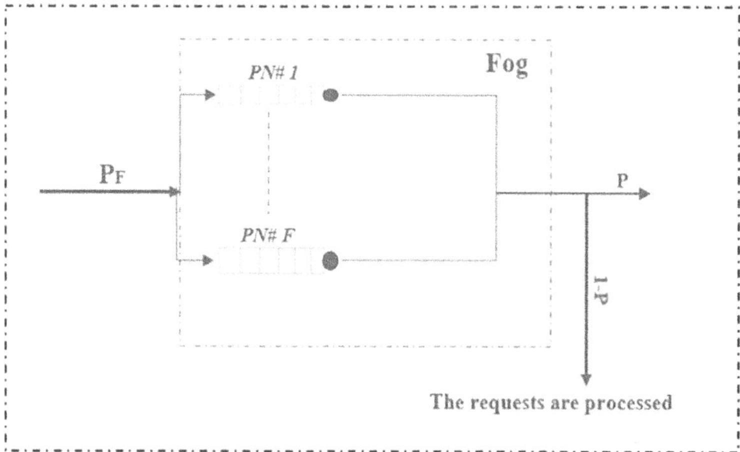

Fig. 5. The queuing model for the Fog.

Public Cloud Queuing Model

Comparatively, the public cloud has more capabilities and resources than the Fog and the private cloud. In the public cloud, it is easier to scale up the infrastructure if there is an increase in traffic. Therefore, we assume the queuing model for the public cloud is M/M/N, where the public cloud features several processing nodes (B) and various VMs, and each processing node has an infinite waiting buffer. Figure 6 depicts the queuing model for the public cloud.

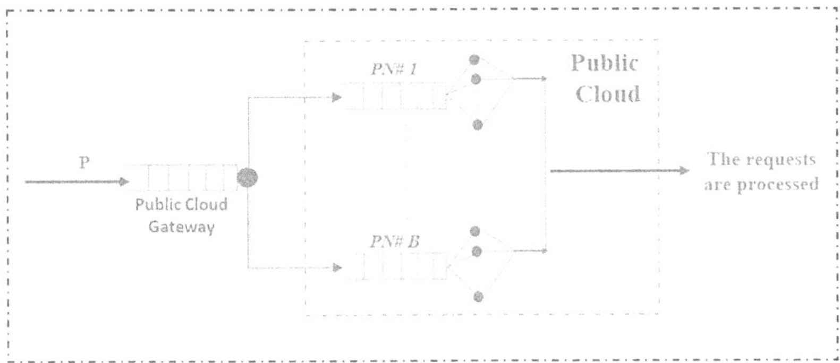

Fig. 6. The queuing model for the public cloud.

Overall Queuing Model & Key Parameters of the Monitoring System

The table describes the queuing model for each component by using the Kendall Notation. Figure 7 illustrates the queuing model for all the elements. The gateways and the public cloud have an infinite queue. Moreover, the private cloud and Fog have a finite queue.

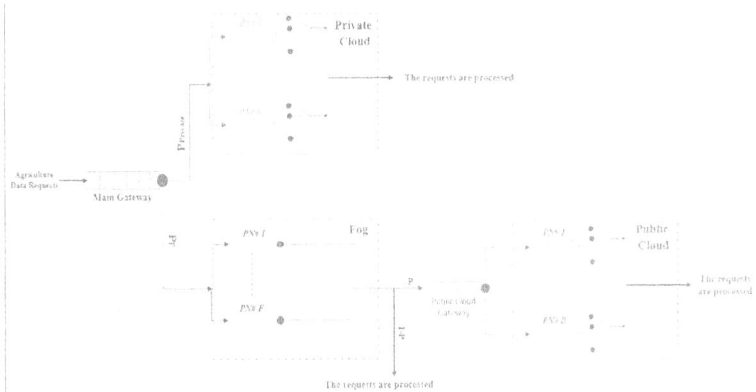

Fig. 7. Queuing model for the agriculture monitoring system.

4 Results and Discussion

This section presents the simulation setup and performance analysis of the agricultural IoT monitoring system. Using the JMT simulator, results for the private cloud, Fog, and public cloud are evaluated across key metrics including response time, throughput, waiting time, and utilization.

4.1 The Tool Setup of the IoT Monitoring System

This subsection outlines the simulator setup and parameter configuration. The Java Modelling Tools (JMT) were installed on a PC with an Intel Core i7 processor and 32 GB RAM. Simulations were executed multiple times to evaluate IoT monitoring performance under workloads ranging from 1000 to 10,000 requests per second. The system model includes four key components—gateway, private cloud, Fog, and public cloud—with performance metrics defined for each. Using these parameters, JMT simulations were repeatedly run to analyze and assess the overall performance of the IoT-based agriculture monitoring system (Table 1).

Table 1. The performance measurements for the JMT simulator

Parameters	Values
$1/\mu GW$	0.0001
Pprivate	0.4
$1/\mu 1$	0.001
R	4
N	5
PF	0.6
$1/\mu F$	0.01
F	5
1-P	0.4
P	0.6
$1/\mu PublicG$	0.0001
B	5
N	6

4.2 Response Time of the IoT Monitoring System

The response time in the proposed system represents the duration required for servers across different clouds (private or public) to respond to IoT devices, including both transmission and processing delays. As a key performance metric, high response time indicates possible issues in resource allocation, link utilization, or latency. As shown in Fig. 8, with 40% of IoT traffic directed to the private cloud, response time increases with workload but decreases as resources scale. For example, at 2000 IoT requests/s, response time drops from 0.38 s with 20 VMs to 0.02 s with 30 or 40 VMs. While minimizing response time enhances performance, it also increases resource costs.

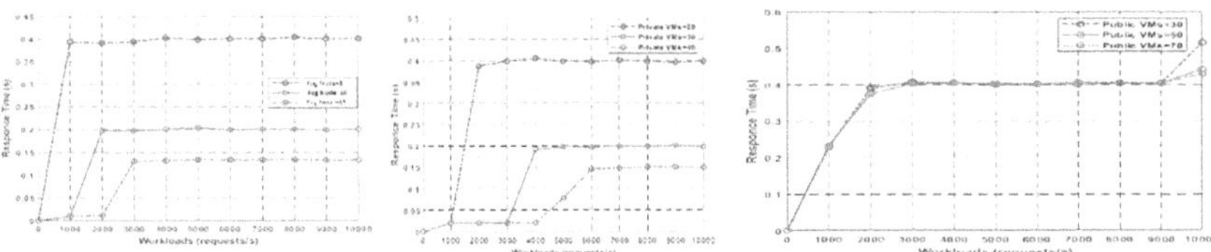

Fig. 8. The response time of the private cloud, the response time of the Fog and the response time of the public cloud

Figure 8 presents the response time performance of the Fog and public cloud. In the Fog layer, where IoT traffic probability is 60%, response time increases with workload but decreases as node count grows—from 0.39 s with 5 nodes to 0.19 s with 10 nodes and 0.02 s with 15 nodes at 2000 requests/s. Similarly, at 5000 workloads, response time drops from 0.4 s (5 nodes) to 0.23 s (10 nodes) and 0.12 s (15 nodes), showing that additional resources reduce delay but raise cost. In the public cloud, response time remains relatively stable due to greater capacity, varying slightly from 0.4 s (30 VMs) to 0.36 s (70 VMs) at 2000 requests/s, and from 0.52 s to 0.42 s at 10 000 requests/s.

4.3 Throughput of the IoT Monitoring System

Throughput, another key metric for evaluating network performance, measures the number of IoT agriculture data requests processed per second. As shown in Fig. 9, increasing resources in the private cloud enhances throughput—from 1249 req/s with 20 VMs to 2010 req/s with 30 VMs and 2502 req/s with 40 VMs.

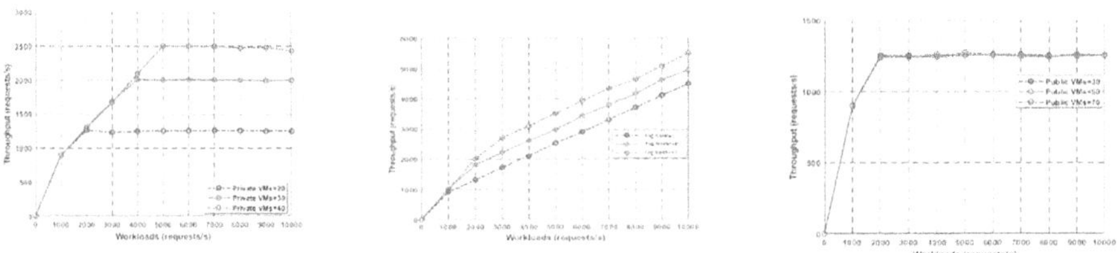

Fig. 9. The throughput of the private cloud, the throughput of the Fog and The throughput of the public cloud

Figure 9 shows the throughput performance of the Fog and public cloud. In the Fog layer, throughput rises from 2516 req/s with 5 nodes to 2966 req/s with 10 nodes, and 3509 req/s with 15 nodes, indicating that higher node counts enhance processing capacity. In contrast, the public cloud maintains nearly constant throughput—about 1250 to 1260 req/s—as the number of VMs increases from 30 to 70, reflecting its already ample resources and processing capability.

4.4　Utilization of the IoT Monitoring System

This subsection presents CPU utilization, a key indicator of network performance. High utilization can affect metrics such as response time. As shown in Fig. 10, CPU utilization decreases as resources increase—from 52% with 20 VMs to 28% with 30 VMs and 20% with 40 VMs at 1000 workloads/s. At 4000 workloads/s, utilization reaches 100% for 20 and 30 VMs and 80% for 40 VMs.

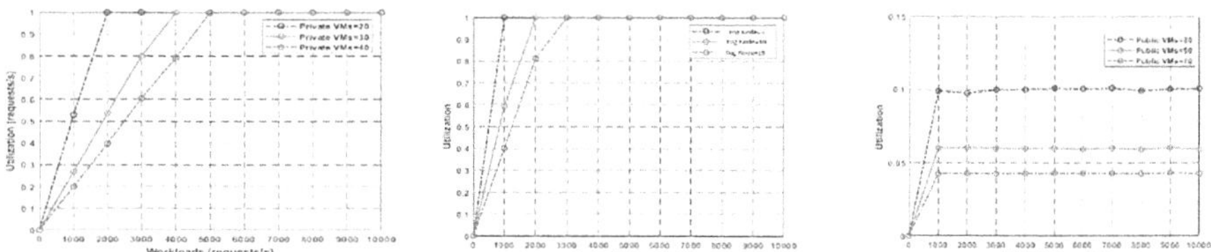

Fig. 10. The Utilization of the private cloud, the Utilization of the Fog and the Utilization of the public cloud

Figure 10 shows the utilization performance of the Fog and public cloud. In the Fog layer, utilization reaches nearly 100% with 5 nodes at 1000 workloads/s, decreasing to 60% with 10 nodes and 40% with 15 nodes. At 2000 workloads/s, utilization remains 100% for 5 and 10 nodes but drops to 80% for 15 nodes due to limited resources. In contrast, the public cloud shows minimal utilization—about 10%, 6%, and 4% with 30, 50, and 70 VMs, respectively—reflecting its higher resource capacity.

4.5　Waiting Time of the IoT Monitoring System

Waiting time is considered one of the primary key performance metrics. As explained earlier, the private cloud and the Fog have a finite queue. Meanwhile, the gateways and the public cloud will have an infinite queue. The waiting time performance metric depends on the processor's capability and the number of resources in the cloud. For instance, the public cloud will almost have no waiting time because there are several resources compared to the Fog and private cloud.

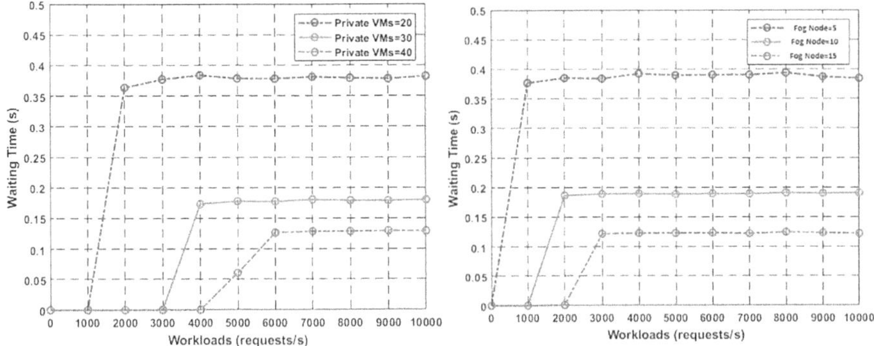

Fig. 11. The waiting time of the private cloud and the waiting time of the Fog.

Figure 11 illustrates the waiting time performance of the private cloud and Fog. In the private cloud, waiting time decreases from 0.39 s with 20 VMs to 0.18 s with 30 VMs, and approaches zero with 40 VMs, stabilizing once resources are fully utilized. Similarly, in the Fog layer, waiting time drops from 0.39 s with 5 nodes to 0.19 s with 10 nodes and 0.11 s with 15 nodes, remaining constant beyond full processor utilization.

5 Conclusion

The increasing number of IoT-connected devices, fueled by advancements in 5G technology and its applications, emphasizes the need for efficient IoT monitoring systems. This study thoroughly explores IoT architecture, including key layers and monitoring systems such as Multi-Access Edge Computing (MEC), Network Function Virtualization (NFV), and 5G Network Slicing. The proposed IoT agriculture monitoring system comprises gateways, private cloud, Fog, and public cloud components, with a queuing model defined for each. The system's performance was evaluated using key metrics such as response time, throughput, utilization, and waiting time. Various scenarios were analyzed by altering resources within private, Fog, and public cloud environments to assess their impact on network performance.

In future work, we will investigate the connectivity layer using both wired and wireless technologies, comparing LoRa and NB-IoT to optimize access networks and improve IoT monitoring performance. Additionally, we will integrate deep learning techniques [35–38] to enable predictive analytics for utilization, failure, and latency in large-scale IoT systems.

Disclosure of Interests. The authors declare that there is no conflict of interest regarding the publication of this paper.

References

1. Kakkavas, G., Diamanti, M., Stamou, A., Karyotis, V., Bouali, F., et al.: Design, development, and evaluation of 5G-enabled vehicular services: the 5G-HEART perspective. Sensors **22**(2), 426 (2022)

2. Yang, J.: 5G Network for a Variety of Vertical Services. In: 5G Verticals, Wiley, 2020, pp. 25–56

3. Veedu, S.N.K., Mozaffari, M., Hoglund, A., Yavuz, E.A., Tirronen, T., et al.: Toward smaller and lower-cost 5G devices with longer battery life: an overview of 3GPP Release 17 RedCap. IEEE Commun. Stand. Magaz. **6**(3), 84–90 (2022)

4. Alturki, R., Munshi, A., Alshawi, B., Agarwal, K., Khan, F., Khan, S.: CardioBERT: a cardiac identification using fusion features in consumer healthcare. IEEE Trans. Consum. Electron. **71**(2), 3522–3530 (2025). https://doi.org/10.1109/TCE.2025.3575522

5. Khan, S., Dilshad, N., Ahmad, N., Noor, S., AlQahtani, S.A.: Integrating AI in security information and event management for real time cyber defense. Sci. Rep. **15**(1), 35872 (2025). https://doi.org/10.1038/s41598-025-19689-x

6. Morchid, A., El Alami, R., Raezah, A.A., Sabbar, Y.: Applications of internet of things (IoT) and sensors technology to increase food security and agricultural Sustainability: Benefits and challenges. Ain Shams Eng. J. **15**(3), 102509 (2024)

7. Jangam, A., Bhosale, V.: Internet of Things (IoT): definitions, challenges, and recent research directions. Int. J. Adv. Res. Sci. Commun. Technol., 276–281, January 2023

8. Lu, H., Huang, K., Azimi, M., Guo, L.: Blockchain technology in the oil and gas industry: a review of applications, opportunities, challenges, and risks. IEEE Access **7**, 41426–41444 (2019)

9. Anas, S.A.B., Singh, R.S.S., Kamarudin, N.A.B.: Designing an IoT agriculture monitoring system for improving farmer's acceptance of using IoT technology. Eng. Technol. Appl. Sci. Res. **12**(1), 8157–8163 (2022)

10. Arvanitis, K.G., Symeonaki, E.G.: Agriculture 4.0: the role of innovative smart technologies towards sustainable farm management. The Open Agric. J. **14**(1), 130–135 (2020)

11. Balram, G., Kumar, K.K.: Crop field monitoring and disease detection of plants in smart agriculture using Internet of Things. Int. J. Adv. Comput. Sci. Appl. **13**(7) (2022)

12. Zafar, S., Miraj, G., Baloch, R., Murtaza, D., Arshad, K.: An IoT based real-time environmental monitoring system using arduino and cloud service. Eng. Technol. Appl. Sci. Res. **8**(4), 3238–3242 (2018)

13. Kamienski, C., Soininen, J.-P., Taumberger, M., Dantas, R., Toscano, A., et al.: Smart water management platform: IoT-based precision irrigation for agriculture. Sensors **19**(2), 276 (2019)

14. Wang, L., Wu, W., Xiao, J., Huang, Q., Hu, Y.: Effects of different drip irrigation modes on water use efficiency of pear trees in Northern China. Agric. Water Manag. **245**, 106660 (2021)

15. Phasinam, K., Kassanuk, T., Shinde, P.P., Thakar, C.M., Sharma, D.K., et al.: Application of IoT and cloud computing in automation of agriculture irrigation. J. Food Qual. **2022**, 1–8 (2022)

16. El Kafhali, S., Salah, K.: Performance modelling and analysis of Internet of Things enabled healthcare monitoring systems. IET Networks **8**(1), 48–58 (2019)

17. Alam, S., Shuaib, M., Ahmad, S., Jayakody, D.N.K., Muthanna, A., et al.: Blockchain-based solutions supporting reliable healthcare for fog computing and Internet of Medical Things (IoMT) integration. Sustainability **14**(22), 15312 (2022)

18. D. Gowda V, Sharma, A., Rao, B.K., Shankar, R., Sarma, P., et al.: Industrial quality healthcare services using Internet of Things and fog computing approach. Measurement: Sensors **24**, 100517 (2022)

19. Aazam, M., Huh, E.N., Zeadally, S., Harras, K.A., AbuKhousa, E., et al.: Multistage adaptive control strategy based on image contour data for autonomous endoscope navigation. Comput. Biol. Med. **149**, 105946 (2022)

20. Khan, S., AlQahtani, S.A., Noor, S., Ahmad, N.: PSSM-Sumo: deep learning based intelligent model for prediction of sumoylation sites using discriminative features. BMC Bioinform. **25**(1), 284 (2024)

21. Rasheed, A., Joo Chong, P.H., Ho, I.W.H., Li, X.J., Liu, W.: An overview of mobile edge computing: architecture, technology and direction. KSII Trans. Internet Inf. Syst. **13**(10), October 2019
22. Wang, X., Li, J., Ning, Z., Song, Q., Guo, L., et al.: Wireless powered mobile edge computing networks: a survey. ACM Comput. Surv. **55**(13s), 1–37 (2023)
23. Ranaweera, P., Jurcut, A., Liyanage, M.: MEC-enabled 5G use cases: a survey on security vulnerabilities and countermeasures. ACM Comput. Surv. **54**(9), 1–37 (2022)
24. Rejiba, Z., Masip-Bruin, X., Marín-Tordera, E.: A survey on mobility-induced service migration in the fog, edge, and related computing paradigms. ACM Comput. Surv. **52**(5), 1–33 (2020)
25. Villamil, S., Hernandez, C., Tarazona, G.: An overview of internet of things. TELKOMNIKA (Telecommunication Computing Electronics and Control) **18**(5), 2320 (2020)
26. Murakami, M.: Optical network technology for future ultra-high-capacity communications in the beyond 5G and big data era. NTT Techn. Rev. **20**(6), 43–51 (2022)
27. Folgado, F., Calderón, D., González, I., Calderón, A.: Review of industry 4.0 from the perspective of automation and supervision systems: definitions, architectures and recent trends. Electronics **13**(4), 782 (2024)
28. Altulyan, M., Yao, L., Wang, X., Huang, C., Kanhere, S.S., et al.: A survey on recommender systems for internet of things: techniques, applications and future directions. Comput. J. **65**(8), 2098–2132 (2022)
29. Wang, K., Jin, J., Yang, Y., Zhang, T., Nallanathan, A., et al.: Task offloading with multi-tier computing resources in next generation wireless networks. IEEE J. Sel. Areas Commun. **41**(2), 306–319 (2023)
30. Uddin, I., Awan, H.H., Khalid, M., Khan, S., Akbar, S., et al.: A hybrid residue based sequential encoding mechanism with XGBoost improved ensemble model for identifying 5-hydroxymethylcytosine modifications. Sci. Rep. **14**(1), 20819 (2024)
31. Abbas, N., Zhang, Y., Taherkordi, A., Skeie, T.: Mobile edge computing: a survey. IEEE Internet Things J. **5**(1), 450–465 (2018)
32. Ali, B., Gregory, M.A., Li, S.: Multi-access edge computing architecture, data security and privacy: a review. IEEE Access **9**, 18706–18721 (2021)
33. Yousaf, F.Z., Bredel, M., Schaller, S., Schneider, F.: NFV and SDN—key technology enablers for 5G networks. IEEE J. Sel. Areas Commun. **35**(11), 2468–2478 (2017)
34. Shen, X., Gao, J., Wu, W., Lyu, K., Li, M., et al.: AI-Assisted network-slicing based next-generation wireless networks. IEEE Open J. Vehicular Technol. **1**, 45–66 (2020)
35. Noor, S., AlQahtani, S.A., Khan, S.: XGBoost-Liver: An intelligent integrated features approach for classifying liver diseases using ensemble XGBoost training model. Comput. Mater. Contin. **83**(1), 1435–1450 (2025). https://doi.org/10.32604/cmc.2025.061700
36. Khan, S., et al.: Deep-ProBind: binding protein prediction with transformer-based deep learning model. BMC Bioinformatics **26**(1), 88 (2025). https://doi.org/10.1186/s12859-025-06101-8
37. Khan, S., et al.: XGBoost-enhanced ensemble model using discriminative hybrid features for the prediction of sumoylation sites. BioData Min. **18**(1), 12 (2025). https://doi.org/10.1186/s13040-024-00415-8
38. Noor, S., Awan, H.H., Hashmi, A.S., Saeed, A., Khan, S., AlQahtani, S.A.: Optimizing performance of parallel computing platforms for large-scale genome data analysis. Computing **107**(3), 86 (2025). https://doi.org/10.1007/s00607-025-01441-y

Design and Research of Multiuser and Multimodal Virtual Fitness Equipment Based on VR

Shihong Yao[1], Shuqing Zhang[1], Jun Hou[2], Zhonghua Xiang[1], Linhua Jiang[2(✉)], and Attila Vidács[3(✉)]

[1] Huzhou Vocational & Technical College, Zhejiang, China
[2] Xidian University Hangzhou Institute of Technology, Zhejiang, China
`jianglinhua@xidian.edu.cn`
[3] Budapest University of Technology and Economics, Budapest, Hungary
`vidacs.attila@vik.bme.hu`

Abstract. To address the issues of insufficient interactivity, scarce scenarios, and limited fitness types in traditional spinning bikes, this paper proposes a multiuser and Multimodal virtual fitness system. Through Multimodal interactions such as cycling and rowing, as well as multiuser online interactive technology, the user experience is significantly enhanced. The system hardware employs an Arduino development board to collect multi - source sensor data including heart rate, blood oxygen, and speed, and utilizes a Bluetooth module for wireless data transmission. The software is developed based on the Unity 3D engine, and Mirror is used to achieve multiuser and Multimodal network - based interactive functions. The design of this system enriches the types of fitness available to users, enables multiuser virtual fitness across different locations, and provides a novel solution for indoor fitness.

Keywords: Virtual Reality · Fitness System · Multimodal Interaction · Multiuser Online Connection

1 Introduction

In 2023, Teyi Tsai [1] developed a low-cost virtual bicycle system based on the Internet of Things (IoT) interface. This system utilized the IoT infrastructure to construct a prototype of a low-cost rehabilitation system for the elderly, which was capable of acquiring and processing bicycle data from the cloud in real time. In the same year of 2023, the team led by Amanpreet Chander developed a method that calculated the speed and RPM of the pedals through the acceleration data generated by mobile phones [2], and then transmitted the data wirelessly to the virtual system. The virtual bicycle could imitate the motion postures of real cyclists, thus achieving virtual fitness exercises with extremely simple hardware equipment.

However, traditional spinning bikes fail to meet evolving user demands. This study introduces a Multiuser and multimodal virtual fitness system that combines cycling,

Z. Lin et al. (Eds.): INSAI 2025, CCIS 2894, pp. 266–278, 2026.
https://doi.org/10.1007/978-981-95-9299-9_20

rowing, and networked interactions to enhance immersion and engagement. Moreover, through multiuser virtual fitness exercises, this system can promote diverse social interactions and provide good emotional value.

2 System Design

2.1 Overall Architecture

The design of the Multiuser and multimodal virtual fitness system includes both hardware and software aspects, as shown in Fig. 1. The hardware design mainly focuses on collecting relevant human motion vital sign data such as speed, heart rate, blood oxygen level, and posture angle. The data are collected and wirelessly transmitted by using an HC-05 Bluetooth module and an Arduino development board [3]. The software design is to develop a Multiuser online system based on virtual reality technology by utilizing the Mirror framework, and integrate multisource sensor data to drive the Multiuser and multimodal virtual fitness system.

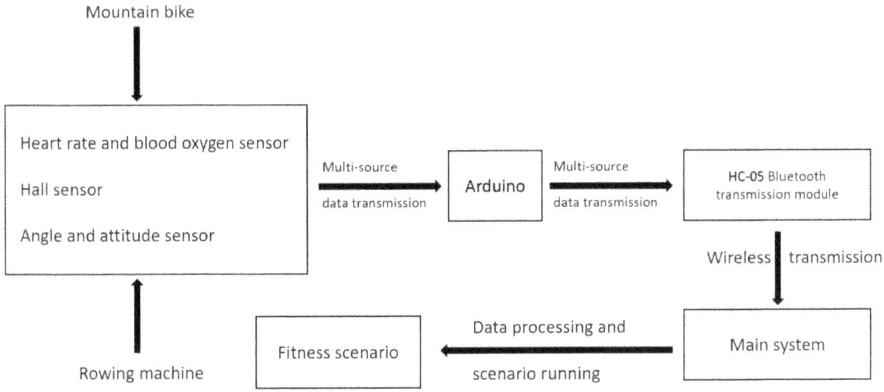

Fig. 1. System Architecture

2.2 Hardware Design

This system uses a mountain bike for virtual cycling and an indoor rowing machine for virtual rowing. As shown in Fig. 2, it is a schematic diagram of the installation of relevant sensors. The mountain bike is fixed on a magnetic resistance cycling stand, and a Hall sensor is fixedly installed on one side of the bracket at the rear wheel of the mountain bike. As depicted in Fig. 2, the signal acquisition end of the Hall sensor [4] should be kept perpendicular to the rear wheel hub. Two sets of symmetrical magnets are attached to the rear wheel. Each time a magneta passes by the Hall sensor, a data collection will be carried out. For obtaining the posture angle of the handlebar, a JY61 posture angle sensor is used, and the posture angle sensor is fixed at the center of the handlebar. The heart rate and blood oxygen sensor [5] adopts a MAX30102 sensor module. The heart rate and blood oxygen sensor is fixed on the left side of the handlebar. When in use, it is only necessary to fix the left index finger to the heart rate and blood oxygen sensor.

Fig. 2. Sensor Installation

Sensors for measuring speed, angle, heart rate, and blood oxygen level collect data via an Arduino [6]. Table 1 below shows the connections between the relevant sensors and the IO ports. The acquired data is then transmitted to the main system through a Bluetooth module. Specifically, the HC - 05 Bluetooth module is adopted, which consists of two parts: HC - 05 - USB and HC - 05. The HC - 05 module is embedded in the development board, while the HC - 05 - USB module needs to be plugged into the USB port of the host. The fast interconnection data transmission mode between the master and slave modules can significantly reduce data loss and features low latency and a strong signal.

Table 1. IO Port Allocation

Sensor	Speed Sensor	Posture Sensor	Health Sensor	Bluetooth Module
Digital Port	D1	Rx/Tx	D6/D7	D8/D9
Signal Type	Pulse	Byte Stream	Byte Stream	Byte Stream

The speed of the virtual cycling device takes the average speed of the rear wheel as the reference standard. The real-time cycling speed is calculated by using the changes of high and low pulses generated when the magnet is continuously monitored by the Hall sensor during the movement of the rear wheel. The principle is that the Hall sensor generates a high level when the magnet is close and a low level when the magnet is not close. As shown in Fig. 3, every time the wheel rotates one full circle, it passes the Hall sensor twice, and each time it passes, the average speed for a half-circle can be obtained [7]. Here, we assume that the maximum radius of the wheel is r, and the circumference of a half-circle of the wheel is πr. The time period between two pulses is

T, and the counter value generated between two half-circles is n. Then the time for the wheel to rotate a half-circle is nT. From this, we can conclude that the average speed V of the wheel rotating a half-circle is $V = \pi r/nT$. Since the rotation speed of the wheel is very fast during normal cycling, the average speed is close to the instantaneous speed of virtual cycling in the system, thus enabling real-time synchronization between the actual cycling speed and the cycling speed in the virtual fitness system.

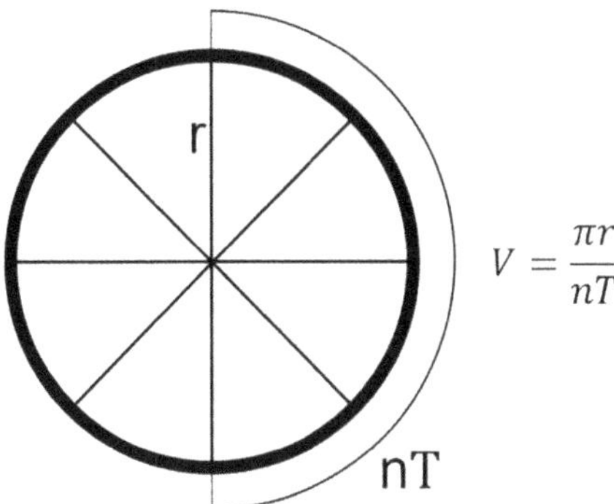

Fig. 3. The principle of wheel speed measurement

For the speed collection of the rowing machine equipment, as shown in Fig. 4, the system fixes the rowing handle to the VR handle. The motion frequency generated by the back - and - forth swinging of the rowing handle synchronizes with that of the VR handle. When users perform rowing movements on the rowing machine, pulling the rowing handle backward generates the forward propulsion for rowing, and the average speed at which the VR handle is pulled backward represents the rowing speed.

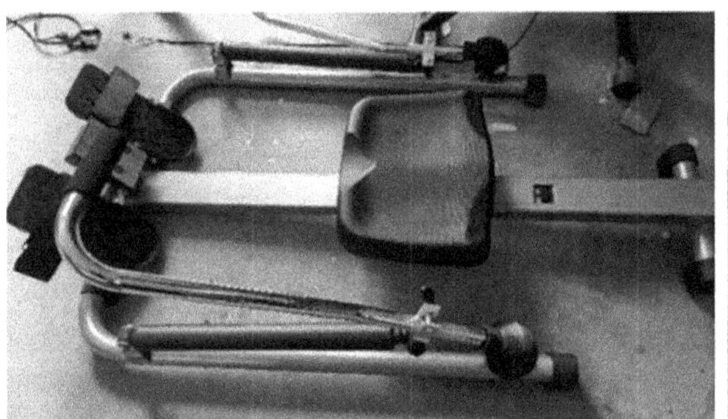

Fig. 4. Rowing machine fixed VR handle

When the VR handle is bound to the rowing handle, the initial position of the rowing handle is set as L1, and its final position after pulling back is L2. The entire pulling - back process of the rowing machine takes time T. Then, the average speed V, which represents the average speed of one rowing cycle, can be calculated using the following formula:

$$V = \frac{L2-L1}{T} \tag{1}$$

2.3 Software Design

The UI interface of this system is designed by using the UGUI components of the Unity 3D. As shown in Fig. 5, the UI interface of the multimodal fitness system mainly consists of three major modules: the main interface, the scene and character interface, and the virtual fitness interaction interface. The main interface includes single-player and multi-player fitness interaction modules, allowing users to choose between a personal roaming scene and a multiplayer online interaction scene. The scene and character interface provides a 3D micro-model scene selection function, as well as a module for choosing between the cycling and rowing systems. The virtual fitness interaction interface enables users to directly view their interaction data, including relevant information such as user names, avatars, ranking list information, cycling speed, heart rate, and blood oxygen level. This system integrates two different fitness systems, three types of characters, and six scenes with different styles, which significantly enhances the interestingness and immersive experience of virtual fitness.

Fig. 5. UI interface diagram

The system employs gaze interaction technology to achieve interface interaction functions. The gaze interaction technology makes use of the virtual rays emitted from the center of the field of view of the VR headset to interact with the UI interface. As depicted in Fig. 6, it is the flowchart of the gaze interaction between the VR headset and the UI interface. Users can interact with the interface simply by turning their heads, and they are also able to observe the surrounding environment in all directions [8]. This not only enhances the safety of users during virtual fitness but also significantly improves their sense of immersion.

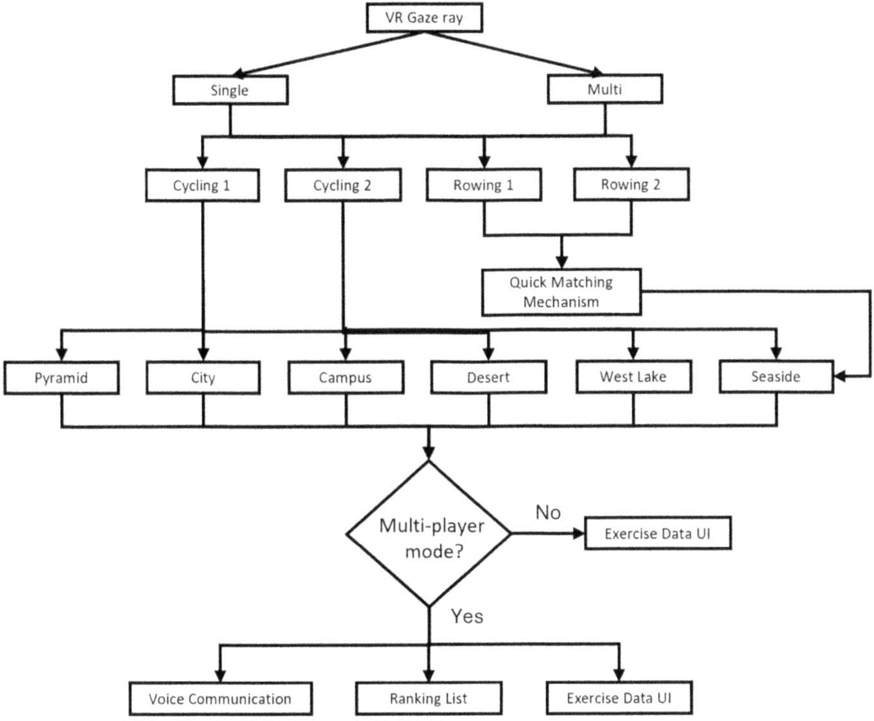

Fig. 6. UI interface interaction flowchart

2.4 Scene Construction Based on Micro-model

2.4.1 Map Creation

This system has set up six types of micro-model scenes, including various micro-model scenes such as the West Lake, the Pyramid, the Desert, the Seaside, the City, and the Campus. The scene content utilizes the Terrain component in Unity to create different terrain structures, such as flatlands, mountains, basins, and other various landforms. 3D models like lakes, roads, and buildings designed with 3DMax software are integrated, and appropriate texture materials are added. Finally, a variety of micro-model scenes are obtained.

2.4.2 Construction of Character Models

Create models of a mountain bike and a rowing machine in 3ds Max, and also create a human character model. Bind the bones to the character model as shown in Fig. 7. Then import these models into Unity. Use the Animator in Unity to create and record animations for the combined model of the character and the virtual fitness equipment. This includes recording normal driving animations for the cycling system, left - turn and right - turn animations, and designing rowing actions for the rowing machine. To ensure that the Multimodal devices can synchronize with the movement speeds of the Multimodal virtual models in the virtual system scene during use, we need to conduct multiple rounds of debugging and set the playback speed of the motion animations to achieve synchronization of the motion postures.

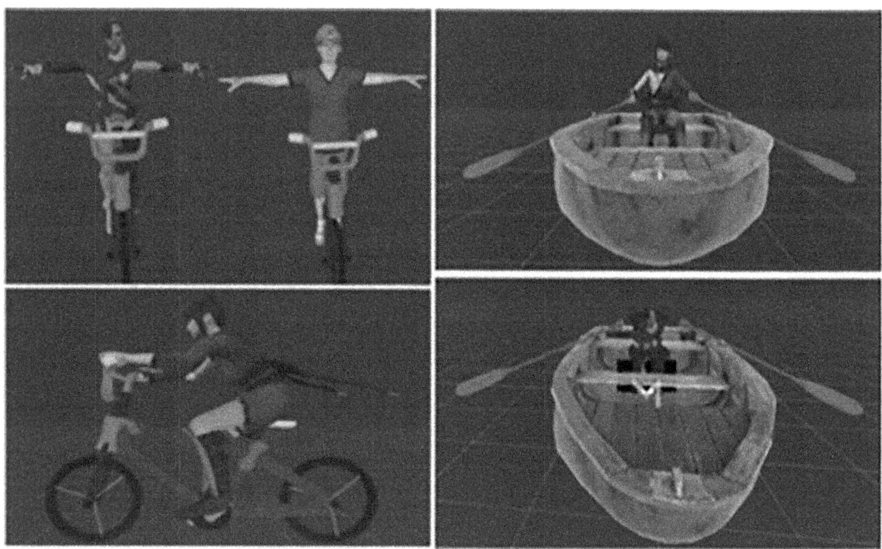

Fig. 7. Character and Equipment Model

2.5 Multiplayer Online Strategy

In order to enhance users' sense of interaction and make the experience more interesting, based on the traditional stand-alone virtual fitness system, this system has designed a Multiuser and multimodal online interaction mode. The Multiuser online function is realized through the Mirror plugin in Unity. The server side of the Multiuser and multimodal system is set up on the cloud server. Relevant data such as the speed, blood oxygen level, heart rate, posture data, ranking list information, etc., generated when users conduct movement interactions on the client side, are transmitted to the server side in real time. Then, the server side sends the data to all other users in the same scene, achieving real-time synchronization and transmission of Multiuser and multimodal data.

The Multiuser and multimodal online system requires the establishment of the system on the cloud server side. This system uses the LeanCloud cloud server to manage the background data [9]. The platform provides various game solutions, such as online battles, ranking lists, and player data storage, which can fully meet the design requirements of the system and improve the design efficiency of the system.

This system adopts the strategy of directly and quickly matching rooms. Users are randomly assigned to multiple existing rooms, and they can also create their own rooms, thus achieving fast and efficient Multiuser online virtual fitness. The principle of creating different online rooms is to set different random port numbers on the remote server to bind the corresponding rooms, with each port number corresponding to an online room. The fast matching strategy is to select the room with the least number of people from the list of existing online rooms for matching and entry. This can greatly avoid problems such as packet loss in data transmission and lag and stuttering caused by an excessive number of people.

The implementation of the system data synchronization mechanism involves adding relevant attributes such as Mirror's Network Manager and Kcp Transport to an empty object in the main scene. The Network Manager attribute can control the online scene, the address of the cloud server, and the binding of player prefabs. It can provide prefab selection for virtual scenes and characters in the multi - player and Multimodal system. The Kcp Transport attribute can bind the port number of the cloud server to determine each online room, achieving a unique match between the port number and the online room. This strategy enables independent data transmission between multiple scenes, enhancing the stability and robustness of the system. Each prefab has two core attributes: Network Identity and Network Transform. These respectively determine the unique identity of the player prefab in the network and control the real - time position information of the player prefab in the scene.

Data such as users' avatars, nicknames, and exercise mileage in the multiplayer and multimodal online system need to be synchronously and visually displayed among all clients through the cloud server. For the visual display of Multiuser data, on the one hand, a UI interface is required to achieve the visual effect. More importantly, two features in Unity, [Command] and [ClientRpc], are used to realize the synchronous transmission of multisource data. The [Command] feature enables the client side to send instruction information to the server side. The method is called on the client side and executed on the server side. The [ClientRpc] feature allows the server side to send instruction programs to all client sides. The method is called on the server side and executed on the client side [9].

Information such as users' avatars, nicknames, and mileage in the leaderboard is transmitted from the client side to the server side using the [Command] feature, and then the user data is sent from the server side to all client sides by using [ClientRpc]. For the users' exercise mileage data, it is necessary to bind and obtain the prefabs corresponding to all users on the server side. The Position attribute of the Curvy curve of the movement path is used to obtain the relative distance value of each prefab on the scene route. The effect is shown in Fig. 8 below. By ranking the mileage values in this way, the ranking of users in the exercise leaderboard can be obtained. Moreover, the users' exercise data is visually displayed through UI design, enriching the content and interestingness of virtual fitness.

Fig. 8. UI Interface Design

3   Performance Test

3.1   Test Plan

In this project, two college student testers are invited: Tester 1 (male) and Tester 2 (female). Both of them are in good health (without diseases such as hypertension or depression that have a significant impact on cardiopulmonary function, BMI, and emotions). The two testers are not allowed to engage in strenuous exercise within two weeks before the test and should try to maintain the same environment and physical and mental state.

We will conduct tests on the two testers in three aspects: cardiopulmonary endurance, BMI, and emotions. Data will be collected for the first time when they first use the virtual system, and the second data collection will be carried out when they have used the system for 10 days.

3.2   Experimental Results and Analysis

3.2.1   Test Results and Analysis of Cardiopulmonary Endurance

The physical sign of human heart rate is one of the standards for a person's health. Accurate heart rate data can provide a clearer understanding of the user's exercise state [10]. To ensure the reliability of the data, the real-time cardiopulmonary conditions of the two testers were obtained under the same load. As can be seen from the heart rate data in Fig. 9 and Fig. 10 below, the abscissa represents time (in seconds) and the ordinate represents heart rate (in beats per minute).

The heart rate change data before and after using this system show that: The resting heart rate of Tester 1 decreased from 78 beats per minute before exercise to 72 beats per minute after exercise. Under the condition of constant exercise intensity, the average heart rate during exercise decreased from 129 beats per minute before using this system to 124 beats per minute. The resting heart rate of the other test subject (Tester 2) also showed an improving trend, decreasing from 72 beats per minute in the initial record to

66 beats per minute. Moreover, during the test with the same amount of exercise, the average heart rate during exercise decreased from 125 beats per minute to 123 beats per minute.

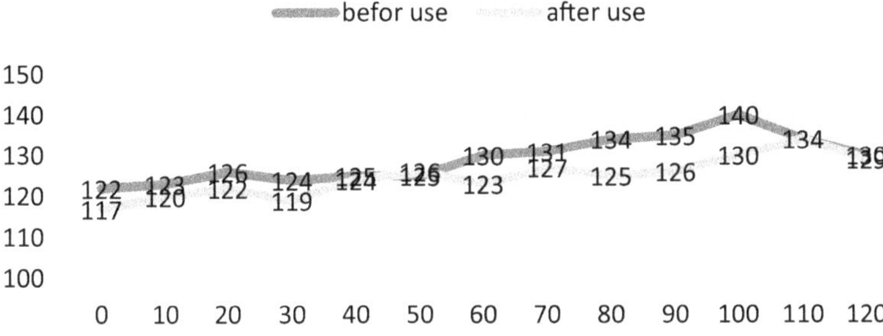

Fig. 9. The Change of Exercise Heart Rate of Tester 1 before and after Use

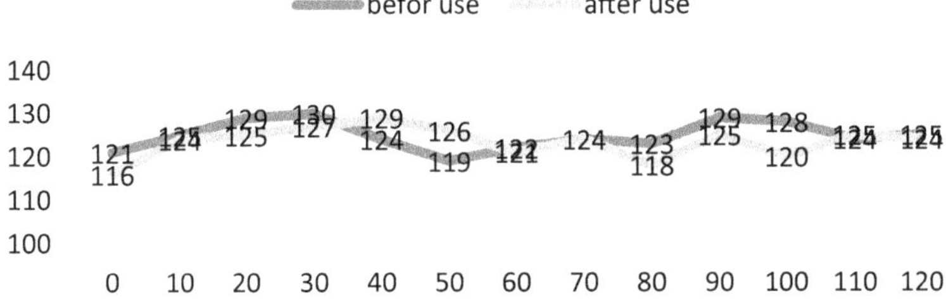

Fig. 10. The Change of Exercise Heart Rate of Tester 2 before and after Use

The comparison of the two groups of data shows that after regularly using this virtual system, both the resting heart rate and the exercise heart rate indicators have been optimized. This indicates that the equipment of this system can significantly improve the cardiopulmonary endurance of the human body.

3.2.2 Experimental Results of BMI

The body weight of a person has an important impact on the state of energy balance [11]. Therefore, it is more scientific to evaluate a person's health status through the Body Mass Index (BMI) indicator [12]. Before the formal system test, this study collected the basic physical sign data of the two testers: Tester 1 (with a height of 1.80 m and an initial weight of 80 kg) and Tester 2 (with a height of 1.75 m and an initial weight of 65 kg). The calculated Body Mass Index (BMI) values of Tester 1 and Tester 2 were 24.6 and 21.2 respectively.

After exercising using this system, the re-measured data showed that the height dimensions of the two testers remained stable (Tester 1 was still 1.80 m and Tester 2 remained 1.75 m), while the weight indicators showed positive changes: Tester 1's weight decreased to 78 kg, and Tester 2's weight dropped to 64.5 kg. The corresponding BMI values were 24.0 and 21.0 respectively.

The experimental data reveal two key conclusions: Firstly, this system has no significant regulatory effect on the height parameters of adult individuals, which is consistent with the law of human skeletal development. Secondly, the BMI indices of the two testers both decreased after using this system, confirming the effectiveness of this exercise program in terms of weight management.

3.2.3 Experimental Results of Emotional State

Different emotions bring about negative or positive subjective states [13]. Currently, the application of VR technology to promote rehabilitation psychology has gradually become the norm [14]. Emotional regulation training [15] is also one of the psychological intervention treatment methods in mental rehabilitation [16], which can help patients with mental rehabilitation achieve a healthy reintegration into society as soon as possible. Based on the subjective characteristics of emotional measurement, this study uses selfevaluation to assess the emotional state. A multidimensional emotion recording tool has been specially designed (see Tables 2 and 3). An evaluation framework is constructed from four basic dimensions: pleasure, anger, sadness and anxiety. Each dimension adopts a 10-level scoring mechanism for the quantification of subjective intensity.

Table 2. Tester 1 Self - Emotion Scoring

Status	Tester	Happiness	Anger	Sorrow	Fear
Before Fitness	Tester 1(Male)	9	0	1	0
After Fitness	Tester 1(Male)	9	0	0	0

Table 3. Tester 2 Self - Emotion Scoring

Status	Tester	Happiness	Anger	Sorrow	Fear
Before Fitness	Tester 2 (Female)	6	0	4	0
After Fitness	Tester 2 (Female)	8	0	1	0

The experimental data show that the dimensions of anxiety and anger remained at zero throughout the experimental period, and the main changing data were related to the two aspects of happiness and sadness. Before the test, both testers had a certain degree of sad emotions, which may be related to various factors such as the research pressure of postgraduate students and the fast pace of life. After the test using this system, the happiness of the two testers increased, and their sadness significantly decreased. These findings confirm that the multiplayer and multimodal virtual fitness system has a two-way regulatory effect on emotional health - it can not only enhance the experience of positive emotions but also effectively relieve the state of psychological stress.

4 Conclusion

This system focuses on the development of a Multiuser and multimodal virtual sports interaction system. In the hardware design, various sports equipment such as rowing machines and mountain bikes are integrated, and multisource sports vital sign data including speed, angle, and heart rate are collected. The HC-05 Bluetooth module is used to wirelessly transmit the data to the host system. In terms of software design, the development of Multiuser online fitness scenarios has been realized, enriching the content design of virtual characters and sports scenes. This system enables multiplayer online fitness and allows for communication among users. For example, the leaderboard can enhance users' sense of competition, and a variety of beautiful scene contents can make users feel more pleasant.

However, there are still areas in the current system that urgently need optimization. For example, how the existing system can perform dynamic damping regulation based on the terrain materials of the virtual scene roads will become a key technical challenge for enhancing the realism of the sports experience.

Acknowledgments. The research was supported by the Huzhou Vocational & Technical College University-Level Planning Project (No. 2024YB20) and partly supported by the National Natural Science Foundation of China (No. 62175037).

References

1. Tsai, T., Finkelstein, J.: Design and implementation of a low-cost virtual biking system using IoT interface. In: 2023 IEEE 9th World Forum on Internet of Things (WF-IoT), Aveiro, Portugal, pp. 1–7 (2023)
2. Chander, A., Airan, A., Sahani, A.: A virtual reality based system for a more engaging indoor exercise biking experience. In: 2023 IEEE International Instrumentation and Measurement Technology Conference (I2MTC), Kuala Lumpur, Malaysia, pp. 01–06 (2023)
3. Yao, S., Long, W., Hu, L., et al.: Research on sports data acquisition and transmission technology based on VR. In: 2021 International Conference on Networking Systems of AI (INSAI). IEEE, pp. 278–283 (2021)
4. Cao, J.: Design of power control system based on hall sensor. Inf. Technol. Informatization, 79–81 (2021)

5. Chen, Y., Yuan, H., Xu, Y.: Design and implementation of VR smart bicycle fitness system based on sports health management mode. J. Hangzhou Normal University (Natural Science Edition), pp. 374–380 (2021)
6. Chuan, X., Dandan, Z., Ziming, P.: Design and development of spinning bike game based on VR technology. In: 2020 IEEE 5th International Conference on Image, Vision and Computing (ICIVC)
7. Wang, T.: A VR Rree Riding System Based on Panoramic Video. HuZhou University (2022)
8. Wang, Z., Xu, Y., Chen, H., et al.: Design and implementation of immersive spinning bike system. J. Fujian Comput., 136–137 (2020)
9. Yao, S.: Panoramic Style Riding System Based on Virtual Reality Technology. HuZhou University (2023)
10. Yao, S., Long, W., Hu, L., et al.: Research on sports data acquisition and transmission technology based on VR. In: 2021 International Conference on Networking Systems of AI (INSAI). IEEE, pp. 278–283 (2021)
11. Wang, K., Xie, Y., Qin, P.: Research on the progress of fat loss under the combined intervention of exercise and nutrition. Adv. Phys. Sci. **10**, 419 (2022)
12. Li, J.: Effect of CrossFit training on physical health of sedentary people in the workplace. HeNan University (2022)
13. Zhang, L.: Research on Influencing Factors of Privacy Information Disclose Intention of Ecommerce's Users Based on Cognitive Theory of Emotion. Central China Normal University (2022)
14. He, Z., Xiong, C.: Design and application of rehabilitation psychology practical teaching system based on VR technology. In: 2021 3rd International Conference on Machine Learning, Big Data and Business Intelligence (MLBDBI), Taiyuan, China, pp. 553–556 (2021)
15. Chen, W., Han, B.: Psychological intervention treatment in psychiatric rehabilitation. In: Proceedings 2011 International Conference on Human Health and Biomedical Engineering, Jilin, China, pp. 353–356 (2011)
16. Guangli, L.: Design and development of VR-based psychological problem intervention system. In: 2024 IEEE 2nd International Conference on Image Processing and Computer Applications (ICIPCA), Shenyang, China, pp. 501–505 (2024)

Author Index